William Pitt, Earl of Chatham
This portrait hangs in the court room of Pittsylvania County

THE HISTORY

of

PITTSYLVANIA COUNTY

VIRGINIA

BY

MAUD CARTER CLEMENT

Baltimore

REGIONAL PUBLISHING COMPANY

1987

Originally Published: Lynchburg, Virginia, 1929
Reprinted: Regional Publishing Company
Baltimore, 1973, 1976, 1981, 1987
Library of Congress Catalogue Card Number 72-10443
International Standard Book Number 0-8063-7989-8
Made in the United States of America

DEDICATION

TO MY HUSBAND

NATHANIEL E. CLEMENT

AND TO THE MEMORY OF
OUR ONLY DAUGHTER

ELIZABETH LANIER CLEMENT
1904—1927

TABLE OF CONTENTS

ILLUSTRATIONS

PREFACE

My purpose in writing this book has been to show the part borne by the people of Pittsylvania County, Virginia, in the settlement, growth and development of our country.

In tracing the great movement of peoples—when waves of unrest have swept through the country, and in telling the story of the wars and all the great crises in our history, it has been impossible to restrict this history to county lines, so that the earlier part of the book is largely a record of the people of Southern Piedmont Virginia, that is, of Halifax, Pittsylvania, Henry, Patrick, Franklin, Bedford and Campbell Counties.

Years of research have been spent in uncovering the facts here recorded, and when at last assembled they form a story of hardihood, perseverance and high courage of which posterity may well be proud.

M. C. CLEMENT.

May 19th, 1928.

CHAPTER I

THE INDIANS

Pittsylvania was once the home of the red man. Indian villages have stood along the banks of the streams and Indian corn fields waved over the rich bottom lands. The stillness of the primeval forest has echoed to the hunter's cry and the returning warrior's shout of victory. The countless arrowheads and bits of pottery found today throughout the county are mute reminders of the day of his dominion.

But the Indians were gone—their villages deserted and farm land abandoned e'er the white settlers came into this upland region to make their homes. The time of their going, however, had been of such recent date that the site of the villages and farm lands could be located and were often mentioned as pointers in early land grants. But with the passage of time all knowledge of these local tribes was lost, and it has been only through the research of recent years that their identity has been established and their tragic story brought to light, revealing to us a people renowned for honor, courage, and bravery, who, through the vicissitudes of war, were finally overcome by their ancient enemies.

We learn with surprise that the Indian tribes of Midland Virginia belonged to the great Siouian[1] race found today on the far western plains. It is a tradition of their race that they once lived in the east, probably on the Ohio River, and far back in history a migration took place—a part of the nation crossing the mountains over into Midland Virginia, while others moving down the waters of the Ohio and Mississippi rivers, gradually spread through the west. The Sioux is the greatest buffalo hunter of all the American Indians, and it is thought by some[2] that it was their love of the buffalo chase that lured them from their mountain home to the more level plains of Virginia and the west; but it is more probable that wearied by the constant wars waged by the northern Indians, they sought relief in a more distant home. The Siouian Confederacy extended through Midland Virginia from the Rappahannock River down into the Carolinas. The eastern part of Virginla was held by the Powhatan Confederacy, who were of the Algonquin race.

Captain John Smith gives the first account of the Virginia Siouian tribes when he visited the falls of James River in 1607, and found the Monocan Indians living near. He said that the Powhatan Confederacy

[1]Mooney's "Siouian Tribes of the East."

[2]*William and Mary Quarterly*, Vol. 19, page 172.

extended to the falls while beyond lay the Monocan Confederacy, and that between the two constant war was waged.

The Monocans told Smith that they lived in mortal dread of the Massowomacks, who were a great nation beyond the mountain; and begged Smith and his company to free them from their tormentors, of whose cruelty they bitterly complained. The Massowomacks were the Iroquois, or Five Nations[3] of the North, who waged continual war upon the Virginia tribes.

When Captain John Smith explored the Rappahannock River he encountered another Siouian tribe, the Manahock Indians who were friends and confederates of the Monocans on the James. One of the Manahock warriors was captured and when questioned by Smith as to who the English were, replied: "We heard you were a people come from under the world to take our world from us," which Smith said was a fair guess for the savage.

When asked further how many worlds there were, the Manahock replied: "No more but that which is under the skies that cover me, which are the Powhatans, the Monocans, and the Massowomacks higher up the mountain." The Monocans, he said, were their friends and neighbors, but the Massowomacks who dwelt upon a great water with many boats, "had so many men they did make war with all the world."

Smith said that the Monocans were the chiefs of the league or confederacy of the upland Indians against the power and tyranny of the Powhatans.

The Indian tribes of South Midland Virginia were far enough removed from Tidewater not to be disturbed by the constant war waged by the whites against the tribes prior to 1650, but the existence of these tribes was known to the English by means of the fur trade. From the beginning of the colony there had been men with the vision and foresight to see that the fur trade was an industry of much financial worth. At an early date Henry Fleet and William Claiborne extended the trade up the Chesapeake Bay until Maryland suppressed their efforts. Then the men of southside Virginia opened a trade with the Indians of the unknown south and west.

[3]The Five Nations were a confederacy formed in 1575, of the Seneca, Oneida, Cayuga, Onondaga, and Mohawk tribes, hence the name Five Nations. The Virginia government made repeated efforts to protect her tributary Indians from the fury of these northern savages. In 1677 Colonel Henry Causey, representing Virginia and Maryland, met them in conference at Albany, New York. Again in 1679 and 1684 Virginia agents held conferences with them, but their agreements were not kept by the Iroquois. Later treaties were made with them by Virginia in 1722 and 1744. (*Va. Mag. History*, Vol. 312, 13.)

In June, 1641, Walter Austin, Rice Hoe, Joseph Johnson and Walter Chiles[4] petitioned the General Assembly "for leave and encouragement to undertake the discovery of a new river of unknown lands bearing west southerly from Appomattox River." Their petition[5] was granted in March, 1642, with a right to enjoy all profit from their adventure for fourteen years. "West southerly" from Appomattox would lead to Pittsylvania and its vicinity, where the Sapony and Occaneechi Indians lived, who were famed for their trade.

The Indian uprising and massacre of 1644 caused a break in the fur trade, but in the Indian treaty of 1646 arrangements were made to take care of the trade through the erection of four forts along the frontier to which the Indians were permitted to come and barter. Fort Henry was located on the south side of James River, on the Appomattox, and put under the command of Captain Abram Wood, who was allowed to keep the fort free of taxes for a number of years, but was required to maintain a small force there at his own charge, probably his trading force, which should be a garrison for the fort. Across the river from the fort was the home of Captain John Flood who at that time was chief interpreter in Indian affairs for the colony.

Captain Abram Wood was a southside man of military experience and for many years a trader and explorer, who had learned that in order to secure the trade of the Indians it was necessary to go after it. In 1650, with his partner Edward Bland, a merchant, he explored in a southwestwardly direction from Fort Henry to the rapids of Roanoke River in North Carolina. Bland kept a diary[6] of the trip from which we learn something of interest concerning our local tribes. In reply to questions about the Roanoke River, which the Indians called "Hocomawananch," one of the Indians told Wood and Bland that the river ran a great way up into the country; and that about three days' journey further to the southwest there was a far greater branch (Staunton) "so broad that a man could hardly see over it (Indian exaggeration), and bended itself to the northward above the head of James River into the foot of the great mountains on which river there lived many people upwards, being the Occomecheams and the Nessoneicks, and that where

[4]Walter Chiles, Sr., emigrated to Virginia before 1638, and was granted lands in Charles City County, along the Appomattox River. He served as a member of the House of Burgesses for ten years, was Speaker of the Assembly and a member of the Council. He died in 1653 leaving a son Walter Chiles, Jr. More than a hundred years later John, Henry and Rowland Chiles, descendants of Walter Chiles, made their homes in this section where their forefather was granted the right to trade with the Indians. (*Va. Mag. History,* Vol. 19, p. 105.)

[5]Hening's "Statutes," Vol. I, p. 262.

[6]Bland's "Discovery of New Britain."

some of the Occanecheans lived, there is an island within the River three days' journey about, which is of a very rich and fertile soil, and that the upper end of the island is fordable, not above knee deep, of a stony bottom, running very swift and the other side very deep and navigable." (Narratives of early North Carolina, page 16.)

The Occaneechi Island, so plainly described by the Indian guide, is situated at the junction of Dan and Staunton Rivers, and still retains its name of Occoneechi Island.

From the report which Wood and Bland gave of this trip they were granted a monoply of the trade in an Act of the Assembly of July, 1653,[7] stating:

"Whereas an act was made in Assembly of 1642 for the encouragement of discoveries to the westward and southward giving them all profits for fourteen years, and is since discontinued, it is now ordered that Major Abram Wood and Edward Bland and their associates may discover and shall enjoy such benefits and trades for fourteen years as they shall find out in places where no English ever have bin and discovered, nor have had particular trade."

A like order was granted at the same time to Colonel William Claiborne and Captain Henry Fleet.

So great was interest at this time in the discovery of new places that this same Assembly of 1653 directed, "Whereas diverse gentlemen have a voluntarie desire to discover the mountains and supplicated for lycense to this Assembly, it is granted unto any for so doing, provided they go with a considerable party and strength both of men and ammunition."

The Dutch,[8] who were carrying on an extensive fur trade, had been wont to buy their pelts from Wood and Bland until they were excluded from Virginia trade by an Act of the General Assembly. They then turned to their kinsmen in New York, and continued their southern fur trade through the agency of the Susquehanna Indians living at the head of Chesapeake Bay, whom they employed as runners to trade with the southern Indians.

An Act of the Assembly, 1662, recites that the northern Indians frequently came "to the heads of our rivers whereby plain paths will soon be made which may prove of dangerous consequences." The "plain paths" across Virginia so feared by the Assembly led from the north across James River at Manakin Town and ended at the Occaneechi

[7]Hening's "Statutes," Vol. I, p. 376.
[8]"Land Marks of Prince William," by Fairfax Harrison.

Island. It is of interest[9] to note that this early trade route across Midland Virginia, opened first by the Indians, continues a main artery of travel today, for the Southern Railway from Richmond to Danville follows this way.

The northern Indians were forbidden by an Act of the Assembly to trade with the southern Indians; but naturally they paid no heed to this law of Virginia, and in 1663 Governor Berkeley stated that their trade amounted to "200,000 beaver skins from our own precincts." To secure these pelts the Dutch supplied the Indians with a greater amount of ammunition than the Virginians had themselves.

In order to retain some of their trade Major Abram Wood petitioned the Assembly for the right to trade in firearms with the native tribes, and the Act of Assembly[10] of March, 1658, repealing the law against the sale of firearms, recites:

"That the neighbouring plantations both of English and forrainers do plentifully furnish the Indians with gunns, powder and shott, and do thereby draw from us the trade of beaver to our great loss and their profitt, and besides the Indians being furnished with as much of both gunns and ammunition as they are able to purchase. It is enacted that every man may freely trade for gunns, powder and shott; it derogateing nothing from our safety, and adding much to our advantage."

We may assume that the Indians of Pittsylvania and the adjacent territory were known to the English through the trader from 1640 onward.

There is mention of these local tribes in connection with the Rechahecrian invasion in 1655. The Rechahecrians are thought[11] by some to have been the Cherokees, who lived across the mountains in the Tennessee country, and claimed that their territory extended eastward as far as the Peaks of Otter. Others[12] suppose the Rechahecrians to be the Requa Indians of Erie, who were driven out of their home in 1655. History gives no reason for the invasion and the Act of Assembly for March, 1655,[13] simply states: "Many western Indians are drawn from the mountains and lately sett down neare the falls of the James River to the number of six or seven hundred."

The colonists became very much alarmed at the close proximity of so many strange Indians and the upper counties were authorized to raise

[9]"Land Marks," by Fairfax Harrison.
[10]Hening's "Statutes," vol. I, p. 543.
[11]Bureau of Ethnology "Hand Book of American Indians, 'Cherokee'."
[12]Parkman's "Jesuits in America."
[13]Hening, Vol. I, p. 452.

a force which was put under the command of Col. Edward Hill, whose home was at Shirley, to treat with these Indians to get them to retire by peaceable means if possible, if not by force. The allied Indians were called upon for aid, and one hundred Pamunkey warriors marched under their King Totopotomoi. A battle was fought at Bloody Run, where Richmond now stands, in which the English were defeated and King Totopotomoi and the greater part of his warriors were slain. Lederer, an early historian, said that Totopotomoi, the Pamunkey chief, was slain while fighting for the English against the Mahocks and Nahyssans, Indian tribes of this section. Thus it would seem that the Siouian tribes and the Rechahecrians were friends and allies, and it is possible that the latter crossed the mountains on the invitation of the Midland Virginia Indians, who, viewing the growing power of the whites and the waning power of the Powhatans, thought it an opportune time to attack.

The unknown south and west remained a matter of keen interest, and in 1669 Governor Berkley himself planned a trip of western exploration, but said that his plans came to naught from continued rains. (Alvord's Western Exp., page 175.) The following year he sent out a party of gentlemen under the command of Major William Harris for the purpose of western exploration. A member of the party, John Lederer, a German, kept a diary[14] of the trip written in Latin, from which is gained the first real knowledge of our local tribes of Indians. Harris's party first visited the chief village of the Monocans, which spread out about three miles along the south bank of the James, in the present county of Powhatan; and the site is still known as Manakin Town. Taking a course due westward from there, the party traveled several days until they came to the country of the Mahocks, and fearing some hostile outbreak from the Indians all turned homeward except Lederer, who with a single Indian guide named Jackzetavan, continued the journey alone.

After going four days in a southwestern direction and meeting no one they came to Sapon, a village of the Nahyssan tribe, "scituate upon a branch of Shawan, alias Rorenock, River." Lederer describes Sapon as having "all the attributes requisite to a pleasant and advantageous seat; for tho' it stands high, and upon a dry land it enjoys the benefit of a stately river, and a rich soyle, capable of producing many commodities, which may hereafter render the trade of it considerable." Their king's residence, called Pintahae, was not far distant and equally well situated

[14]Translations have been made of Lederer's Diary, and can be seen in the State Library, Richmond.

upon the same river. It is difficult to locate these places from Lederer's description. Mooney, the authority on the Siouian tribes of the east, suggests Otter River in Campbell County as the site of Sapon Town; but it is more probable that it was upon Staunton River that these Indian villages were located, for Staunton at this time was known as Sapony River, and can indeed be described as a stately stream. Judging from the number of Indian relics found in the neighborhood of Altavista one is led to believe that this section of Campbell and Pittsylvania counties lying along Staunton River was once the site of an Indian settlement, for a privately owned collection[15] of Indian relics gathered in the vicinity contains several hundred arrow heads, many tomahawks, hoes, and other implements of Indian use. Pintahae, not far distant and equally well situated upon the same river, may well have been on the old Gordon plantation a few miles up the river near Leesville, where many Indian relics have also been found.

Lederer said that he had heard that the Nahyssans had been at war with the whites for ten years, probably since the Rechahecrian invasion, but he ventured among them trusting to his trading goods which he thought would please them. They questioned him closely, and deciding that he meant no harm, welcomed him warmly, and were so pleased with his friendliness and honesty that they wished to adopt him into their tribe.

Lederer recorded many interesting things of these Indians, of their manner of living and their customs. He said that they were tall and warlike and Colonel Byrd[16] who knew them in later years said, "They were the bravest and honestest Indians Virginia ever knew,"—that there was something "great and venerable in their countenances, beyond the common mien of savages."

The Nahyssan tribe was rich. In their little temples or oratories was a great store of unbored pearls, which had been taken in warfare from the Florida Indians and which were prized as highly by the Indians as the whites. They were a powerful and aggressive people and made war upon the tribes far to the south.

These Indians were not dull or wanting in understanding, but had good intelligence. The history of their tribe was preserved in the form of a narrative handed down from father to son, and the children were required to learn by heart all the tribal traditions. The young men were

[15]Owned by Miss Juliet Fauntleroy of "Avoca."
[16]Byrd's "The History of the Dividing Line."

trained in oratory by their wise men, and their chiefs were men of great eloquence. Lederer said that though they lacked the training that the study of books gives, not to think they were lacking in knowledge of rhetoric, physics, and government. He said, "I have been present at some of their consultations and have heard their seniors deliver themselves with as much eloquence and judgment as I should have expected from men of civil education and literature."

Each Indian tribe in Virginia had its own tribal sign, which was worn painted on the shoulders as a distinguishing mark when away from home. The tribal sign of the Nahyssans was three arrow heads.

After spending about three weeks at Sapon Town, Lederer left, promising to return next year, and directed his course to the Occaneechi village, an island about fifty miles eastward upon the same river, the Roanoke. The Occaneechi, a kindred tribe of the Siouian nation, were a very wealthy people, being the merchant traders for all this part of the east. Their language was the trade language of the east, as Mobilian was the trade language of the Gulf States and was used by the medicine men of the various tribes in their ceremonies, as Latin is used by the priests of the Roman Church. (Beverley.) The Occheneechi Trading Path extended from the James River to Augusta, Georgia. We are told that "it was[17] the mart for all Indian trade 500 miles around"; that they had on hand no less than a thousand beaver skins at a time. They raised immense crops of corn and always kept on hand a year's supply of provisions. Here the native tribes brought their pelts to barter for the guns and ammunition, beads, trinkets and cloth supplied by the Dutch of New York, by Major Wood, by Captain Byrd and by other Virginia traders.

The following year, 1671, these local Indians were again visited by explorers with a commission, when Thomas Woods, Thomas Batts and Robert Fallan were sent out by Major Abram Wood "for the finding out the ebbing and flowing of the waters on the other side of the mountains in order to the discovery of the South Sea."

They set out from Appomattox[18] Town on September 1, 1671, and traveled from the Occaneechi Path due west two days and came to the Sapony Indian Town, about two o'clock. In the evening they reached the Saponeys west (probably Pintahae) where they were "joyfully and kindly received with firing of guns and plenty of provisions." After

[17] Mass. 1.
[18] Journal of Batts and Fallom.

securing a Sapon guide to show them a nearer way to the Toleras than usual they continued their journey about twenty-five miles and came "to the town of the Hanathaskies, lying west by north, in an Island in the Sapony River, rich land." Twice more in one day they passed the Sapony River; but after crossing the mountains the river became the Roanoke, a curious custom which it follows today. The river is called Roanoke at its head until it breaks through the Blue Ridge Mountains, when it becomes the Staunton until its conjunction with the Dan a hundred miles lower down; then it again becomes the Roanoke, which name it bears until its mighty waters reach Albemarle Sound.

The travelers discovered a great river flowing north by west, which they named in honor of their chief, Wood River (now New River), and after taking possession of all this western domain in the name of the English monarch, they returned home by the same route, visiting the towns of the Tolero, Hanathoskies, and Saponies where they were well and kindly received. On October first they reached Fort Henry and closed their diary with the pious exclamation, "God's Holy name be praised for our preservation!"[19]

In 1673 Wood sent out two more explorers into the southwest, James Needham and Gabriel Arthur, and an account of their trip is preserved[20] in a letter written by Major Wood to his friend John Richards, in 1674. The explorers followed the Occoneechi Trading Path from Fort Henry to the island home of this industrious trading tribe, who resented the trading activities of the English and tried to block the way of Wood's men. But meeting with a band of Tomahitan Cherokees the English made the long arduous trip with them across the mountains into the Tennessee Country, and were the first white men to explore Tennessee. Leaving Arthur to learn the language, Needham hurried back to Virginia to report to Wood, and on his way out again he was murdered by his Occaneechi guide, Indian John or Hasecoll. "So died," wrote Major Wood, "this heroic Englishman whose fame shall never die if my pen were able to eternalize it, which had adventured where never any English-

[19]In his "Remarks on the Journal of Batts & Fallom" John Mitchell states in 1755:

"From this Town of Appomattuck they set out along the path that leads to Accaneechy, which is an Indian Town on the Borders of Virginia and Carolina, marked in all our maps; from which path they traveled due west. Now you will see both these roads laid down in our Map of North America, and exactly as they are described in this Journal, they being the two roads that lead from the Falls of Appomattuck River southward to Carolina and westward to our settlements on Wood River in Virginia.

"The road that goes to the westward, which was the one that our travellers went, crosses three branches of Roanoke River, a little below the mountains, just as it is described in the Journal, as may be seen by comparing the Journal with our map. This branch of Roanoke River is called Sapony River in the Journal, which has been called Staunton River (in memory of the Lady of the late Governor of Virginia) ever since the survey of these paths in running the boundary line between Virginia and North Carolina in 1727."

[20]Alvord's "From Alleghany Explorations," p. 197.

man had dared to attempt before him, and with him died 144 pounds of my adventure. I wish I could have saved his life with ten times the value."

Young Captain William Byrd succeeded to the business of his Uncle Thomas Stegg, about 1671, and became an active competitor of Major Wood for the Indian trade to the south and west. While Batts and Fallam were at the Tolera Towns in 1671, they heard that "Mr. Byrd and his great company's Discoveries" were three miles away. Besides the great companies of traders, there were also the independent traders, such as Henry Hatcher, who had reported to Major Wood details of Needham's death at the hand of the Occaneechi. When Col. Byrd visited his estate of Eden in North Carolina in 1733, he saw cut upon a great beech the following inscription, "J. H., H. H., B. B., Lay here the 24th of May 1673." The initials read Joseph Hatcher, Henry Hatcher and Benjamin Bullington, three Indian traders who had camped under that tree on one of their trips to trade with the Indians sixty years before.

From the foregoing narrative we learn that this section was well known to the traders by 1675, with well marked trade paths leading through to the west.

Sapon Town was the village of the Sapony clan of the Nahyssan tribe, who taking their name from their village, in later years were known as the Saponies. We have seen that Staunton River was formerly known as Sapony River and conjecture that the towns of Saponi, east and west, were located respectively near Altavista and Leesville.

The location of other Indian settlements in this section are shown in the early land grants in which they are named as pointers in marking boundary lines.

There was an Indian Town on Pigg River, as shown by the following entry:

"1747. Surveyed[21] for Tucker Woodson 400 acres at the mouth of a branch that comes into Pigg River on the south side near the Indian Town, thence up and down the river and branch."

There was also an Indian fort on Pigg River:

"1748.[22] For Roger Turner, jun, 400 acres at the Indian fort about 3 or 4 miles above the mouth of Hatchet Run on Pigg River." Hatchet Run is a branch of Pigg River, on the north side of the river in what is

[21]Surveyor's Record, p. 59.
[22]Surveyor's Record, p. 90.

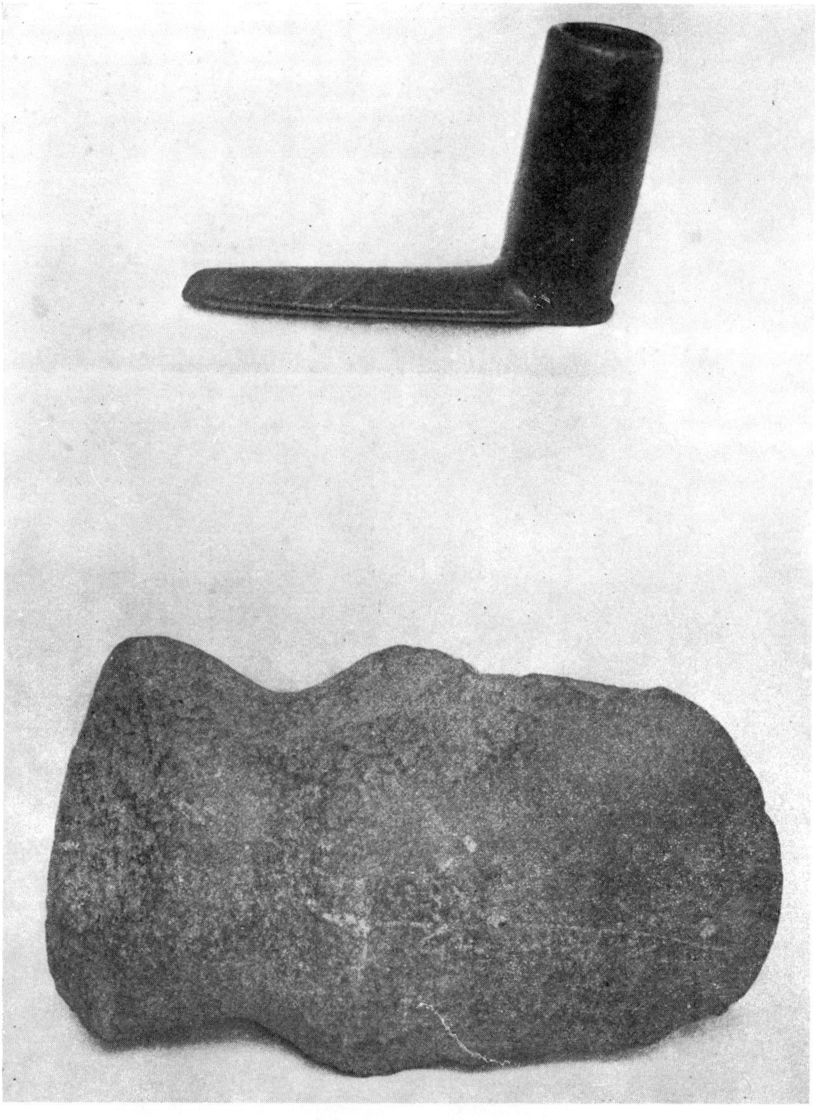

Indian Pipe Found on Banister River
Indian Stone Axe Found at Coles' Hill
Both once used by the Sapony Indians

now Franklin County. When the English colonists first landed in Virginia they found the Indians using the fort for protection against their enemies.

Another Indian[23] fort is mentioned in a grant on Rutledge's Creek of Dan River:

"To William Wynne, May 1753, leave is granted to take up 2000 acres joining the lines of his survey on Dan River, Beginning at a branch below the old Indian Fort running up Rutledge's Creek."

Rutledge's Creek, now a tributary, was at that time all of Pumpkin Creek, which flows through Schoolfield and enters Dan River on the outskirts of Danville.

There is mention of an Indian[24] town on Otter Creek of Smith River:

"1748, To Daniel Rion 200 acres beginning at the Indian Town on the south branch of Otter Creek."

There was undoubtedly an Indian settlement where Pigg River flows into Staunton, judging from the many relics found in the fork of the rivers. The junction of two rivers was an ideal site for an Indian town.

The Virginia Indians did not live in tents, but built for themselves arbor-like houses of saplin poles, which were bent at the top and tied with white oak thongs, giving a curved roof; all then was closely covered with bark and mats, which kept out the wind and rain perfectly. Beverley said of their houses, "they are warm as stooves but very smoky, yet at the top of the house there is a hole made for the smoke to go out right over the fire."

The Indians fixed upon the richest ground for their villages with a view to the fertility of their nearby gardens and fields. It has been thought that they lived by hunting and fishing and it is with surprise that we learn[25] how industrious a farmer was the Virginia Indian, growing in his fields many varieties of corn, peas, beans, pumpkins, cymblings, watermelons, muskmelons, and potatoes.

From the Surveyors' Records we learn the location of many Indian farm lands. In the northern part of the county, along Sycamore Creek were Indian fields, and a branch of Sycamore Creek was called Indian Field Branch. There were Indian fields on Potters Creek of Pigg River, "above the great fork," which were probably adjacent to the Indian town on Pigg River. There were great Indian fields on Reedy Creek of Smith River and Indian Fields Mountain along Smith River was of course

[23]Surveyor's Record, p. 195.
[24]Surveyor's Record, p. 90.
[25]Beverley.

named for nearby fields. On the north and middle forks of Mayo River, in Henry County, were Indian farm lands; also on the south side of Blackwater River, in Franklin County—all probably belonging to towns near by. We learn from a deed[26] of 1807 that there were Indian fields on a branch of Cherrystone Creek between Concord and Chatham, and on a slight eminence below the station at Chatham are to be found many broken pieces of pottery and arrow heads, indicating a former settlement there.

There were, of course, other villages and farm lands near which no boundary lines were run and therefore not mentioned by the surveyors. With the countryside to choose from the Indian selected the most fertile lands for his farming operations. An early[27] writer said, "wherever we meet with an old Indian field or place where they have lived we are sure of the best Ground."

The farm work[28] was done chiefly by the women and clearing the ground for fields and gardens cost them much labor. The undergrowth was pulled up by hand while the larger trees were killed by bruising and removing the bark at the base with stone mallets. Then with the use of stone hoes they cultivated around the dead trees, removing each year the fallen branches, until finally the trunks themselves would come down and the field stand cleared. By this slow process hundreds of acres of farm lands in Pittsylvania were cleared by the Indian farmers.

We are told by Col. Byrd[29] that the women were not beautiful but were straight and well proportioned and had an air of innocence and bashfulness that was charming. Besides using the skins of animals for clothing the women wove a coarse cloth from silk grass of which they made skirts, leaving a fringe of grass at the bottom, and these they wore quite gracefully.

As a means of exchange the Indians used bits of shell called peake and roanoke. Beverley wrote that peake, which was both white and purple, was cut from the same shell, highly polished, and drilled through the center forming small cylinders. The purple peake was of greater value than the white, bringing eighteen pence a yard, the white nine pence. The peake or string beads, was used in various ways for ornaments such as coronets, bracelets, belts, to adorn tomahawks and to lace

[26]Pittsylvania County Deeds, Book 15, p. 434.
[27]Hugh Jones "Present State of Virginia," p. 9.
[28]*William and Mary Quarterly*, Vol. 19, p. 79.
[29]Byrd's "Dividing Line."

up garments. Roanoke,[30] of less value than the peake, consisted of flat pieces of shell which were drilled through and largely used for ornamenting the garments made of skins. It was for this shell money that Roanoke River was named.

In 1676 came that upheaval in Indian affairs occasioned by Bacon's War, which not only broke the power of the Indians but left in its wake a long line of evils for the colonists themselves. With the decimation of the tribes, passed the great epic of fur trading, and its glamour of adventure and discovery. The trade was continued by a hardy race of hunters, who went into the wilderness and secured pelts with their own rifles, and who being generally illiterate, left no record of their adventures in journals or letters.

Bacon's War was brought about by an invasion of the Susquehannas who lived at the head of the Chesapeake Bay and who had been driven out of their homes by the attacks of the Iroquois and the whites. They fled down into Virginia, which they well knew through their trading, and began murdering the outlying settlers and plundering their homes. Governor Berkeley did not permit any armed resistance to the Indians, so they grew bolder in their attacks until several hundred Virginians had been slain. Then the Susquehannas moving southward, the men of southside Virginia rose, and under the leadership of Bacon pursued them to the island home of the Occaneechi, whither it was thought the Indians had fled in search of powder.

The Occaneechi had long been on friendly terms with the Susquehannas in their many trade transactions and received them kindly. But the crafty Susquehannas, probably lured on by the rich stores of food and furs, treacherously attacked their hosts and were only driven out of the islands after a sharp fight.

When the English arrived the Occaneechi,[31] who had always maintained friendly relations with the colonists, joined forces with them and defeated the Susquehannas. Then affairs took a strange turn which it is hard to understand at this distant day.

Some of Bacon's men departed for home as soon as the Susquehannas were overcome but the greater number remained in the hope of procuring food, their own being exhausted. Rosseechy, king of the Occaneechi, promised the whites food, but continued to put them off and insisted

[30]Calendar of Virginia State Papers, Vol. I, p. 113. "Roanoke is shell money fixed upon skins. Peake is shell money strung upon cords."

[31]Mary Newton Standard's "Bacon's Rebellion."

on their remaining six days. In the meantime the king sent out and gathered together his people, and manned his forts, of which there were three on the island. While matters were in this tense state a shot was fired from the banks killing one of Bacon's men, and this was the signal to open battle which raged fiercely for a night and a day. The Indians were severely beaten. King Rosseechy of the Occaneechi and the king of the Monocans were slain, with one hundred warriors and many women and children.

In Bacon's own account of the battle he says that they fell upon an Indian town of three strong forts. It is possible that Bacon, having been in this country only a year, did not sufficiently discriminate between the friendly and the hostile tribes. Had an old experienced trader like Colonel Abram Wood commanded that day, these friendly tribes would not have been so needlessly annihilated.

We may suppose that the warriors of the Sapony tribes fought by the side of their kinsmen, the Occaneechi, in that great battle of May, 1676, for in the treaty drawn up with the Indians in 1677, the articles of agreement were signed, along with other kings and chiefs, by "Mastagonoe, young king of the Saponees," and by "Tachapoake, chief man of the Saponees," the Pittsylvania tribes thus becoming tributary to the government of Virginia for the first time in their history.

In the treaty[32] the Indians acknowledged themselves subject to the King of England and to hold their lands by patent from His Majesty.

It was further agreed that if their holdings were not sufficient for their huntings, more would be granted unto them:

That no Englishman should be allowed to settle within three miles of an Indian town:

That any injury or hurt done by the English should be reported to the Governor, and he would administer punishment:

That the Indians should have the right to fish, oyster, gather puccon, tuckahoe, wild oats or anything else for their natural support upon the Englishman's land, provided they first reported their business to the Magistrate:

That each King and Queen should have equal power to govern their own people, except the Queen of the Pamunkeys, who had power over several other tribes:

That their warriors should be ready to assist the English in their marches against their enemies:

---

[32] *Va. Mag. Biog.*, Vol. 14, pp. 289-296.

That Indian Kings and Queens should pay a yearly tribute of twenty beaver skins, and that when their Kings and Queens and great men and attendants should come to visit the Governor and council they should be treated with respect and entertained at the public charge:

And to prevent mistakes and misunderstandings that one out of each of the neighboring tribes should learn to speak the English language to be their interpreter.

Mastogonoe, young King of the Saponies, signed the treaty with his mark thus, "E," while his chief man, Tachapoake, used the letter "S" for his signature.

The other tribes acknowledging the agreement were the Pamunkeys, Nottoways, Appomattox, Weyonokes, Nansemunds, Meherrins and Monocans. We note the absence of the Occaneechi and the Tutelos.

The Indians suffered severe losses in the conflict with Bacon, and the Five Nations of the North, taking advantage of their weakened condition, harassed them cruelly.

The Great War Trail of the Iroquois led down the Valley of Virginia, crossed the Blue Ridge Mountains at the water gap of Staunton River, and passed eastward of the mountains through the counties of Franklin and Henry into North Carolina. Thus you will see that the Indian tribes of Pittsylvania, living in their frontier position at the base of the mountains must have suffered constant attacks from their northern enemies.

Of these northern tribes it was said[33] that they felt an implacable hatred for the southern Indians; that "their wars are everlasting, without Peace, enmity being the only Inheritance among them that descends from Father to Son, and either Party will march a thousand miles to take their revenge upon such Hereditary Enemies."

About this time the Sapony[34] and Tutelo tribes abandoned their villages and fields and moved eastward to the junction of the Dan and Staunton Rivers and established themselves near their kinsmen, the Occaneechi. In the river at this point there are three islands of rich soil, and on the central one the Occaneechi had long made their home; the Saponys occupied the lower and the Tutelo the upper islands. Early travelers describe the islands as an ideal place for Indian settlement, with rich soil and fine timber, well defended from enemies by the swift current of the river.

It was probably the losses which these tribes sustained in the battle with Bacon which caused them to join forces, for Colonel William Byrd

[33]Byrd's "Dividing Line."

[34]Mooney's "Siouian Tribes of East."

who knew them in later years said that they found themselves too weak separately for their own defense, so they agreed to unite. Formerly they were each a distinct nation, or "rather a clan of the same nation, speaking the same language, and using the same customs, but their perpetual wars against all other Indians in time reduced them so low as to make it necessary to join their forces."

Colonel Cadwallader Jones of Rappahannock, who carried on an extensive trade with the Occaneechi and Tuscarora Indians, wrote[35] to Lord Baltimore from Mount Paradise, Virginia, February 2, 1681, asking permission for the bearer, Thomas Owsley, to trade for him at "Nanticoke only for Roanoke and Peak," explaining, "I have an inland trade about four hundred miles from here S. S. W. This year the Indians will need Roanoke and I have a considerable trade with them. Through it I learned six weeks since of the motion of the Seneca Indians about 300 miles S. S. W. from here. They took from an Indian town 35, and 4 or 5 from several small towns under the mountains near 500 miles (from hence). They have so oppressed the Indians that they have made no corn this year. They are now in a full body returning home. By reckoning, they may be in your country on their return when the turkeys gobble, by the information of those that were here."

Even with the protection of the river as a barrier, the Occaneechi and kindred tribes were unable to maintain themselves on their island homes against their enemies, and in 1700 were found living[36] down in South Carolina. The daughter of the Tolero King was the last of her nation and fearing lest[37] she be not treated with the respect due her rank, poisoned herself with the root of the Trumpet Vine. Her father had died two years before, and by his daring exploits had made himself feared by all Indians.

These tribes suffered not only from the fury of the northern Indians, but from southern tribes as well. Colonel Byrd said, "all the nations round-a-bout bearing in mind the havoc these Indians used to make among their ancestors in the insolence of their power, did at length avenge it home upon them, and make them glad to apply to the governor for protection."

We would infer from the following letter[38] written by Benjamine Harrison in 1709, that the Saponeys had returned to Virginia at this time:

[35] *Va. Mag. History,* Vol. 30, pp. 326-327.
[36] Mooney.
[37] Byrd.
[38] Va. Calendar State Papers, Vol. 1, p. 179.

"The King of ye Sapponeys was at my house, and ye Nottoways and Meherrins likewise; ye Sapponey King complained that ye Nottoways and Tuscaradas had killed two of his people and demanded ye delivery of the murtherers."

The Nottoways in answer said that the Saponeys had killed three of their men and wounded two others, and when the Saponeys protested it was not they but Toteros, the Nottoways replied that the Sapponeys and Toteros were as one people. The Nottoways further said that they had engaged the Sapponeys to assist them in cutting off the Toteros and had paid them a quantity of roanoke, and would pay them still further for their aid.

The Meherrin and Nottoway tribes lived in Virginia on the rivers of those names, and the Tuscaroras in North Carolina; all three tribes belonged to the Iroquoian Race, and were ancient enemies of the Saponeys.

After the three tribes of Occaneechi, Tolero, and Saponey united they were known by the single name of Saponey. Governor Spottswood felt a great pity for these friendly Virginia Indians who had once been so powerful and were now so helpless and took them under the protection of the government, settling them in Brunswick County about three miles from the Roanoke River. He had a good opinion[39] of their fidelity and courage and believed that they would be a barrier in that part of the country against the incursions of foreign Indians. In 1714 he built Fort Christiana for them and made an attempt to educate and Christianize their children, employing Mr. Charles Griffin, a schoolmaster, at a salary of fifty pounds yearly.

In a letter[40] written by Governor Spottswood in 1715 to Governor Hunter of New York he said:

"I have no reason of late to complain of ye Senecas yet as they pass frequently along our frontiers, I can not but be apprehensive of their giving disturbance to our Indians: Especially to the Saponies, a nation of all our Tributaries the best disposed to the English, and which I am more concerned to protect, in regard of their readiness to let their children be bred up Christians, and that in order thereto there are 100 of them at a school I have lately set up at their town."

---

[39]Byrd.

[40]Va. Calendar State Papers, Vol. 1, p. 179.

Mr. Griffin the schoolmaster is described[41] as "a man of good family, who by the innocense of his life, and the sweetness of his disposition, was perfectly well qualified for the undertaking. Besides he had so the art of mixing pleasure with instruction that he had not a scholar who did not love him affectionately."

Hugh Jones, who wrote "The Present State of Virginia," in 1722, knew Mr. Griffin and Fort Christiana well, and said that all that he wrote of the Indians was told him by Mr. Griffin who gained his information from the Saponeys."

Jones said: "I have seen seventy-seven Indian children at a time at school under the careful management of the worthy Mr. Charles Griffin. These children could all read and say their cathechism and Prayers tolerably well." Again, "The Indians so loved Mr. Griffin that I have seen them hug him and lift him up in their arms, and fain would have choosen him for a King of the Saponey nation."

But the school at Fort Christiana came to an end through Mr. Griffin's being called to William and Mary College to instruct the Indian boys there, and so this good and benign influence in the lives of the Saponeys was lost.

Jones, again speaking of the Saponeys, said: "They have tolerable good notions of natural Justice, Equity, Honor and Honesty to which Rules whereof their great men strictly adhere; but their common people will lye, cheat and steal."

Their belief in the ancient custom of an eye for an eye, is illustrated in the following occurrence: "Major (Joshua) Wynne was shot and killed by an Indian because one of our servants had killed one of their great men, and upon the trial of the Indian they pleaded that we were the aggressors and that they never rest without revenge: and that now they said they and we were equal, having each lost a great man: wherefore to avoid more bloodshed there was a necessity to Pardon the Indian."

Despite the protection of the government the Saponeys continued to suffer attacks from the northern savages. In 1717 Fort Christiana was beset by a party of Iroquois who killed six and carried off a man and a woman. In 1719 Governor Spottswood wrote[42] to the president of the Council of New York complaining of the constant depredations of the Five Nations and said that if the Governor of New York could not restrain them that the Virginians would do so, even though an Indian war followed.

[41] Hugh Jones.

[42] *Va. Mag. History,* Vol. 13, p. 9.

In 1722 Governor Spottswood was instrumental in having the Treaty[43] of Albany drawn up with the governors of New York and Pennsylvania and the Five Nations, in which the Iroquois were restricted in their travels through Virginia to the west of the Blue Ridge, "not upon pain of death to molest the tributary Indians of the Colony. It is furthermore agreed upon by the Indians that whenever they shall make a fire in the woods, they will place a stone in the midst of the fire as a sign that none but friends have been there."

This treaty, however, failed to restrain the Iroquois, for the following spring the militias of the frontier counties were put in a state of defense, fearing an attack from the northern Indians.

The records[44] of this time reveal what pains the government of Virginia took to protect these tributary Indians and to keep the peace among the various tribes. Nathaniel Harrison, of Surry County, was Indian agent for the tribes between the James and Roanoke Rivers. He represented to the Council in February, 1726, that the Saponeys complained that when a party of their Indians went hunting on the Roanoke River they were attacked in the night by the Tuscaroras, and seven of their men captured or slain.

In April, the great men of the Saponeys appeared[45] before the Council and repeated their complaint against the Tuscaroras, praying that if the government could not obtain satisfaction, that they be allowed to take their revenge in their own way. The great men of the Saponeys also complained to the Council that the English brought rum to their town to sell to their young men, causing great disorder among them. Colonel Byrd wrote that the good purpose of Governor Spottswood in gathering the Indians at Christiana had been to a large extent frustrated by the way in which the white people of the neighborhood corrupted their morals and ruined their health with rum. Strong drink was continually causing them to break the laws of the Colony.

One of the great men of the Saponeys committed a murder while drunk for which he was tried in the courts and hanged, in 1728. Governor Gooch of Virginia reported[46] the occurrence to the Lords of Trade of England, saying:

"The murder was committed while the Indian was drunk which they look upon as a just excuse, because, as they say a man is not accountable

[43]*Va. Mag. History,* Vol. 12, pp. 339-340.
[44]*Va. Mag. History,* Vol. 32.
[45]*Va. Mag. History,* Vol. 32.
[46]*Va. Mag. History,* Vol. 28, p. 300.

for what he did while he was deprived of his reason. Yet they readily delivered him up to justice, upon my first message, and he has since been tried and executed without any sign of resentment although he was in much esteem among them. I had ordered some of the nation to be at the tryal who did attend, and by an interpreter were made to understand that the Proceedings in the court against them were the same as in like case they would be against a white man."

But Governor Gooch was mistaken, the Saponeys felt great grief and indignation at the ignominious death suffered by one of their great men, and threatened[47] to drive the whites across James River. The following year they left Virginia and went to live with their friends, the Catawbas, in Carolina.

But in the spring[48] of 1732 the Saponeys again sought the protection of the Virginia government, and were permitted to settle on either the Roanoke or Appomattox rivers, on any lands not already granted to His Majesty's subjects. No sooner had they returned, however, than trouble began with the neighboring Nottoways, who attacked their fort in the month of August with divers foreign Indians (Iroquois). On account of these disorders the Council enacted:

"Whereas the Nottoways frequently entertain members of the Five Nations of New York, who by their Treaties of Peace are bound not to pass eastward of the mountains, they are to forbear entertaining or giving encouragement to the coming of any of these foreign Indians."

But despite these precautions again in December of the same year information was brought before the Council that the northern Indians were on the frontier plantations of Brunswick, lying in wait to cut off the Saponey Indians, and for the defense of the inhabitants as well as for the Saponeys the militia from the several frontier counties was ordered out.

In June, 1733, the Saponeys and Nottoways represented[49] to the Council that they wished to form a treaty of peace, and include the Tuscaroras of North Carolina. The Nottoways and Tuscaroras being members of the Iroquoian race, were ancient enemies of the Saponeys (of the Siouian race), and we may suppose that the latter felt themselves no longer able to contend against their hereditary foes, and surrendered to them.

---

[47]Calendar Virginia State Papers, Vol. 1, p. 215.
[48]*Va. Mag. Hist.*, Vol. 13, p. 11.
[49]*Va. Mag. Hist.*, Vol. 13, p. 294.

Mr. Robert Hix of Surry, an experienced Indian trader, was appointed to attend the Saponey Indians in the making of the treaty, and to report the terms to the Council. Leave was granted the Saponeys to go and live with the Tuscaroras, but if at any time they wished to return to Virginia, lands would be granted them along the Roanoke River. But never again did the Saponeys return to their native land, and in 1740 removed with the Tuscaroras to the north where[50] in 1753 they were incorporated into the body of the Iroquois, becoming the Sixth[51] Nation of the North. The measure was approved by Sir William Johnson, the English representative, and from this time the Saponey chiefs sat in the Council of the League on equal terms with the Iroquoian chiefs.

Thus passed from Virginia this noble tribe of red men, leaving to us who have succeeded to their domain but a faint outline of their tragic story.

[50]Mooney.

[51]When the Tuscaroras were adopted by the Senecas, they formed the Sixth Nation in the League.

CHAPTER II

NATURAL CONDITIONS

Pittsylvania County is centrally situated in south midland Virginia, touching on the North Carolina line. Its greatest dimension from north to south is forty miles, from east to west twenty-eight miles, giving a total area of 1,012 square miles. It ranks first in size among Virginia's one hundred counties.

Pittsylvania lies wholly in the Piedmont plateau, having a rolling surface, broken by many small mountain ridges. The first range of hills westward from the coast of sufficient size to dignify with the name of mountain is a gentle ridge traversing the southeastern part of the County, called the White Oak Mountain. A score of miles further on rise Turkey Cock Mountain in the west and Smith Mountain in the northwest, both rugged and steep; while across the northern part of the county stretch Jasper, Farmers and Brushy Mountains, well defined ridges standing several hundred feet above the surrounding upland country. In between these low ranges and rolling hills are fertile valleys watered by many streams.

Pittsylvania is well drained by three water systems; Dan River in the southern part, Banister River in the central part, while Staunton River forms the northern boundary of the county.

The first written description of this section is given by John Lederer when he made his explorations in 1670, and visited the Indians here; for those other early explorers and traders, Colonel Abram Wood, Colonel William Claiborne, and their associates, left no written account of their adventures.

Lederer wrote that the country near the Virginia and North Carolina line "tho' high[1] is level, and for the most part a rich soil, as I judge by the growth of the trees, yet where it is inhabited by Indians it lies open in spacious plains." It is surprising to find how much open land was found by the early explorers throughout Virginia, large areas of cleared spaces and meadows being often met with, which were called savannahs.

Beverley wrote[2] that the explorers of midland Virginia "found large level plains with fine savannahs three or four miles wide, on which there were an infinite quantity of turkeys, deer, elk and buffalo, so gentle and

[1]Lederer's.

[2]Beverley's "History of Virginia."

undisturbed that they had no fear at the appearance of men, but suffer them to come almost within reach of their hands." And again he said: "In some places lie great plats of low and very rich ground well timbered, in others, large spots of meadows and savannahs wherein are hundreds of acres without any tree at all, but yield grass and reeds of incredible height."

Mr. John Fontaine records a trip he made to Fort Christiana in company with Governor Spottswood April, 1716:[3]

"We saw this day several fine tracts of lands and plains called savannahs, which lie along the river side, much like our low meadow lands in England. There is neither tree nor shrub that grows upon these plains, nothing but good grass which, for want of being mowed or eaten down by cattle, grows rank and coarse. These places are not miry but good firm ground."

Colonel William Byrd of Westover, a member of the commission which surveyed the dividing line between Virginia and North Carolina, in 1728, wrote a delightful[4] account of the expedition in which he told many interesting things of that section of Virginia which later became Pittsylvania County.

After leaving the inhabited part of the country Colonel Byrd named all the streams over which they passed, and said: "On October the 10th, we crossed the south branch of the Roanoke River for the first time and named it Dan. It was about 200 yards wide where we forded it and when we came over to the west side we found it lined with a forest of tall canes." It cost them some time and labor to cut a passage through the canes, but in the meantime they had "leizure to take a full view of this charming river. The stream which was perfectly clear ran down about two miles an hour. The bottom was covered with a coarse gravel spangled very thick with a shining substance—It made the river exceedingly beautiful."

The point at which they crossed the river is the southeast corner of Pittsylvania County.

Two miles further on they came to a creek which they named Cane,[5] "from the prodigious quantity of tree canes that fringed the banks of it." Colonel Byrd described these canes as growing from twelve to sixteen feet high, as thick as a man's wrist, and keeping green winter

[3] "Memoirs of a Huguenot Family," 270-271, Maury.

[4] "A History of the Dividing Line," by William Byrd.

[5] Cane Creek, a tributary of Dan River, lies in the southeastern part of Pittsylvania County.

and summer for six years when they seeded and died. The following spring they began to shoot again and the second or third year regained their former stature. "They grow so thick, and their roots lace together so firmly that they are the best guard that can be of the river bank, which would otherwise be washed away by the frequent inundations that happen in this part of the world." It is singular that the growth of canes which nature provided to conserve the soil and protect the banks of the streams has entirely disappeared from this county.

After going two miles further on the surveying party again crossed the Dan, "still a beautiful stream, rolling down its limpid and murmuring water among the rocks." Near by from one of the highest hills was made the first discovery of mountains to the northwest, which looked like "ranges of blue clouds rising one above the other."

Col. Byrd remarked here upon the number of wild grapes found growing in the woods, which made their going difficult. He said, "they make it evident how natural both the soil and climate of this country are to brier." Today the "muscadine" and the "sloe" still grow abundantly through the woods, burdening the September air with the heavy fragrance of their delicious perfume. Byrd further remarked, that, "our Indian killed a bear two years old that was feasting on these grapes."

Again within a few miles the Dan was crossed twice more which proved to be a bend of the river, where the party encamped for the night. The view of the river here was so beautiful that they kept climbing to a small hill nearby to enjoy it the more. Here Colonel Byrd noted that the wild geese were beginning to arrive from the north where they summer around Hudson Bay; on their first coming they were lean, but soon fattened on the grass of the river banks. The Indians, he said, called them "Cohonks" from their cry, and marked the New Year by their coming.

Soon again the surveying party crossed the Dan for the fifth[6] time, and observed several small Indian fields nearby, where they supposed the Saura Indian had been used to plant corn, for their town in which they formerly lived was only seven or eight miles south. Colonel Byrd described these fields as producing a sweet kind of grass excellent for horses; and added that the "Indian killed a fat buck, the men brought in four bears and a brace of wild turkeys, so that this was truly a land of plenty." The stream on which this plentiful amount of game was

[6]The southern boundary line of the county is crossed by Dan River five times, the river making two bends.

found was named Cascade[7] by reason of its waterfalls. The Indian employed to keep the party supplied with meat was a Sapony from Fort Christiana, called Bearskin.

The haziness of the atmosphere was now marked by Col. Byrd, which he said was due to the firing of the woods by the Indians, "for we are now near the route the northern savages take when they go out to war against the southern nations." (Byrd referred to the great War Trail of the Iroquois which crossed through Henry and Franklin Counties.) He said the reason fire made such havoc here in the wilderness was because the woods were not burnt every year, as they generally were amongst the inhabited areas; and the accumulated trash and leaves of years, when finally set fire to by some passing Indians, made such a conflagration that it swept all before it. Wood[8] firing was the besetting sin of the Virginia Indian, but it was done for economic reasons, making living conditions easier for him. He depended upon the wild game of the forest for the meat for his table, and by regularly firing the woods the undergrowth was killed out, only the larger trees being able to survive his periodic burnings. This produced an openness of woods which was favorable to the growth of berries and grass upon which the game fed, and also made travel through the woods less troublesome. It is said[9] that "freedom from undergrowth was one of the most notable features of the original woods of Virginia." In the descriptions of eastern Virginia left by the earlier writers frequent mention is made of the open parklike appearance of the forests, large trees standing some distance apart, with grass and flowers growing underneath. Wherever the Virginia Indian was accustomed to go he fired the woods, and when the explorers pushed into the back country they found he had been as industrious with his forest fires there as elsewhere, and the meadows and savannahs met with were due to his firings.

Louis[10] Michel made a journey through Virginia in 1702, of which he wrote: "The forests (of Virginia) are convenient to ride or hunt in. The trees are far apart, with no undergrowth on the ground, so that one can ride anywhere on horseback. The game is easily discovered because of the openness of the forest. The hunting of the Indian helps to clear the forest and pasture." He then described "fire hunting," in which the woods are fired in a circle, driving the game to the center,

[7]Cascade Creek lies in the southwestern part of the county.

[8]*William and Mary Quarterly,* Vol. 19, page 86.

[9]Dr. Philip Alexander Bruce's "Economic History of Virginia in the 17th Century."

[10]*Virginia Mag. History,* Vol. 24, p. 41.

where it is easily slaughtered. The openness of the early forests of Pittsylvania is a tradition[11] handed down today.

The surveying party now passed beyond the present confines of Pittsylvania County and became very fearful of encountering some of the northern Indians, for they saw signs of their encampments, but happily none of the savages were met with. The next two rivers were named Irwin and Mayo in honor of the two surveyors, Alexander Irwin and William Mayo.

Six fat bears were brought in the night they camped on Mayo River, one bear being so fat that there was no way to kill him except by firing into his ear. The surveying party brought their bread with them and depended upon the game of the country for meat, which was found in abundance after reaching the section which later became Pittsylvania—deer, bear, buffalo and wild turkey were plentiful since no settlers had yet come in to disturb them. And to show their gratitude for being thus fed "by Heaven in the great and solitary wilderness," they agreed to wear in their hats the maosti, which is in Indian language the beard of the wild turkey cock, and on their breasts the figure of the bird with wings extended, holding in his claws this motto "Vici Coturnicum," which meant that they were fed in the wilderness like Moses and the children of Israel, but with wild turkey instead of quail.

Upon reaching the mountains (now western Patrick County), the surveying party turned back, having run the line 241 miles.

On their return they halted again at the bend of the Dan, for "there was no passing the angle of the river without halting a moment to entertain our eyes with that Charming Prospect." Byrd marked the richness of the soil here and said: "All the land we travelled over this day, and the day before, that is to say from the river Irvin (Smith) to Sable Creek (the bend) is exceedingly rich, both on the Virginia side of the line, and that of Carolina. Besides whole forests of canes that adorn the banks of the rivers and creeks thereabout, the fertility of the soil throws out such a quantity of winter grass that horses and cattle might keep themselves in heart all the cold season without the help of any fodder. Nor have the low grounds only this advantage but likewise the Higher Land.

"I question not but there are 30,000 acres at least lying altogether as fertile as the lands were said to be about Babylon. But this hath the advantage of being a higher and consequently a much healthier situation than that.

[11]Mr. James Carter and the Rev'd Chiswell Dabney.

"Besides grazing and tillage, which would abundantly compensate their labor, they might plant vineyards upon the hills.

"They might too produce hemp, flax and cotton in what quantity they pleased, not only for their own use, but likewise for sale. They might raise very plentiful orchards of both peaches and apples * * *. In short everything will grow plentifully here to supply either the want or wantonness of man."

This glowing praise was given to the lands of southwestern Pittsylvania County, along the dividing line and across on the North Carolina side.

"Happy will be the People," exclaimed Byrd, "destined for so wholesome a situation, where they may live to fulness of days, and which is much better still with much content and gaiety of heart."

After passing the last ford of the Dan, at the present dividing line between Pittsylvania and Halifax Counties, Byrd said "the men grieved sorely for they reckoned themselves out of the latitude of bears, which like not the neighborhood of merciless man."

Five years later Colonel Byrd again visited this section of the state when he came with a party of friends in 1733 to view a purchase of 20,000 acres which he had made in North Carolina, bordering on the dividing line, south of Pittsylvania, and which he named[12] the Land of Eden. These lands were a part of those he had so praised on his former trip. Byrd's party proceeded to the forks of the Dan and Staunton Rivers and on the three Indian islands there (Tutelo, Occoneechi and Sapony) they found the soil rich, the timber large, and a kind of pea growing, "very grateful to cattle and horses which holds green all the winter." In the old fields where the Indians lived grass grew as high as a horse and rider. In the wooded parts they found a "vetch that is green all winter and a great support of horses and cattle though it is feared the hogs will root it all up."

Six miles beyond the forks they came to the house of Peter Mitchell, who was "the highest inhabitant up"; then for six miles they rode "through charming Low Grounds to a large stream which we agreed to name Banister River." Mr. John Banister was a member of Colonel Byrd's party and no doubt it was in his honor the stream was named.

On revisiting the scenes of his former expedition, Byrd found that the canes which had formerly lined the banks of the streams had withered and died, but that new shoots were already springing up.

---

[12]William Byrd also wrote an account of this trip which he called "A Trip to the Land of Eden."

The plat of the Land of Eden was in the shape of a wedge, measuring one mile across at the east end (the bend of Dan River), three miles across at the west end (where Smith River crosses the dividing line), and fifteen miles in length. Upon this trip Byrd's party had the prodigious luck to bring down a young buffalo, upon which they made a great feast.

On their return Colonel Byrd visited a man named Aaron Pinston, living on Tewahominy (now Aaron's Creek) who was "the highest inhabitant up" on the south side of Dan River. Byrd wrote,[13] "he reacons himself perfectly safe from danger, and if the bears, wolves and panthers are as harmless as the Indians his stock might be safe too."

Further proof of the great abundance of game once found here is given in the Surveyor's Book of Land Grants, the earliest record in Pittsylvania Court House, dating from 1737, four years after Colonel Byrd's last visit. The country being all one vast wilderness in order to describe the metes and bounds of the grants, the surveyors frequently made mention of the natural conditions met with, and in doing so unconsciously left for us a description of the country before man made his home here.

There were still many buffalos roaming the hills, leaving their well marked trails through the forests to feeding grounds and watering places. There is mention of these buffalo paths in the early grants. In 1743 there was surveyed for William[14] McClain 400 acres on the ridge between Difficult and Stewart Creeks, "beginning a mile above the old Buffalo Path." In 1745 there was surveyed for John Coles[15] 400 acres, "beginning at the head of Terrible Creek, thence down the Buffalo Path." These grants were located in eastern Halifax County. There was a buffalo path mentioned on Chestnut Creek, in Franklin County.

Time has preserved one of these long ago buffalo paths in the southeastern part of the county. Across the broad lawn of Mr. John White, who lives near Laurel Grove, there runs a slight depression which can be readily discerned in the smooth green turf. This trace is said to be an old buffalo path that led to a nearby stream.

An old frontiersman[16] said of buffalo roads: "In the neighborhood of all licks with which I have been acquainted there are roads of very ancient appearance which were made by the animals, and it is sometimes

[13]Byrd's "Trip to Eden."

[14]Surveyor's Record, page 10.

[15]Surveyor's Record, page 18.

[16]*Virginia Mag. History,* Vol. 7, p. 9.

the case that the roads are located with a good deal of judgment when crossing a hill or ridge." No doubt many of these buffalo paths became the first roads of the settlers.

There was a well known place on Wynne's Creek called "the buffalo bed," which must have been a favorite retreat for the herd; while there were "buffalo rowls" (rolls) on Jonakin Creek, and "buffalo camp" on Mill Creek. (Thomas Jonakin was an early settler.) Buffalo "licks" were numerous and named on various streams throughout this section; there were upper and lower licks on Sandy and Miry Creeks, and great licks on Wynne's Creek and Cane Creek; others were mentioned on Whitethorn, Tomahawk, Pye Creeks of Pigg River, Chestnut, Allen and Catawba Creeks.

An early writer[17] described licks as being commonly on the banks of rivers, creeks or spring heads, where the clay or earth is impregnated with salt. "These licks are natural openings of a few acres in extent quite destitute of timber, not a tree, not even a vestige of one, to be perceived in them; but the ground therein is always covered with an abundance of excellent long grass. They are frequented by deer, elk, buffalo, horned cattle and horses which daily resort to them to lick the earth or clay with their tongues."

From a road order we learn that a ford on Pigg River was known in 1774 as the Buffalo Ford; today there is a Buffalo Ford on Banister River, near "Coles' Hill."

Fearing the presence of man, with the coming of the settlers the buffalo retired westward and passed over the mountains, seeking freer range. A gap of the Blue Ridge in western Franklin County was named Buffalo Gap.

The surveyors also made mention of the bears found here, referring to trees which had been felled for catching them, as for instance: "To John Nicholds[18] four hundred acres on Sycamore Creek, beginning at a White Oak cut down for a bair."

"1754. To Robert[19] Pusey four hundred acres on Otter Creek of Irwin River beginning at a forked poplar with a hole near the root made to take out a bear."

So numerous were the bears that there was a place on Sandy River known as Bear Garden: "1745. To Richard[20] Green 200 acres on both

[17]J. F. D. Smythe's "Travels," pages 140-41.
[18]Surveyor's Record, p. 91.
[19]Surveyor's Record, p. 206.
[20]Surveyor's Record, p. 18.

sides Sandy River, beginning at the lower end of Bear Garden." This property later came into the possession of Colonel John Wilson, who in his will of 1820 bequeathed Bear Garden to one of his sons.

There were beaver dams and beaver ponds on Banister, Mayo, Pigg, and Stinking Rivers, and on Tomahawk Creek. These were the little animals whose fur was so prized by the trader that in his search for it he made long and perilous trips into the unknown interior. Fish dams, elk shoals, goose ponds and wolves dens were named as pointers on various streams throughout the county, and so numerous were the wolves that in order to exterminate them a reward per head was offered as late as 1800.

Turkey Cock Mountain was so named from the many flocks of wild turkeys once found there, and in 1746 a place on Pigg River was called Turkey Bottom. It is with pride we note the return of these noble birds to Pittsylvania, where they were once so plentiful, and then all but exterminated through the greed of the hunter. Several flocks have been seen in the "Meadows."

The "Meadows" are a peculiar formation of country, many miles in breadth and length, which extend through the eastern part of the county. It is crossed by many streams, and is thought to be the bed of a prehistoric lake. They have always been a favorite feeding ground for game, and as late as the beginning of the last century Indian arrow points could be gathered from the fields almost like gravel. (Captain Issac Coles authority). As late as 1840 deer were still found there. A very early hunting path led up Banister River, probably to the "Meadows."

In the original growth of our forests there were trees of tremendous size. In a grant of 1748 to Isaac Cloud, mention is made of a "hollow chestnut tree in which said Cloud and Smith used to camp, on the grounds between a branch of Banister and Turkey Cock." This tree stood near Callands and it was necessarily of great size to admit of sleeping quarters for two men. Again we gain an idea of the size of the original forest trees from the great width of the boards with which some of the oldest houses in this section are ceiled; as for instance the Carter home of "Green Rock" and the Abram Shelton home at Chalk Level.

Col. Byrd remarked upon the many nut bearing trees found in this section, the walnut, hickory nut, scaley bark, pig nut, and chestnut trees growing in so great abundance that he thought the industry of nut-oil (similar to olive-oil) might be profitable. The early grants refer to "black walnut bottoms," and there was a "while walnut puncheon camp" on Mayo in 1754. These noble trees have all but disappeared from our forests.

The pawpaw, a tree native to this section, has the very unusual property of striking fire. This was known to the Indians, whose method of using it, Byrd tells us, was as follows: "They hold one of these dry sticks in each hand, and by rubbing them hard and quick together, rarify the Air in such a Manner as to fetch Fire in ten Minutes." This fire was always used in their sacrifices and ceremonies, since it was a profanation to make use of a fire already kindled. The pawpaw is a small tree found growing along the streams and in the fall of the year bears a fruit somewhat like a banana.

CHAPTER III

FIRST SETTLEMENT

At the end of the first one hundred years following the landing of the colonists at Jamestown, the settlement of Virginia had not extended westward beyond Tidewater, though the back country had been explored and was well known to the traders.

Colonel Cadwallader[1] Jones, who had long conducted an extensive fur trade from his settlement on the Rappahannock River, in 1698 presented to Governor Nicholson a plan for trade with the Indians of the Great Lake regions, accompanied by a map of the country. On this map was traced the two mountain systems in the west with the Valley of Virginia lying between, and the six great rivers of the State taking their rise in the mountains. Jones named the more western range the Appalachian Mountains but to the Blue Ridge he gave different names in different localities, and in this section called it the Occaneechi Mountains for the local tribe of Indians with whom he had been trading; he also named the Roanoke River the Occaneechi River.

The Governor and Council took no action at this time in regard to the development of the western lands; but it is very probable that Jones's map fell into the hands of Alexander Spottswood when he became Lieutenant Governor of Virginia, 1710, for Spottswood said in a despatch of Feb. 1st, 1719-20:

"I have many[2] mapps and Draughts drawn from my Observation in my travels through the inhabited parts of this colony. I have others from the Information of the most credible and Intelligent persons I have met with here: Some from the Acco'ts of our Traders and others from the Relations of the Indians."

Spottswood, being a man of action and foresight, set about developing the resources of the colony and in 1716 led his Golden Horse Shoe party of gentlemen explorers across the state to the top of the Blue Ridge and saw the promise of this western country. As a result of this expedition two counties, Spottsylvania in the north and Brunswick in the south were established by Acts of Assembly in November 1720, which recited[3] that the frontiers toward the Blue Ridge were exposed to "dangers from the Indians and the late settlement of the French toward the west-

[1] *Virginia Magazine History,* Vol. 30, page 336.

[2] Spottswood's Letters II, 332. In his will he left his books, maps and mathematical instruments to William and Mary College.

[3] Hening's "Statutes," Vol. 4, pp. 77-79.

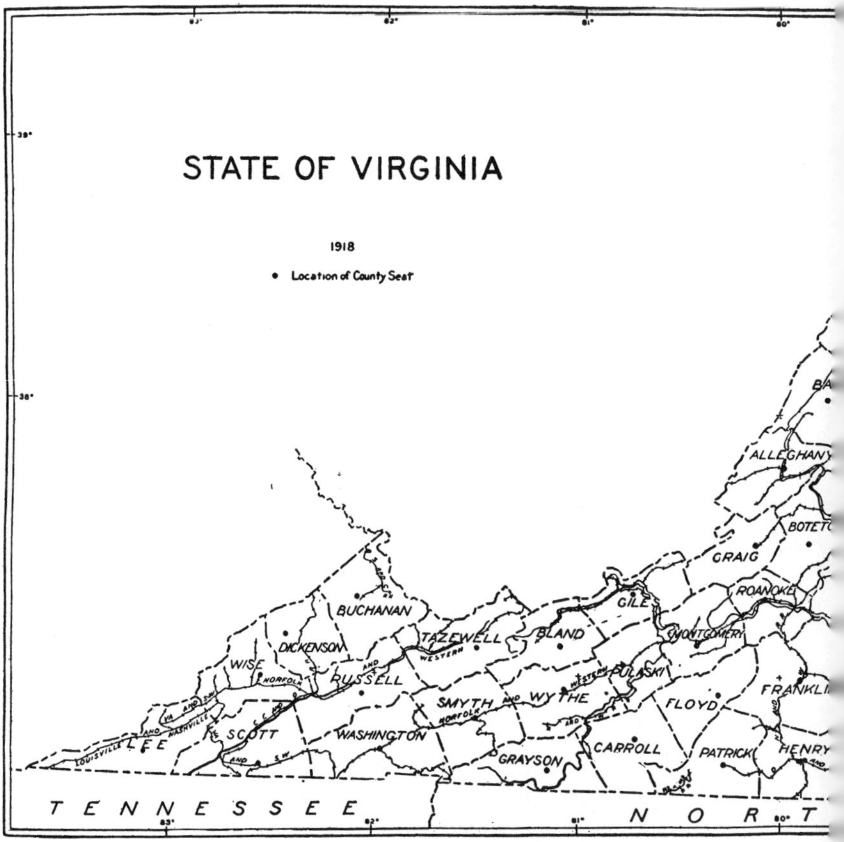
STATE OF VIRGINIA
1918
Location of County Seat
BUCHANAN
DICKENSON
WISE
LEE
SCOTT
RUSSELL
TAZEWELL
BLAND
SMYTH
WYTHE
WASHINGTON
GRAYSON
CARROLL
PULASKI
MONTGOMERY
FLOYD
PATRICK
HENRY
CRAIG
ROANOKE
ALLEGHANY
TENNESSEE
NORFOLK
WESTERN
LOUISVILLE
NASHVILLE
83°
82°
81°
80°
39°
38°

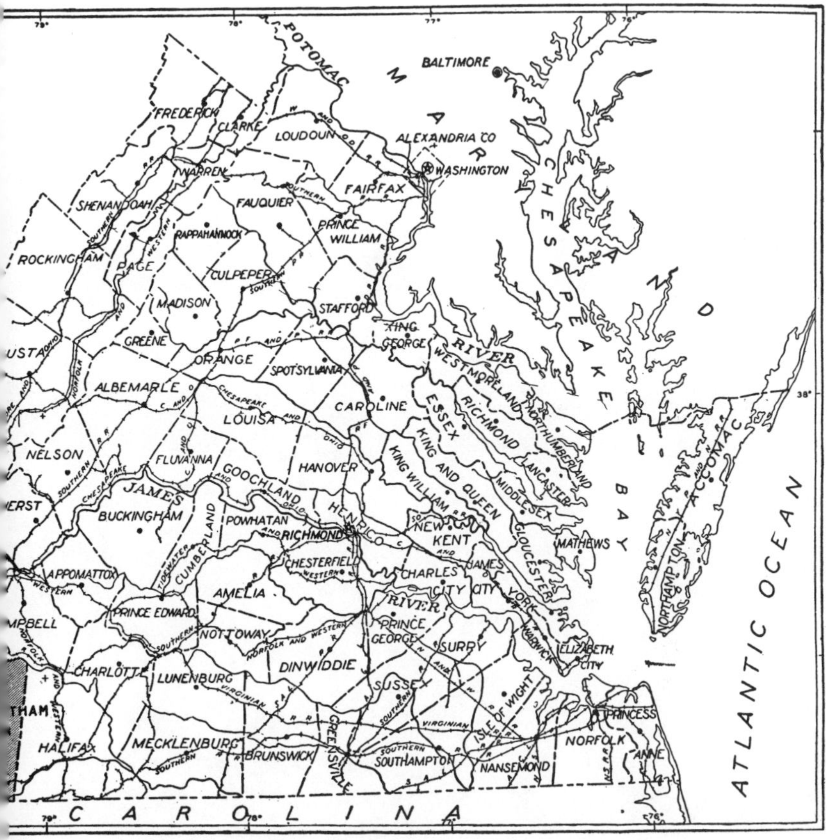

POTOMAC
MARYLAND
BALTIMORE
ALEXANDRIA CO
WASHINGTON
CHESAPEAKE BAY
FREDERICK
CLARKE
LOUDOUN
WARREN
FAIRFAX
SHENANDOAH
FAUQUIER
PRINCE WILLIAM
RAPPAHANNOCK
ROCKINGHAM
PAGE
CULPEPER
MADISON
STAFFORD
KING GEORGE
GREENE
RIVER
WESTMORELAND
ORANGE
SPOTSYLVANIA
ALBEMARLE
LOUISA
CAROLINE
ESSEX
RICHMOND
NORTHUMBERLAND
NELSON
FLUVANNA
HANOVER
KING AND QUEEN
KING WILLIAM
LANCASTER
MIDDLESEX
ACCOMAC
JAMES
GOOCHLAND
BUCKINGHAM
CUMBERLAND
POWHATAN
RICHMOND
HENRICO
NEW KENT
GLOUCESTER
MATHEWS
NORTHAMPTON
APPOMATTOX
CHESTERFIELD
CHARLES CITY
JAMES CITY
YORK
AMELIA
RIVER
PRINCE EDWARD
NOTTOWAY
PRINCE GEORGE
SURRY
WARWICK
ELIZABETH CITY
CHARLOTTE
LUNENBURG
DINWIDDIE
SUSSEX
ISLE OF WIGHT
PRINCESS ANNE
HALIFAX
MECKLENBURG
BRUNSWICK
GREENSVILLE
SOUTHAMPTON
NANSEMOND
NORFOLK
ATLANTIC OCEAN
CAROLINA
79°
78°
77°
76°
38°

ward of the mountains." The French settlements referred to were Kaskaskia and Cahokia in Illinois, founded in 1700; Detroit founded in Michigan in 1701; and Vincennes in Indiana in 1705, and these were regarded as a menace to the future development of the colony.

The boundaries of Brunswick were not definitely stated but were to be defined by the Governor with the consent of the Council; the Act stated however, that the initial point of the County should be the Roanoke River where that stream flowed into North Carolina, and should extend westward to the Blue Ridge Mountains, and include the "Southern Pass," which was probably the water gap of Staunton River where it breaks through the Blue Ridge. The lines were never defined with certainty, and can only be determined by the legislative acts establishing new counties. Roughly speaking, the boundaries of old Brunswick were the State of North Carolina on the south, the Blue Ridge Mountains on the west, the upper reaches of the James River on the north, and on the east a straight line drawn from the James to the point where the Roanoke flowed into North Carolina. From this territory were later formed the counties of Lunenburg, Mecklenburg, Charlotte, Halifax, Pittsylvania, Bedford, Campbell, Henry, Franklin, Patrick, Prince Edward and a part of Amelia.

The heads of Virginia's government began to feel that the French settlements to the west of the mountains constituted a real menace to the future development of the colony, and inducements were offered to settlers who would brave the dangers of the wilderness and make their homes in the two new counties.

In the Acts for establishing the counties in 1720 £1,000 of public money was ordered to be set aside for the use of the "Christian tithables" who settled in the new counties, to purchase arms and ammunition for their defense. In 1723, the Lords[4] of Trade of London, upon the petition of the Virginia Council, exempted the inhabitants of Spottsylvania and Brunswick from the payment of quit rents and the purchase of land rights for the space of seven years. The quit rents were a yearly tax of one shilling for every fifty acres of land, payable directly to the Crown; the land rights were customary fees due for taking out land grants. In the same order the Crown limited land grants to 1000 acres per person; this was intended to encourage actual settlers along the frontier, rather than the forming of huge estates. Later acts showed that this policy was changed, for grants of immense holdings were permitted, but the principle

[4] *Virginia Magazine History,* Vol. 12, page 346.

was maintained in requiring three out of every fifty acres to be cultivated, or when that was not practical, three head of cattle to be maintained, or a house of certain dimensions to be built. The policy of the government was to extend the frontier line as quickly as possible.

Settlers at once found their way up the fertile valley of the Rappahannock and made their homes in Spottsylvania, but the development of Brunswick was much slower for the reason that the streams which watered old Brunswick flowed south into North Carolina, and the line of settlement in Virginia ever led up its water courses which formed convenient highways for travel. The would-be settler of Brunswick, having no water highway at hand for his use, must needs hew one out through the wilderness. This being so arduous a task, it was only through the gradual development of the country that the frontier line was made to recede year by year, and the fertile valleys of the Roanoke and its tributaries at length to become the home of man.

Brunswick was so sparsely settled that it was not until 1732, twelve years after its establishment, that a court for the county was organized. The first justices chosen for the great southern county were Henry Fox, Henry Embry, John Wall, John Irby, George Walton, William Wynne, Richard Birch, Nathaniel Edwards, Charles King, and William Maclin. Richard Birch qualified as Sheriff and Drury Stith as Clerk, but Stith later became surveyor of Brunswick, a position of much trust and authority in the uncharted wilderness. His deputies were Peter Fontaine, a son of the rector of Charles City County, Robert and Sherwood Walton. With the opening of the western country to settlers land speculation became rife, and Monette said, "In none of the provinces had the infatuation for western lands been carried to a greater extent than in Virginia."

Judge Chalkley[5] said of Virginia at this period, "A bureaucracy or cabal was in complete control (of the colony) and there was the opportunity to establish families and fortunes through grants of large tracts of lands, which were no sooner marked out than they were taken under the military protection of the colony * * *. The leaders were men of large caliber and great force and had a motive sufficiently exacting to keep them active. It must be admitted that the main object of the leaders was self-aggrandisement."

While the men who sat in executive council in Williamsburg issued orders of council for many thousands of acres of lands for themselves,

[5]*Virginia Magazine History,* Vol. 30, page 190.

they also brought in the emigrants—the Scotch-Irish, the Germans and the Swiss to settle upon their lands, and extended Virginia's frontier line with amazing rapidity.

In 1732 Colonel Beverley was granted 100,000 acres in what is now Augusta County and brought in a band of Scotch-Irish emigrants from Pennsylvania for settlers.

Colonel William Byrd, who had seen for himself the fertility of Brunswick's western lands, petitioned the Council[6] on June 11, 1735 for 100,000 acres along Roanoke River, between the waters of Birch Creek and Irwin River, on which to settle a number of Switzers and other foreign Protestants whom he speedily expected. The land lying between Birch Creek and Irwin River is southern Pittsylvania County.

Many delays attended Colonel Byrd's plan of bringing in a body of emigrants, and at a meeting of the Council on November[7] the 3rd, 1737, he petitioned for a further time of one year for seating his lands on Roanoke River. In that year he published a book in German called "New Found Eden in Virginia,"[8] telling of the advantages of Virginia climate and soil in his efforts to attract Swiss and German settlers. But misfortune followed Colonel Byrd's attempt. The vessel bringing in the Swiss emigrants, after having safely braved the dangers of the long sea voyage, was overtaken by a severe storm in Lynnhaven Bay and badly wrecked, many of the colonists losing their lives. The *Virginia Gazette* gave an account of the disaster and said that ninety of the survivors proposed, however, to go on to the place of settlement.

But Colonel Byrd was not to be daunted by defeat and again in October,[9] 1738 he petitioned the Council of Virginia for further time "for saving and seating his lands on the Roanoke for the settlement of a number of Swiss emigrants who he is advised are now at sea." Another year's time was granted him for "bringing said Switzers upon land aforesaid since it may be impractical for them to go thither to dwell during the ensuing winter."

At a meeting of the Council in October, 1739, another petition from Colonel Byrd was read and twelve months time was allowed him.

There was one other grant of land in western Brunswick of like proportion to Colonel Byrd's, when 100,000 acres[10] were granted in 1753

[6]Cal. Va. State Papers, Vol. 1, page 223.

[7]*Va. Mag. History,* Vol. 14, page 15.

[8]*Va. Mag. History,* Vol. 13, page 282.

[9]*Va. Mag. History,* Vol. 14, page 120.

[10]Surveyor's Records of Pittsylvania, page 195.

to John, James and William Maclin, John Willis, Henry Morris, William Twitty, Charles Lucas, Francis Willis, John Smith and Robert Throckmorton in Halifax and Augusta counties, to be surveyed by the surveyor of Halifax, "beginning at the head of the South Fork of Roanoke running thence to a river known by the name of Dan, thence to the head of New River, supposed to be the Waters of the Mississippi River, and four years' time allowed them to survey and pay Rights for same."

In 1738 William Randolph[11] and the merchants, Walter King and John Harmer, were granted 10,000 acres "along Wart Mountain, under the Blue Ledge" (Patrick County), which was probably the most westerly grant in this part of the country. In December of the same year 24,000 acres were granted them joining their former grant.

In 1740 Peter Jefferson, Ambrose Smith and Charles Lynch were granted 15,000 acres joining Colonel Randolph's order. In 1745 Archibald Cary, David Bell and others had orders of Council for 35,000 acres on Irwin River; William Wynne, Clement Reade, and Robert Jones for 36,000 acres; and Colonel Lomax's company for 15,000 acres.

In 1748 David Bell,[12] Joseph Bell, Archibald Cary and Walter King were granted 60,000 acres along Peter's Creek (Patrick County); Samuel Morris[13] (Hanover), William Sims (Hanover) and others were granted 40,000 acres along Doe Creek; Richard Lane, Sr., Thomas Davenport, James and Joseph Terry 20,000 acres on Turkey Cock Creek. To various persons there were innumerable grants ranging from one to ten thousand acres, besides the customary 400 acres allotted to each settler.

The men of eastern Brunswick and adjacent counties, taking advantage of their close proximity to the unclaimed wilderness, secured many orders of Council for various sized holdings. Major Drury Stith, the surveyor of Brunswick, and his deputies, being in a position to know where the unpatented lands lay, took up large bodies of land.

These early surveyors lived a hardy life in the open, tramping countless miles up hill and down dale through the virgin forests. His spirit must have been touched by the beauty of this upland landscape who wrote in 1753 of a certain point on Sandy Creek, describing it as "a cleft of rocks in a cloister of pines."

[11]William Randolph was of "Turkey Island," James River, and a member of the Council.

[12]Surveyor's Record, page 100.

[13]Surveyor's Record, page 161.

The governing powers of the colony took note of the slow development of Brunswick's western lands and in order to encourage settlement along the Roanoke, in November, 1738, enacted (Hening's "Statutes," Vol. 5, 57):

"Whereas the lands lying upon Roanoke River on the southern boundary of this colony are for the most part unseated and uncultivated; and a considerable number of persons, as well as his Majesty's natural born subjects, as foreign protestants, are willing to import themselves with their families and effects, and to settle upon the said lands, in case they can have suitable encouragement for their so doing: And whereas this settling of that part of the country will add to the strength and security of the colony in general * * * therefore, Be it inacted that all persons whatsoever who within ten years next after the passing this Act shall import themselves into this colony, and settle upon the Roanoke River, on the south branch (Dan) of the same above the fork; and on the north branch of the said river, above the mouth of Little Roanoke, and the lands lying between them, deemed to be in Brunswick County, shall be exempted from the payment of all levies for ten years, and be at liberty at all times hereafter to pay the officers fees in money at the rate of three farthings per pound of tobacco.

"And that letters of naturalization be granted to any alien settling there, upon a certificate from the Clerk of the County of his having taken the oath appointed by parliament, instead of the oath of allegiance and supremacy; any law to the contrary notwithstanding.

"Provided that the persons so settling upon the lands before mentioned shall during the said ten years support their own poor and make and maintain their own bridges without any charge upon the rest of the parish of St. Andrews and County of Brunswick."

The "Aliens" to whom the government was offering the above inducements to settle in old Brunswick were the Germans,[14] the Quakers and the Scotch-Irish who were then moving in great numbers from Pennsylvania down into Virginia. Under the benign wisdom and leadership of William Penn, Pennsylvania had become the asylum for the oppressed peoples of the old world. Thither had fled the Quakers from England; the Germans from Alsace-Lorraine and other States of the upper Rhine; and the Scotch-Irish from Ulster, who sought relief from governmental restrictions. It was to these wanderers that Virginia offered homes and relief from taxes, and great numbers came between the years 1730-40, settling

[14] *Virginia Magazine History,* Vol. 18, page 40.

mainly in the Valley of Virginia, though many crossed the Blue Ridge and made their homes east of the mountains.

Who were the hardy souls who dared to go into the wilderness of western Brunswick, and braving all the hardships of frontier life, there to make their homes? The forest trees must needs be felled to build the rude cabins which housed these first comers. As there were no roads worthy of the name the settlers were isolated, miles from neighbors, stores and church. Again we turn to the surveyor's records and it is surprising to find how many of the families found in the county today were those who first settled here, and who were largely instrumental in converting the wilderness into the abode of man.

Colonel Byrd said the inhabitants highest up in 1733 were Peter Mitchell and Aaron Pinston, living in what is now eastern Halifax. The surveyor's records open November 1737, with two surveys of 200 acres each, to Robert Kilkrouse and Robert Humphrey on Morris' Creek, adjoining Colonel Byrd's survey; and Humphrey's Path became a well known early way. On November the 17th of the same year Michael Young entered for 400 acres below the second fork of Banister and Thomas Marlow for 100 acres in the fork of Roanoke a little below Peter Mitchell's Path.

In June 1738 William Wynne, one of the justices of Brunswick County, entered for 200 acres on the southside of Dan River; and in 1746 Wynne and others had orders of Council for 4,000 and 5,000 acres on Beaver's Creek. William Wynne later moved with his family to this new country; and Wynne's Creek of Dan River and Wynne's Falls where the City of Danville stands were named in his honor.

In November 1738, Henry Embry, another justice of Brunswick County, had by assignment from Cloud 200 acres on the southside of Banister River, touching Humphrey's line. This order shows that the Clouds, Isaac, Joseph and Isaac, Jr., were in this section at the early date of 1738, and would indicate that some of Colonel Byrd's efforts to advertize this section were not fruitless, for the Clouds were from Pennsylvania, as is shown by the following record:

"At a court held for Pittsylvania in July, 1770, Richard Thrasher being first sworn, Proved in Court that Elizabeth Layne is the eldest daughter of Isaac Cloud and that he was the eldest son of Joseph Cloud, and that the said Cloud has no male heir living. And that the said Clouds were of the Province of Pennsylvania, in the County of Chester."

The history[15] of Chester County states that the Clouds[16] were English Quakers and that they came to America between 1683-85. The Quakers of Pennsylvania formed a company in 1730 under the leadership of Morgan Bryan[17] and Alexander Ross for the purpose of making settlements in Maryland and Virginia, and were granted 100,000 acres along the Shenandoah. Associated with Ross were Joseph Ballinger, James Wright and Evan Thomas. Permission was gained from the Quarterly Meeting of Chester, Pennsylvania, to build a meeting house in Virginia and the Hopewell Monthly Meeting of Frederick was formed in 1734. This settlement of Friends flourished for many years.

The Clouds being Quakers from Chester, Pennsylvania were probably members of Ross's company of Friends, who exploring down the Valley, found these unclaimed lands of western Brunswick full of promise and made their homes here. Morgan[18] Bryan later moved down the Valley, settling awhile in Roanoke County, and in 1748 removed to the Yadkin, North Carolina, where he was joined by the Boones. A very early road through this section was called Morgan Bryan's Road, and when the Moravian Brethren came through here in 1753 on their way to North Carolina, they followed this road of which they said "Morgan Bryan first came this way."

The Clouds made several entries for land along Banister River, where they first made their homes; in 1744 Joseph Cloud entered for 200 acres "on both sides the fork that the path to Isaac Clouds goes up, beginning at the Buffalo Lick."

In 1740 Gideon and Daniel Smith made several entries for land along with the Clouds. Gideon Smith, Sr., died about 1755, when the church wardens[19] bound his two orphan daughters, Peninah and Keziah, to Daniel Smith. It was probably for these two early settlers and hunters, Daniel and Gideon Smith, that Smith Mountain in the northern part of the county, and Smith River were named. Smith River had first been

[15]"History of Chester County," by J. Smith Futhey & Cope.

[16]"The History of Family Ancestors," by T. Marshall Potts, contains the information that the Clouds of Pennsylvania were from Calne, Wiltshire, England, and were Quakers. William Cloud died about 1702 and his will is on file in Philadelphia. He had the following children: William, Jeremiah, Joseph, Robert, John and Susannah. At a Court held for Halifax County, May 1752, it was ordered that "Thomas Mustein, Joseph Ironmonger, Groege Whiffon, and Daniel Smith do appraise the estate of Isaac Cloud, deceased."

Isaac Cloud of Pittsylvania left no male descendants according to a Court Record. Joseph Cloud probably left some, William and Isaac Cloud, for a deed of Patrick County shows that William and Isaac Cloud, brothers, owned 5,000 acres on Elk River, Tennessee, and in 1818 gave to William Cloud, Jr., of Hawkins County, Tenn., a power of attorney to sell the land. (Patrick Co. Records.)

[17]*Va. Mag. History,* Vol. 13, page 127.

[18]Morgan Bryan came from Ireland to Chester, Pennsylvania in 1719; he had sons William, James Joseph and Morgan. (Henderson's "Winning of the Southwest.")

[19]Halifax County Records.

called Irwin River by Colonel Byrd's surveying party, but as early as 1743 we find its name being changed, for in that year William Buttram was granted 400 acres "on the north side of Smith River, beginning at the lower end of an Indian field," also 400 acres on the southside "including the Bent"—(Page 8, Surveyor's Book).

In 1748 Joseph Cloud, James Terry and John Dawson were granted 12,000 acres on the Tararat River (Patrick Co.), and in early 1800 several members of the Cloud family were living in Patrick County.

Another first settler who probably also came down the Valley was John Stuart who patented lands on Terrible Creek in 1737, and on Banister River in 1738. It was probably for Stuart that Stewarts' Creek of Halifax was named, for his name is spelled both ways in the records. His interest seemed to lead him westward for we find Stuarts' Camp on Smith River in 1745, and Stewarts' Camping Creek ran at the foot of the Blue Ridge. A road order of Sept. 23, 1768, appointed a surveyor of the road from Stewart's Levels to Bull Mountain in Patrick, and in August, 1769, John Stewart, Gent., Will Stewart, and Joshua Barton were appointed to view a road from the said Barton's to Stewart Gap. The inventory of John Stewart, Gent., in 1776, named nine Bibles and a Confession of Faith, indicating that he was of Scotch origin.

When John Stewart transferred some entries of land that he had made in 1737-38, Thomas Finny was a witness to the transaction. Finny was another very early settler and patented much land throughout the county, but more especially along Banister River, where he seemed to make his home. In 1746, William Harris was overseer at "Finnywood," and at this time Finny conveyed to him several entries of land. On one occasion Finny Isaac Winston, Jr., a "pistole" for 400 acres on Bye Creek of Banister River, a pistole being a spanish coin worth $4.67. This could hardly indicate the value of lands at that time.

On March 13, 1738, there was surveyed for Joseph Morton, Jr., 400 acres on the southside of Staunton River, at the mouth of the first great creek above the mouth of Otter River; also 400 acres on the first south fork of Staunton River above the mouth of Goose Creek. This is the first notice we have of the upper reaches of Roanoke River being called Staunton River. We note that Goose Creek and Otter River had also received their names. A patent of 1751 shows that Joseph[20] Morton made his home on a branch of Sandy River.

[20]The will of Joseph Morton, Sr., dated 1749, was proven in Halifax Court March 20, 1753, naming wife Elizabeth, daughters Jane Royle (Royall), Martha and Anne; to son John 400 acres on Sandy River bought of Joseph Cloud; to son Joseph 400 acres on Sandy River including the home

In 1739 William Buttram entered for 400 acres on Banister River beginning at the "Great Low Grounds." In 1743 he made several entries on Smith River, and Buttram Town Creek, or Town Creek as it is known today, was no doubt named for his settlement there. Other settlers of this year were John and William Russell, who gave their name to Russell's Creek of Smith River; and Thomas Seymour whose path on Terrible Creek was mentioned in 1744.

In 1740 Thomas Rutledge, probably from Pennsylvania, was patenting land here, while other members of the Rutledge family passed on through on their way to South Carolina, where they became eminent in the history of the nation. Rutledge's Creek, near Danville, signifies where Thomas Rutledge made his settlement. Another Scotch-Irish settler from Pennsylvania was Israel Pickens, who in 1745 patented 400 acres on Chestnut Creek, and in 1746 was living on Banister River (Surveyor's Book, p. 15). David Logan was also a Scotchman, and in 1748 had an order of Council for 1,000 acres on Elkhorn Creek, where the old Logan settlement is still standing, surrounded by hoary boxwoods.

However, not all early settlers were from Pennsylvania; in 1741 John Pigg, of Amelia County, entered for "400 acres on the north side of the south fork of Staunton River, beginning opposite the mouth of Snow Creek." The south fork of Staunton River had not been named at this time and took its name from John Pigg, becoming Pigg River; Snow Creek, a tributary of Pigg River had already received its name. At this same time David, William and Thomas Caldwell, of the "Caldwell Settlement," Will Rogers and Adam McCoule made entries for land on Snow Creek.

John Wall, a justice of Brunswick County was interested in the western lands; in 1743 he patented several tracts along Difficult and Terrible Creeks in which mention is made of "Walls' Camp." The surveyors frequently referred to camps, some of which were probably hunters' camps, others of land prospectors and still others of the settlers coming in. They also mentioned old cabins and cabins where some one had formerly lived, as though the first comers with the world to choose from frequently changed their abiding place.

Will Hogan had a camp on Banister, and as early as 1741 had entered for 800 acres on Dan River. Hogan's Creek, across the North Carolina

---

place; to son Jehu 400 acres on Sandy River; Executors Captain Charles Anderson, Joseph Morton, Jr., wife and son John. Witnesses to will were Thomas Morton, Sam Morton and Joseph Morton, Jr. Joseph Morton, Sr., is said to be the brother of John Morton, of Henrico (father of Samuel Morton, and Joseph Morton, Jr.), and Thomas Morton, Sr., of Henrico County (father of Thomas Morton, witness to will).

line, was probably named for him. Joseph White had an early camp on Sandy Creek, and John Russell on Mayo River; Hamon Critz was camping on Spoon Creek (in Patrick) in 1747, where he settled and became a leading citizen. He was one of the first justices of the peace of Pittsylvania County.

These camps were rudely constructed cabins built for the comfort of the campers. On page 174 of the Record we read:

"1754. Surveyed for John Ward (Albemarle Co.) 400 acres on the south fork of Mayo River beginning at White Oak, marked R. I., near a camping place where Robert Jones camped and made said camp of White Walnut puncheons."

In 1746 Hugh Henry had a chestnut puncheon camp on Banister River. Occasionally the early settler built for himself a rock house, but whether a dwelling or meat house it is not known. They were mentioned as pointers by the surveyors, as:

"1746, James Woods enters 400 acres opposite to the Rock House, running up and down Banister River.

1746, Edward Sizemore enters 400 acres on the South side Banister River beginning a little below the little Rock House about the mouth of little Polecat.

1754, Henry Sizemore 400 acres on Head of Upper Fork of Great Polecat between said Polecat and ye Branches of Sandy Creek Beginning at a Rock House.

1754, Richard Witt 400 acres on South side Dan River Beginning at the Rock House."

In 1741 Benjamin Clement, of Amelia, patented land on Sycamore Creek of Staunton River, where a few years later he made his home. The names of William Blevin, Richard Echols and William Muncus, three first settlers, appear on the surveyor's record at this time; also Mary, Henry and Ephriam Sizemore, one of whose patents was on Peter Mitchell's Creek, beginning at "the Roads"; and another included the place on which Ephraim lived.

In 1744 John Donelson of Accomac County patented 200 acres "on both sides of Sandy Creek, between Robert Moon's line and Joseph Cloud." He made his home on the banks of Banister River, and for 35 years was an outstanding figure in the life of the section. Hugh Henry, probably also of Accomac, became a settler here at the same time. In the same year Thomas Calloway entered for 200 acres "including the place he lives on"; and Joseph Ironmonger was settled on Sandy Creek.

In 1745 Elisha Walden patented 400 acres on Cherrystone Creek, and the following year lands on Irwin and Smith River where he made his home at a place called the Roundabout.[21] Walden became a well known "long hunter" and explored Tennessee and Kentucky. John Kennon and John Moore were now living near Miry Creek, and there was a path connecting their homes. Redmon Fallen had made his home on Sandy Creek of Dan River and Joseph Mays was living on Staunton River.

In 1746 William Randolph was granted 4,000 acres along Staunton River, including the Long Island. From a road order we learn that Randolph established a plantation at Long Island under the charge of an overseer. At this time John Owen had two plantations on Staunton River.

There were not a great many surveys made in this section between the years 1737-1745, and the greater number of these were of land speculators. In 1745 Brunswick County was divided and all this western country became a part of Lunenburg County, and it was from this date on that the settlement of this section became active.

While the wandering "aliens" from Pennsylvania and New Jersey had largely constituted the first settlers of old Brunswick's western lands, with the formation of Lunenburg we find more and more settlers from Tidewater Virginia, especially from the peninsula between the James and York Rivers. The Quit Rent Rolls of Virginia which listed the land ownership in each county on which a tax of one shilling for each fifty acres was payable directly to the Crown, were sent annually to England. Only the Rolls for the year 1704 have been found and they constitute an excellent source for tracing early Virginia families.

In the Rolls for King and Queen County are the familiar names of Daniel Coleman; Nicholas, Edmond, Thomas and George Dillard; John Loving; Peter Lyon; Zachery Lewis; Jacob Lumpkin; Edward, John, and Henry Pigg; Thomas Tunstall and Samuel Walden.

In King William County Rolls were listed John Marr; Thomas, Stephen, and James Terry; William and John Hurt; William Douglass; William Coates.

In the lists of tithables (tax lists) of Henrico County, 1679 are the following familiar names: Nicholas Perkins, James Royall, Mr. Kennon, Thomas East, Abram Womack (son of William), James Akin, William Harris, Mr. George Worsham, Charles Clay, Godfrey Ragsdale, Henry Pruit, Mr. Richard Ward, and John Millner.

[21] *Va. Mag. History*, Vol. 7, page 249.

In 1746 the names of many well known families appear in the surveyor's records; James and Joseph Terry, who made their homes near Peytonsburg; Peter Wilson who settled on Dan River and operated a ferry there; Major John Coles, whose sons Isaac and Walter later lived here; Richard Tredway, Sr., and son John Tredway; Robert Been, who moved in later years to Tennessee. In this same year appeared some families from Maryland,[22]—Richard Lane, Sr., Richard Lane, Jr., Tidence Lane and John Fuller Lane who patented lands along Elkhorn. In 1748 Dutton Lane, Robert Sweeting, Edward Sweeting and Dutton Sweeting entered for several grants along Banister River. Sweden, or Sweetings Fork, a stream in the eastern part of the county is probably named for this family. Dutton Lane was a pioneer Baptist minister of Pittsylvania County, and a sketch of his life is found in Taylor's "Lives of Baptist Ministers." In 1771 Robert Sweeting gave a power of attorney to Dutton Lane to go to the province of Maryland to demand and receive for him any lands and estates to which he was entitled.

In 1748 Samuel Harris, of Hanover, who also became a noted Baptist pioneer preacher, patented land on Sandy River where he made his home and became a leading and influential citizen. James Hunt of Lunenburg and Daniel Coleman, Senior and Junior, of Cumberland also patented lands here in that year, to which their families came some years later.

There were a number of settlements at this time on Smith River, of western Lunenburg. John Hicky had made his home there and opened a store. John Reddy had a home and plantation on the river, and it was probably for him that Reddie's Gap of Smith Mountain was named. James and Daniel Blevin, well known hunters, had homes on the river and their wagon road was referred to by the early surveyor. Abram Little, whose name appears on the Quit Rent Rolls of Essex County, 1704, was probably a hunter and fur trader, for his "Meat House," on Leatherwood Creek, was an early landmark. It was perhaps for him that Little River of Floyd, was named. Robert Pusey[23] had taken up lands on Otter Creek of Smith River, where he made his home; and John Frederick Miller was already settled on Mayo River.

[22]Dutton Lane, of Baltimore County, Maryland, married Pretiosa Tidings, daughter of Richard Tidings, and made his will in 1726 naming wife Pretiosa and sons Richard, Dutton and Samuel Lane. (Baltimore Wills.) Dutton, Richard and Tidence (Tidings) Lane of Pittsylvania were probably sons of Dutton Lane of Baltimore.

[23]Caleb Pusey was a leader among the Quaker settlers of Pennsylvania from the time of his coming in 1682 until his death forty-five years later. He lived at Chester, the home of the Clouds, and was survived by a family. From the papers gathered and preserved by Pusey during his long and eventful life, Proud compiled his history of Pennsylvania. Among the members of Pennsylvania's early assembly are many names familiar to Pittsylvania and adjoining counties, such as Thomas Pemberton, John and Edward Bennett, Joshua Fearne, Griffith Owen, Robert Jones, Joseph Boothe, James Logan, and Richard Hill (Proud's "History of Pennsylvania.")

So numerous a settlement had been made at the foot of the Blue Ridge Mountains (in Western Patrick), that in 1749 the court of Lunenburg ordered a road cut from the Court House to the settlement.

The water courses with their rich bottom lands drew the early settlers as they had drawn the Indians, and settlers were found at an early date upon the streams of the extreme northwestern section of Lunenburg, that lay adjacent to the Blue Ridge Mountains. This section is watered by Blackwater River, Chestnut Creek, Snow Creek and Pigg River, and today forms the southern part of Franklin County. Through Magotty and other gaps of the Blue Ridge it is accessible to and in touch with the lower Valley of Virginia.

In 1746 Augusta County ordered a road to be built in the lower valley, then included within the county's limits. This was to extend from the ridge dividing the waters of the New River from the waters of the south branch of the Roanoke (Blackwater River), to end in a road leading over the Blue Ridge which was the main highway to the markets of the James, and known as the "Warwick Road." Warwick was a place of tobacco inspection on the James below Richmond. Among the workers appointed for the road were Thomas and Tasker Tosh, whose name is perpetuated in Pittsylvania today in the village Toshes. Peter Rentfro settled on the western side of the mountains, but James and Joseph crossed over and established their homes on Blackwater, where they operated a mill. Rentfro's Path along Blackwater was frequently mentioned by the surveyors. A road, probably "the Warwick," led from James Rentfro's across the Blue Ridge to Little River, as is shown by the following patent: "1754. Benjamin Pyborn, 400 acres, beginning at a Sugar Tree marked T. D. (near the spring of an old cabin formerly used), above James Rentfro's under the Mountain on the Road Way to the Little River."

In 1747 Thomas Jones, Roger Turner, and David Griffith were on Pigg River, and Isaac Atkinson, William Owen and Robert Hooker had settled plantations there. William Atkinson was now operating a mill on Harping Creek. At the same time Patrick Johnson, Peter Elliott (or Ellet) Benjamin Ray, Thomas Gill, Thomas Hall and John Miller had cabins on Magotty Creek, and John, Mark and Stephen Cole and John Hilton were on Blackwater. Thomas Duncan was living on Staunton River above the mouth of Blackwater, and Nicholas Scott had a cabin on Turkey Cock Creek. A little later James Standeford established his home on Blackwater.

While eastern Lunenburg (i. e. the present Lunenburg, Mecklenburg, Charlotte, Halifax and eastern Pittsylvania) numbered among its early settlers many families from eastern and Tidewater Virginia, as well as the Scotch-Irish of the Buffalo and Cub Creek settlement, we may safely assume that the first settlers of Lunenburg's western lands (i. e. Patrick, Henry, Franklin, Bedford and western Pittsylvania) were the Quakers, Germans, Welsh and Scotch-Irish of Pennsylvania, who having made their way down the Valley of Virginia, crossed through the gaps of the mountains into Piedmont Virginia.

Settlers from Pennsylvania continued to move to Pittsylvania lands until the end of the century. Harmon Cook,[24] who purchased large tracts of land on Tomahawk Creek and Pigg River, was a colonizer who brought in many families from Pennsylvania in the latter part of the century. Cook petitioned the General Assembly of Virginia in 1788 for a town to be established on his lands in Pittsylvania, "at the forks of the roads leading from Houlston to Pennsylvania and Petersburg," stating that many traders had already settled there. Young Abram Rohrer, son of Abram Rohrer,[25] a native of Switzerland, followed Cook from Pennsylvania to Virginia, and marrying Cook's daughter, founded the Rorer family of the county.

Among the later Pennsylvania emigrants were George Craft,[26] a man of means who settled on the Pigg River Road (near Climax), building a handsome brick home; John Schelhausen, a German, whose name has been Americanized to Shelhorse; and Jacob Berger, whose headstone records that he was born in Germany. The latter settled on Frying Pan Creek and his old home "Clifton" stands today, overlooking the stream.

There were three well marked lines of travel over which the early settlers journeyed on their way to Pittsylvania, all of which followed the way of old Indian trails. One led from the east—the more settled parts from Brunswick, and followed the line of the Occoneechi Trading Path. Another led from the northeast across James River in the direction of the "plain paths" of the Susquehanna Indian traders. Along this way came

[24]The will of Harmon Cook was recorded May 21, 1810. He bequeathed his property to his three sons, John, Harmon and Abraham Cook; and to his daughters, Catherine Wright, Mary Razor and Nancy the wife of Abram Rorer.

[25]Abram Rorer and his wife had issue four sons, Rudolph, Charles, David and Abram. David studied law and removed to Iowa, where he became a distinguished jurist. Abram, Jr. married Mary Wright and settled near his father in the northwestern part of the county. In his will proven September 17, 1855, he named son Ferdinand Rorer and daughters Angeline James, Elvira Harvey, Aquella Ann Lipscomb and Malitta Miller.

[26]A tradition has been handed down in the family that Pamelia, the wife of George Craft, was a near relative of Dr. Benjamin Rush, of Philadelphia, the friend of the Revolutionary Cause.

many of the families from counties north of the James, some of whom settled for awhile in Amelia and Cumberland counties before journeying on further south. The third way led down the Valley of Virginia, and across the Blue Ridge Mountain into southern Piedmont Virginia, following the line of the Great War Trail of the Iroquois. Along these three routes came the first settlers with their belongings, choosing from out the wooded countryside the sites upon which they would found their homes.

Chapter IV

A PART OF LUNENBURG COUNTY, 1745-1752

As the line of settlement pushed westward it became necessary to divide the old counties and form new ones, and in February, 1745, the General Assembly of Virginia enacted:[1]

"That whereas divers inconveniences attend the upper inhabitants of Brunswick County by reason of their great distance from the Court-house and other places usually appointed for public meetings, * * * that the County be divided by a line to be run from the County line, where it crosses Roanoke River, to strike Nottoway River at the fork, * * * and the part above the said line to be one other distinct county and called by the name of the county of Lunenburg."

The Act further stated that, "Whereas the Assembly, for the encouragement of settlements along the southern boundary, had enacted that all persons who within ten years after the passage of the act, should import themselves into the Colony and settle either upon the south branch of the Roanoke River above the fork (Dan River), and on the north branch above Lickinghole (the Staunton River), including the lands between, should be exempted from all levies, those persons now pray that this Act be repealed."

A court for the new county was organized and held on May the 5th, when the following gentlemen took the oath of justice[2] of the peace—William Leonard, Matthew Talbott, Lewis Delony, John Phelps, William Hill, John Caldwell, Cornelius Cargill,[3] Abraham Cooke,[4] Hugh Lawson, Thomas Lanier,[5] and William Caldwell.

John and William Caldwell represented the Scotch-Irish settlements made on Cub Creek ten years earlier. Cornelius Cargill had probably moved into this new section from Surry County of Tidewater, for he

---

[1]Hening's "Statutes," Vol. 5, page 383.

[2]Order Books of Lunenburg County.

[3]In 1753 Cornelius Cargill married Hannah Blanks, widow. Her will in 1757, shows that her husband was living at that time.

[4]The will of Abraham Cooke is recorded in Lunenburg in 1748, naming wife Sarah, and sons Charles and Benjamin.

[5]Thomas Lanier was the son of Nicholas Lanier of Brunswick, and grandson of John Lanier, the emigrant, whose will was proven in Prince George County 1717, naming sons John, Sampson, Robert and Nicholas. Thomas Lanier was born about 1722 and married Elizabeth Hicks in 1742, issue: Robert, born 1742; Molly, born 1744; Sarah, born 1748, married first Col. Joseph Williams, second Robert Williams; Betty, born 1750, married Col. Joseph Winston; Caty, born 1752; Patsy, born 1754; Rebecca, born 1757, married Col. Joseph Williams, brother of Robert Williams; Thomas, born 1760; Susanna, born 1763; Lewis, born 1765; Fanny, born 1767; William, born 1770. Thomas Lanier moved to Greenville County, North Carolina, where his will was probated August, 1805. (Wheeler's "History of North Carolina.")

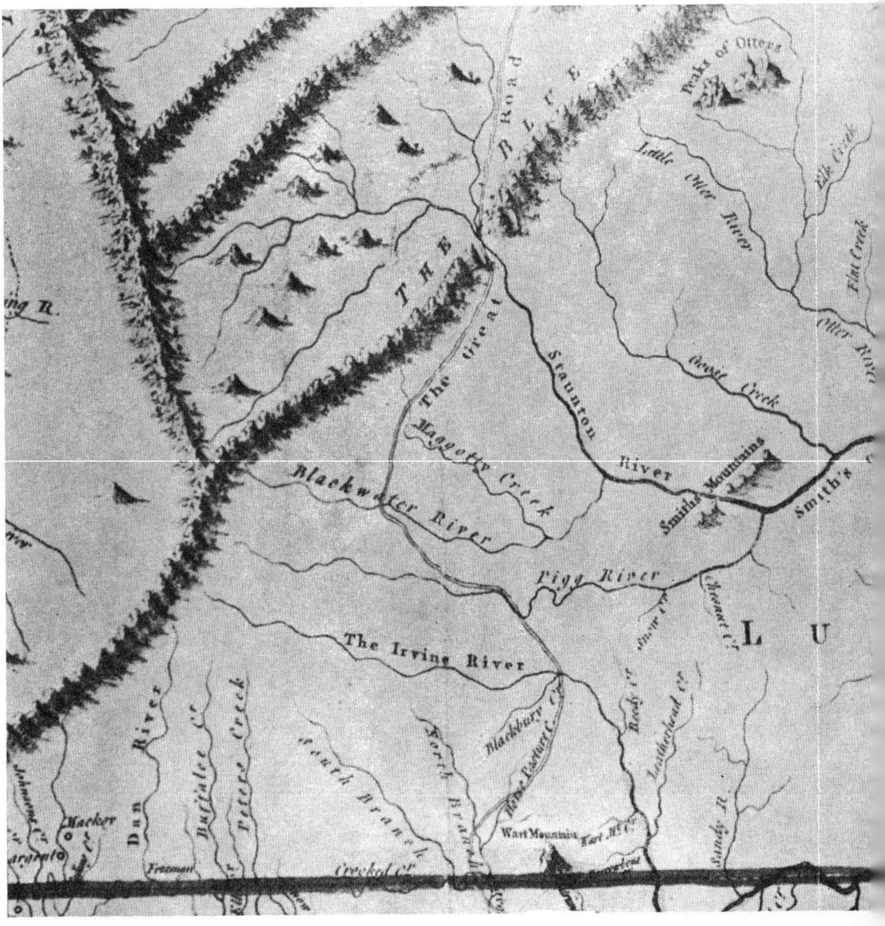

MAP OF LUNENBURG COUNTY
Section of Map of Jefferson and Fr

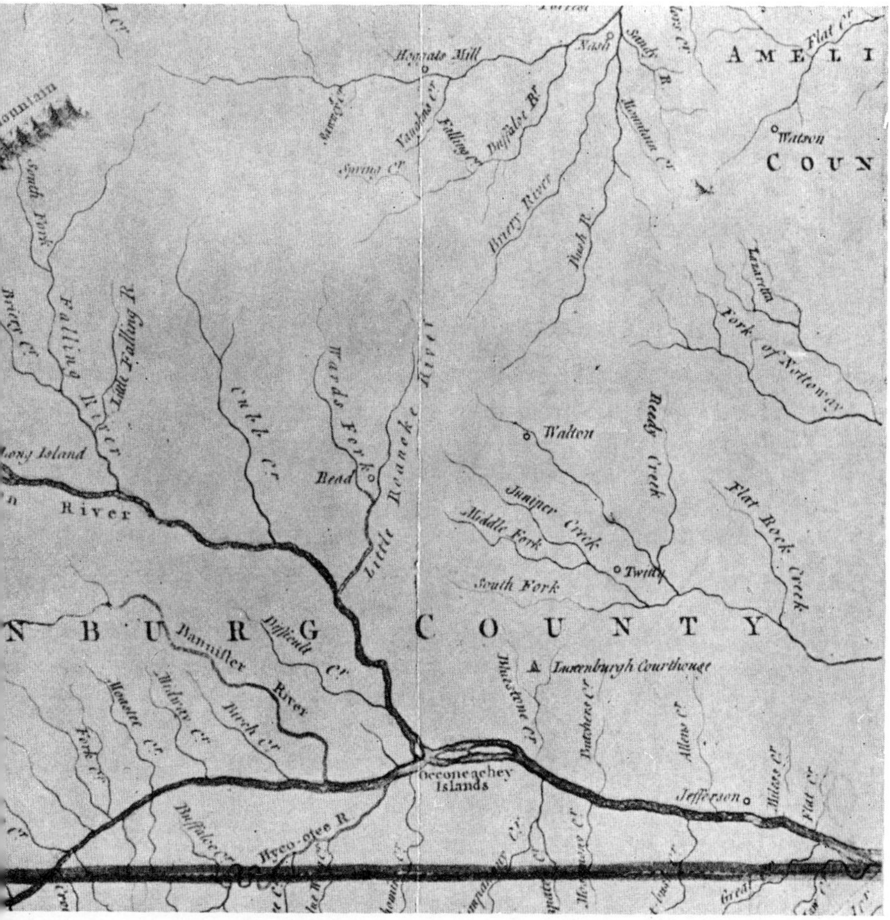
AMELI
COUN
Watson
Flat Cr.
Hoggats Mill
Nash
Sandy R.
Vaughans Cr.
Falling Cr.
Buffaloe Br.
Spring Cr.
Mountain Cr.
Briery River
Bush R.
South Fork
Falling River
Little Falling R.
Briery Cr.
Long Island
River
Cubb Cr.
Wards Fork
Bead
Little Roanoke River
Walton
Reedy Creek
Juniper Creek
Middle Fork
South Fork
Twitty
Flat Rock Creek
Fork of Nottoway
NBURG COUNTY
Bannister River
Difficult Cr.
Birch Cr.
Luxenburgh Courthouse
Bluestone Cr.
Butchers Cr.
Allens Cr.
Occoneachey Islands
Jefferson
Miles Cr.
Buffaloe Cr.
Hyco-otee R.
Fork Cr.
Mulberry Cr.

is thought to be the son of the Rev'd John Cargill who went from England to the Leeward Islands in 1708, and later settled in Surry. Thomas Lanier represented the Huguenot family of John Lanier who settled about 1685 south of James River.

The County Courts were presided over at this time by justices of the peace who were appointed by the Governor from among "the most able, honest and judicious citizens of their respective counties," according to Act of 1661. Bruce[6] says, "there are innumerable proofs that they were drawn from the body of the wealthiest, most capable and most respected men to be found in the whole community, and the office was looked upon as being so purely honorable that as in England it carried no salary."

Another duty of the justices was to take "the lists of tithables," or tax lists, each in his own district. A tax of 21 pounds of tobacco was laid by the government upon each tithe, that is upon every male of 18 years and over, and upon every slave of 16 years and over. The lists of tithables for the county were ordered to be taken in the following manner:

"William Caldwell, Gent, is ordered to take the lists of Tithables in the County from the mouth of Falling River to the mouth of Little Roanoke River.

"Cornelius Cargill, Gent, is ordered to take the list of Tithables from the mouth of Little Roanoke River to the mouth of Blewstone to the County Line, also in the fork of Roanoke.

"William Hill, Gent, from the mouth of Blewstone to the mouth of Allen's Creek.

"Lewis Delony, Gent, from the mouth of Allen's Creek to the line that divides this from Brunswick County.

"Hugh Lawson, Gent, from the line that divides this from Brunswick County, upwards to the mouth of Hounds Creek.

"Liddal Bacon, Gent, from the mouth of Hounds Creek to the extent of the County upwards."

Clement Read[7] was appointed clerk, Thomas Bouldin,[8] sheriff, and Gideon Marr,[9] King's attorney for the new county. John Hall was

[6]Bruce's "Institutional History of Virginia in the 17th Century."

[7]Clement Read patented large bodies of land in western Lunenburg; in 1744 Read with others had orders of Council for 10,000 acres "in the Ford of Irwin River at the Great nap of Reeds"; 10,000 acres on Banister River, beginning at the mouth of Stinking River; 20,000 on the head waters of Banister, running toward Turkey Cock and Snow Creeks.

[8]Col. Thomas Boulding and his wife Nancy Clark left many descendants throughout the United States. Col. Wood Boulding of the Revolutionary War was his son.

[9]In the Amelia County Marriage Bonds is recorded the marriage of Gideon Marr to Sarah Miller, September 4, 1743. In 1768 he bought lands on Dan River from William Bean, where he made his home. His will was proven at Pittsylvania Court House, March 22, 1777, naming wife Sarah, sons John and Richard Marr, and daughter Agatha, wife of Constant Perkins.

named surveyor of the north district and Peter Fontaine surveyor of the south district of the county; two years later James Terry was appointed deputy surveyor to Peter Fontaine.

The following constables were appointed at this time: Richard Calloway, Daniel Dodd, Silvanus Walker, William Hunter, Richard Griffen and James Coleman. In 1746 Isaac Cloud was appointed constable for the upper part of Banister River (in Pittsylvania County); and in 1748 Elisha Walling (Walden) was appointed constable "in this County on Smith's River and the Wart Mountain" (Henry and Patrick Counties).

Since Lunenburg was a newly settled section all the inhabitants had come from elsewhere. Let us pause for a moment and see what is known of some of these early county officers.

Clement Read, a man of parts and a leader in the development of the section, first settled here in 1733, making his home on Little Roanoke River. The first that is known of him is his landing at Williamsburg, a small lad. Being a sprightly and prepossessing youth, Speaker Robinson took a fancy to him and sent him to William and Mary College, where he graduated. He amassed a large estate and was the ancestor of a distinguished family.

Thomas Bouldin, who was appointed sheriff, had only come to the county the year before from Maryland. He was the son[10] of an Irishman of Pennsylvania, and with his wife Nancy Clarke Bouldin, had travelled by boat down the Chesapeake Bay, and then upwards a hundred miles across country in a wagon to his new home. Upon their arrival there was nothing to house them but a rude cabin, but as soon as possible a commodious mansion house was built, and upon its completion a great housewarming was held to which the whole countryside was invited, the following hospitable invitation being posted at the cross roads: "All are welcome who choose to come." Preparations for the guests were made on a lavish scale. An ox roasted whole was one of the items for the feast, which lasted a night and a day, with dancing and frolicking. Col. Bouldin was a man of executive ability and a leader in his community.

Peter Fontaine, the surveyor of the south district, was the son of the Rev'd Peter Fontaine, a French Huguenot, and rector of Westover Parish, Charles City County, where young Peter was probably reared. Peter Fontaine, Jr. married Sarah Winston, and settled in the new

[10] Powhatan Boulding's "The Old Trunk."

county to practice his profession. James Terry, the deputy surveyor, was probably from the county of King William, for in the Quit Rent Rolls of 1704 there are listed Thomas, James and Stephen Terry. Richard Calloway, one of the constables is said to be the son of a Welch emigrant; we have seen that Isaac Cloud, another, was a Quaker from Pennsylvania.

In the year 1745 Daniel Smith came into Court and moved that his name be added to the list of tithables; at the same time it was ordered that the names of George, Zacheriah and John Ashworth, George and Thomas Shadwell be also added.

At the August Courts of 1746, James Dochey, lately of Bristol, England, came into Court and proved his importation; Henry Sage, lately of London, proved his importation; John Freeman, lately of Worcester, England, proved his importation; and George Ireland, lately of Shropshire, proved his importation. At the same time Peter and Sher Torian, and Silvester Gianane took out papers of naturalization.

Life in those pioneer days was simple and direct, and the courts a place to redress grievances, and many were the suits brought regarding trespass, debts and boundary lines. Among the suit papers we see the now familiar names of Thomas Finny, Israel Pickens, William Bean, David Logan, Ephriam Sizemore, Thomas, Richard and Francis Calloway, Elisha Wallen, John Donelson, Richard and Tidance Lane, and Joseph Cloud.

In the County Levy laid in December 1746 the lists of those who were paid for a wolf's head contain the names of Gideon Smith, Thomas Finny, Joseph Rentfro, Joseph Cloud, Hugh Henry and William Calloway.

The making of roads has been a problem with which man has grappled from earliest times, and the Court of Lunenburg was faced with the necessity of providing highways through the large and thinly populated county. The distance across the county from its eastern boundary to the western limit, now Bedford, Franklin and Patrick counties, measured all of 150 miles; and this vast extent of territory was broken by countless streams and hills which rose higher and higher in magnitude until the mountains themselves were reached.

At a Court held in March, 1747, it was ordered:

"That a road be cleared the best and most convenient way from William Bean's on Dan River to the Banister River, thence to North River at Cargills' Horse Ford, thence to the Court House.

Peter Wilson is appointed surveyor of that part of the road which leads from the said Bean's to Sandy River (near Danville).

"William Hogan is appointed surveyor of that part of the road leading from Sandy River to Double Creek (eastern Pittsylvania).

"William Wynne is appointed surveyor of that part of the road leading from Banister River to North River at Cargills'."

This road led in the same direction of the road that runs today from "Oak Hill" to Danville, where turning to the northeast it continued across Halifax.

A second road leading from William Bean's home on Dan River was laid off three years later, in July, 1750:

"William Bean is appointed surveyor of the road leading from his house to the head (mouth?) of Sandy River.

"Tidence Lane is appointed surveyor of the road from the head of Sandy River to the lower falls of Banister River.

"William Russell is appointed surveyor of the road from the falls of Banister to Fuqua's Ford (on Staunton River)."

William Bean's house on Dan River was established on the northern side of the river near the present station of Wenonda. In 1768 Bean sold his lands in this section to Col. John Payne of Goochland, Nicholas Perkins, Gideon Marr, and others and moved out to the new country of the Tennessee. Phelan, in his "History of Tennessee" said of him:

"Captain William Bean of Pittsylvania County, Virginia, advanced further into the wilderness than anyone who had preceded him, and his son Russell Bean was the first white child born in Tennessee. With the erection of his cabin near the junction of Watauga and Boone's Creeks in east Tennessee began the history of Tennessee."

Bean was probably from Augusta county for his name is listed in 1742 in the Militia Company of Captain George Robinson of Augusta, along with those of Stephen, Peter and James Rentfro and John and James Cole, who were also first settlers of Lunenburg's western lands.

There were three very early roads which led across Pittsylvania to the west, known as Hickey's Road, the Irish Road, and the Pigg River Road. Hickey's Road led from a point on Staunton River in northern Halifax to the settlement that had been made at the foot of Wart Mountain in western Patrick, a distance of near 120 miles. The Wart Mountain is now called Bull's Mountain and lies east of the main range of the

Blue Ridge, as shown on Jefferson's and Fry's map. Mayo River takes its rise near by and for this reason the settlement was called the Mayo settlement.

When the Englishman J. F. D. Smythe journeyed through this section in 1774 he was told of the marvelous extent of view to be had from the summit of Wart Mountain. He made the ascent and felt amply repaid for the perils and fatigue of the trip. He described the view—"On the east you could perceive the deep and broken chasms where the Dan, Mayo, Smith, Banister and Staunton Rivers direct their courses; some raging in vast torrents, some gliding in silent gentle meanders. On the north you can see the Blackwater, a branch of the Staunton. On the northeast you will observe with great astonishment and pleasure the tremendous and abrupt break in the Alleghany Mountains through which the mighty waters of the New River pass. * * * On the south you can see the Dan, the Catawba, the Yadkin and the Haw breaking through the mighty mountains that appear in confused heaps and piled on each other in almost every direction.

"Throughout the whole of this amazing and most extensive perspective there is not the least trace of art or improvement to be discerned. All are the genuine effect of nature alone and laid down on her most extended and grandest scale."

Smythe and his guide crossed over the mountain and pursuing their journey in a northwest course crossed the Blue Ridge through a gap used only by the hunters, some twenty miles southwest "of the gap that the great trading path goes over" (Magotty Gap). Smythe recounted that wild turkeys were so numerous a whole company of men could have subsisted on them. (It has been thought that Wart Mountain was a peak of the Blue Ridge, but this evidence of Smythe's shows it to have been Bull Mountain, an outlying spur of the Blue Ridge).

Hickey's road was authorized at a court held for Lunenburg in June, 1749:

"It is ordered that a road be laid off and cleared the best and most convenient way from Staunton River to the Mayo Settlement at the Wart Mountain, and it is ordered that Joseph Mayes and all the male Laboring Tithables convenient to the said road forthwith mark off and lay open the best and most convenient way from Staunton River to Allen's Creek and keep the some in repair according to law.

"Richard Parsons is appointed surveyor of that part of the New Road leading from Staunton River to the Mayo Settlement at the Wart Mountain, to-wit from Allen's Creek to Banister River.

"Elizha Walling is appointed surveyor of the part of the New Road from Staunton River to the Mayo Settlement, leading from Banister to Smith River.

"Joseph Cloud is appointed surveyor of that part of the New Road leading from Staunton River to the Mayo Settlement, to-wit: from Smith River to the said settlements."

This road led from a point on Staunton River in Northern Halifax, by Mount Airy, Chalk Level and Chatham, crossing Banister River near the Poor Farm, and turning west led across Henry and Patrick counties. The eastern part of this road continues a well known highway today. It took its name from John Hickey,[11] who had made a settlement and opened a store near its western limits.

The Mayo Settlement was no doubt made by Pennsylvania settlers. At the same court which authorized Hickey's Road, a road was ordered to be built from what is now Bedford to western Franklin County, "from the Fish Dam on Otter River through the Meadows on to Magotty Creek, to the Burying Place at the End of the Road, Joseph Rentfro, William Morgan and John Meade are appointed surveyors to lay off and clear said road." Magotty Creek breaks through the Blue Ridge Mountain, forming the well known Magotty Gap, through which passes an old roadway. The "burying place at the End of the Road" would indicate that many newcomers passed that way and camped awhile, leaving behind them tragic reminders of their passage in the graves of their loved ones.

The Irish Road led in the same general direction of Hickey's Road, east and west. Some of the very early land plats contain sketches of these three roads, and from them we find the Irish Road leaving a ford on Banister River near old Pigg's Mill, running thence to Whitmell and on into Henry County, crossing Grassy Creek to the west. It probably took its name from the early Irish settlers.

The Pigg River Road led from Elkhorn by Whittles, Green Bay Church and Red Eye in a northwesterly direction across Pigg River and serves as a main thoroughfare today. It was later continued across Franklin County to Little River of Floyd County. Along these three

---

[11]John Hickey's will was proven in Henry County, December 25, 1784, in which he named sons John, Joseph, James, Cornelius, Benjamin, Elijah, Michael, and Joshua; daughters Mary and Jane Heard. Appointed wife Mary and William Heard, Jr., executors.

roads traveled the early settlers, some moving westward from the more thickly settled sections of the east; others having traveled down the valley, crossed the mountains and moved eastward.

The making of early roads and paths is described in the following manner by J. F. D. Smith, the Englishman: "Roads and paths are marked out by blazes on trees, cut alternately on each side of the way every 30 or 40 yards. A blaze is a long chip slized off the side of a tree with axe; it is above 12 inches in length and through the bark and some of the sapwood, and by its white appearance when first made serves to direct the way in the night as well as in the day. The first blazed paths originated in this way: when any person went from one place to another through the woods when it would have been difficult to return upon his track, he fell upon the method of blazing each side of the trees at certain distances as he passed on, and thereby retraced his way in returning without the least trouble."

In 1748 George Currie was granted leave to keep a ferry on Great Roanoke River from Munford's Quarter to the Occaneechi, the island formerly occupied by the Indians of that name.

In 1749 John Boyd was given leave to keep a ferry on Dan River; and here in 1781 was enacted one of the leading events of the Revolutionary War, when General Greene and his army escaped across the river from Cornwallace's pursuing hosts.

Charles Carter and Dame Maria Byrd, executors of the will of Colonel William Byrd, deceased, began in 1746 to sell his lands north and south of Dan River, which were a part of the Order of Council for 105,000 acres granted to Col. Byrd in 1735. This great tract of land was called "The Havila," and the records of the sales fill many pages of the deed books of Lunenburg and Halifax Counties. Among the first purchasers were Alexander Irvine, Hugh Lawson, William Douglas, William Fuqua, Gideon Smith, David Evans, John Boyd, Hugh Moore and the Echols'.

When the lists of tithables were ordered to be taken in 1750, John Phelps, Gent, was ordered to take the lists from Falling River to Goose Creek, which led up Staunton River and included northern Halifax and Pittsylvania and southern Charlotte and Campbell Counties. Nicholas Hayle, Gent, was ordered to take the list from Goose Creek, upwards, including Bedford and Franklin Counties. This list contained 105 names, among which were William, Peter and Joseph Bennett, the Rentfros, Patrick Johnson, the Griffeths and other first settlers.

William Caldwell, Gent, was ordered to take the lists from the Little Roanoke River up the Fork. This list contained 334 names among which were James Hunt, John East, John Mullin, Richard Tredway, Thomas Mustein, William Glass and Thomas Finney.

Cornelius Cargill, Gent, was ordered to take the lists from the Forks (Roanoke River) to the Upper Line (Mountains), including southern Halifax, Pittsylvania, Henry and Patrick Counties. The lists numbered 274 names, but a part of the sheets are missing. In the 95 names preserved were Hugh Henry, the Irvines on Dan River, the Blevins on Leatherwood, Gideon Smith, Abraham Little, Redmon Fallen on Sandy River, Ephraim Sizemore, William Hogan, William Russell and Captain William Irby.

Chapter V

A PART OF HALIFAX COUNTY, 1752-1767

So great was the influx of new settlers into Lunenburg County that seven years after its establishment it was deemed necessary to divide this great domain and create a new county. Accordingly in February, 1752, the General Assembly of Virginia enacted:[1]

"That all that part thereof lying on the south side of Blackwater Creek and Staunton River, from the said Blackwater Creek to the confluence of the said river with the river Dan, and from thence to Aaron's Creek to the County line, shall be one distinct County and parish, and called and known by the name of Halifax and parish of Antrim; and all that other part thereof on the north side of Staunton River, from the lower part to the extent of the county upwards, shall be one other distinct county, and retain the name of Lunenburg and parish of Cumberland."

The domain that later was to be Pittsylvania now lay within the bounds of the great new county of Halifax, and the courthouse, after several changes, was located in the eastern part of the county. As generally happens, the place of holding court drew settlers and tradesmen, and in 1759 100 acres[2] belonging to James Roberts, the younger, and adjoining the courthouse were laid off into a town and named Peytonsburg. The trustees appointed for the town were James Roberts, Theophelus Lacy, Robert Wade, Jr., and Nathaniel Terry. With the establishment of the courthouse and a duly constituted town in this (Pittsylvania) section, the inhabitants ceased to be so isolated and remote from the world of affairs. For the monthly court drew lawyers and men of property from other sections, bringing a touch of the outside world; while the ubiquitous trader was present at any gathering of people. The military organization of the county was effected at the courthouse, with its attendant musters to the music of fife and drum. All this added interest and color to the life of the inhabitants.

---

[1]Journal, House of Burgesses, 1752-3, page 33.

[2]Hening's "Statutes," Vol. 7, page 305.

The justices of the peace appointed for the new county were William Byrd,[3] William Wynne,[4] Peter Fontaine, Jr.,[5] William Irby, James Terry,[6] Nathaniel Terry, Robert Hampton, Andrew Wade, and Sherwood Walton. In the following year Thomas Dillard,[7] Thomas Calloway,[8] Samuel Harris,[9] Benjamin Clement,[10] Peter Wilson[11] and Robert Pusey[12] were recommended to the Governor as fit and able persons to be added to the Commission of Peace, all of whom lived in that part of the county that later became Pittsylvania. Of these first gentlemen justices of

---

[3]William Byrd, the third, whose father William Byrd, the second, was granted 105,000 acres in southern Halifax.

[4]William Wynne is thought to be a descendant of Captain Robert Wynne who in his day was one of the most influential men in Virginia. He was a member of the House of Burgesses for Charles City County, 1657-60; and Speaker of the House from 1661-1674. His sons were living and married early in the 18th century. Thomas Wynne, Gent., was living in Prince George County in 1707, aged fifty years. Major Joshua Wynne was a justice of Prince George in 1708. These brothers are believed to be the ancestors of the Wynns of southern Virginia. The will of Captain Robert Wynne was proved in 1678; he desired to be buried in Jordan's Church as near as possible to son Robert; to son Thomas he bequeathed a farm near Canterbury, England, and two homes in Canterbury; to youngest son Joshua he left a house and Oatmeal Mill in Canterbury and two other houses there; rest of estate in Virginia and England to wife Mary.

[5]Peter Fontaine, Jr., was born in Virginia in 1720. He was deputy surveyor of old Brunswick, part surveyor of Lunenburg, and surveyor of Halifax County, performing his office in this section of Virginia for more than twenty-five years. During these years he patented for himself about 10,000 acres; and for his father, the Rev. Peter Fontaine three tracts containing 6,000 acres, who held them for an inheritance for the sons of a late marriage.

Peter Fontaine, Jr., served as justice of the peace and county lieutenant of the military forces of Halifax County. He lived for many years in Lunenburg County, but when appointed surveyor of Halifax, he moved in 1754 to the County and made his home on the south bank of Staunton River, a few miles above the mouth of Double Creek. Upon his father's death in 1757 he became his executor, and finding the distance from Halifax to Charles City too great to properly look after his father's affairs, Col. Fontaine moved to Hanover in the fall of '57, where he spent the remainder of his days.

Peter Fontaine, Jr., married Eliza Winston and had issue: 1. William Fontaine who married Anne Morris and settled in Hanover. 2. John Fontaine who married Martha, daughter of the orator Patrick Henry, and made his home in Henry County, probably on his father's patented lands.

[6]James Terry was an early settler and patented large bodies of land in this section. In 1757 he moved to Orange County, North Carolina. In 1764 (Halifax Deed Book) he sold to Nathaniel Terry, Hugh Innes, Robert Wooding, Thomas Dillard, Sr., Thomas Dillard, Jr., Ed. Booker, John Bates, James Dillard, Archibald Gordon, George Watkins, John Donelson, Thomas Tunstall, vestrymen of Antrim Parish, for £350, 794 acres on Sandy Creek, where the said Terry formerly lived, for a Glebe for Antrim Parish.

[7]Thomas Dillard, Sr., died in Pittsylvania in 1774.

[8]Thomas Calloway, Richard Calloway, William Calloway and Francis Calloway were brothers and early settlers of this section. They were the sons of a Welsh emigrant (Dinwiddie Papers, Vol. 2, page 109). In 1746 Thomas, Charles, James and Richard Calloway entered for 4,800 acres on Beaver's Creek; in 1754 Thomas, Sr., Thomas, Jr., Charles and Richard Calloway entered for 10,400 acres on Johnson's Creek: In the first list of tithables taken for Pittsylvania County in 1767: "Thomas Calloway, sons Charles and Thomas Land, 3 tithes, 100 acres."

William Calloway settled in Bedford, when he patented 15,000 acres; Richard Calloway went to Kentucky with Daniel Boone. "Calloway's Level," situated on the Chatham and Lynchburg Highway about four miles north of Chatham was an early Calloway settlement. Matilda Calloway, a daughter of this house, married Mr. James Poindexter, and they built and settled the beautiful old place which still overlooks south Chatham, surrounded by wide lawns and oaks, now owned by the Pattersons.

[9]Major Samuel Harris died in 1799, and his will is probated in Pittsylvania Court House, Oct. 21st of that year. He left his estate to sons Nathaniel, Samuel and Benjamin and daughters Mary Buckley and Elizabeth Perkins.

[10]Benjamin Clement made his home on Staunton River in 1748.

[11]Peter Wilson was patenting land along Sandy Creek of Dan River in 1746. He made his home on Dan River (about 6 miles above the city of Danville) where he established Wilson's Ferry. His will is recorded in Halifax, in 1762, in which he named wife Alcey, sons John, Peter and William, and daughters Nanny, Isbell, Margaret and Agnes Perkins, wife of Peter Perkins. Family tradition records that Peter Wilson and his wife Alcey were Scotch-Irish emigrants. The left a distinguished progeny among whom were Governors Albert M. Scales and Robert Brodnax Glenn of North Carolina and Governor Wilson Lumpkin of Georgia.

[12]Robert Pusey was probably from Pennsylvania where Caleb Pusey was for many years a leader among the Quakers.

Halifax, William Byrd and Peter Fontaine, Jr., were of Charles City County; William Irby, William Wynne, and Sherwood Walton were of southside Virginia; Nathaniel and James Terry and Benjamin Clement from King William County; Samuel Harris from Hanover County; Robert Hampton, Andrew Wade, Robert Pusey, Peter Wilson and Thomas Calloway were probably from Pennsylvania.

The clerk was instructed[13] to purchase one dozen volumes of Webb's "Virginia Justice" for the use of the magistrates so that they might be instructed in their duties.

The other officers appointed for the county were George Currie, clerk, with William Wright, deputy clerk; Nathaniel Terry, sheriff, with Samuel Harris, deputy sheriff; Clement Reade, of Lunenburg King's attorney; Peter Fontaine, Jr., surveyor, with Sherwood Walton and William Sims deputy surveyors.

A letter[14] from Peter Fontaine, Jr., to relatives in England, tells of his appointment as surveyor for the new county:

"Lunenburg, July 9, 1752.

"My district for surveying lies, i. e. the chief of it in Halifax County, in the fork of the River Roanoke, so that I now live out of my County and by means of the indulgence granted me of having assistants, I do not go at all into the woods. Though my living 150 miles from Williamsburg forces me frequently to take very tedious rides."

Two years later Peter Fontaine moved to Halifax, settling on the south side of Staunton River near the mouth of Double Creek.

One of the first duties of the new justices was to take the tax lists, or lists of tithables, which was ordered as follows:

"William Irby is ordered to take the lists of tithables from the Point of Fork up to Buffalo (eastern Halifax).

"James Terry is ordered to take the lists of tithables from the mouth of Buffalo up Staunton River to the extent of the county." (This included northern Halifax and Pittsylvania and southern Franklin counties.)

"Hugh Moore (?) is ordered to take the lists of tithables from the mouth of Miry Creek up Dan River to the extent of the county" (including southern Pittsylvania, Halifax, Henry and Patrick Counties).

The tithables for the county numbered 634 and the poll tax of 21 pounds of tobacco amounted to 13,314 pounds, out of which the expenses

[13] Order Books of Halifax County.

[14] "Story of a Huguenot Family," by Maury.

of the county government were paid. The names of Joseph Mayes, Henry Short, Robert Crump, Charles Sowder, Charles and David Lessonby, Hamon Critz, John Frederick Miller and John Henry Stone were ordered to be added to the lists of tithables.

In 1756 Governor Dinwiddie[15] sent the lists of tithables of all the counties in Virginia to the Lords of Trade at London, and gave for Halifax 629 whites and 141 blacks (total 870); for Bedford 357 whites and 143 blacks (total 500); for Lunenburg 1,209 whites and 983 blacks; for Brunswick 1,299 whites and 976 blacks.

The Church of England being the established church of the colony, as new counties were formed new parishes were laid out co-extensive with the counties, and the parish of Antrim was established in Halifax, probably taking its name from Antrim, Ireland, former home of the Irish settlers. Certain official duties were entrusted to the vestrymen, such as the care of the poor and the marking of boundary lines. The following gentlemen[16] took the oath of vestrymen and entered upon their official duties: James Terry, Richard Echols, Thomas Dillard, Thomas Calloway, Richard Brown, William Irby, Merry Webb, William Wynne, John Owen, Peter Wilson, John Guillington, Paul Carrington, Samuel Harris and George Curry.

There were many dissenters, probably the Scotch Presbyterian, and they petitioned in 1755, for leave to build a meeting house, and were granted[17] the right to erect one on the land of William Russell on Difficult Creek, but the history of the church is not known.

The early settlers attacked the wilderness in grim earnest, hewing down the trees for clearings, making real homes with gardens and orchards such as they had known in those parts of the colonies where civilization was well established. In 1753 Thomas Calloway and others were ordered to view the improvements made on Leatherwood Creek (Henry County) by Ralph Elkins, and found 26 acres under cultivation, 20 head of neat cattle, fences, orchards, buildings and other improvements to the values of £396. In 1754 Obadiah Woodson had 304 fruit trees set out on his plantation on Snow Creek. Pioneer life was necessarily primative, and the first homes were cabins, which were soon succeeded by the story and a half weatherboarded house, of dormer windows, usually dignified by the term of "mansion house," in the wills of the builders.

[15]Dinwiddie Papers, Vol. 2, page 352.
[16]Order Book of Halifax, No. 1.
[17]Order Book of Halifax.

The question of roads at once engaged the attention of the court. At a court held on October 17, 1752, a petition was presented by "Thomas Calloway and the inhabitants of this county, setting forth that the old Road leading from Banister to Smiths River is so hilly and broken that it is most impassable for carriages, and praying that Henry Lunsford, John Russell and Joseph Ironmonger may be appointed to view and mark the best and most convenient way from the head of the south fork of Sandy River on the south side of Banister Mountains to the place appointed for the Court House." The Banister Mountains were of course "White Oak" Mountain, and the "old Road from Banister to Smith River" was no doubt the Hickey Road opened in 1749. This road petitioned for was ordered to be opened and cleared and it probably led from the Irish Road near Whitmell across by Chestnut Level, said to be a very old roadway.

William Bean was again ordered to mark and lay off a road from his house on Dan River to the Falls of Banister, this road having previously been ordered by the Lunenburg Court in 1750. Bean's home on Dan River seems to have been a point of peculiar interest judging from the number of roads ordered to be built from this place. It was probably the center of numerous settlements along Dan River. Peter Wilson and Nicholas Perkins were neighbors of Bean's.

In July, 1753, William Bean, John Stone and Redmon Fallen were ordered to mark a road from Bean's on Dan River to the Court House, and in October they reported the road viewed and marked. Thereupon the court ordered: "Peter Wilson is appointed Surveyor of that part of the said road as leads from John Russell's Mill to Fall Creek, and Samuel Harris is appointed surveyor of that part of the said road as leads from Fall Creek to Sweeting's Fork." The surveyors were ordered to open and clear the roadway using the following tithables, who lived in the vicinity of the road: John Russell and son, William Mobberly, James Duncan, David Lane, George Chadwell, Lambeth Dodson, Thomas Williamson, John Yates, William Stevens, Silvester Junal, Thomas Smith and son, Isaac Little and son, Abram Little, Charles Little, William York, James Wady, John Railey, James Cargill, Redmon Fallon and son.

The order further read: "Benjamin Terry is appointed surveyor of the road from Sweeting's Fork to the Court House, to use his own tithables with those of James and Nathaniel Terry, Griffith Dickerson and James Scott."

This road lead in a northeastern direction, across eastern Pittsylvania.

Settlers from Pennsylvania and Maryland were continuing to pour south, seeking homes and cheaper land, and many now settled in western Halifax. They came bringing all they owned. The prosperous drove big wagons in which were packed all their household goods and farming utensils, and in which the women and children rode. "The men walked,[18] or rode on horseback, driving before them such cattle as they owned. Some had no wagons and traveled on horseback, or walked with a pack horse carrying bedding, a few simple farming implements, cooking utensils, a bag of corn, and the Bible. Some, lacking even a pack horse, walked all the way, carrying their entire property.

"The emigrants usually left Pennsylvania in the early fall, after harvest was over, reaching Virginia or North Carolina before hard winter set in. Almost all were farmers, but were artisans as well, making almost everying they needed. The Germans were industrious and economical; the Scotch-Irish, ambitious, alert and grasping."

These upper inhabitants of Halifax had increased in numbers until now they began to petition for more roads. In March,[19] 1753, Richard Parsons and William Adkins were ordered to mark a road from the mouth of Snow Creek to Hickey's Road. In July the inhabitants on Pigg River and Snow Creek (Franklin County) petitioned for a road from the uppermost of the inhabitants to the Snow Creek Road, and Thomas Hall and William Hill were ordered to lay off the road. The following year the same inhabitants begged that the road laid off by Hall and Hill be extended to the top of the Blue Ridge, which was accordingly ordered, with Tully Choice as surveyor. This road led across Franklin County to the mountains.

At this time the inhabitants about Wart Mountain petitioned, "that a road be run from Hickey's Road at or near the plantation of Merry Webb the nearest and best way to intersect Hickey's old road at Horse Pen Pasture Creek," and Charles Sowder, John and Will Blevins were ordered to mark the way and report at the next Court. The surveyor's records contain references to Hickey's Old Road and Hickey's Road, showing that there were two roads bearing Hickey's name.

There is mention of a visit[20] to Hickey's Store made by the Moravian brethren, in 1753, when the first colony traveled from Bethlehem, Pennsylvania down to North Carolina to occupy the grant of 72,000 acres made to them by Lord Granville. This settlement is now Winston-

[18] "The Building of an Empire," by J. G. Roulhac Hamilton.

[19] Order Book of Halifax, No. 1.

[20] *Virginia Mag. History*, Vol. 12, pages 273-79.

Salem. The brethren made the journey down the Valley of Virginia, crossed the Blue Ridge Mountains at Magotty's Gap and continued through Franklin and Henry Counties into North Carolina. A rude wagon way had been cut out before by Morgan Bryan[21] whom it had taken three months to travel from the Shenandoah to the Yadkin, clearing his way as he went, and for years this road bore his name, being called Morgan Bryan's Road. Bryan, after leading a body of Quakers from Pennsylvania into Virginia, in 1748 moved with Martha, his wife, and eight children, to the Yadkin in North Carolina.

Over Bryan's rough way traveled the Moravians with their long bodied wagon, experiencing many difficulties in crossing the streams and getting up and down the steep mountains which they encountered. They kept a diary of their journey written in Latin in which they mentioned the unvarying kindness of the people along the way, in whom we recognize some of the earliest settlers.

They record: "Near by Magotty Creek dwells Benjamin Ray,[22] an old man of some ninety years, and his wife, who is about a hundred years old. They are both active and cheerful people who gave us milk to drink and were very kind." Close by the house they came upon the "Werrick Road which runs mostly westward and is a pretty good road." Over this road the back settlers conveyed their tobacco, and probably other produce, to market, at Warwick on the James.

The following day the brethren came to Mr. Robert Cole's place, a justice of the peace (Lunenburg) from whom they bought some corn; and a little further on they crossed Blackwater, "a large creek with steep banks," and missing the way came to an old mill race at Rentfro's Mill. A few miles on and they stopped at the plantation of Robert Johnson to buy hay, who told them he had not heard a sermon in nine years.

They crossed Smith River in the northwestern part of what is now Henry County, and after going forward several miles stuck fast in a mud hole. They wrote that "Mr. Hiccki (John Hickey) who lives half a mile from here and keeps a store (which is the nearest house at which we can buy salt) came to us and showed himself very friendly. We had a miserable road to his house. Here we bought some provisions."

After passing Horse Pasture Creek they drove four miles and, "ate dinner at Adam Loving's plantation. Here we bought ten bushels of

[21]Archibald Henderson's "Conquest of the Great Southwest" states that Morgan Bryan came from Ireland to Chester, Pennsylvania in 1719, with sons William, Joseph, James and Morgan. After settling on the Yadkin in North Carolina, the Bryans were joined by the Morgans and Boones. Edward Morgan had come from Wales; his daughter Sarah married Squire Boone and among their children was Daniel, the hunter.

[22]Benjamin Ray had a cabin on Magotty Creek in 1747.

corn. The people were very friendly to us." A few miles on and the brethren entered North Carolina.

This grant to the Moravian Brethren lay ten miles from the Yadkin, "on the upper Pennsylvania Road." There was a well known roadway already established, from Pennsylvania to North Carolina, called "the Great Road from Pennsylvania to the Yadkin." This road was traced on the map of Virginia made by Jefferson and Fry in 1751, and followed the direction of the great war trail of the Iroquois, crossing the Blue Ridge at the Staunton River water gap and passing through Bedford, Franklin and Henry Counties. Along these two roads, Morgan Bryan's and the Great Road, passed thousands of families from Pennsylvania, Maryland and New Jersey, seeking homes in the south. For forty years, from 1735-1775, this migration of Germans and Scotch-Irish continued in wave after wave. In one year it was estimated that more than a thousand families entered North Carolina from Pennsylvania by way of Virginia.

In the midst of these peaceful plans of development—the making of roads, clearing farm lands and planting orchards, there suddenly burst upon the colony the horror of Indian warfare. War is always a great disturber of the settled order of affairs, but in Indian war there was added the constant terror in each household of a surprise attack from the savages. Halifax being the most southern frontier county suffered greatly both in the loss of inhabitants who fled southward and in the general turmoil which put a stop to all internal improvements. Peter Fontaine wrote, "the last two years I lived in Halifax (1755-57) I had very little to do in surveying owing to the unsettled condition of the County due to the war."

Chapter VI

THE FRENCH AND INDIAN WAR

In 1754 trouble arose with France over the boundary lines of the French and English possessions, which resulted in the conflict known as the French and Indian War. Many of the northern Indians taking the part of the French waged a cruel warfare against the defenseless inhabitants of frontier Virginia.

The butchery of his fellow countrymen so moved the heart of young Colonel George Washington that he wrote to the governor of Virginia: "The tears of the women and the petitions of the men melt me into such deadly sorrow that I solemnly declare I would offer myself a willing sacrifice to the butchering enemy, provided that would contribute to the peoples' ease."

Upon the arrival of General Braddock and his English force early in 1755, the spirits of the people rose high for they deemed deliverance from their savage foes at hand. In the early summer, on the eve of Braddock's march, the following letter[1] of instruction was sent by Governor Dinwiddie to the county-lieutenants of all the frontier counties, of which Halifax formed the most southern:

"Sir,

Whereas it has been signified to me by his Excellency Gen. Braddock, y't is suspected w'h our army is far advanced the French and their Indians will fall upon the frontier Settlements of y'r Colony, for the better guarding ag'st the dangerous consequences of such an Attempt You are hereby required to keep a diligent Look out and send me Speedy Advice if any number of men shall appear in Arms on our Frontiers, and give a proper Alarm to the Neighborning Counties."

When the dire news of Braddock's defeat on the Monongahela spread through the Colony, consternation seized upon the back inhabitants, for they well knew the havoc which would be wrought among them by the savages in the wake of this victory. The upper inhabitants to the number of thousands forsook their homes in the Valley and across the Blue Ridge in Piedmont Virginia, and fled to the Carolinas. "Not only[2] did hundreds of families desert the exposed lands adjacent to the upper waters of the Potomac, James and Staunton Rivers, but thousands poured

[1]Dinwiddie Papers, Vol. 2, p. 67.

[2]Bruce, Tyler, and Morton's "History of Virginia," Vol. I, p. 360.

out of the foothills of Piedmont and set their faces resolutely toward the same regions of the Carolina."

The Rev'd James Maury of Louisa County in a letter[3] to Philip Ludwell, of February, 1756, described this condition in Piedmont Virginia: "By Bedford Courthouse in one week, 'tis said, and I believe truly said, near 300 Persons, Inhabitants of this Colony, past, on their way to Carolina * * * Scarce do I know a neighborhood but what has lost some Families, and expects quickly to lose more." They agreed that if fifty[4] savages could without resistance drive off 2,000 cattle and horses, and destroy all buildings standing here and there over a wide area of country, what devastation of life and property could not one thousand accomplish.

The Virginia settlers fled to the Carolinas because they expected to find in the shelter of the friendly Catawbas and Cherokees protection against the inroads of the northern Indians. It was probably owing to this exodus that we find many of the Scotch names listed in the tithables of western Lunenburg missing from the records a few years later; such as McDead, McCusick, McCanes and McDavid and so on.

Colonel William Byrd,[5] the third, was county lieutenant of Halifax and in charge of all military activity in the county. His home was at "Westover" in Charles City County, more than 150 miles distant, but he still owned a great part of the 105,000 acres granted to his father, and this, with his known ability, was the occasion of his being appointed a justice of the peace and presiding military authority in the frontier county of Halifax. He was a man of great wealth but this did not dull the edge of his patriotism and he served his country actively throughout the war, undergoing great hardships and filling positions of great trust. He was naturally absent from Halifax a great part of the time and the inhabitants of the county, amid their anxious fears at this time appealed through their justices of the peace to the Governor. He replied in the following letter[6] to Col. William Byrd:

"Sir.— "July 22, 1755.

I have a long Representation from the Justices of the Co'ty of Halifax in regard to the barbarous murders committed in the Co'ty of Augusta and their Fear of being attacked by these savages. They com-

[3]*Va. Mag. History & Biog.*, Vol. 19, pp. 292-300.

[4]Bruce, Vol. 2, p. 361.

[5]A letter of General Forbes to William Pitt, July 10, 1758, said of Byrd: "As he has a large and opulent fortune in Virginia, he joined the Earl of London early after his arrival in America. He accompan'yd the army to Halifax last year and sett a noble example to all the gentlemen of the continent who had either inclination or ability to serve their King and Country." (*Va. Mag. Hist.*, Vol. 16, p. 133.)

[6]Dinwiddie Papers, Vol. 2, p. 110.

plain of want of Officers for the Militia. As you are Lieut. of the Co'ty I enclose You some blank Commissions to fill up to such as You think are most Worthy. They also complain of want of Ammunit'n. I have ordered all the Militia of Co'ty to be muster'd and a report to be made to me of their numb's and how provided with Guns, Ammunit'n etc. When you make a return to me of y'r Co'ty Militia, I shall endeavor, all in my Power to supply their Wants."

In response to this letter we may suppose that Col. Byrd journeyed up from Westover and reorganized the County Militia for at the August Court[7] for Halifax, 1755, the following officers were elected:

William Irby, Colonel of the Militia.

Nathaniel Terry, Major of the Militia.

Thomas Dillard, Major of the Militia.

Benjamin Clement and William Lawton, Captains of Companies of Rangers. The duty of the rangers was to "range" along the frontiers through the forests in search of hostile Indians.

Col. Clement Read, whose home was in Lunenburg, but who served as King's attorney for Halifax County was active in the defense of the frontiers. He advised[8] Governor Dinwiddie in August that the people of this section had raised a volunteer company of fifty men, and also agreed to pay them for six months service. Nathaniel Terry of Halifax was appointed Captain of the company, and his commission was accompanied by the following[9] instructions from the Governor:

"Sir, "August, 1755.

You hav'g rec'd a Com'e to Com'd a Co'y of Volunteers raised on purpose to repel and revenge the many cruel Murders and Outrages committed by several Strangling French and Ind's, who if not soon defeated, our Inhabit's in the frontier Counties, already greatly intimidated may be obliged to abandon their Plantat's, and as it has pleas'd God to give you courage and Resolution to Oppose those Invaders of Y'r Co'try I hope it will be y'r first and principal Care to keep up a just sense of Religion y't you may with confidence go forth under the Protect'n of the Supreme Being who is always ready to assist those who call upon him with a true penitent."

The Governor admonished him "to be careful of the Powder and ball"; and to use every caution against molesting the friendly Cherokees

[7]Minute Book of Halifax Co. Va., No. 1.
[8]Dinwiddie Papers, Vol. 2, pp. 156-8.
[9]Dinwiddie Papers, Vol. 2, 158-9.

and Catawbas in ranging through the forests, for, he said, as soon as a person who understood their languages could be procured, he would send an Express to these friendly Nations to advise them of our men being out against the French and Northern Indians.

The Cherokees lived in the Tennessee Country and the Catawbas in the Carolinas, and both nations had long maintained friendly relations with the colonists. The French were now making overtures to them in the hope of inciting them to war against the English, while Virginia was making every effort to retain their friendship.

The Governor had sent[10] up from Williamsburg for the use of Captain Terry's Company four and one-half barrels of powder, two barrels of shot and fifty swords, and wished the men to stay out on a ranging expedition until November. A commission was also sent at this time to Captain John Phelps to command a company of Bedford Militia.

It is probable that Captain Terry for some unknown reason did not march at this time, for in a letter[11] to Col. William Calloway, of Bedford, the Governor stated:

"Sept. 20, 1755.

"Sir,—

Am much surprised y't C't Phelps and C't Terry have not marched out agreeable to their and Y'r Proposal. You now recommend one Robt. Wynne for a Com'd. The money I sent up can not be made use of as the men are not marcht."

For the defense of the frontier inhabitants the General Assembly[12] enacted in March, 1756, "that whereas the frontiers of this colony are in a very defenseless condition and openly exposed to the incursions and depredations of our cruel and savage enemies who are daily destroying the lives and estates of the inhabitants of that part of the colony, and it is necessary that forts should be erected in those parts, to put a stop to those violent outrages of the enemy, * * * That a chain of forts be erected to begin at Henry Enochs, on Great-Cape-Capon, in the county of Hampshire, and to extend to the South Fork of Mayo River, in the county of Halifax."

These forts were placed not nearer to one another than twelve miles and not further apart than twenty-five miles; there were three erected in western Halifax. In September, 1756, George Washington visited the line of forts and reported to the Governor that he proceeded to

[10]Dinwiddie Papers, Vol. 2, p. 156.

[11]Dinwiddie Papers, Vol. 2, p. 211.

[12]Hening's "Statutes," Vol. 7, p. 18.

Fort Trial on Smith River, the most southerly of the forts. No record or tradition is left in the county of Washington's visit. He probably came with a few riding companions, quietly inspected the forts and returned.

Fort Trial was located[13] at the mouth of Reed Creek, six miles west of the present town of Martinsville, on a small eminence that commands a very fine view of Smith River for several miles. In 1774 the fort was visited by J. F. D. Smythe, the Englishman, who described it in his "Travels":[14]

"The fort resembled a quadrangle polygon enclosed with large timbers and cuts of trees split in two about twelve or sixteen feet high above the ground, standing erect, and about three or four feet in the earth quite close together, with loop holes cut through about four or five feet from the ground for small arms. * * * There was a log hut each side of the gate. Within the area, nearly in the center were two common framed houses and boarded, filled in to the height of five feet with stone and clay on the inside as a defense against small arms." Today one can trace the outline of the buildings by the rocks that formed the inner walls.

The other two forts of western Halifax were named Mayo Fort and Hickey's Fort, and all three were built[15] by Nathaniel Terry. Mayo Fort was located on the plantation of John Frederick Miller,[16] who petitioned[17] the General Assembly in 1759 for redress because of the damages he suffered on account of the fort. He stated that by order of the commanding officer of Halifax County a fort had been erected on his plantation which enclosed his dwelling house and other houses, and was garrisoned by a company of militia, who "to render it more secure from the approach and attacks of the enemy, cut down a large Orchard, burnt one house, and 1,600 Fence Rails and made use of 118 feet of plank about the Fort," besides doing him many other damages. He stated that the fort was still in the possession of the militia and rangers. Hickey's Fort was probably located on the plantation of John Hickey.

---

[13]*Va. Mag. Hist.*, Vol. 22, p. 426.

[14]"Travels in America," by J. F. D. Smythe, pp. 178-9.

[15]Hening's "Statutes," Vol. 7, p. 220.

[16]John Frederick Miller was a native Scotchman, and ancester of George Mercer Miller, who on October 10th, 1833, married Laura McClelland and had issue: Margaret Ellen Miller married Mr. Tarr; William B. Miller; Thomas Stanhope Miller, Charles Edwin Miller, never married, resided at "Sharswood," Pittsylvania; Parke Miller married in 1865 Judge Horation Davis, of Wilmington, N. C., brother of Bishop Davis of South Carolina and left three sons, Frederick, William and Charles.

[17]Journal of the House of Burgesses.

That only one of the forts was manned at this time is shown by the following letter[18] from the governor to Colonel Read:

"Nov. 1756.

"As it is represented to me the absolute necessity of hav'g a F't garrisoned in Halifax, the Inhabit's of y't Co'ty being greatly Expos'd to the Inroads of the En'y, I therefore give You Orders to garrison one of the three Forts built on the Front's of Halifax, with a Captain, Lieut., Ensign, two Serjeants, two Corporals, and forty men; y't you acq't me of a proper Person to Com'd, who will keep the men under proper Discipline and to your Duty, not to leave the F't but wh'n sent out on Scout'g Parties; the Compa's to remain in pay till the first of Mar. next, and the men to be pick't good men, y't will obey com'ds, and do y'r Duty. As I understand there is a great waste in Provis's, You are to order y't y'r Provisions be weighed out to 'em, vig't 1½ lbs. Beef and 1 lb. Bread per Day. The 100 Beeves you have sent there I suppose will serve y't Garrison to the Time above."

Captain Nash was put in command of this fort, and served throughout the winter and the following summer.

Volunteer forces, who called themselves Associators, were raised in the summers of 1756 and 1757 for the purpose of carrying war into the Shawnee Country, and destroying their towns along the Ohio River. The frontier inhabitants feared that with the march of the Associators they would be left in a defenseless condition and open to attacks from the enemy.

In February, 1757, the Governor wrote[19] to Colonel Clement Read, who continued active in the Colony's defense:

"I am of the opinion you have Arms suffic't for the Associators, those Arms lent to Colonel Fontaine and Stalnaker ought to be called in for the use of the Expedit'n and as Col. Lewis has orders to raise three compan's on the frontiers of Augusta and Captain Nash in Halifax with Captain Hogg's Comp'y I think sufficient for the defense of the frontier until the return of the Associators."

Both expeditions proved to be failures, the Associators failing to reach the Shawnee Country, and during the summer of 1757 the enemy again appeared on the frontiers. In August letters[20] from Halifax, Bedford and Augusta notified the Governor that the Shawnees had murdered seven and carried off captives eleven of the inhabitants. The

[18]Dinwiddie Papers, Vol. 2, p. 557.
[19]Dinwiddie Papers, Vol. 2, p. 589.
[20]Dinwiddie Papers, Vol. 2, p. 678.

Governor thereupon ordered[21] Colonel Peter Fontaine who was now county lieutenant of Halifax to send out two companies of militia.

That the fears of the inhabitants of Halifax were not without reason is shown by the following letter[22] of Peter Fontaine, written from Halifax in June, 1757:

"The County of Halifax is threatened by our enemy Indians, and the people in the upper part of the county, which by the late encroachments of our enemies have become a frontier, are in great consternation and all public business at a stand. The poor farmers and planters have dreadful apprehensions of falling into the hands of the savages, as indeed considering the treatment those have had who have had the misfortune to be surprised by them, they have good reason.

"We have amongst us two or three who have made their escape from the Shawnees (a tribe of Indians that live on the Ohio, to the Westward of Halifax), the Indians suspected that one of them whose wife and children had been inhumanly murdered, would attempt to escape, to prevent which they cut deep gashes in his heels and as soon as the man was like to get well and be in order to travel again they cut other gashes across the former, and by that means and at other times searing his feet with hot irons, kept him a continual cripple. The man, however, being of an enterprising spirit, providentially made his escpae * * * Such cruelties they practice upon our people that all had rather perish than be taken alive."

A dispute arose at this time between the justices of Halifax and Governor Dinwiddie over some point about which we can now only surmise. The Governor was a doughty Scotchman in whom the national trait of economy was pronounced and he loudly complained of the expense entailed in the defense of the frontiers of the colony. In the spring of that year (1757) the people of Halifax had suffered losses and cruel indignities at the hands of the Indians, and the question in dispute was no doubt one of more protection and security, which the justices of Halifax demanded.

The Governor, in his choleric wrath, turned the offending justices out of office and said in a letter[23] to Colonel Fontaine:

"Cou'd they expect any other return than turning out those that have been refractory and I now send a new Comm'o which I hope will answer my Intent's for the Service of the County."

[21]Dinwiddie Papers, Vol. 2, p. 678.
[22]"Memoirs of a Huguenot Family," Maury.
[23]Dinwiddie Papers, Vol. 2, p. 680.

In the new commission of peace for Halifax the governor named Colonel Bland, who owned a "Quarter" in the county, and this further exasperated the people, who in their exposed and unhappy condition needed an ever present authority and not one many miles distant from this section.

In a letter to Col. Bland,[24] the Governor voices his complaint of Halifax, as he frequently did of Augusta, and the other frontier counties and officers:

"Sir,—

I am much offended at the arrogance and ill manners of several of the justices of the Peace in Halifax Co. I expected they would have been very thankful on my including a Gent of y'r good Sense and Capacity to be a Magistrate there, which I am convinced they greatly want. Cou'd they have expected that I sh'd have notified their clamours otherways than turning the refractory out of command."

The Governor, safe in his palace at Williamsburg, failed to appreciate the anxious dread under which the people of the exposed counties labored. Those "refractory" justices seemed not to fear his royal authority, though he used it vigorously against them, for a justice was appointed for life.

In the spring of 1758 the Shawnees made another attack upon frontier Halifax, seizing and carrying into captivity one of the leading citizens of the county, Robert Pusey, a justice of the peace. Pusey was a large land owner as shown by his patents; he made his home on Otter Creek of Smith River. In a petition[25] to the General Assembly in 1775, he stated that he and his wife and child were captured by the Shawnees in March, 1758, and carried into captivity where he was held a long time until he redeemed his liberty. He thereby lost all of his property and prayed for some relief.

Following upon this tragedy the militia companies of Lunenburg and Halifax were ordered to the frontiers, as the following order[26] to Captain Thomas Bouldin of Lunenburg shows:

"April 18, 1758.

"Capt. Bouldin,—

"You with the men under your command are to march to Halifax Court House, there to joyn a company raised by Col. Maury, whose orders you are to receive:

[24]Dinwiddie Papers, Vol. 2, p. 688.

[25]Journal of the House of Burgesses, p. 1775.

[26]"An Old Trunk," Powhatan Bouldin.

"I am informed that Major Samuel Harris has received cash and orders from the government to furnish such forces as are sent to the assistance of Halifax County with provisions. To Col. Maury then you are to apply for his orders to Major Harris for a supply for your men. In the meantime you are to take steps appointed by law to procure those necessary.

"Col. Maury will meet you at the Courthouse and give you directions when to march to the relief of the frontier of this county.

"I am your humble servant, Clem't Read."

"P. S. You must cause your Lieutenant to keep an exact journal of all your marches * * * that it may be returned to the President at Wmburg according to order."

Major Samuel Harris was commissary of the three forts of Halifax at this time.

Col. Peter Fontaine who had been county lieutenant had moved from the county to Hanover and his cousin, Abram Maury, succeeded to the position.

Captain Robert Wade's company of Halifax Militia took a range along the frontier in the summer of 1758. John Echols,[27] a member of the company, was probably detailed to keep a record of the expedition, for in his journal we read that in the month of August, "Capt. Robert Wade march't from Mayo Fort with 35 men in order to take a range to the New River in search of our enemy Indians. We marcht about three miles that day to a Plantation where Peter Rentfro formerly lived and took up camp. Next morning we marcht along to a place called Gobling Town where we Eat our Brakefast, and so continued our march and took up our camp that night at the Foot of the Blew Ledge (Blue Ridge).

Next Day we crossed the Blew Ledge and marched to Francis Eason's Plantation and continued there that night. Our hunters brought in a plentiful supply of venison. Next morning being Tuesday the 15th we marcht down to Richard Ratcliff's plantation on Meadow Creek where we continued that night. Next morning sent out Spyes and hunters to Spy for emeny signs and to hunt for provisions."

Echols told how they spent several days there, and then one day five Indians came very unexpectedly upon them. He said the Indians "stood

[27]Calendar of Virginia State Papers, Vol. I, p. 254. John Echols, the author of the Journal, was probably a son of one of the four Echols, Richard, Abram, Joseph and William who in 1728 with others, patented 6,000 acres in Spottsylvania County on Bent Creek. In 1745-6 Richard, Abram, Joseph and William Echols patented lands in Pittsylvania and adjacent counties.

in amaise and Reason they had, for I suppose there were twenty guns presented at them. They said they were Cherokees. I made signs to them to shew me their Pass But they had none. They had with them five head of horse and Skelps that appeared to be whitemen. Four of the horses appeared as tho' they had been recently taken, the other was vary poor."

There was a hunter with them named Abraham Dunkleberry who said the Indians were Cherokees, but that they evidently were rogues. The Captain was doubtful of what he should do, but finally allowed the Indians to depart, which greatly displeased the men who said there was no use in ranging if the enemy were to be allowed to go after catching them. So after the hunter Dunkleberry had packed up his skins and gone the Captain appointed twelve[28] men to go after the Indians, and overtaking them in an Orchard they killed four and wounded the other. Then finding so many Indian signs about and their ammunition running low, they decided to return home.

On Tuesday the 22nd they ate dinner on Blackwater Creek and spent the night at Robert Jones' Plantation at the head of Pigg River. The following day "myself and four more left the company and went across by Gobling Town and came to Mayo Fort that night. The Captain and the rest of the men tells us that they came to Hickey's Fort that night and the next day to Mayo Fort. I remember no more worth making a Remark of, so courteous Reader, I Rem Yrs. etc.

John Echols."

Virginia's plan of defense for the colony consisted in keeping companies of rangers out along the frontiers in search of enemy Indians, the line of forts manned by the militia and two regiments of a thousand men each under the commands of Colonel George Washington and Colonel William Byrd which co-operated with an English force in an active campaign against the French. Each county was called upon to furnish by draft its proportion of soldiers called for in making up the regiments.

Throughout the winter of 1758-9 these three forts of Halifax were manned by detachments of the militia while companies of her rangers were out on duty. This is shown in the petition of Abraham Maury[29]

[28]The twelve men appointed to follow the Indians were Adam Herman, David Herman, Adam Hall, Richard Hall, Richard Hall, Jr., Tobias Clap, Philip Clap, Joseph Clap, Benjamine Angel, David Currie, Richard Hines, James Lyons.

[29]Colonel Abram Maury was the son of Matthew Maury who was born in Dubling and died in Virginia in 1752, and his wife Mary Anne Fontaine, daughter of the Rev. James Fontaine of England and Ireland. Abram Mary married Susanna Poindexter and left many descendants.

(Journal of House of Burgesses) Nov. 13, 1759, who stated that he entered into contract with the governor to furnish the militia and rangers of Halifax and Bedford counties with provisions from November, 1758 to March, 1759. He further stated that upon the reduction of Fort Duquesne the detachments of militia were recalled from the forts, leaving the provisions in the forts unguarded; that the rangers were so long in returning that before their arrival the provisions had been destroyed.

The Rev'd James Maury wrote of Col. Maury in 1759:

"My brother is concerned in victualizing the troops stationed in the southwestern frontier of the colony, and by his prudence, activity and spirited conduct has greatly contributed to keep the remote inhabitants from abandoning their habitations" (Bouldin).

A tradition of these troublous times has been preserved[30] in the story of the capture by the Indians of a young maiden named Mary Crawford who lived in the northern part of the county in the neighborhood of Hurts, where the incident is still remembered and told. The story runs that an attack was made upon the neighborhood by the Indians, who having secured much plunder and many prisoners, retreated across the mountains. Mary Crawford, a young woman who made her home with a family by the name of White, was among those who were captured. It is told that she was rescued by young Captain Henry Stanton, who fled with her down Staunton River and returned her safely to her people.

Hale tells in his Narratives that in the year 1760 a party of Indians crossed the Blue Ridge and murdered people living east of the mountains in Bedford and Halifax Counties. They took several women and children prisoners and loading their horses with plunder escaped by way of New River. However, their camp was discovered, the alarm given, and the whites overpowering the Indians, the captives were released. The capture of Mary Crawford probably occurred at this time.

After many disasters the direction of the war was given over to William Pitt, the English statesman, and under his energetic and wise guidance the whole character of operations at once changed. Upon the fall of Fort Duquesne the name of the fort was changed to Fort Pitt (now Pittsburg) in his honor. Victory crowned the arms of the American Colonies in 1760, though peace was not concluded until 1763, when the treaty of Paris was drawn up, giving to England all the territory north of New Orleans and east of the Mississippi River.

[30]This story was told by Col. Abner Anthony, who was born in 1812, and died in 1908. He was the son of Mark Anthony, of Anthony's Ford, on Staunton River, and his wife who died at the age of 99 years, as a result from a fall from her horse. (Related by Miss Juliet Fauntleroy of "Avoca.")

In 1758 the General Assembly[31] provided that the soldiers who had seen active service in the war should be paid. The following list of officers was given for Halifax; unfortunately the muster rolls of the companies were not preserved:

Pay to Lieut. Thomas Green and a party of militia under his command in Halifax, as by muster rolls	£ 42.
Pay to Thomas Spragin as a lieutenant and a party of militia of the said county under his command, as per muster roll	5.10.
Pay to Captain Robert Wooding[32] and a party of militia of said county under his command as per muster roll	32.
Pay to James Dillard[33] as a lieutenant and a party of militia under his command, as per muster roll	102. 4.8
Pay to Captain Peter Wilson and a company of militia under his command of said county, as per muster roll	35. 3.4
Pay to Captain Robert Wade, Jr.,[34] for pay to himself, his officers, and a company of militia of said county under his command, as by muster roll	475. 8.6

[31]Hening's "Statute," Vol. 7, pp. 219-20.

[32]Captain Robert Wooding was for many years a leading and influential citizen of Halifax County. There is a tradition in the family that Robert and his brother John, when small boys in England were returning home from school one day when they were accosted by two men on horseback, each of whom asked the boys to break for him a riding switch. Upon handing the switches to the strangers the boys were suddenly seized by the men who lifted them to their horses and hid them under their long riding cloaks. The boys never saw their home again and were sold to Virginia. Kidnapping was a nefarious trade practiced in England for many years.

Robert Wooding married Mrs. Elizabeth Hill; his will was proven in Halifax May 14, 1796, in which he named as legatees James and Mary Taylor; James Chappell, son-in-law; Elizabeth Hill; son Thomas Hill (Wooding) brother John Wooding; Benjamin Rogers, husband of Nancy Hill; Porterfield Kent, husband of Elizabeth Hill; Mrs. Elizabeth Hill (Wooding), son Thomas Hill Wooding, Executor.

[33]Captain James Dillard (3) of Halifax militia, vestryman and justice of the peace, is said (Hill's "History of Henry County, Va.) to be the grandson of James Dillard (1) an English emigrant, and the son of James Dillard, Jr. (2), who married Lucy Wise in 1724, and had issue: Thomas (3), Nicholas (3), James (3) (born 1727), Stephen (3), John (3), and William Terry Dillard.

In the Quit Rent Rolls of King and Queen County, 1704, are listed: Thomas, Nicholas and Edward Dillard. In 1752 Thomas Dillard, Sr., James Dillard, Edward Dillard and Thomas Dillard, Jr., patented about 5,000 acres in Halifax along Staunton River and Straightstone Creek.

Thomas Dillard, Sr.'s will was proven at Pittsylvania Court House, 1774, bequeathed his estate to his sons James and Thomas Dillard, naming Thomas executor. Also mentions Thomas, the son of his son James, and James' other children.

John Redd said in his "Reminiscences" that John Dillard of Henry County, was "grandson of Captain Dillard of Pittsylvania, Sen." Captain James Dillard, of Indian Wars, was very probably the son of Captain Thomas Dillard, Sr., of Pittsylvania; he is said to have spent his latter years in Amherst Couty, where his will is recorded.

[34]It is interesting to note the following excerpts from McCalls' address before the Pennsylvania Historical Society, 1832. (Hazard's Hist. Register, Vol. II, p. 193.)

"Prior to Penn's settlement, a settlement of Quakers was made in Chester County. In 1675 Robert Wade accompanied by some followers of the sect, established himself at Uplands. It is upon record that the first monthly meeting of Friends in Pennsylvania was held in Wade's house in 1681."

Robert Wade, Jr., of Halifax County, was the son of Robert Wade Sen., whose will was proven at Halifax, C. H., April 19, 1770, in which he named wife Elizabeth, daughters Sarah Stokes and Mary Hunt, sons Stephen Wade, Charles Wade, Edward Wade, Hampton Wade and wife Jean, and Anne Wade, the widow of Robert Wade, Jr., deceased.

Robert Wade, Jr., died in 1764, naming in his will daughters Sarah and Betty Wade and son Hampton and Robert Wade. To wife Anne he left "the choice of either of my two plantations, the place where I now live or the place where my Father lives"; named as executors Clement Reade, Paul Carrington, William Stokes, Memucan Hunt and Hampton Wade.

Pay to Captain James Dillard and a company of militia under command of said Dillard, as by muster roll	414.11.4
To Captain Thomas Calloway	6.18
Lieut Wm. Edwards, Ensign Hugh Harris.	
James Elkins and John Edwards, Sergeants.	
To Nathaniel Terry,[35] the balance of his pay for attending the militia and building three forts	29.
To Colonel Abraham Maury for 28 days service in riding to the Forts and settling townships	14.

The pay allowed[36] the militia was ten shillings a day for a colonel, major and captain; five shillings a day for a lieutenant; one shilling a day for a private.

[35]Nathaniel Terry was the son of Benjamin Terry whose will was dated 1760 and proven at Pittsylvania C. H. in 1771, naming sons Nathaniel, Benjamin, Peter, Joseph and Robert Terry; daughter Mary, Elizabeth and Sarah Terry; Lavinia King and Kezia Murphy; wife Elizabeth Irby (Terry).

Nathaniel Terry died in 1782 when the inventory of his estate was taken. The legatees were named in a deed in Halifax in 1801 as follows: William Terry, Joseph Terry, Nathaniel Terry, Robert Terry, Berryman Green who had married Nancy Terry, Keeble Terry who had married Sally Terry, and James Thompson who had married Polly Terry.

[36]Hening's "Statutes."

Chapter VII

THE CHEROKEE WAR—WESTERN EXPLORATION

In the hope of enlisting the aid of the friendly Cherokees and Catawbas in the struggle against the French and their Indian allies, Governor Dinwiddie appointed Colonel William Byrd and Colonel Peter Randolph to visit the two nations.

This they did in the summer of 1756, carrying with them many gifts, and successfully concluded a treaty with the tribes whereby they agreed to furnish Virginia with 500 warriors in return for the erection of a fort for the protection of their wives and children against the assaults of the northern Indians. Virginia at once fulfilled her promise, and Fort Loudon on the Tennessee was built the same summer.

In the spring of 1757 when the long promised Indian aid arrived it was found to consist of but 400 warriors and of these only 180 remained at the fort at Winchester, the others immediately returning home. They had evidently become disaffected towards the Virginians through French influence, and now were bent upon mischief, for in their march back and forth through Virginia they committed many acts of violence upon the inhabitants, and slew and tomahawked[1] one of their own members in Col. Clement Read's yard.

When they reached western Halifax and Bedford Counties they became bolder in their defiant attitude and robbed the inhabitants of their horses, plundered their homes, and offered brutal insults to their persons.

The people of Halifax were placed in a most trying position, for it was well known and understood that the Cherokees were our friends and allies, and that their warriors had marched to our aid; yet here were marauding bands of more than a hundred warriors straying over the country and boldly robbing the inhabitants, who hesitated to offer resistance to the intruders for fear of provoking them to war. We may know that the Cherokees were keenly sensible of the plight in which these Virginians were placed, for they remained several weeks terrorizing the countryside.

A letter[2] of Colonel Fontaine to relatives in England, dated June 11, 1757, said: "Those of the Indians that call themselves our friends do despise us, and in their march through our inhabited country, when going to our assistance, insult and annoy. It is not above a month ago since a

[1]Dinwiddie Papers, Vol. 2, p. 609.

[2]"Memoirs of a Huguenot Family," by Maury.

party of about a hundred and twenty Cherokees, in passing through Lunenburg insulted people of all ranks."

When Col. Read[3] notified the Governor of the presence and behavior of the Cherokees his Excellency advised reasoning with them in a mild way for fear of provoking them to open warfare, which he said "would prove of fatal consequences; however the people are not to be robbed and insulted."

But when the people, acting upon the Governor's advice, attempted to reason with the Indians, their peaceful overtures were repulsed and bloodshed followed.

A letter[4] from the Governor to Col. Fontaine, County Lieutenant, in regard to the situation stated:

May 7, 1757.

"Sir,—

I received y'r L're of April 20, last night and am very sorry for the aprehensions the frontiers are under an attack from the Indians. It is a surprise to me that the People allow Indians to come so frequently among them: the very examining of the Co'try and the Peoples Houses was Suspicion Sufficient to raise the militia and Take 'em all Prisoners. I approve of your sending out James Dillard with fifty men; and please order him to continue out aranging."

The citizens of Bedford County petitioned[5] to be allowed to kill the Indians, and asked for soldiers to be stationed among them for protection, but their petition was denied in the hope of preventing open conflict.

Governor Dinwiddie's term of office expired January, 1758, and Mr. Blair, president of the Council, became the presiding official of the colony until the arrival of Governor Fauquier in the following June. Blair ordered an investigation into the origin of the troubles in Halifax and Bedford Counties with the Cherokees, and for this purpose a especial court was held at Mayes Ferry (now Booker's Ferry), on Staunton River, in Halifax County, on June 1, 1758, when the following depositions[6] were taken of those who had suffered from Indian outrages or taken part in the conflicts with them:

"Halifax County }
to-wit— }
At Mays's Ferry on Staunton River June the 1st, 1758, was taken by Order of Mr. President Blair—The State cause and process of the three several Engagements,

[3]Dinwiddie Papers, Vol. 2, p. 612.

[4]Dinwiddie Papers, Vol. 2, p. 619.

[5]"North Carolina Hist. Review," Vol. 2, p. 443.

[6]"Indian Book," Vol. 6, pp. 153-59, at Columbia, South Carolina.

had between several parties of militia of Halifax and Bedford Counties, in Company with part of Captain Hawkin's men, with several parties of Indians in their march thro' those Counties which is as followeth, to-wit,

John Wheeler, William Verdiman, John Hall, Richard Thompson, William Verdiman Junr, Robert Jones Junr, and Henry Snow being first sworn, as to the first of the three Engagements they deposed in Substance as followeth.

First John Wheeler aged about 50, John Hall and Richard Thompson aged about 25 each, swore that having been robbed of some Horses sometime in the begining of May, being at a neighbours House, were informed by him, that several Indians were seen to pass thro' the Neighbourhood with a great number of packed Horses, and that several other Horses were missing of that Neighbourhood, to the number of 20 at least That they had Robbed several Houses, and had as was supposed murther'd or—Captivated a family near that Neighbourhood, as the family was missing, and could not be heard of, and that they called themselves Shawanees; Whereupon these three Deponents with four others agreed to go after the Indians, and in a friendly manner demand the Horses, and other things Stolen; That these three Deponents, being on Horse back, the rest on foot, came up with the Indians, And the Deponent Wheeler calling them Brothers, desired to treat with them. The Indians painted and sullen, put themselves in a posture for Battle, And sternly asked if they were for War, The Deponents replied they were not, That they were friends and Brothers and desired peace and quiet delivery of their Horses, and asked the Indians of what Nation they were; upon that they instantly set up the War Whoop; The deponent Wheeler seeing his Horse in the Hands of an Indian took hold of the Bridle, and whilst they were strugling for him, other Indians came up and seized him and the Horse he rode, which he was forced to quit to them after receiving several Blows with a Tomahawke—fled on foot, three Indians pursued him, and three Guns were fired, as he supposed at him and his Companions, as he heard a Bullet whistle by him, and he and his Companions made their escape without any other Hurt or loss, then that of two more Horses, which were then taken from them by the Enemy, That in their flight they met the rest of the Company on Foot, coming to them upon which reinforcement, they came to a resolution once more to follow the Indians, and being joyned afterwards by a few others, did so, making up the Number Eleven tho' some of those Eleven were without Guns, That they came to Staunton River, and when there, these several Deponents, to-wit; John Wheeler, William Verdiman, John Hall, Richard Thompson, William Verdiman, Junr, Robert Jones, Junr, and Henry Snow, Swear that when they arrived at the River Bank they as they imagined heard the Indians WarHalloo on the other side, that they proceeded to pass the River, that when they gott over, on rising the Bank on the other side, they found a small fire just kindled, and at some little distance from thence, they observed the Enemy, upon which all the Deponents say that Old William Verdiman aged about sixty, went foremost, and that they all followed close at his heels, that when they came up to the Enemy they found they had tyed their Horses, pretty many in Number to the Bushes, that most of the Indians were painted and others then painting, some black some Red, but mostly black, that when they came near Old Verdiman pulled off his Hatt and Bowed and accosted them in terms of peace, and Friendship, and said Gentlemen we come in a Brotherly manner to ask you for our Horses, and other Goods, that you have taken from us, that the Indians gave a kind of a Grunt, and appeared determined for mischief, stripped themselves threw out the priming of their Guns, fresh primed and Cocked them, struck their Tomahawks into Trees, and in an angry manner demanded of the Deponents if they would fight; that whilst Verdiman who was still uncovered Bowing and Treating with them, the Enemy Indeavored to Inviron them, and had actually got them into a half Circle before the Deponents were aware upon which, and young Verdiman observing that two Indians had pointed their Guns, they the Deponents all retreated backwards with their Faces to the Enemy, and took to trees, that on their retreat, the Indians threw their Tomahawks, and that two of them narrowly missed two of their men, that one of them would have hitt Old Verdiman, but that he luckely parried it with an Elder Stick he had in his hand (for he was one of the number of those that had no Guns) and the Indians pursuing and they retreating in Order, they were near drove to the River Banck, where they must have inevitably perished had they then attempted to have crossed, that on the retreat a Gun was fired upon which the Engagement insued, and many Guns discharged on both sides, in which Engagement the Father of John Hall one of the deponents fell, and being mortally wounded soon after died, that during the Engagement those of the Deponents who had Guns were obliged to fly from tree to tree to one another for a shott of Powder and Lead both being very scarce among them, that in the Engagement three Indians fell, that at last their Powder and Lead being Expended they fled back over the River in different places, and being all met again on the other side, they went to a Neighbours House, supplied themselves with more Ammunition, and went back again to place where the Engagement was to look for their wounded friend, who they found expiring, three Indians dead in the Field and much plunder, that they scalped the Indians, threw their dead Bodies into the River, and brought away their dying friend and the plunder, and that their Friend soon after dyed, the account of Spoil found in the Field consisting of Horses, Saddles, Bridles, Mens, and Womans apparel &c., is herewith sent Contained in two papers Numbered 1. 2.

To give the particulars and cause of the second Engagement William Morgan, Pinkethman Hawkins, Thomas Overstreet, and George Thomas were sworn.

Pinkethman Hawkins on his Oath deposed, that being Ordered out by Colonel Talbot to join Captain Mead, to go in pursuit of the Enemy who had killed Hall, stole many Horses, Robbed and plundered many Families in Bedford and Halifax Countys, and was supposed to have killed or Captivated other Families who were then missing, in his March he fell upon the House of one Standiford (where he found one Byrd whose wife the Indians had taken and threatned to carry her away as a Squa, though she afterwards luckily made her escape, whilst the Enemy was Busy in plundering her Husbands House) and he found the House of Standiford strip of everything, the Bed Ticks ripped open and carryed away, and the feathers scattered all over the House, and the Family gone, whilst there he heard a hollowing and noise of Indians. Ordered his men then with him fifteen in Number to go with twenty five of the Inhabitants, who had collected themselves, and way lay the Indians at a pass he was advised by his Guide, they must go through, and extend a line along the Ridge by that pass as long as the number of men would admit of, and wait the coming of the Indians; for that he himself and another, namely one Tarbro, would go to the Indians (who by the noise he imagined was over the River not far of) and treat with them in a Friendly manner about the Prisoners and Plunder they had gott, and that he charged them, if they should see the Indians pass by with him a Prisoner, or, that they should hear of his death, or, if they should pass by with their Horses Packed, they might conclude his Treaty with them had proved ineffectual, and Ordered them if either of these things should happen, to treat the Indians (more especially as all along their March, they had declared themselves Shawanees), as Enemys, and on the March of his men, in consequence of such Orders, He Hawkins, with Tarbro, as was concerted proceeded forwards to treat with the Indians, that when they came to the River Eight or Ten Indians came over the River to them, that he endeavoured to come to terms with them, proposed peace and Friendship, and called them Brothers, they surlily answered, no, no, no Brothers, English damned Rogues, and clapping their Hands, on their Breats called themselves, and making signs signifyed to them, there was a great many Shawanees all about them, that the wood and Mountains were full of them, that he still mentioned peace and told them that he and Tarbro were unarmed and came as Brothers, but the Indians not withstanding his mentions for peace, Striped him of his Coat, Waiscoat, Shirt, Shoes, Stockings, and Hatt, and gave him several Blows with their Tomhawks and ordered him away, he remembering that in his Breeches (which was all the Coaths they had left him) he had about five shillings in Cash, gave it to one of the Indians, who thereupon returned him his Coat, upon which the Deponent Hawkins thinking they were in a better humour, again proposed to treat with them, upon which they beat him and Tarbro very severely, and Cut him thro' the upper Lip with a Blow of a Scalping knife, led them both by the Hands up the River Banck and ordered them to run away or they would kill them, which Order they readily Obeyed, and being at two great a distance, and as they were bare footed did not come up with the men till the Battle with the Indians was over.

William Morgan on his Oath deposed that being one of the Twenty five that had joined Hawkin's Men excited thereto by the Complaints of the People for the continual and repeated Robberies committed among them by the Indians, and more particularly on Account of the several Familys missing supposed to be killed or Captivated by the Indians, and of the Caption of Byrd his Neighbours Wife, he with the others on the receipt of Hawkins's Order, marched under the direction of one Shoat who was their Guide to take possession of the Ridge, mentioned in Hawkins's Deposition, where they posted themselves, very advantageously, that whilst they were there waiting for the Enemy, Byrd, who had watched the Fate of Hawkins and Tarbro, came to them and informed them of the abuse received by them from the Indians, and directed them to be ready prepaired for the Enemy was approaching, in a very little time after they heard the Indian War Whoop and a Gun fired upon which a runing fit began, that the Indians tryed to get them into a half moon three times which at last they effected and that in the

Engagement he saw two Indians fall, that at last the Enemys half moon being broken, both parties fled from each other.

Thomas Overstreet swore in Substance as Morgan the foregoing Deponent George Thomas being sworin Deposed in Substance as followeth, That the Indians had Stole a Stallion from one John Echols, that Echols bought a Horse of the Deponent to follow the Indians to give them in Exchange for his Stallion, that the Indians took him from Echols also, and Shot at him, that their Number to about forty had a large Number of Pack Horses with them; That they Robbed Striped one Wollocks and beat him; That being sent by Colonel Talbot for relief of Men, in his way met some men who had been striped and beaten by the Indians, that he went with them to the House of one Morgan, a Brother to Morgan one of the Deponents, which they found open and plundered, and all the Family missing, that he found abundance of Feathers Strewed about the Yard, that in the path a little distance from the House they found a Childs Shirt and Cap, and some pieces of Rope and Hickory Bark, on which they concluded the Family was bound taken and carryed away Prisoners; that a little further they found the Patent of Morgans Land and some paper money; That they proceeded to the next House which they found in the same order and condition, with the Feathers thrown about, and the Family missing; That they went farther to other Houses and found them empty, the Family's gone and the Doors of their Houses Tomahawked and cut with many other signs of wanton Mischief, That these appearances induced him to join the twenty four who joined Hawkins' fifteen (the rest of Thomas's Deposition was the same in Substance as Morgans and Overstreets with respect to their Orders and the Engagement with the Indians, only with this addition) that the day after the Engagement, he this Deponent with others came to View the Field were the Engagement happened, where they found one Indian dead which was scalped, Nineteen fine Horses, and much plunder, and among the plunder a French Scalping Knife, note, that this second Engagement happened soon after the first but not with the same Indians.

To the third Engagement were examined upon Oath George Watts, Charles Brigh, Samuel Brown, and John Craig.

George Watts on his Oath deposed that on or about the 23[d] day of May one Franciscae, having informed the people in his Neighbourhood that he was Robbed of his Horse by Twelve Indians, that they had burnt a House and Tomhawked a woman; a Sergeant belonging to

Captain Haristones Company in Bedford, with Nine men of which these Deponents were a part were Ordered to follow the Indians, to know who they were and treat with them about the delivery of the Horses and things Stolen. That they went in search of them, and when they came in sight of them which was but a few miles from Bedford Court House, the Sergeant and four of the others would proceed no farther, not liking the looks of the Indians, but that he with the three others the Deponents, proceeded to march up to them; That when they came near (as they were Ordered) they demanded of what Nation they were, and they answered Cherockees, they therupon told them they were Brothers, and as a Token they were so Grounded their Firelocks and told the Indians to do so to and meet and shake Hands and talk about their Horses &c[a] they had taken from the White men their Friends, upon which the Indians immediately striped themselves (as is their Custom when determined for Battle) took to Trees, and prepared to Engage. That this Deponent being foremost, took, as they rest also did, to a tree, that an Indian fired at him, that he returned the fire and saw an Indian fall, they they these Deponents gave Ground and at last ran, that the Indians did not pursue, that they ran to a Plantation near, where were some women and Children, and in a small time returned to the Place where they fought the Indians, and found them gone and some Plunder and Stolen Horses left behind them, which they took and carryed away.

Charles Bright Swore the same in Substance with Watts, only with this Circumstance added, to wit, that before the Indians fired and Watts had returned the fire on which an Indian fell, the Indians had got them into a half Moon, and that the Bullet shot by the Indian at Watts went between Watts's head and the Bark of the Tree he stood behind and beat of much of the Bark.

Samual Brown deposed the same in Substance as Watts and Bright. John Craig deposed the same in substance as Watts, Bright and Brown, with this addition, to-wit; the twelve as he supposed, Cut thro' the Roof of his House and Robbed it.

Now follows the Substance of some Depositions taken to prove many Robberies committed by the Indians on several of the Inhabitants, and to prove they called themselves Shawanees, taken at the Instance and request of the persons concerned in the several Engagements.

John Wallocks being sworn deposed in substance as followeth: That having heard of much Mischief being done and of many Robberies being committed, by the Indians in Bedford and Halifax County's, the Neighbourhood where he lived collected themselves together at one of the Neighbours Houses till the Indians should pass by, or the fright be over, that whilst he was there some people came to them who had been just Striped, Robbed and beaten by the Indians, and that they believed the Indians by the Rout they took would pass that way, along a Road that ran near the Plantation where they then were, that he excited by an Imprudent Curiosity to see them, went to the road along which he supposed they would pass, and hideing himself in convenient place, waited their coming, he presently heard them rideing Hallooing and whooping, and when they came pritty near him they stopped in an open convenient part of the road to try the Horses they had but just Stolen, and continued their sometime, paceing up and down the Road diverting themselves, till he, skipping from one hiding place to another, the better to discover what they were about, was unhappily espied by them and catched; when they catched him they Stripped him of every thing but his Shirt, took away his Gun Powder-Horn and Shot Bag, shook their Tomhawks over his head, and calling themselves Shawanees beat him pritty much, and dismissed him, ordering him to run, and he running pleased at his Escape fell upon another Indian who took his Shirt, gave him another threshing, and sent him off Stark naked Ordering him to Run and as he fled, threw a Stone at him which had well nigh knocked him down, and cut his Back in a terrible manner.

John Yates being sworn deposed, that he in company with one Philip Preston were rideing along the road together not having heard anything about the Indians, or suspecting anything about them. He heard a Gun fired close behind him, and turning about discovered three Indians close at his Heels, That they could have made their Escape, But on the Indians calling out Cherrockees and holding out their hands in token of friendship, and fearing to be fired at should they attempt to Escape, they stopped; The Indians came up to them and Shook hands, and then instantly pulled them off their Horses, beat them with Sticks, Stripped them naked, took all they had from them, pointed their Guns at them, and Ordered them to run which Order they instantly Obeyed.

Philip Preston being sworn deposed the same in substance as John Yates.

Patrick Johnson being sworn, deposed that a parcel of Indians of what Nation he knew not, came to his House shot a Bull in his yard. Robbed him of eight Horses and all he had in the World.

Hartman Doran on his Oath deposed that he was Robbed by the Indians of all that he had.

James Moore on his Oath deposed that the Indians came to his House, set up the War Whoop, and called themselves Shawanees, that he saw in their possession the Horse of Robert Lucas his Neighbour Loaded with goods—That they demanded of him his Horse, that they beat him unmercifully that they shot two Guns, that ye Powder of one flew in his face, that they took two mares from him and Robbed him of his goods.

John Allcorn on his Oath deposed that being at home, he heard a Gun fire, heard the War Whoop, that he hid himself, and that they Robbed him of every thing in his House.

George Adams deposed much to the same purpose, and that they Robbed him Adams, of all he had in his House.

Robert Pepper deposed that on the 7th day of May he and his Mother being at home, some Indians came rideing upoto his house that some fired their Guns, others flourished their Tomhawks, that they called themselves Cherrokees and told them many Shawanees were coming, that they took from him three Riffle Guns his Powder-Horn and Shot Bag, Struck his Mother with a Tomhawke, presented a Gun to her, struck him with a Tomhawke and with the But end of his Gun struck out two of his Teeth, knocked down his Mother, and Robbed the House of every thing in it.

The particulars of the several Robberies are Contained in the papers herewith sent, number No. 3. 4. 5. 6. 7. 8. 9. which papers were sworn to, and the Quaker Echol's letter is also herewith sent. In Obedience to His Honour Mr. President Blair's Commands we the subscribers met at Mays Ferry on Staunton River in the County of Halifax on Thursday the first day of June 1758 and caused to come before us the several parties in the several foregoing depositions, named, and on Oath Examined them touching the State, Cause and process of the three Several Engagements between the militia and several Parties of Indians, and have set down as near as possible the sum and substance of the whole.

Witness our hands the 1st day of June aforesaid—

Clement Read.
Mathew Talbot."

One would judge from these depositions that the people of Halifax and Bedford showed much restraint and patience in dealing with the

Indians, suffering great indignities and heavy losses rather than offend an allied nation. A firmer stand might have served a better purpose.

At this time Jeremiah Terry of Halifax appointed[7] his "Trusty Friend Nathaniel Terry to be my true and lawful attorney, to act, do and perform all such matters and things to me in any wise relating," stating that he was "about to depart the colony and bound for the Cherokee Nation." He was probably a member of some commission appointed to confer with the Cherokees.

Virginia's overtures of peace were without avail and the Cherokees became more and more estranged from their white friends. They were both alarmed and irritated by the ever encroaching settlements of the whites who had purposely sought the Cherokee neighbourhood that they might enjoy the protection of these Indians against the cruel Shawnees. It was but natural for the French emissaries, in their efforts to win the aid of the Cherokees for themselves, to point out that the white settlers would never rest until they possessed the red man's territory, for they had already made great inroads upon his hunting grounds.

The final break was caused by the arrest of a chieftain while in conference with Governor Littleton of South Carolina, whereupon the Catawbas and the Cherokees took up the tomahawk against the white settlers. Peace was just settling over the country; men were feeling free once more to go about their daily affairs of sowing and reaping and building and road making, when this second Indian War burst upon them.

Col. Peter Fontaine[8] writing in 1760 of this second Indian conflict said:

"Several families that had since the former troubles returned to their settlements on the frontiers, are again frightened and have left them—so that Halifax is much confused and as unfit for my business (surveying) as when I left it. Our Colonies are raising men to go against them.

"The Indians have fallen upon our poor scattered unprepared frontier settlements * * * and 'tis said they have brake up more frontiers, come lower down to do mischief and killed as many people as in the last war."

In this emergency Virginia organized a regiment of a thousand men, which was put under the command of Col. William Byrd. The Cherokees were defeated in the battle of Etchoe, in 1761, and peace following, in January 1762, the General Assembly voted[9] to the regiment in apprecia-

[7]Halifax County Deed Book.
[8]"Memoirs of a Huguenot Family."
[9]Hening's "Statutes."

Joshua Worsham purchased land on Dan River in this year.

tion of their valor and bravery, and the hardships they had undergone "one full year's pay over and above what shall be due them."

In the year 1761, as soon as the state of affairs with the Cherokees and Catawbas would admit of hunting in the wilderness, Elisha Walden[10] and a party of 18 men, made up of his friends and neighbors, formed themselves into a company for the purpose of taking a "long hunt." Walden[11] lived on Smith River at a place called the "Round-a-bout," about two miles west of Martinsville; we have seen that in 1748 he was appointed constable of western Lunenburg, from Smith River to the Wart Mountains. He had married a Miss Blevin, the daughter of a neighbor, Will Blevin a noted hunter, and in the hunting party were some members of the Blevin family, Henry Scags, Newman, Charles Cox, and others of western Halifax and Bedford.

"Long-hunting" is described by the old frontiersman, John Redd, in the following manner:[12]

"The (long) hunter set out about the first of October, and each man carried two horses, traps, a large supply of powder, led and a small hand vise and bellows, files and screw plates for the purpose of fixing the guns if any of them should get out of fix, they returned about the last of March or the first of April * * *. In their hunts there rarely ever went more than two or three in a company, their reason for this was very obvious, they hunted in the western part of Virginia and Kentucky. The country they hunted in was roamed over by the Indians and if they happened to be discovered by the Indians two or three would not be so apt to excite their fears about having their game killed up, besides this small parties were mutch more sucksesful in taking game than large ones."

Long hunting was an occupation that required much hardihood, courage and endurance, but in return yielded a good profit, for Haywood[13] says "an industrious hunter would return with peltry enough to bring 16 or 1700 pounds, an immense sum of money in those days."

John Redd was a neighbor and knew Walden well, and said[14] of him in his Reminiscences: "In 1774 he had been a long hunter for many years and hunted on a large range of mountains to the east of Powells Valley and from Walden the mountains took its name, and to this day

[10]Judge Haywood's "History of Tennessee," p. 45.
[11]*Virginia Mag. History,* Vol. 6, p. 338.
[12]*Virginia Mag. History,* Vol. 7, p. 248.
[13]Haywood's "History of Tennessee," pp. 38-39.
[14]*Virginia Mag. History,* Vol. 7, p. 249.

goes by the name of Walden's Ridge. He always returns home with his horses heavily laden with skins and furs."

Two other long hunters known to Redd were William Pittman and Henry Skags, of whom[15] he said, "they were men of high sense of honor and vary great truth." Both probably lived for awhile in this section for Pitman's Creek is a branch of Blackwater River, and several members of the Skags family, John, Charles and Zacharich, were given in the first list of tithables[16] for Pittsylvania County.

It is very probable that Walden and his friends had served in the recent Indian campaign and ranging along the frontiers had seen for themselves the great abundance of game that lived undisturbed in the virgin forest of Southwest Virginia. They remained on this hunt eighteen months, ranging over southwestern Virginia and eastern Tennessee and Kentucky, naming the mountains and streams as they came to them. Powell's Mountain was so called from[17] seeing the name of Ambrose Powell cut on a beech tree there; Powell had accompanied Dr. Thomas Walker of Albemarle when he explored that section in 1750. They also named the adjacent river and valley Powell. Walden's Ridge was named for Walden; Scag's Ridge and Newman's Ridge were named for other members of the company. They crossed the mountains through Cumberland Gap into the Kentucky country and all agreed that Walden should name the gap, which he did calling it Cumberland for his former home in Cumberland County, Virginia.

On their return the following year they crossed the Blue Ridge Mountains at Flower's Gap in Franklin County, and found few settlers west of the mountains, the murderous attacks of the Indians having driven them eastward and southward. They hunted this year on the Clinch River, which they named for the following amusing incident:

"An Irishman was a member of the company; in crossing the river he fell from the raft into it and cried out, 'Clinch me! Clinch me!' meaning lay hold of me. The rest of the company, unused to the phrase, amused themselves at the expense of the poor Irishman and called the river Clinch."

In the year[18] of 1764 the Blevins went up into Kentucky and hunted near Crab-Tree Orchard on Rock Castle Creek, where they found the game so plentiful that they continued to hunt there for several years.

[15] *Virginia Mag. History,* Vol. 7, p. 250.

[16] In the List of Tithables taken for Pittsylvania County in 1767 were John, Charles and Zacheriah Scaggs.

[17] Haywood's "Tennessee."

[18] Haywood's "Tennessee."

Daniel Boone, who was living on the Yadkin, came among the hunters that year, saying that he was employed by the Henderson Company to explore the country. Henry Skags was afterwards employed by the Hendersons for the same purpose.

Draper[19] said of Skaggs that he and his brothers Charles and Richard were a family of noted hunters, and nothing but hunters, who kept pace with the advancing wave of settlements. He described Skaggs as "possessing a large bony frame, he was bold, enterprising and fearless." In the winter of 1771 Henry Skaggs and a man named Knox made a station and hunted in Greene County, Kentucky. One day when absent from the station on a hunt their camp was plundered by a half-breed Cherokee named Will Emery. When they returned to find the result of their winter's labors gone, they carved on a tree, "Fifteen hundred skins gone to ruination." Skaggs[20] and his brother later settled in this section of Kentucky, where they lived to a ripe old age.

Daniel Boone's is the romantic figure associated with Kentucky's early history, but this band of intrepid hunters from western Halifax first blazed the way into that unknown country, and braving the dangers of Indian attacks, lived year after year in the heart of the wilderness. They marked the Indian trail through Cumberland Gap, followed in after years by countless thousands of homeseekers bound for the west—the Gap now so famed in the annals of our early history.

We have seen that traders from Virginia and the Carolinas found their way into this western country in the latter half of the preceding century, and traded with the Indians for furs. Later there grew up a hardy race of hunters who went into the wilderness with their own guns and secured the pelts for the fur market. They were the explorers of the western country, naming the mountains and streams; they were the forerunners of the settlers, often acting as guides through the wilderness over which they had so often hunted.

It was probably the favorable reports of the far western country brought home by Walden's Company that induced Captain William Bean to forsake the security of his home in Pittsylvania, and make the first white settlement in the wilderness of Tennessee.

Walden[21] himself moved out to this new country and made his home for awhile on the Holstein River, 18 miles above Knoxville. But having grown to love solitude, when the settlements around him grew numerous, he traveled on further into the west and settled in Missouri.

[19] Draper's Manuscripts.

[20] "Cyclopedia of Biography," Vol. 5, p. 813, says of the Skaggs family that they were of Scotch descent and many of them settled in Maryland.

[21] *Virginia Mag. of History,* Vol. 6, p. 338.

Chapter VIII

PITTSYLVANIA BECOMES A COUNTY IN 1767

The call of the western country with its undeveloped resources was strongly felt alike by the inhabitants of eastern Virginia and the settlers of Pennsylvania and Maryland. A spirit of restlessness and adventure led men here and there, setting up their household goods first in one place and then in another. Youth and age both fared forth to travel the rough roads that led to the upland country; the penniless young man hoped to carve a fortune out of the wilderness, while the well-to-do man of family planned to increase his estate. When Pittsylvania was their destination we can imagine their satisfaction upon beholding from some eminence their new home—the gently rolling hills which lost themselves in the blue distance, the murmuring waters of the crystal clear streams and the broad sweeps of rich meadow lands.

There is a tradition handed down by the elder[1] people of the county that when the first settlers came in they found this a veritable land of plenty, for not only did the woods still abound with game of every kind for their subsistance, but growing through the woods and fields was a wild vetch that provided ample food for the stock all winter; that the horses, after being worked through the day, were belled at night and turned into the woods to graze, and with no other food than this wild vetch they kept in good condition. Colonel Byrd mentioned seeing vetch growing wild on his trip to Eden, but feared it would be destroyed by the hogs. Vetch, of course, was found only where the forests were open and the sunlight came in, being another proof of the openness of the woods. The common name today for this vine is "partridge pea," and when we see it growing here and there by the road side, with its modest purple blossoms, we should not be unmindful of the worthy part it played in the settlement of our country.

An early writer[2] records of this section, "that the inhabitants give their cattle and stock salt once a week to gentle them, for in this mild climate where there is no occasion to provide food for them in the winter, they would go entirely wild, for they live in the woods."

[1]The Rev'd Chiswell Dabney and Mr. James Carter of Chatham.

[2]J. F. D. Smythe's "Travels in America," page 143.

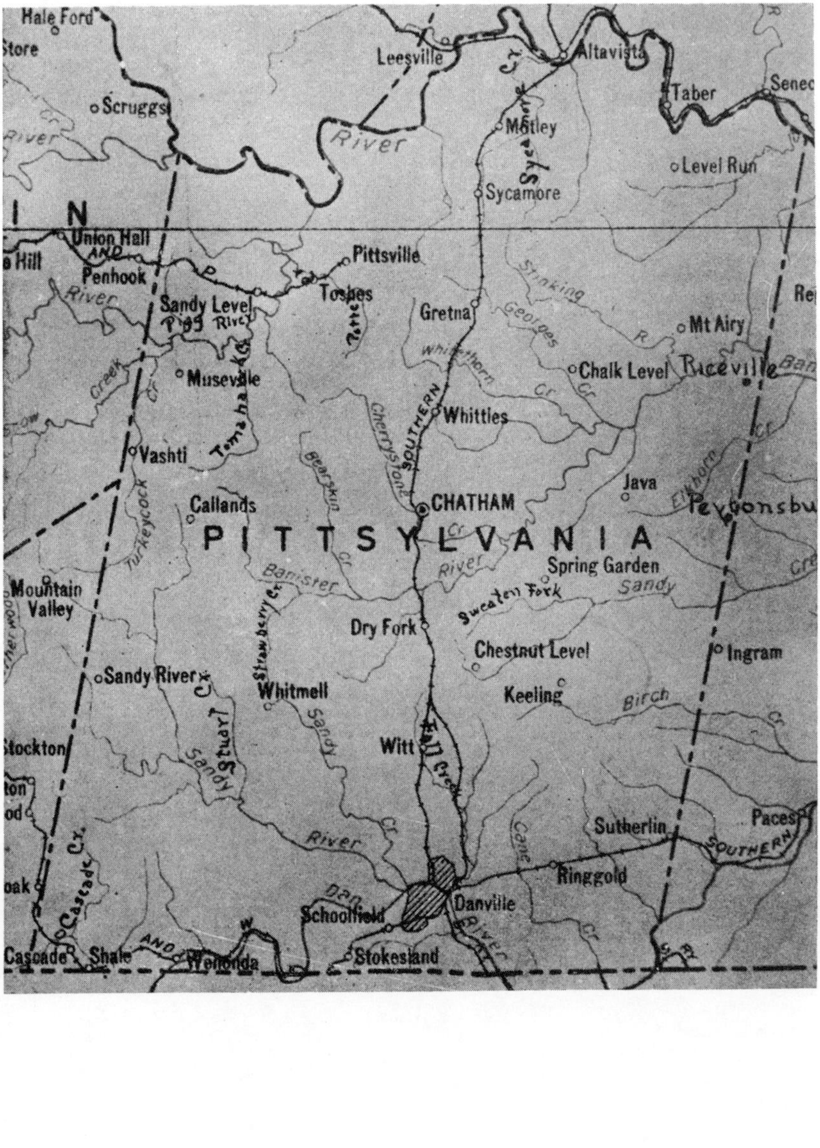

Hale Ford
Store
Scruggs
River
Leesville
Altavista
Taber
Senec
Motley
Sycamore Cr.
River
Level Run
Sycamore
N
Union Hall
AND
Hill
Penhook
Pittsville
River
Sandy Level
Pigg River
Toshes
Gretna
Stinking
Georges
R
Mt Airy
Chalk Level
Riceville
Musevile
Whitethorn
Cr
Cr
Tomahawk Cr.
Cherrystone
SOUTHERN
Whittles
Vashti
Bearskin
Java
CHATHAM
Elkhorn
Callands
Turkeycock
Peytonsbu
PITTSYLVANIA
Spring Garden
Mountain
Valley
Banister
River
Sandy
Sweaten Fork
Dry Fork
Chestnut Level
Ingram
Sandy River
Strawberry Cr.
Whitmell
Keeling
Birch
Cr
Stockton
Sandy
Witt
Fall Creek
Sandy
Sutherlin
Paces
Cascade Cr.
River
Cane
SOUTHERN
Ringgold
Dan
Schoolfield
Danville
River
Cascade
Shale
AND
Stokesland

As the settlement of the colony extended westward it was found necessary to form still another county out of the original domain of old Brunswick; and so we read in the Acts of the Assembly[3] for October, 1766:

"Whereas, many inconveniences attend the inhabitants of the county of Halifax by means of the extent thereof; and the said inhabitants have petitioned this General Assembly that the said County may be divided; Be it enacted, that from and after the first day of June next, the said county of Halifax be divided into two counties by a line to be run from the mouth of Straightstone Creek on Staunton River, to the Country line, near the mouth of Country Line Creek on Dan River: and that all that part of the said county, which lies on the upper part of the said line shall be one distinct county, and called and known by the name of Pittsylvania; and that the other part which is below the said line shall be one other distinct county, and retain the name of Halifax. Be it further enacted that after the first day of June a Court for the said county of Pittsylvania be constantly held by the Justices thereof, upon the fourth Friday in each month."

And so on June 1, 1767, Pittsylvania entered the sisterhood of Virginia counties, and was named in honor of the great English statesman, William Pitt, who had shown himself to be a friend of the colonies. He was strongly opposed to Englands laying a tax on the American Colonies and held that America contributed to England's resources by the monopoly of her trade, for it was to England alone that the colonies could sell.

When the Stamp Act was passed, Pitt was at home ill in bed; on his return to Parliament he strongly denounced the measure, and said:

"In my opinion this kingdom has no right to lay a tax on the Colonies. America is obstinate. I rejoice that America has resisted; three million of people so dead of all feeling of liberty as to voluntarily submit to be slaves would have been fit instruments to make slaves of the rest."

"He spoke," said a looker-on, "like a man inspired," and ended by calling for an immediate repeal of the act. In February, 1766, Pitt succeeded in having the Stamp Act repealed, in spite of the opposition of the King and his friends. It was in grateful recognition of this service that the new county in Virginia was named Pitt's Woods.

When the dividing line was run between Pittsylvania and Halifax, it was found that Peytonsburg, the country seat of Halifax, lay in

[3]Hening's "Statutes," Vol. 8.

Pittsylvania, and here at Halifax old Court House was held on Friday, June 29th, the first court of Pittsylvania County. A commission[4] had been received from Governor Fauquier appointing justices or judges, to preside over the courts, which read as follows:

"Virginia, to-wit:

George the Third, by the Grace of God, of Great Britian, France and Ireland, King, Defendant of the faith, and so forth, To Thomas Dillard, Sr.,[5] James Roberts, Jr., Archibald Gordon,[6] Thomas Dillard, Jr.,[7] Hugh Innes,[8] John Donelson,[9] Theophilus Lacy,[10] John Wilson,[11] Peter Cope-

[4]The original commission has been preserved.

[5]See note 33, Chapt. VI.

[6]Colonel Archibald Gordon was a native of Scotland, and lived in the Western part of the county near the present Franklin and Henry County line. He was never married and took a keen interest in county affairs. He was very regular in his attendance upon court as a presiding justice, and his name was frequently signed to the court proceedings, written in a neat scholarly style.

Major John Redd, a neighbor, said of him in his Reminiscences: "Colonel Gordon was superseded as Colonel of Pittsylvania under the new order of things that took place in the beginning of the revolution. I don't know whether it was owing to his old age or because he was not sufficiently American in his feelings. He was born in Scotland and I don't think he ever saw any military service. He was rather below ordinary height, coarse features. By those who knew him he was regarded very honest and correct in all of his transactions."

[7]Thomas Dillard, Jr., was the son of Thomas Dillard, Sr., and was executor of his father's will. He took an active part in the life of the country, serving as county lieutenant of the militia, justice of the peace and vestryman of the Established Church. He commanded a company of Pittsylvania Militia in the Indian Campaign of the Revolutionary War, and was so pleased with the more western part of the colony that he later moved with his family into that section of the county.

[8]Hugh Innes was a man of ability and prominence, representing this County in the House of Burgesses from 1769 to 1774. The Surveyor's records show that Captain Hugh Innes was patenting land on Panther Creek in 1763. He owned two plantations on Pigg River where he made his home, and after the division of the county in 1777 his residence lay in that part that later became Franklin County.

His will was probated at the April Court of Franklin, in 1797, in which he named sons Robert, Hugh, James and Harry Innes, daughter Elizabeth Eggleston Innes and Mrs. Turley. He directed that his lands in Bourbon County, Ky., and Patrick County, Virginia, be sold to complete the education of sons James, Hugh and Harry and daughter Elizabeth Eggleston Innes. He named as executors of his estate son Robert Innes, friend Samuel Calland and Harry Inness of Kentucky. He left a large estate in lands and his inventory included a "Library of Books," two desks and a riding chair. Captain Hugh Innes was probably a son of James Innes, a brother of the Rev. Robert Innes of Caroline, both of whom were natives of Scotland. James Innes settled in Richmond County, where his will was proven in 1710, naming daughters Sarah, Elizabeth and Hannah (wife of Charles Brent), sons Enoch and James; wife and small children. Hugh is a name much used in the Brent family.

[9]Colonel John Donelson married Rachel Stocklay, of Accomac County and has issue: 1. Captain John Donelson, who married Mary Purnell and had Mary, who married General John Coffee, and Sandy. 2. Catherine who married Captain Thomas Hutchings of Pittsylvania; their son Captain John Hutchings was a business partner of President Andrew Jackson. 3. A daughter who married Captain John Hay. 4. Rachel who married President Andrew Jackson. 5. Samuel. 6. William. 7. Severn.

[10]Theophilus Lacy was sheriff of Pittsylvania County in 1773. He married Martha Cocke, daughter of Abram Cocke of Amelia County, Nov. 28, 1759 (Amelia M. Bonds). The inventory of his estate in Pittsylvania was taken Nov. 24, 1777, and included ten slaves. The inventory of his estate in Guilford County, North Carolina, amounted to £1,031. In the division of his property were named his widow Martha Lacy, and children Hopkins, Theophelus, John William, and Polly, son Bathcocke and daughter Betsy.

[11]John Wilson was the son of Peter Wilson and Ailcy, his wife, early settlers of Pittsylvania, who made their home at Wilson's Ferry on Dan River. Their son John was born in 1740, about the time of their coming to this section.

John Wilson was an active man of affairs, and acquired large wealth in land and negroes. He served as county lieutenant of the militia forces of Pittsylvania during the Revolutionary War from 1778 to its close; represented his country in the House of Delegates in 1778-79-82, and was a member of the Constitutional Convention of Virginia in 1788, when the Constitution of the United States was adopted.

In 1767 John Wilson married Mary Lumpkin, a daughter of George Lumpkin, of Marrowbone Creek, and made his home at "Dan's Hill," near the Ferry. Here he reared his large family, who intermarried with the leading families in the State. John and Mary Wilson had issue: 1. Peter Wilson, who married Ruth Stovall Hairston, daughter of Peter Hairston and Elsie Perkins, and lived at "Berry Hill." 2. John. 3. William. 4. Nathaniel, married Winnefred Tunstall, daughter of William Tunstall, Jr., of "Belle Grove," and settled "Belle Grade," on Dan River. 5. Clement.

land,[12] John Smith,[13] John Dix,[14] George Jefferson,[15] Peter Perkins,[16] John Vanbibber,[17] Hamon Critz,[18] John Hanby,[19] John Wimbush,[20]

6. George, married Elizabeth Brodnax, and settled "Laurel Cliff." 7. Robert, married Catherine Pannill, daughter of Samuel Pannill, of "Green Hill," Campbell County, and lived at "Dan's Hill." 8. Mary, married Col. John Clark. 9. Patsy, married Alex. Cunningham. 10. Nannie, married Robert Brodnax. 11. Isabella, married James Anderson Glenn.

John Wilson died in 1820 and is buried at "Dan's Hill."

[12]Peter Copland was a merchant from Caroline County, who settled in the western part of this County (now Henry) about 1756, and operated a store there. In the Surveyor's Record, we read: "1756. To Peter Copland (Merch't of Caroline) 400 acres between Lomax and Company Line and Irvine River." He made a deposition in 1755 that he was an emigrant from Great Britain in 1743; probably being an agent for some Scotch merchant.

[13]John Smith, see note.

[14]John Dix lived on Dan River and operated Dix's Ferry. He commanded a company of militia from Pittsylvania during the Revolutionary War. His will was probated in 1784 in which he named wife Kerenhappuch, sons William and Larkin, daughters Susannah who married Benjamine Turner, Sally married William Wilkenson, Martha married William Payne, Henrietta Dix and Matilda Francis Dix.

[15]George Jefferson was the son of Field Jefferson of Lunenburg, whose will was proven in Mecklenburg County in 1765, naming sons George, John, Peterfield, and Thomas Jefferson. Field Jefferson and his brother Peter were the sons of Thomas Jefferson of Henrico, whose will was proven in 1731. Field Jefferson made his home in Lunenburg County, while his brother Peter Jefferson moved up to Albemarle, where he married, Jane, the daughter of Isham Randolph, and became the father of President Thomas Jefferson.

George Jefferson, the son of Field, patented large bodies of land in Pittsylvania, a part of which he later sold to his brother, Peterfield Jefferson. In the first list of tithables taken in Pittsylvania County we find:

"List of Tithables taken by George Jefferson in Pittsylvania County, Camden Parish, year 1767," and in the list occurs the following item: "George Jefferson (Mecklenburg) John Davis overseer and negroes to-wit, Sam, Chance, Pompey, Phillis, Pat, Sary. Tithes, 7. Acres, 8,000."

George Jefferson lived and died in Mecklenburg County, but the fact that he owned much land in Pittsylvania, constituted his elegibility for holding the office of justice of peace. Peterfield Jefferson, after purchasing several tracts of land from his brother George, moved to Pittsylvania and made his home near Turkey Cock Creek. He left no will, but his wife, Mrs. Elizabeth Jefferson (who was the daughter of Samuel Allen of Cumberland County) left a will dated 1828, in which she named sons Field, John, Samuel Allen, Alexander, Archer and Thomas Jefferson.

[16]Peter Perkins was the son of Nicholas Perkins and his wife Bethenia Harden, who settled on Dan River in 1755. Nicholas Perkins served as a justice of the peace of Halifax County in 1759, and his will is proven there in 1762, in which he named sons Peter, Nicholas, Constant, Thomas Harden Perkins; daughters Anne, Bethenia, Susanna, Mary and Elizabeth. He willed to son Peter Perkins the upper half of his tract of land on the north side of Dan River and to son Nicholas the lower half of said tract; to son Constant Perkins the upper half of lands on the South side of Dan River, "where I now live," and to son Thomas Harden Perkins, the lower half of said tract.

Nicholas Perkins' children, married as follows: 1. Peter, married Agnes Wilson, daughter of Peter Wilson. 2. Nicholas, married Sarah Pryor. 3. Constant, married Agatha Marr. 4. Thomas Harden, married Mary O'Neal. 5. Bethenia, married in 1762, Absolam Bostick. 6. Susanna, married John Marr. 7. Mary, married Thomas Hardiman. 8. Anne, married Joseph Scales. 9. Elizabeth, married, 1st, William Letcher in 1778, 2nd, Major George Hairston.

Peter Perkins established his homes on the lands bequeathed him by his father, on the north side of Dan River, on an eminence overlooking the river. His home, called "Berry Hill," is standing today, and is a beautiful example of early American architecture. He was an ardent patriot and during the Revolutionary War served first as captain and later as colonel of the Pittsylvania militia; and also threw open his home to be used as a military hospital. He was a man of wealth owning great bodies of land, both in Virginia and North Carolina; and about 1795 removed to North Carolina, making his home in Stokes County. Peter Perkins and his wife Agnes had issue: 1. James Perkins. 2. Elizabeth Perkins, married in 1782 to John Pryor; and in 1798 Henly Stone. 3. Bethenia Perkins married in 1778 Lemuel Smith. 4. Elsie Perkins, married Peter Hairston of Upper Saura Town, North Carolina, and had issue one child, Ruth Stovall Hairston, who married her cousin, Major Peter Wilson, of Pittsylvania, and went to live at "Berry Hill." Their only child, Agnes John Peter Wilson, married Samuel Hairston and settled beautiful "Oak Hill."

[17]John Van Bibber lived in the western section of the county.

[18]Hamon Critz, an early settler, lived on Spoon Creek (now Patrick County) and died in 1802.

[19]John Hanby and Jonathan Hanby were brothers, and lived in the western part of the county that later became Patrick County. Jonathan is said to have been one of the followers of Marion, "the Swamp Fox" of the Revolution. John Hanby's will is probated in Patrick County in 1817, naming sons Samuel, William, Gabriel and John; daughters Nancy, who married Charles Clement of Pittsylvania, Sally who married William McCraw, Jane, Mary and Susannah.

[20]John Wimbish lived at Peytonsburg where he owned and operated some stores, and the village was sometimes called Wimbish's Stores. He married on Sept. 18, 1766, Mary Brady, the daughter of Owen Brady (Halifax Marriage Bonds). He accumulated large wealth in his lifetime and his will is recorded Dec. 20, 1802, in which he named, wife Mary, son John Wimbish, and daughters Polly Wimbish and Nancy Pannill, who had married John Pannill, of "Chalk Level." He willed to wife

Robert Chandler[21] and Benjamin Lankford[22] of the County of Pittsylvania. Gentlemen, Greeting. KNOW YE, That whereas we have constituted and assigned you our Justices of the Peace for our County of Pittsylvania. We do therefore authorize and appoint that the Commission being read as usual, and one of you the said Thomas Dillard, Sr., James Roberts, Jr., Archibald Gordon, Thomas Dillard, Jr., Hugh Innes, John Donalson, Theophilus Lacy, John Wilson, Peter Copeland or John Smith, having first taken the Oaths appointed by Act of Parliament to be taken, instead of the Oaths of Allegiance and Supremacy, the Oath appointed to be taken by act of Parliament made in the sixth Year of our Reign, together with Oath appointed by a late Act of Assembly to be taken by Justices of the Peace, which the said John Dix and George Jefferson, or any Two in the Commission above named are hereby required, authorized, and empowered to give and administer to you; you administer to the above Justices and every of them, the above-mentioned Oaths and Tests, together with the Oathes appointed by the said late Act of Assembly, to be taken by Justices; And we do farther give and grant unto you full Power and Authority, from Time to Time, to administer the Oaths to all other Officers, Civil or Military, who by Law are required to take the said Oaths, and subscribe the said Tests, or any of them; of the Performance whereof you are to cause due entry to be made in the Records of your Court, and here also to keep this Commission until farther Direction shall be given, causing your Clerk to return to our Secretary's Office of our said Colony, from Time to Time, the Names of the Justices, who take the said Oaths, and of those who refuse to take them. WITNESS our truly and well beloved Francis Fauquier, our Lieutenant Governour and Commander in Chief of our said Colony and Dominion, at the Council-Chamber in Williamsburg, under the Seal of our said Colony, the eighth day of May, One Thousand Seven Hundred and sixty-seven, in the Seventh year of our Reign.

Fran. Fauquier."

The law of the colony enjoined that the justices be appointed from among the most able and judicious citizens in the county, and history

"the tract of land I now live on, containing 670 acres, including the town of Peytonsburg, reserving the rents of the Ordinary House, the use of the Store and the Lumber Houses."

[21]Robert Chandler lived in the western part of the county that later became Henry.

[22]Benjamine Lankford was chosen first sheriff of Pittsylvania County in 1767. In 1775 when the county was put in a state of defense, Lankford was appointed captain of a company of militia and a member of the Committee of Safety. In 1777 he was made major of the county militia. He represented the county in the General Assembly from 1774-1790. In Jan., 1771, he married Henrietta Booker, the widow of Edward Booker of Halifax County. His will was probated September 17, 1810, in which he named the following children: sons Benjamin and Stephen Lankford, daughters Mary Todd (widow of Richard Todd), Anne Madison, Sarah Browne, Kitty Turner and Henrietta Lankford.

bears record that the governors followed this injunction in making their appointments. The county courts became the most influential body in the colonial system of government. "To the[23] character of the courts as an institution was undoubtedly due the great satisfaction of the people with the administration of the judicial affairs of the community." While the original appointments were made by the royal governors, vacancies in the body were filled upon the recommendation of the court itself, so that in this way the body was self-perpetuating.

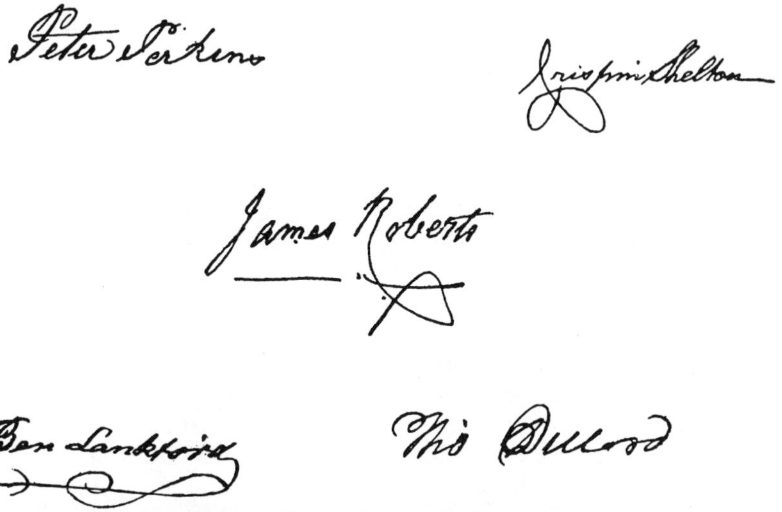

SIGNATURES OF EARLY JUSTICES OF PITTSYLVANIA

Benjamin Lankford was chosen sheriff, John Donelson, surveyor, and William Tunstall,[24] clerk of the county. The Tunstall family

[23]Bell's "Old Free State, Lunenburg County."

[24]William Tunstall, first clerk of Pittsylvania County, was the son of William Tunstall and his wife Anne Hill of King and Queen County. He married Elizabeth (Betsy) Barker, daughter of Colonel Thomas Barker of Edenton, N. C., and settled in the western part of the county.

William Tunstall was a man of wealth and like many gentlemen of his day maintained a fine stable. In 1766 he imported from England Koulihan, a horse of finest blood. William Tunstall and his wife, Betsy, had issue: 1. William Tunstall, Jr., born 1772. 2. Peyton Randolph Tunstall. 3. James Tunstall. 4. Nathaniel Tunstall. 5. Thomas Tunstall. 6. George Tunstall. 7. Elizabeth Tunstall. 8. Anne Tunstall, married Edmond Tunstall, son of Thomas Tunstall of Pittsylvania. 9. Lucy Tunstall, married Henry G. Williams of North Carolina. After the death of Col. William Tunstall, his wife returned to Bertie Co., North Carolina, taking all of her family with her except son William Tunstall, Jr., who succeeded his father as clerk of Pittsylvania. William Tunstall, Jr., married Sarah Pugh of Bertie County, North Carolina, and settled prior to 1800 Belle Grove, a very handsome estate, with fine brick mansion. They had issue: 1. William H. Tunstall, served as clerk from 1830 to 1852. 2. Whitmell Pugh Tunstall. 3. Thomas Barker Tunstall, married Sarah Sullivan 1824. 4. Anne married Samuel W. Tunstall. 5. Eliza, married Col. George Townes. 6. Winnefred, married Nathaniel Wilson, son of Col. John Wilson, settled "Belle Grade" on Dan River and had issue: Mary Wilson, married Richard Baptist. Isabella Wilson, married Henry Hobson Lumpkin, son of Governor Lumpkin of Georgia. Anne Eliza Wilson, married William Lea. George Wilson. Martha Wilson, married Dr. John Roy Cabell. Virginia Wilson, married Garland Jeffries. Indiana, Winnefred, Maria, Agnes, John, William and Nathaniel Wilson.

seemed to have a peculiar fitness for the office of county clerk; in Tidewater Virginia members of the family often filled the position. The clerkship of Pittsylvania was held by the Tunstalls for eighty-three years, through three generations. William Tunstall was succeeded in 1791 by his son William Tunstall, Jr., who built and settled beautiful "Belle Grove," a mile east of Chatham. He was in turn succeeded by his son William H. Tunstall, in 1830, who established the home now owned by Mr. Hunt Hargrave, of Chatham.

The lists of tithables which were straightway taken by the justices have been preserved and show who were Pittsylvania's first citizens. They numbered 938 whites and 316 slaves, giving a total of 1,254. In 1773 the lists of tithables numbered 2,198, showing the rapid increase in settlement. This increase in population was largely brought about by an influx of settlers from Tidewater, who were restlessly turning their eyes westward. Dodd[25] says "the hill counties of Louisa and Pittsylvania were teaming with a restless population and most gentlemen of the older lowland counties had patents to great tracts in Watauga, Kentucky and Augusta Counties, great areas which we know respectively as Tennessee, Kentucky and West Virginia, and the lawyers had much to do to keep things straight, or perhaps to tangle matters so that another generation would be needed to clear them up."

After the close of the Revolutionary War the restless population of Pittsylvania began to seek those newer western counties and migrated to them in great numbers.

There were resident lawyers who practiced before the early court of Pittsylvania, men of culture, ability and wealth, among whom were Colonel Haynes Morgan, Captain Hugh Innes, Gideon Marr, Robert Williams and William Todd. But Patrick Henry's exceptional powers were everywhere recognized and his opinions were like a court of last appeal. In 1770 Mr. John Smith, of "The Pocket" wrote to his brother-in-law, Captain Arthur Hopkins[26] also of Pittsylvania, who was preparing to take a trip down county: "Tell Mr. Henry I have long expected his opinion on the affair I wrote to him, but have never heard once from

[25]"Statesmen of the Old South," Dodd.

[26]Captain Arthur Hopkins, who settled in the northwestern part of the country, was a son of Dr. Arthur Hopkins of New Kent and Goochland Counties. Dr. Hopkins was born in 1690 and took a degree in medicine from Edinburgh, Scotland; he was justice, sheriff, vestryman and colonel of Goochland. He died in 1765 and by his wife Elizabeth Pettus had issue: Samuel, John, Captain Arthur, of Pittsylvania, James, Lucy, wife of George Robinson of Pittsylvania, Mary, wife of Col. Joseph Cabell, and Elizabeth, the wife of John Smith of the Pocket. Captain Arthur Hopkins, married Judith Jefferson, daughter of Peterfield Jefferson, and had issue, among others James Hopkins, who inherited his father's home and had issue, Reuben, who married successively Frances and Polly Carter, daughters of Jesse Carter of "Oakland," and Judge Arthur Francis Hopkins, born Oct. 18, 1794, in Pittsylvania, graduated in law at Chapel Hill, N. C., and became the first judge of the Superior Court of Alabama.

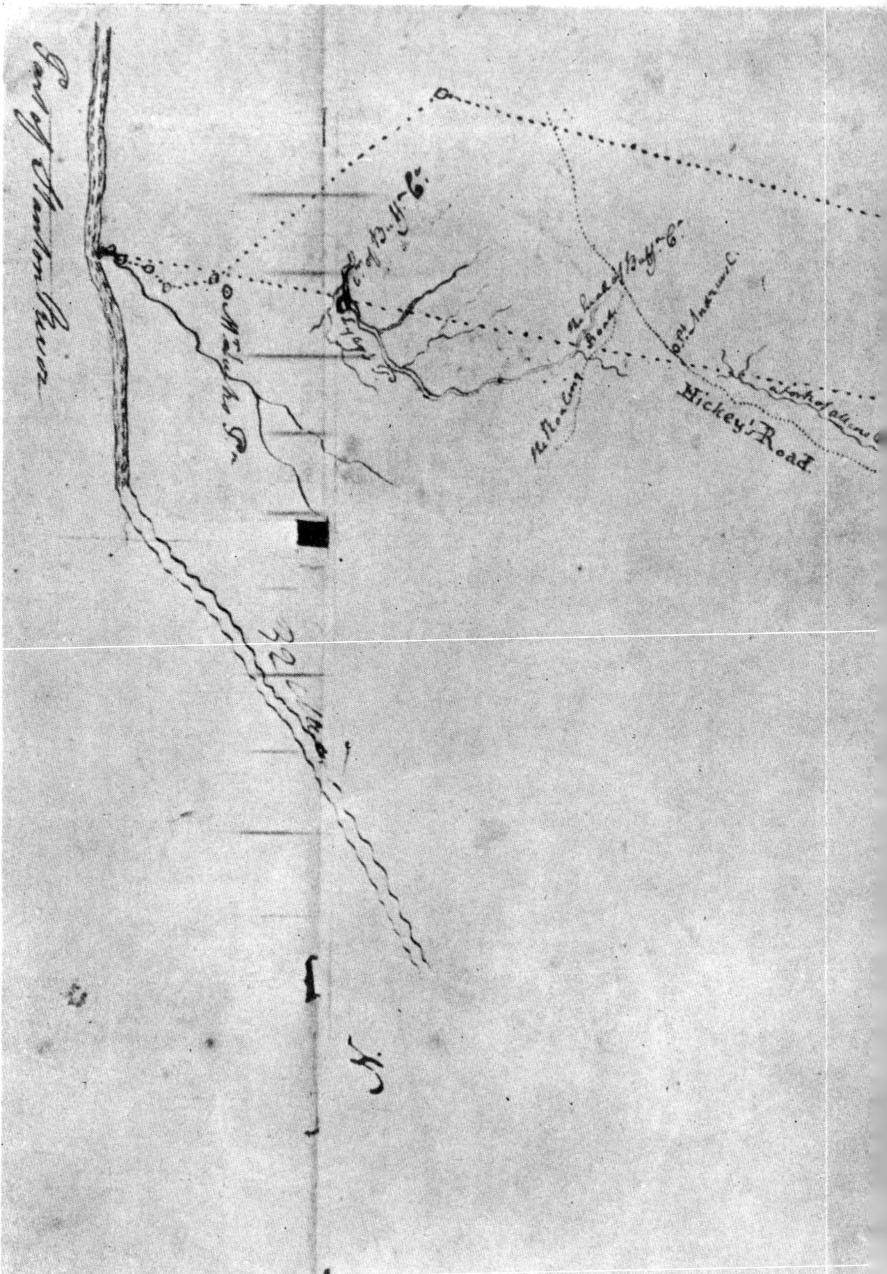

MAP OF DIVIDING LINE

Between Pittsylvania and Halifax Counties, run in 1767 by Col. John Dor

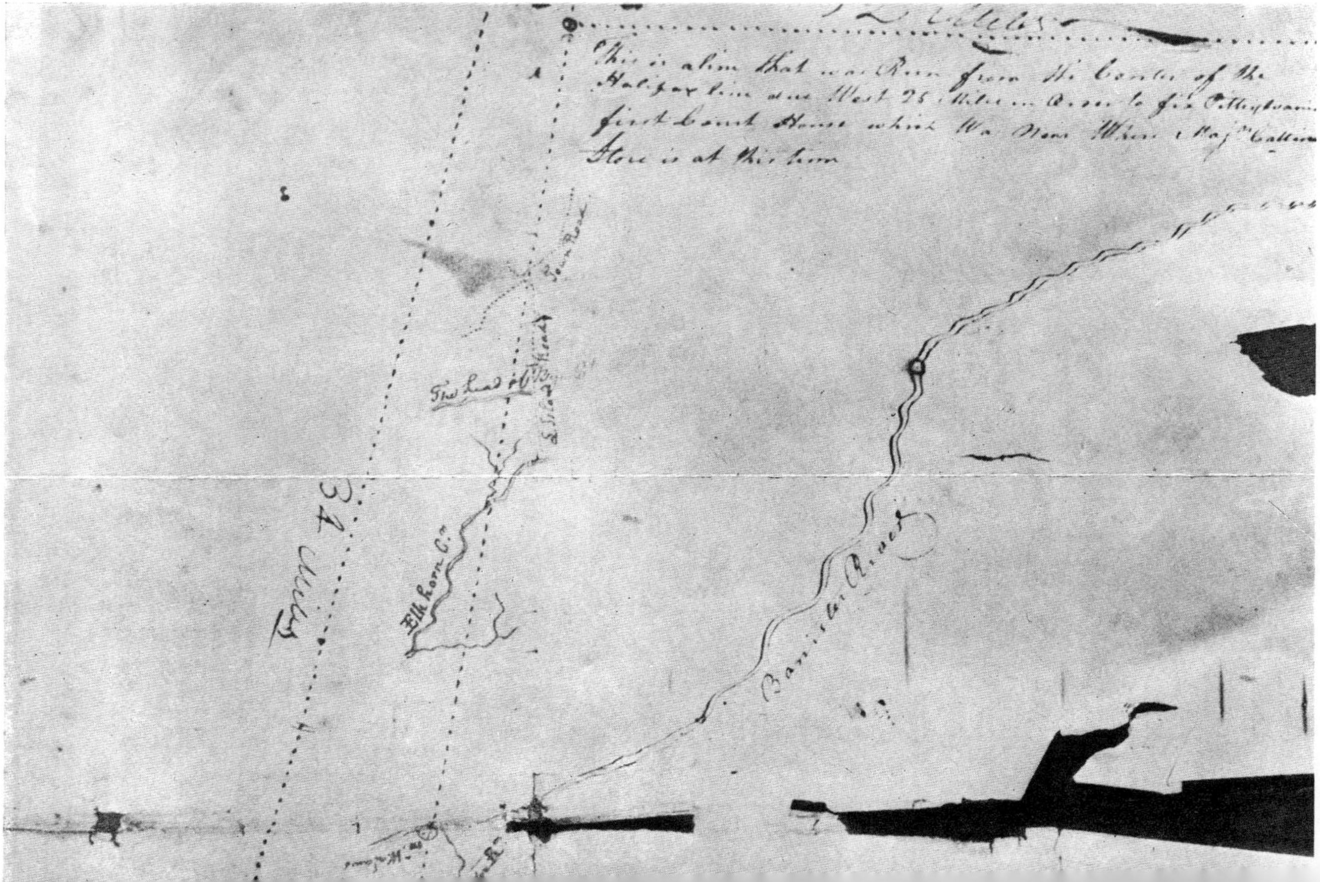
This is a line that was Run from the Center of the
Halifax line due West 25 Miles
first Court House which Was Near Where
Store is at this time
34 Miles
Elk horn Cr
The head of
Banister River

him, tho' the person I wrote by told me he promised to write me an answer in a short time. If he will send it by you, his fee for his Opinion I will send by Mr. Lynch, Burgess for Bedford, next month."

The surveyor of the county was ordered to run a line due west 27 miles from the center of the dividing line between this county and Halifax, and the courthouse to be established at the most convenient place to the end of this line. The court closed with an order that the next court be held "at the Plantation of Captain James Roberts on Sandy River."

At the September Court the sheriff of the county was directed "to wait upon his Honour the Governor to Request him to establish the Courthouse on the Plantation of James Roberts, the court being of the opinion that the said Place is the most convenient." Pittsylvania, like the preceding counties, at first extended westward to the mountains, and at this time embraced within its boundaries the present counties of Patrick, Henry, and Franklin south of Blackwater River, and the point on Sandy River was considered a central and convenient place for holding court for the large county. The place selected is the present site of Callands—here there are bold springs, the head waters of Sandy River, and it was near the convenience of these springs that the court buildings were located.

James Roberts, Jr., agreed to build the courthouse, to be of the same dimensions as Halifax old courthouse, "to be shingled and properly finished. Also a pair of Stocks and Pillary and a sufficient Prison for the use of the county."

The military organization of the county was effected at once. Archibald Gordon, Gent., produced a commission from the Governor appointing him county lieutenant of the militia. The county lieutenant was in command of all the military forces of the county and outranked the colonel of the militia. Colonel Gordon was a native of Scotland, an old bachelor, and lived and died in that part of the county that later became Franklin, near the Henry and Franklin dividing line.

John Donelson, Gent., was appointed colonel, Thomas Dillard, Gent., was appointed lieut.-colonel, and Theophilas Lacy, Gent., was appointed major of the county militia forces. Crispen Shelton, Peter Perkins, Benjamin Lankford, George Rowland, John Cook, Abram Shelton, Elisha Walden, Robert Chandler, William McDaniel, John Wilson, Hamon Critz, Richard Walden, John Pigg, James Lyon, George Jefferson, William Thomas, and Robert Hairston were appointed captains of the militia during the years 1767 to 1770.

The interest that is always attached to court at once drew settlers to the new courthouse and in November, 1769, the General Assembly established a town there. The law read:[27] "Whereas James Roberts of the county of Pittsylvania has laid off fifty acres of his lands where the Court House of the said county now stands, into lots and streets for a town, which would be of great advantage to the inhabitants of that county if established a town for the reception of traders, be it therefore enacted that the said fifty acres shall be established a town to be known by the name of Chatham."

Thus the county seat of Pittsylvania was also named in honor of William Pitt, who was the Earl of Chatham. Mr. James Roberts failed to build the courthouse as he had agreed, and in 1770 the court ordered that unless the courthouse was completed within two months Mr. Roberts would be prosecuted in the General Court. The building of two prisons was let to Michael Rowland for £75, one to be 14 x 12 feet, the other to be 10 x 12 feet.

At a court held on July 24, 1772, leave was granted James Roberts to build large gates "across the Roads near the Springs and the Court House." The location of the courthouse is shown in a plat of land patented by John Rowland on which there is a drawing of the building. It stood on a slight eminence above the branch that flows from the two bold springs, and the outline of a rock foundation can be traced there today. Thomas Bruce was a tavern keeper at Pittsylvania C. H. in 1773.

James Roberts met with financial troubles and the land on which the town of Chatham was built was offered for sale, a notice of which appeared in the *Virginia Gazette,* April 5, 1775: "To be sold on the 4th Thursday in May next, being Pittsylvania Court Day, by virtue of a deed of trust from James Roberts, the tract of land whereon the court house now stands, containing about 1,000 acres, 50 of which are laid off into a town and several houses built thereon. It would be profitable to any person inclined to keep taverns as that without any land but a garden now rents for sixty pounds per annum."

The justices of the peace, sensible of the dignity of their positions as judges of the courts, resented any light behavior toward them in the execution of their office. There are many instances in the records of fines being imposed for such offences.

[27]Hening's "Statutes."

At a court held August 1767:

"William Astin having insulted Mr. Justice Innes in the execution of his office and behaved contemptuously to the court, he is therefore fined £10."

In November 1774, William Young was ordered to lie in the stocks one hour for having behaved contemptuously to the court.

In the settlement of this new country the justices of the peace represented the power to enforce law, order and good morals, and as a body they do not seem to have neglected their duty. Grand juries were summoned at intervals before whom were brought offenders for swearing one oath, two oaths, three oaths and even four oaths; for getting drunk, for selling liquors contrary to law, and for allowing one's slaves to work on the Sabbath Day.

Soon after the establishment of the courthouse on Sandy River a young Scotchman named Samuel Calland[28] opened a store there. He proved to be a man of parts and amassed a large estate, and his name so overshadowed that chosen for the village that in time it was forgotten that Callands ever bore the name of Chatham. Calland's store stood in the broad field to the left of the old Moorman residence where some ancient cherry trees mark the spot. The Calland home was a mile or so distant, near the end of Turkey Cock Mountain, and in the rock walled grave yard there sleep many of the Calland family. The old residence, still standing, is one of the oldest buildings in the county, and is now the home of Mr. Cabell Cobbs.

The early account books of Calland's store give an insight into living conditions and the household needs of the people of this section. On November 21, 1784, Captain Lodowick Tuggle visited the store and purchased for his household:

[28]Samuel Calland was born in Scotland in 1750 and was operating a store at Pittsylvania courthouse before 1774. He married Elizabeth, the daughter of Mr. John Smith, of "The Pocket," and lived a life of much elegance at his home. He left no will but his heirs are shown in the settlement of his estate as follows: Sons Samuel, James, Bowker and Ralph Calland; daughters Elizabeth, the wife of William Calloway, and Matilda, the wife of Henry G. Calloway. His estate was divided into four plantations, listed as the Manor Plantation, the Glebe Plantation (formerly home of the minister of the Established Church), the Dan River Plantation, and the Sandy River Plantation.

The will of Mrs. Elizabeth Calland, widow of Samuel Calland was recorded February 18, 1828, and after making many bequests to different members of her family, she bequeathed "to Doctor Tavenor C. Shelton a small tract of land on Bearskin Creek in Pittsylvania; to my old and respected friend, John Tompkins, of Richmond, nine shares in the Virginia Bank."

1 pr. shoe buckles	£ .2
1 large Punch Bowl	.2
1 small Punch Bowl	.1
1 doz. blue cups and saucers	.6.8
I large blue tea pott	.5
1 blue milk pott	.1
1 flat bottom thimble	.6
1 Testament	.2.4
1 snuf box	.1.3
1 yard ribbon	.1.6
1 fine Hatt	.18
26 yards linen	3.15.6
2 felt hats	.9
3 pr. Best Men's Shoes	1.2.4
1 dozen knives and forks	.7.6
25 needles	.1
4 pair plaid hose	.8
12 yards of plaiding	1.4
2 yards of black mode	1.
1 dish 3 lb. weight	.7.6
10 yards of Osnaberg	.10.5
1 pair shoe buckles	.3
1 pair of knee buckles	.1.3
2 pewter porringers	.4

On December 1st, 1784, Captain James Robert's wife came shopping and purchased:

7 yards finest chintz	£3.17
7 yards finest chintz	3.13
6 yards print linen	1.16
6 yards print linen	1.10
2 fine handkerchiefs	.10
4½ yards Shalloon	1. .3
4½ yards Durant	1.18
2 pen knives	.2
12 yards fine linen	3.18
1 pair men's gloves	.4
1 pair lady's gloves	.3
1 pewter porringer	.3
1 ivory comb	.2.6
3 yards of superfine Shaloon	1.8.4

Colonel William Tunstall, the clerk of the county, made many purchases at Calland's for his household, such as linen, chintz, tea, and so on. Two physicians are noted in the day books of 1784, Dr. Arthur Kezee and Dr. Thomas Gibson, both of whom purchased supplies for their practice. The articles most commonly called for were sugar, molasses, rum, shot, hoes, hats, shoe buckles, linen and osnaberg, the latter being a coarse cotton cloth used for negro clothing.

The goods for the store were brought up from Richmond and Petersburg, and neighboring planters, having waggoned their tobacco down to market, would bring back a load of goods for Calland. The charge for hauling was estimated per pound.

"Nov. 15, 1784, To captain Francis Graves
By carriage of back load 2400..........£4.16
To Daniel Richardson By carriage 2250 from Richmond.......... 4.10"

On March 25, 1785, the old pioneer and hunter, "Captain Elisha Walden of Holston River," (account book) Tennessee, made a call at Calland's store. Probably some business matter had brought him this long distance back to his old home. There is no doubt but that he was warmly welcomed by his friends and old neighbors and plied with many questions about life in the wilderness. How were old friends faring, who had gone out to the Tennessee county? What of the Indians? Were lands cheap? and so on. The purchases made by Captain Walden that day, "a fine apron," "a fine handkerchie," and some black silk were probably gifts for his women folk out in the wilderness.

It was the duty of the court to maintain the county's system of roads, which was done in the following manner: an overseer or surveyor, was appointed for a certain section of road, and it was his duty to see that the road was worked and kept in a passable condition, using the laboring tithables in his district. An overseer was liable to a fine for neglect of duty, and many such fines were imposed by the court.

The following early road orders contain items of interest. At a court held in August 1767, "it is ordered that John Morton, James Blevin, Thomas Calloway and William Roberts mark a road from this courthouse to Hickey's Road leading toward the upper Saura Towns." The Saura Towns belonged to the Saura Indians of North Carolina and this road led from Callands towards the state line.

"Ordered that James Talbott be the surveyor of the Road from John Blevin's on Smith River to Hickey's Old Road below Leatherwood Chapel," a chapel built by the Church of England.

"Adam Loving, John Parr, John Hanby, Frederick Fulkerson ordered to mark a Road from Talbot's Road about ½ mile below his house to the Tararat, crossing Smith River at Bate's and South Mayo at John Parr's." The Ararat River is in southwestern Patrick.

"William Collins is appointed overseer of the road from Dillard's Musterfield (on Staunton River) to Hickey's Road."

"Thomas Watson, Thomas Hardy, and Henry McDaniel ordered to mark a Road from Hickey's Road at or near Great Cherrystone to the Pigg River Road across Elkhorn just above the old ffoard." This is probably the road that runs today from Chatham to Peytonsburg.

In 1768 it was ordered that "James Poteet, Ruban Keith, and Benjamin Watson do view a Road from Robert Hill's to the head of Wiggen to lead to Little River." Little River is in Floyd County, and this road led from western Franklin across the Blue Ridge Mountain.

In 1769 John Lewis[29] (Byrd), William Owen and William Thomas were ordered to view a road from "the Stoney Hill to the Armstrong Road." There were two John Lewises living in the county at this time, one of whom named his home "The Byrd" and the other "the Mountain"; and in order to distinguish between them, the name of the home always accompanied each signature. John Lewis of "The Byrd" named his home for his father's place, "The Byrd" of Goochland County, home of Colonel Charles Lewis.

In 1774 Thomas Black, James Dillard, and Peyton Smith were ordered to "view a Road from Standefer's Track, joining the Road that leads from Blackwater (River) to the Road from Ross's Quarter to the courthouse." This order shows that Standeford maintained a track for racing horses in western Pittsylvania (now Franklin), in 1774. These first citizens of Pittsylvania, whether Virginians from Tidewater or Scotchmen from across seas, brought with them into their new home the gentleman's sport of breeding and raising fine horses. Of the thirty-nine most noted horses imported into Virginia prior to the Revolution (listed in *Va. Mag. History,* Oct. 1927), "Koulihan" was imported in 1766 by William Tunstall, first clerk of the county, which would indicate that he maintained a fine stable. One would judge that horse racing was a customary sport of the day from the casual reference made in the following letter written in 1782 by Henry Innes of Bedford County to Ralph Smith of "The Pocket":

[29]John Lewis of "The Byrd" made his home on Dan River in the southeastern part of the county. In his will proven July 21, 1794, he named sons Robert, Charles and John, daughter Jane, who married Jonathan Read, Mary who married William Williams and Elizabeth who married a Hobson. He bequeathed "to my son Robert Lewis all that tract of land which I purchased of John Lewis, Senior

"Sir, "Col. Calloway's Monday Morning.

I have sent ye bearer over to know if you will take ye stagg which I offerred you as I was returning from Pittsylvania Court. There is a very large Bull in this neighborhood which was formerly the property of Hezekiah Hall, the Stagg you wintered, and a good Beef to weigh 300 lbs. at Ross's Quarter, which Mr. Herndon will deliver at any moment on my order, for these three I will take fifteen dollars. You may take one, two, or three on these terms, and the money I shall be glad to receive at ye Race next Friday. I have heard that Flanagan was about to purchase a small Drove, if you do not incline to purchase he may have them on those terms. I would come over but it is too wett.

I am sir your mo. ob.

Harry Innes."

It was also ordered in 1774 that "a road be viewed from Colonel Donelson's Iron Works to the mouth of Chestnut Creek." These iron works, known as the Bloomery, were located in eastern Franklin County on Pigg River, and were the earliest iron works in this part of Virginia.

In 1776 Henry France was appointed surveyor of the roads "from where Morgan Bryan's Road crosses the South Fork of Mayo to the Carolina Line."

Since the early roads were rough, most of the travel was done on horseback, but a chaise, or "wheel chair" is recorded here and there in the tax lists. Early owners of chaises, between 1770-80 were John Smith, of "The Pocket," John Dix, Capt. Hugh Innes, William Ware, John Briscoe and William Tunstall.

The education of his children was a problem which faced the early settler of Pittsylvania. No smoothly running system of public instruction such as we have today was then in force; on the other hand schooling was an individual problem for each man to solve for his own family. This was accomplished by means of private tutors and the school house was a familiar building on the Virginia plantation. No doubt it was difficult to obtain teachers for the frontier homes of Pittsylvania, so far removed from the established social life of Tidewater Virginia, and one teacher to a neighborhood was the general rule. It was the custom to build the schoolhouse in some abandoned field, given over to broom sedge and thus

of the Mountain." Charles Lewis, son of John Lewis of "The Byrd," married Mrs. Gatrehood Glover Johns, of Milton, N. C., and had issue: Nicholas, Lucy who married Fielding Walker, and Elizabeth who married Warner Williams. His will was proven November, 1817. John Lewis of "The Byrd" of Pittsylvania was the son of Charles Lewis, of "The Byrd" of Goochland, born 1696; and grandson of Colonel John Lewis of Warner Hall, Gloucester, and his wife, Elizabeth Warner, daughter of Col. Augustine Warner.

grew up the name of "old field school," in which the majority of Virginians received their education.

There is mention of several school houses in the surveyor's records, when a line was run nearby and they were named as pointers. There was a school house on Fox Run of Blackwater River, now Franklin County, in 1756; one on Captain James Terry's plantation in eastern Pittsylvania in 1760; another on the South Branch of Mayo River (Patrick County), in 1766; one on Potter's Creek of Pigg River, near Toshes in 1767; one on the Nix plantation, near Straightstone, and another at Peytonsburg. Of course there were many many others, near which no line was run, and of which there is no record.

Mr. William Williams was an early schoolmaster mentioned in a tax list of the Peytonsburg district, in 1775. In a tax list taken by Archelaus Hughes in 1774, who lived in western Pittsylvania (later Patrick), a schoolmaster was included in Mr. Henry France's household.

When a satisfactory tutor could not be found in the colony one sent back to England for a likely young man. A letter from Alexander Stewart,[30] a Scotch merchant at Manchester, to Mr. John Smith, of the "Pocket" plantation, stated in 1766: "Am sending home (England) for a schoolmaster for you, if any is to be got on the terms you state." Among early tutors at "The Pocket" were William Dabney, Robert Townshend, and Justinian Wills; and in a letter of the latter, dated 1772, he stated that Colonel Calloway's children (of Bedford) and others were taught by him at the same time. The children of nearby plantations walked or drove to school, but those living at a distance, as Colonel Calloway's children, boarded in the same home with the teacher. A copy set for some pupil at "The Pocket" on an August day of 1771, and followed in childish scrawl reads: "I promise to pay to Mr. Jacobus Early The sum of Five pounds on demand Witness my hand this 30th day of August 1771." The youthful writer probably pleased with his skill wrote without a copy: "Sir, please send me as much Broad Cloth as will make me a new sute of clothes and Chare it to the account of, Sir your Humble Servant, Bowker Smith.

To Mr. Robert Cowen Merchant. "

Teaching was an underpaid profession then as now, as this receipt shows:

"Feb. 11, 1761."

Rec'd of John Smith, Junior, Forty shillings for schooling his two children the year last past.

William Ryan."

[30]John Smith Papers.

Bruce says, "not infrequently the tutor in a private family was a person under indentures. It was a well known fact to the planters that men of good education were found among the agricultural servants, and even the convicts who were purchased for the purpose of teaching their children." John Williams was a convict schoolmaster belonging to Mr. Henry Williams, of Peytonsburg, from whom he ran away in 1775. His master, Mr. Williams, advertised for his return in the *Virginia Gazette* of August, 1775, saying that as he understood the Prussian Exercises he would probably try to pass as a deserter from his Majesty's troops; that he had taught a reading school at Peytonsburg for the past eight months. His wearing apparel was described as consisting of a claret colored frieze coat, light colored New Market Coat, with beaver coating, leather breeches, and a raccoon cap with green persian lining.

It was not an unusual thing to have a convict schoolmaster, since men were shipped to Virginia and sold into servitude for political offenses and for debt. We may suppose that Mr. Henry Williams, needing a schoolmaster in his family, had gone down to port and purchased one, then did not wish to lose him after such short service. These white servants were known as "indentured," for after serving their masters for a certain number of years they became free. Another instance of indentured servitude is given in the court minutes of May, 1768, when Champness Terry came into court and declared Matthew Durham and Jane his wife to be set free, although they were due him one year's service. Mr. Terry for some reason gave Durham and his wife one year of their servitude, his generosity probably being a reward for faithful duty.

As late as 1790 there is mention of this custom, when Edmund Tunstall, son of Thomas Tunstall certified to the court that "Mourning Gilmore, son of Sabra Gilmore, who served her time to my said Father to freedom, is also free."

The rich mellow lands of the valleys along the Staunton, Dan and Banister Rivers and the light grey soil of the uplands were found alike vastly productive for the culture of tobacco, and the growing of the plant became the important industry of this new county. The market places, however, were far distant, none nearer than Petersburg and points along the James River, such as Osborne, Rocky Ridge (Manchester), Shoccos, and Warwick.

The difficulty of transportation to market was met in three ways, the tobacco was rolled in hogsheads, sent down by boat, and hauled in wagons. In order to send by boat it was first necessary to get the tobacco to Lynch's Ferry on James River, where Lynchburg now stands. The river was probably the chief means of transportation and a hardy race of river men grew up who plied their trade between the falls of James River and the up country, transporting the commodities of the country in batteaux towed by long poles. Much of Pittsylvania's tobacco found its way to market over Ward's Road, an early historic way which led across Bedford County (now Campbell) from Ward's Ferry on Staunton River, a point in northern Pittsylvania, to Lynch's Ferry on the James. This road was named for Major John Ward, who settled at this point on Staunton River about 1750, and is so excellent a piece of engineering that it was not found necessary to materially change its course when taken over as a part of the State's system of highways.

The tobacco was frequently rolled the many miles to market in stout hogsheads, by running a pole through the center and attaching shafts to which a horse was hitched. The cask was then drawn rolling along, and when the roads were rough and frozen there was likelihood of the casks breaking to pieces and damaging the tobacco. On the map of the dividing line between Halifax and Pittsylvania, run in 1767, there is marked "the roaling road," which led in the direction of Ward's Ferry.

At the market places the tobacco was weighed, inspected and stored to await shipment to England, for it was only to England that the colonists could sell their commodities, and only from England that they could buy. Here there were also large stores where goods of every kind, likewise the latest fashions, were bought direct from England. When convenient the Pittsylvania farmer would accompany his tobacco to market, looking after its inspection and storage. Later he visited the stores and made purchases for his family and plantation. When not convenient to go himself, he would send his tobacco down by an overseer, with a memorandum to the stores of his needs, and the merchant would select his goods and pack them securely so that no injury would come to them on the return trip. There were also waggoners who made a business of hauling back and forth to the market. The charge for carrying one hogshead from the Staunton River to Manchester in 1784, and finding provisions, was £3.3.7½.

At Rocky Ridge there were tailors' shops and dress makers' establishments, where men's suits were made and ladies' gowns fashioned. Thrifty Scotchmen[31] were the merchants of that day. They had been excluded

[31] "Landmarks of Old Prince William," Harrison.

from American trade until 1707 when Scotland formed political union with Great Britain; but from that time they were very active and built up an extensive trade. Partners or resident agents were established in Virginia as the trade increased and princely fortunes were made. From 1750 to 1775 was the golden era of Scotland's trade. President Madison in his old age, 1827, said, "Scotch merchants in Virginia used to have a meeting twice a year to decide on the rate of exchange, the price of tobacco, and the advance in the prices of their goods.

From the letters and business papers of Mr. John Smith,[32] of The Pocket, a plantation on Staunton River, a fair idea is gained of life in Pittsylvania from 1760-1776. The Pocket, so called from lying in a bend of the river, was a tract of 713 acres which was first patented by Col. Peter Jefferson, who prior to 1755 sold it to John Smith. Smith at this time was deputy surveyor of Albemarle County under Colonel Jefferson, but the following tax ticket shows that he was maintaining a force of slaves at The Pocket, who no doubt cultivated the rich bottom land under the supervision of an overseer:

John Smith, Jr., To the Sheriff of Hallifax	Dr.
To 8 Levys @ 93lb. Tob. Each.........744 lbs. at 12/6 per.........	£4.13
To Two first Pool Taxs on 7 Tithes @ 5/Each.........	1.15
To 6 Negro Tithes Taxed with 2/Each.........	.12
To Quitrents of 713 Acres of Land.........	.18. 1
To 1/3 per hundred on the said 713 Acres of Land Taxes.........	. 8.11
	£8. 7. 0

Oct. 3, 1756. Recd. of John Smith, Jun. the Above Acct. being in full of all Taxes due from him at this time and the Quitrents of Seven hundred and thirteen Acres of Land and Eight Levys for the year 1755.

Robert King S:Shrf.

---

[32]Mr. John Smith, of "The Pocket," Pittsylvania County, belonged to the family of the Rev. Guy Smith, who was minister of Abingdon Parish, Gloucester County, and died in 1720, having issue: John, baptized June 3, 1701; Guy, baptized Dec. 12, 1704; and Mary, Joanna, Anne, Susanna, Constantine and Lawrence. John Smith, known as Col. John Smith, married Anne—and had issue: John, born September 23, 1725, and died at "The Pocket"; Bowker, who married Judith Cox of Cumberland County, May 22, 1749; and Guy, who married Anne Hopkins of Goochland, on November 20, 1751. John Smith, Jr., married January 27, 1747, Elizabeth Hopkins, the daughter of Col. Arthur Hopkins of Goochland; was deputy sheriff of Albemarle County from 1750-54; deputy surveyor from 1755-58, surveyor of Goochland County from 1758-62, when he moved to Pittsylvania County. Letters from Dr. James Hopkins of Albemarle prescribed the sovereign remedy of riding for weak lungs. Still seeking health, John Smith spent the summer of 1769 at the Warm Springs, Augusta County. He died 1776, at the age of 51 years and is buried at "The Pocket." His business papers show him to have been a man of culture, wide business interest and much property. In his will he named the following children: Ralph Smith, inherited "The Pocket" and died unmarried; Bowker Smith; John Smith, married Camelia Thurman, and lived at "Lewis Island," on Pigg River; Elizabeth Smith, married Samuel Calland; Anne Smith married Captain William Calloway, son of Col. William Calloway of Bedford County; Samuel Smith married Mildred Ward, a daughter of William Ward and has issue among others, Mildred Smith, who married Mr. Richard Jones of Sheva.

The old dwelling house at "The Pocket" which stood in the bend of the river, has long since disappeared. About 1830 Mr. Arch Haley came into possession of the property and built an imposing residence upon the bluff overlooking the bend.

Due to his state of health, in 1762 Smith moved with his family to the Pittsylvania plantation, in the hope that the pine ladened atmosphere would be beneficial to his frail lungs. His record book contains the following items incident to his moving:

Oct. 1762. Riding Cheare bought of Captain Thomas Starke........£ 6
To John Hammond by going to Goochland after my cattle, 11 days gone ....£ 5
To Stephen Woods for building Dwelling House........£45
To Stephen Townes for building two chimneys to the House........£ 6.10
For rebuilding chimney to old House........£ 2

Mr. Alexander Stewart, a Scotch merchant, was in charge of a store at Rocky Ridge (now Manchester) and wrote Mr. Smith in January 1764: "Your tobacco was left fifty or sixty miles above this place owing to a fall of snow that happened on Saturday last and obliged your people to leave it on the road." (Probably being rolled down.)

In July, 1764, he wrote:
"Sir,
I received yours by Cap't Benja. Clement, and agreeable thereto have sent you by this opp't'y articles as per invoice enclosed with the three pounds which you likewise wanted. The articles are all packed in a rum hhd. along with some belonging to Mr. Clement, so I hope they will come safe to hand and in good order. I have also paid Henry Snow 3 3/5 as you desired. the hhd. tob. which he brought now would not do and Mr. Clement (as he was present) can tell you the reason it was refused. The bottle of Spirits of Turpentine will be sent you from Warrick.

I am Sir,

Yours,

Alex. Stewart (Per Cap't Benj[a]. Clement)."

Captain Benjamin Clement and Mr. Smith were neighbors, both having settled along Staunton River.

May, 1765.

"I have just now got a ship come into me with some goods for the summer, should you want anything for summer wear let me know."

May, 1766.

"Your clothes I have at last got out of the Taylor's Shop, have sent them by this opportunity, they are packed up in a light cask with some other small things, where I hope they will not get wet.

"As to any news of the Stamp Act we have not received any certain account of its being repealed but by the last accounts from home it was of the opinion of everybody there that it would be repealed in a few days after the last ship came away, have sent you the last newspaper wherein you'll find the account brought by her."

August, '66.

"I have got the leather for your chair bottom from Norfolk. Likewise procured a quantity of oil and paint which I suppose you'll want for your house. I have forwarded the chintz, measures and stays to Mrs. Young to be made up as desired.

December, 1767.

"Only two hhds. of your tobacco received, the other was left forty miles above on account of the roads being so hard frozen the casks were like to give way, waggons will have to come down to bring them in. This worthless taylor of ours has never got your clothes done, was obliged to send them undone at last.

Wishing you a merry Christmas."

January, 1769.

"The negro fellow Tom shall wait here for an opp'ty to be sent you, the weather has been and is so very cold and bad that I don't care to send him off without I could depend upon the carefulness of the person who carries him up."

May, 1771.

"Five hoghsheads of your tobacco safe to hand, which has been inspected and weighed.

The hair combs I must send to Williamsburg for, as there are none this way. The silver buckles are fashionable but am doubtful one pair may be rather small, if so send them back I shall have a larger pair made. The wilton cloth was sent from this store."

An estimate of the amount of tobacco raised at this early day is gained from the fact that Mr. Smith paid Mr. Joseph Cabell in 1774 £30 for the carriage of 27 hhds. of tobacco from Lynch's Ferry to Westham (now Westhampton), by batteaux.

Mr. Smith at another time wrote:

"Tell Chenault I have sent 5 hhds. to the river, will send five more next Tusday, 6 more go next week and if he does not set off till week following will have 6 more and shall keep rolling them as fast as I can till I get all my tobacco there whilst the weather permits."

In the settlement of Paul Pigg's estate, 1766-69, recorded in Deed Book 1, are the following entries:

Cash for rolling down 1 hhd. tob.	
2 hhds. at Warwick	2154
1 hhds. at Warwick	1066
I hhds. at Blandford	1105
By inspection at Osbornes	525
By 1 hhds. at Osbornes	1035

In the summer of 1771 there came a great freshet in James River, causing much damage to the warehouses and tobacco along the river. A letter from Alexander Stewart to Mr. Smith said:

"The loss of goods and houses that stood upon the banks here and at Warwick was considerable, beside upwards of 2500 hhds. of tobacco entirely damaged. I observe you likewise are a great sufferer from the fresh."

The newspapers reported later that the river rose forty feet and the loss around Rocky Ridge was between 5,000 and 6,000 hhds. of tobacco. The Roanoke, or Staunton rose even higher than the James, and the people living near its course suffered great loss from the flood waters.

While the James River stores gave a greater variety from which to choose, yet there were good stores within the county at this time. We have seen how wide a variety could be found at Samuel Calland's store at the Court House; he had other stores at Tomahawk and Piny Mount. John Hickey and John Rowland were operating stores in the extreme western part of the county on Smith River (now Henry County). John Wimbish and the Terry's had stores at Peytonsburg, and John Wilson had opened a store at his ferry.

Smythe, the Englishman,[33] wrote in 1774 of industrial conditions in the western part of the county. He said a considerable fur trade was carried on, deer skins selling a shilling sterling per pound, racoon skins for 6 pence each, otter for two or three shillings per skin and beaver in

[33] J. F. D. Smythe's "Travels."

proportion. A considerable quantity of tobacco was cultivated which was almost all carried to James River and sold at fifteen, eighteen and twenty shillings per hundred weight, but the principal of their exports was hogs, which were raised in great numbers and driven in droves of one, two, three, four and five hundred together to the falls of James and Roanoke Rivers, as well as to sea ports. The hogs were sold alive for about 20 shillings per hundred weight. "The hogs run wild in the woods and live largely upon acorns or mast, as it is called. Some years there is such an amazing yield of acorns that the hogs are fattened on that alone, but as it tends to make the meat soft, people generally feed them some little time upon corn, before marketing them."

Since the stock was permitted to run at large through the woods a distinguishing mark was necessary, which was duly recorded in the Clerk's office. For instance: "At a Court held September, 1767, Samuel Hall's ear mark, to-wit, a cross and slit in the Right ear and a slit in the left is ordered to be recorded."

CHAPTER IX

EARLY CHURCHES IN PITTSYLVANIA

THE CHURCH OF ENGLAND

Virginia being an English colony the Church of England was established by law as the form of worship for the people of the colony. Parishes were laid out co-extensive with the counties, which were later divided and sub-divided as settlement increased. The administration of the affairs of each parish was in control of a local body of men known as the vestry, which Bruce[1] says "was composed of the foremost men residing in the parish, whether from point of view of intelligence, wealth or social position. As first gentlemen in the county, apart from the prestige they derived from being the principal guardians of the public morals, they were looked up to as the models of all that was most polished and cultured in their respective parishes." Besides arranging and providing for religious worship for the people of the parish and safe guarding the morals of the community, it was also incumbent upon the vestry to care for the poor, collect taxes and mark the boundary lines of land. Occupying positions of such trust and authority, the members of the vestries were obligated on their part to set the people at large an example of exemplary conduct.

The Colonial Church labored under a great disadvantage in that there was never a resident bishop in Virginia—the care of the church in the colonies being assigned to the Bishop of London, a man whose time was already filled with the demands of the churches in that great city. The Bishop was represented in Virginia in the persons of the royal governor and the commissary. Judging from the reports made by Governor Gooch to the Bishop of London during the years 1727-1749 concerning the welfare of the church, the governors tried faithfully to perform their duty in keeping the parishes supplied with ministers of blameless life and earnestness of purpose.

Much earnestness of purpose was needed in those who ministered to frontier parishes, having to ride scores of miles over rugged upland country to reach their appointments in the distant parts of the county. The Rev. Anthony Gavin[2] wrote in 1738 of the work in Powhatan and Goochland Counties, then extending westward to the mountains: "I have

[1]Bruce's "Institutional History of the 17th Century."

[2]*Va. Mag. History,* Vol. 33, p. 210.

three churches 23 or 24 miles from the Glebe, and besides these I have seven places of worship up in the mountains. I go twice a year to preach in twelve places which I reckon no better than 400 miles backwards and forwards."

It is a well known and lamentable fact that many of the Virginia clergy of this era were sadly lacking in consecration and devotion to their calling; but when all is said and done "the spiritual[3] life of the church bore a rich fruitage in the ideals of liberty and righteousness which animated the men who made Virginia great in the days of the Revolution."

Gooch[4] reported favorably upon the morals of the people of the Colony, saying that they were "so well inclined to Religion and Vertue that 'tis a great pity they should want instruction thro' a lack of ministers." This lack of ministers was felt by the English authorities to be due to the refusal on the part of the Virginia vestries to "induct" their ministers into the parishes, an English custom which the Virginians successfully resisted throughout the entire life of the colonial church. When a minister was formally "inducted" the parish became his for life, the people being unable to dismiss him however undesirable or unpopular he might become. To avoid this situation the vestries refused to induct, and engaged their ministers from year to year, ever holding the right of dismissal in their hands. English clergymen knowing how insecure their charges would be did not readily come to Virginia; and of those who came the greater number were of the Scottish Church. Bruce says: "In the long run the vestries proved themselves to be of all the public bodies in the colony the most tenacious of the right of independent action." Meade[5] declared that in the history of vestries can be traced the origin not only of religious liberty, but also of civil liberty. "The vestries which were the intelligence and moral strength of the land had been trained up in the defense of their rights against Governors and Bishops, Kings and Cabinets. They had been fighting the battles of the Revolution for one hundred and fifty years. Taxation and representation were only other words for support and election of ministers."

The life of the church in this section began with the organization in 1746 of Lunenburg County and Cumberland Parish, extending westward to the Blue Ridge Mountains. The vestry was active and during the first two years seven churches were built, one of which was located on

[3]*Va. Mag. History,* Vol. 33, p. 217.
[4]*Va. Mag. History,* Vol. 33, p. 210.
[5]Bishop Meade's "Old Churches and Families in Virginia," Vol. 1, p. 151.

Stewart's Creek (Halifax Co.). Burgess Wall[6] tried in 1747 to patent 400 acres on Stuart's Creek, "including the chappel," but the patent was declared void. A grant[7] to John Ray, in 1750, records that "there is a church a building on Peter's Creek" (Patrick Co.). In a patent[8] of 1767 this church was referred to as "the old church on the south fork of Peter's Creek." However great were the bounds of a parish, the vestry arranged for worship throughout its extent. Besides the regularly appointed services conducted by the ministers, on those Sundays when the minister was not present the service of the Church of England was read by members at churches, chapels, and at private homes in neighborhoods in which no church building had yet been erected. These churchmen, known as "lay readers," were regularly appointed by the vestries and received 100 lbs. of tobacco a year for their labors.

With the organization of Halifax County and Antrim Parish in 1752 the church became more active in the county. The vestry meetings were held at the Courthouse which was located at Peytonsburg, and the home of the minister, called the Glebe, was situated[9] on Bye Creek, also in the eastern part of the county. Six new churches were ordered to be erected at once, one of which was on Pigg River;[10] chapels were built on Snow Creek, Potter's Creek, and Leatherwood Creek. Early vestrymen of Antrim Parrish whose homes lay in Pittsylvania were Thomas Calloway, Thomas Dillard, John Donelson, Peter Wilson, Samuel Harris, Hugh Innes and Thomas Tunstall.

In 1767 Pittsylvania County and Camden Parish were organized and at the first meeting of the vestry, held June 21, 1767, at the courthouse, there were present[11] the following vestrymen, "who subscribed in Vestry to be conformable to the Doctrine and Discipline of the Church of England as by Law Established: John Donelson, John Pigg, Hugh Innes, George Rowland, Crispen Shelton, John Wilson, Peter Perkins, Abram Shelton, Theophilus Lacy, Robert Chandler, and William Witcher." Benjamin Lankford was appointed clerk and Abram Shelton and George Rowland church wardens. No other business was recorded in the minutes of this meeting but from the levy laid six months later we learn that the work of the parish as organized while a part of Antrim

[6]Surveyor's Book of Pittsylvania County.
[7]Surveyor's Book of Pittsylvania County, p. 126.
[8]Surveyor's Book of Pittsylvania County, p. 401.
[9]Surveyor's Book of Pittsylvania County.
[10]Meade's "Churches," Vol. 2, p. 1.
[11]Vestry Book of Camden Parish, Pittsylvania County, 1767, 1785.

Parish was continued, with laymen reading the church service at different points in the county:

The Parish Levy laid February 1768:

To Lewis Morgan a Reader 6 mos. .... 50 lbs. Tob.
To John King a Reader 6 mos. .... 50 lbs. Tob.
To John Salmon a Reader 6 mos. .... 50 lbs. Tob.
To Benj. Lankford for being clerk of the vestry 6 mos. .... 500 lbs. Tob.
To John Madden being sexton 6 mos. .... 200 lbs. Tob.
To Collector for collecting 14,920 lbs. Tob. @ 6% .... 250 lbs. Tob.
To Mark Foster for keeping a pensioner .... 200 lbs. Tob.
To Thos. Roberts for maintaining Alex Consolvo 2½ mos. and burying him .... 510 lbs. Tob.
To Samuel Harris for maintaining Milly Harris a pensioner... 10 lbs. Tob.
To George Rowland for necessaries found Milly Harris .... 33 lbs. Tob.
To James Doss for maintaining Judah May and finding her clothing .... 600 lbs. Tob.
To Peter Perkins for necessaries found Matthew Robinson...264 lbs. Tob.

At this second meeting of the Vestry (Feb. 1768) the points at which the laymen were to read the prayers were named as follows:

"Lewis Morgan is ordered to Read at the Chappels at Snow Creek and at Potter's Creek and at the home of William Heard.

"George Britain is ordered to Read at the Chappel at Leatherwood and at the home of George Meredith on the Horse Pasture (Henry Co.).

"Lewis Shelton is ordered to Read at James Faris and at George Parsons."

Abram Shelton was appointed collector of the levy and a committee of John Pigg, John Wilson, George Rowland, Peter Perkins and Abram Shelton were named "to view good and convenient Lands for a Glebe."

One month later the Rev. Alexander Gordon of Halifax County came before the vestry and agreed "for 16,000 lbs. of tobacco to be levy'd for him to preach at Abram Shelton's, at the meeting house at Potter's Creek (Toshes), at Snow Creek Chappel, at Van Bibber's, at Peter Copeland (Henry Co.), at Hamon Critz (Patrick Co.) and at Edward Smiths." At the same time an application from James Stevenson for "a Title of Orders for this Parish was received and the church wardens were ordered to certifie same to the Bishop of London." James Stevenson further agreed that the vestry was at liberty to choose another clergyman after his return (from London) if they did not approve of him. He was evidently just entering the ministry and it was necessary for him to make the 3,000 mile trip across seas in order to be ordained because of the lack of resident bishops. This perilous sea trip no doubt deterred many worthy native Virginians from entering the ministry.

A meeting of the vestry was called again in November, 1768, for the purpose of appointing processioners, pursuant to an order of court. The custom of "processioning" was an old one brought over from England, and was carried out every four years. The General Assembly[12] of 1661 enacted: "The Vestry of each parish shall divide the parish into so many precincts as they shall think necessary for the neighbors to joyne and all each others marke trees of every man's land be re-newed." The expression came from the act of the people going in a procession to see the boundary trees re-cut. It was regarded that boundaries three times processioned were unalterably fixed. The vestry ordered processioners as follows: "Thomas Dillard, Francis Luck, Edmund King and William Chick are appointed to Procession all the patented land below Doss's Road beginning at Doss's on Staunton River. Thence along Doss's Road to Clement Road, thence along Clement Road to Hickey's Road to Haines' thence along Hickey's Road to County line, thence along county line to Staunton River, up Staunton River to Doss's.

"Benjamin Clement, Jr., Adam Clement and Thomas Robinson is appointed to procession all Patented land up Staunton River from the mouth of Reed Creek to the mouth of Pigg River to the Ridge.

"Thomas Bennett, William Bobbit, William Lawson and William Justice is appointed to Procession all Patented land from the mouth of Pigg River on both sides to the mouth of Snow Creek and on to the Ridges," and so on.

James Stevenson made the trip across seas safely and on July 14th, 1769, was received by the vestry, which ordered that his salary be paid from the 21st day of February last. With a resident minister of their own, the vestry now set about organizing the parish for religious worship and ordered the building of four new churches and two chapels as follows:

"Ordered that John Donelson, Crispen Shelton, Thomas Dillard, Jr., and Abram Shelton do let to the Lowest bidder the building of a church ordered to be built near Thos. Mustein's the size to be 24 by 32 feet. A framed house with clap board roof, a plank floor with a pulpit and desk two doors, five windows in it 12 feet in the Pitch, with a Small Table and Benches in it.

[12]Hening's "Statutes," Vol. 2, p. 102.

"Ordered that Theophilus Lacy, John Wilson and John Pigg do let to the lowest Bidder the building of the Church near Sam'l Harris the same size of the other thats to be built near Thos. Mustein's.

"Ordered that Hugh Innes and William Witcher do let to the lowest bidder the building of the church ordered to be built near Snow Creek Chappel—the size of the Former.

"Ordered that George Rowland, Peter Perkins and Robert Chandler do let to the lowest bidder the church ordered to be built near the Road Foard of Leatherwood the size of the former.

"Ordered that Hugh Innes and William Witcher let to the lowest bidder the Chappell of Ease ordered to be built near John Willcox's place the size to be 24 feet by 20 Round loggs for the Body, a clap board Roof with Benches, and etc.

"Ordered that George Rowland and Robert Chandler do let to the lowest bidder the Chappell of Ease ordered to be built near Captain Hamon Critz the same size of the other that's to be built near Wilcox's place."

It would seem that these vestrymen of Camden Parish were conscious of their grave responsibilities and were discharging their duties to the best of their abilities. Besides regular service at the six new churches, nine points were named in the parish at which laymen were ordered to read the Prayers on Sundays, as follows:

"Ordered that the Rev. James Stevenson preach at Edward Smith's instead of Holms Gwynn and at Thomas Farris instead of Abram Shelton.

"Ordered that Lewis Morgan tend at Snow Creek Chappel when the Rev. Mr. Stevenson preaches there and that he read Prayers the other Sundays at William Herd's and at Potter Creek Schoolhouse.

"Ordered that John King read prayers at Benjamine Terrys.

"Ordered that Thomas Flowers attend the Rev. James Stevenson, when he preaches at the Mayo Chappell and that he read prayers the other Sundays at George Rowlands and the horse Pasture.

"Ordered that John Casterson attend the Rev'd James Stevenson when he preaches at Edward Smiths and that he read prayers the other Sundays at George Chadwells.

"Ordered that John Fulton Read the Service of the Church of England every Sunday at Sandy River Meeting house.

"Ordered that Thomas Dillard, Jun., Selicit the Gentlemen of the Vestry of Antrim Parish in the Joining them to build a house for the poor and nothing further being offered these orders were signed by

John Stevenson, Clk.
George Rowland—C. W.
Abram Shelton " "
Ben Lankford C. V. C. P."

Two months later at a meeting of the vestry held on Sept. 12, 1769, a change was made in the location of all the churches and chapels, with the exception of Snow Creek Church. The church that was ordered to be located near Thos. Musteins "be now built at the old muster place between Abram Shelton's and Stinking River." The Leatherwood Ford Church "be now built convenient to a spring near John Acopps." The church to be built near Sam'l Harris "be now built at the best and most convenient spring between William Munkus's and Jacob Whitter's place." The chapel ordered at Wilcox's "be now built at the most convenient spring near the Cross Roads called the Carolina and Chiswell Roads." The chapel to be built near Captain Critz "be now built convenient to the first good spring four miles above Critz."

The churches and chapels were erected at once and at a meeting of the vestry held on Jan. 26, 1770, accounts for building them were presented and paid in so many pounds of tobacco. Sextons were employed and books bought for the churches which thereafter appeared in the vestry minutes as the Sandy River Church, the Stinking River Church, the Leatherwood Church, the Snow Creek Church, the Stoney Creek Chapel (Patrick) and Mayo Chapel (Henry).

The old musterfield between Abram Sheltons and Stinking River lay just below the William Pannill place of Chalk Level, and here a colonial church stood. Mrs. Nannie Pannill Ballard, a daughter of William L. Pannill, told of going often as a child to see an aged and well beloved slave who lived on the plantation in a small house which she was told had once been a church. This was probably the Stinking River Church. The Rev. James Stevenson after serving the Parish for one year resigned. The ministerial work of this frontier county was arduous, requiring powers of great physical endurance on the part of the minister who was probably constantly in the saddle; for the parish embraced in area not only what is now Pittsylvania but also Henry, Patrick and the southern half of Franklin County, the western part of which was rugged and broken by numerous mountain ridges.

Mr. Stevenson was succeeded in 1771 by the Rev. Lewis Guilliam, a native Scotchman whose unsavory conduct brought shame upon both himself and his calling. In the records of the court are many petty law suits in which he figures and in which he was invariably the loser. As no home had been provided for the minister of the parish, Mr. Guilliam was boarded in the home of Mr. John Pigg at a charge of 340 lbs. of tobacco a month, which was paid in addition to his salary of 16,000 pounds of tobacco. Two years later the vestry purchased land for a glebe for the parish of Richard Chamberlayne of New Kent, through his attorney John Pigg, buying 588 acres for 180 pounds current money. This land lay near the Sandy River Meeting House and the building of the glebe dwelling house and out buildings was begun at once.

The work of the parish as outlined by the vestry was carried forward; there were services each Sunday at the various places appointed, and the poor and afflicted were cared for until the year 1776, which ushered in the period of the Revolution. The Church of England and the English government were so closely associated in men's minds that the people of the county with patriotic fervor turned from the Established Church and embraced the new faiths of the Baptist and Methodist Churches. This is evidenced in the minutes of the vestry by the resignations of vestrymen which now began to appear. For nearly twenty years the Baptist faith had been preached through the county by able and earnest men, one of whom, Samuel Harris, was a former vestryman; congregations were being established and churches built. And so far as we know the Church of England in Camden Parish and the Baptist Church labored side by side in peace and amity for the cause of Christ.

After 1778 the old Vestry Book no longer held any entries concerning the churches, only those dealing with the care of the poor. There is one last vestry entry of the year 1785, when a meeting of the Vestry of Camden Parish was held at the home of James Roberts on April 1st, and Haynes Morgan and Abram Shelton, Gents., were appointed to attend a convention to be held in the city of Richmond the 18th day of May. The convention was called by those Virginians who remained true to the faith of their fathers, for the purpose of re-organizing the church which now was called the Protestant Episcopal Church. Thereafter the overseers of the poor "of Camden Parish" as they continued to call themselves, kept the minutes of their meetings in the old Vestry Book up to the year, 1850, when the pages of the book were filled.

After the close of the Revolutionary War and the establishment of our freedom the glebes of the Established Church in Virginia were ordered to be sold by an act of the General Assembly. But prior to that act a committee appointed by Pittsylvania and Henry Counties, composed of William Todd, William Witcher, Archelaus Hughes and Abram Penn had sold the glebe on October 19, 1779, to Epaphraditus White of Halifax for 5150 pounds. The glebe tract was sold again in 1804, when Samuel Calland became the purchaser for 30 pounds, 4 shillings. It was described in the deed as being on both sides of Banister River, crossing Robin's Branch, Little Creek and Wet Sleeve Creek; crossing Hickey's road twice; and being "known by the name of Pittsylvania Old Glebe." The tract contained 588 acres and lay a few miles east of Rondo.

The Episcopal Church now almost disappeared entirely from the county, but there were a faithful few like the Smiths, Slaughters, Millers, Sheltons and the Coles who about 1800 built old Saint Andrews Church at Mount Airy that they might have an occasional service from a visiting clergyman, at the same time freely offering the use of the building to any other denomination. With the coming of Dr. George Washington Dame into the county in 1840 and through his boundless zeal the Episcopal Church was re-established here where it had once been so potent an influence in the lives of the people.

The Presbyterian Church

Many of Pittsylvania's first settlers were of the Presbyterian faith, being Scotch and Scotch-Irish emigrants from Pennsylvania. The Synod of Philadelphia was not unmindful of the brethren who had settled in Southern Virginia and the Carolinas, and from time to time appointed ministers to visit them. In 1753 Mr. Donaldson[1] and Mr. McMordie, young men of Pennsylvania were directed to visit these southern settlements and the following year four other ministers were sent on the same mission. They did not visit eastern Virginia, but coming down the Valley, crossed the Blue Ridge and passed through Bedford and Halifax into North Carolina. As there was a settlement of Scotch-Irish on Staunton River near Leesville, it is almost certain the families of that section were visited.

At this early day the settlements in the county were few and widely separated, and the visit of a minister was a matter of importance. Friends of like faith were sent for and prayers held in private homes, while the children were examined as to their knowledge of the catechism

[1]Records of the Synod of Philadelphia, kept at Philadelphia.

and the scriptures, and the elders exhorted to stand firm in the faith. The Synod of Philadelphia, which held jurisdiction over Virginia at this time, made earnest efforts to watch over the distant flocks, and when we remember that it took six weeks to make the trip on horseback, it is surprising that so many ministers visited this section.

No congregation was organized, however, until the year 1755, when the Rev. Hugh McAlden was sent out to labor within the bounds of Hanover Presbytery, which included most of Virginia and North Carolina. He organized a congregation in this section known as the County Line Creek Church. As no church building could be erected without permission of the court, it was probably for this church that the inhabitants of Halifax petitioned in 1755:

"On the motion of Sundry inhabitants (being Dissenters) leave is granted them to build a meeting House on the lands of William Russell, on the Drafts of Difficult Creek."

Difficult Creek flows into Staunton River on the line between Halifax and what was then Lunenburg County, so that a branch of Difficult would most likely be called County Line Creek. The subsequent history of this church is not known, but having no resident minister it probably fell into disuse.

The first church to be established on Pittsylvania soil was old Wet Sleeve, near Callands, which was organized soon after the Revolution. When the young Scotchman, Samuel Calland, opened his store at Pittsylvania Court House and made his home in the county, he became a power in establishing the Presbyterian faith here. While a man of keenest business sense, who by his industry amassed a fortune, he was at the same time a man of strict piety. On one occasion when one of his patrons sent on Sunday for some articles left at the store, he replied by note:

"Dear Sir, I have you the things you left here the other night by Your Son. The other things that you sent for I have not Got the quarter of and I have not sent any as I make it an unalterable rule never to deal of Asunday. I am Sir Respect Yr H. Serv,

Sam'l Calland

3rd July, 1785."

It was through Callands efforts that the congregation at Wet Sleeve was organized and the Rev. David Barr called to be the resident minister. The church building was probably erected in 1784 for in that year Mr. Barr returned to Callands Store 1,000—10^{d} nails, which we may suppose were more than were needed for the work. Mr. Barr married a young lady of the neighborhood, a Miss Fulton[2] and established his home on Sandy River, on lands gotten from his father-in-law John Fulton. He frequently made purchases for himself and family at Calland's store.

Calland's Day Book has the following entry:

"To Rev. David Barr.

Dec. 14, 1784, by Samuel Calland for his subscription..............................£1.4."

A few days earlier Calland had paid Mr. Barr £1 for William Mitchell, which was probably also a subscription. Mitchell's home was at Callands, where he had built a substantial brick residence, and no doubt his family were members of the Wet Sleeve congregation.

In 1785 David Barr was granted by the Pittsylvania Court a license to perform the marriage ceremony. He did not tarry long in the county but moved to North Carolina, and in 1796 he sold his properties here. The Wet Sleeve church was then ministered to by the Revs. James Mitchell and James Turner of Bedford County, who traveled on horseback the three score miles to give the congregation an occasional service. Wet Sleeve never again had a resident minister, and with only an occasional service from a visiting preacher, the congregation languished. When the Calland family, its main stay, passed away, the church passed too, and this early work is today but a memory.

Samuel Calland's obituary appeared in the *Virginia Gazette,* December 2, 1808:

"Departed this life lately at his seat in Pittsylvania County, Samuel Calland, Esq., High Sheriff of the county aforesaid, in 59th year of his age. Mr. Calland was a native of Scotland and came to this country just before the Revolutionary War. By trade since the War he has acquired a very large property * * *. He possessed a vigorous mind, highly improved by reading and an extensive intercourse with the most enlightened part of society * * *. But he was most admired when seen at home, there no one ever visited him without leaving him with the impression that he was a man formed for the enjoyment of happiness; as a husband he was affectionate; as a father, kind; as a master indulgent; as a friend warm; his hospitality was proverbial * * *. His death will be long lamented by his family and numerous friends, and the public will lose in him a diligent, intelligent and virtuous public servant."

---

[2]The will of John Fulton, proven in 1788 named children James Fulton, Jane Shields, Martha Fulton, Elizabeth Fulton, Edith Robinson, and Mary Barr. In 1797 the Rev. David Barr of Mecklenburg County, N. C., sold 248 acres in Pittsylvania County on Little Stewart's Creek of Sandy River.

A church was established at the town of Danville in the early part of 1800, and devout members of the faith who lived in the county would worship there. But no doubt the Synod continued to care and watch over the faithful ones and at intervals to send out visiting preachers to minister to their needs; for in the early part of the past century licenses to marry were issued by the Pittsylvania Court to John Terry, William L. Turner, James Tompkins, William Plummer, and William McElroy, Presbyterian preachers.

Among those faithful few who adhered to the Presbyterian faith despite their lack of church and minister were Mr. William Clark and his wife, Mrs. Jane Clark, of Pineville, and the families of Thomas and Richard Jones. Upon the tombstone of Mrs. Jane Clark, in the family burial plot at "Pineville," there is inscribed the statement that she was a member of the Presbyterian Church.

In 1846 a church was built and a congregation organized at Pittsylvania Court House. The Rev. William Matthews was soon called to the church and throughout his long and saintly life labored among the people of Pittsylvania County, who hold his memory in reverence and affection.

The Baptist Church

Pittsylvania has played a distinguished part in the founding and spread of the Baptist faith in Virginia; for upon its soil was established in 1760 the first Separate Baptist Church in Virginia, "which," said Semple, "was in some sense the mother of all the rest"; and here also lived two of the earliest Virginia preachers, Dutton Lane and that man of God, Samuel Harris.

The Separate Baptist (so called because of their separation from the Established Church) took their rise in New England about 1744. The spread of their teachings began in the South with the removal of Shubal Stearns and Daniel Marshall, two New England preachers, to Guilford County, North Carolina, in November, 1755, where they at once established the Sandy River Church with sixteen members. From this point Stearns and Marshall traveled through the adjacent country, preaching and exhorting the people to repentance, and on their first trip to Virginia made many converts, one of whom was Dutton Lane of Pittsylvania (then Halifax Co.). Shortly after Lane's conversion he began to preach—a revival followed and at one time 42 persons were baptized. In 1760 these converts were organized into the Dan River Church, the first Separate Baptist Church in Virginia. It is not known at this day just where this early historic church of Pittsylvania stood, for it has long since ceased to exist; but to followers of the Baptist faith the site of that ancient meeting house should be hallowed soil.

Semple[1] said of the Dan River Church—"the church prospered under the ministry of Mr. Lane. They endured much persecution but God prospered them and delivered them out of the hands of all their enemies." Dutton Lane, the minister, was a native of Maryland, and was born November 7, 1732, near Baltimore, and moved with his father's family down to Pittsylvania when a small lad. In 1746, when this section had just been incorporated in the county of Lunenburg, Richard Lane, Sr.,[2] Richard Lane, Jr., Tidence Lane and John Fuller Lane patented lands along Elkhorn Creek; and from 1748 to 1770 Dutton Lane was granted lands in different sections of the county.

The Separate Baptists believed in the immediate working of the spirit of God, and taught that to those who earnestly sought God gave "evident tokens of his will." They spoke with deep feeling and strong gestures, and being deeply affected themselves, Semple says, "correspondent affections were felt by their pious hearers which were frequently expressed by tears, treblings, screams, shouts and acclamations. * * * And the people were greatly astonished, never having seen things in this wise." The earnestness of their exhortations won hosts of converts in Pittsylvania for the new faith. After several churches had been established Elder Shubal Stearns "conceived[3] that an association composed of delegates from all these would have a tendency to impart stability and uniformity to the whole." Accordingly the first association was held in January 1760 at Stearn's church in North Carolina, the Sandy River Meeting House, to which eight churches sent delegates, two of which were in Virginia, the Dan River Church, represented by Samuel Harris and the Lunenburg County Church, represented by William Murphy.

Samuel Harris of Pittsylvania County was the foremost man of Virginia in establishing the Baptist faith in this state, and was so recognized and held in the highest esteem by the church. From the time of the organization of the Virginia Association in 1771, until overcome by the frailties of age, about 1790, Harris almost invariably served as moderator of all meetings of the Association and general committees. And when in 1774 it was decided that the church should have an

---

[1]Semple's "History of the Baptist in Virginia."

[2]Dutton Lane was grandson of Dutton Lane of Baltimore County, whose will was proven in 1726, naming wife Pretiosa Tidings and sons Dutton, Tidence and Samuel. John Fuller Lane married Elizabeth Cloud, daughter of Isaac Cloud, and had issue: Dutton, Tidence and Sarah Lane, who married Zacherias McCubbin, son of William McCubbin, also of Baltimore County, Maryland.

[3]Semple, p. 6.

apostolic head, Harris was unanimously chosen for the position, and termed "the Apostle of Virginia." The office, however, was afterwards abolished.

Samuel Harris was born in Hanover County, Jan. 12, 1724. Semple said of him: "Few men could boast of more respectable parentage. When young he moved to the County of Pittsylvania; and as he advanced in age became a favorite with the people as well as with the rulers. He was appointed church warden (vestryman of the Established Church), Sheriff, a justice of the peace, burgess for the County, Colonel of the militia, Captain of Mayo Fort and commissary for the fort and Army." His conversion to the Baptist faith is described[4] as follows:

"On one of his routes to visit the forts in his official capacity he rode up, splendidly attired in his military habit, as the people were collecting at a small house near Allen's Creek on the road leading from Booker's Ferry on Staunton River to Pittsylvania Courthouse (Peytonsburg's).

'What is to be done here, gentlemen?' said Harris.

'Preaching, Colonel.'

'Who is to preach?'

'The Murphy boys, sir.'

'I believe I will stop and hear them'; whereupon Harris dismounted." The house was small and in one corner stood a loom, behind which he seated himself, not wishing to appear in a conspicuous manner. He was deeply affected by the preaching, and in great agony of thought cast away his sword and other insignia of his office. This probably occurred in 1757, for it was during the period of the French and Indian War; and he was baptized in 1758, by Elder Marshall. The following year, relinquishing all his wordly honors, he entered the ministry and gave himself wholly to preaching the Gospel.

Harris devoted the first seven years of his labors to his own county and section, and it was during these years that he together with Dutton Lane and the Murphy boys carried the message through Henry, Patrick, Franklin and Bedford counties. (When these four counties became the Strawberry Association, was the name chosen in honor of Harris's home on Strawberry Creek?) About 1765 Harris widened his field and traveled extensively through Virginia and Carolina, exhorting the people and winning hosts of souls to the new faith. It is said "there is scarcely any place in Virginia in which he did not sow the Gospel seed." Ireland said[5] of him:

[4]Semple.

[5]Taylor's "Lives of Baptist Ministers," Vol. 1, p. 32.

"He was like another Paul among the churches. No man was like minded with him. As the sun in his strength, he passed thro' the State displaying the glory of his adorable Master, and spreading his light and heat to the consolation of thousands." Harris spoke with great power and conviction, and Semple said "his manners were of the most winning sort, * * * with a talent for touching the feelings; * * * perhaps even Whitfield did not surpass him in addressing the heart."

Harris's home in Pittsylvania was situated in the southwestern part of the county, on the head waters of Strawberry Creek. He was a large land owner, and in the year[6] 1777 he paid taxes on 4,000 acres and ten slaves. "Being[7] in easy circumstances when he became religious he devoted not only himself but almost all of his property to religious objects. He had begun a large new dwelling house, suitable to his former dignity; which as soon as it was covered in he appropriated to the use of public worship, continuing to live in the old one. After maintaining his family in a very frugal manner he distributed his surplus income to charitable purposes." Although Harris devoted his new dwelling to public worship there is no record of a church and congregation being organized there. At the first Virginia Association, 1771, fourteen churches were represented, two of which were the old Dan River Church and the Falls Creek Church, both of Pittsylvania. The Falls Creek Church sent as delegates Samuel Harris and Jacob Metciff, and reported 62 members. It is hardly probable that Harris's dwelling on Strawberry Creek would be named the Falls' Creek Church.

Many anecdotes have been preserved concerning this remarkable man. It is told[8] that soon after Harris' conversion to the Baptist faith he went to Fort Mayo to preach to the soldiers and officers there whom he had known well in his official capacity. "In the course of his harangue an officer interrupted him saying, 'Colonel, you have sucked much eloquence from the rum cask today: Pray give us a little that we may declaim as well when it comes to our turn.' Harris replied, 'I am not drunk,' and resumed his discourse. He had not gone far when he was accosted by another in a serious manner, who looking in his face said:

'Sam, you say you are not drunk, are you not mad then? What the devil ails you?'

Colonel Harris replied in the words of Paul:

'I am not mad most noble gentlemen.'

He continued speaking publicly and privately until one of the gentlemen received such impressions as were never afterwards shaken off."

[6]List of Tithables of Pittsylvania County, 1777.
[7]Semple.
[8]Semple, p. 38.

The following incident[9] occurred towards the end of his ministry. "A criminal who had just been pardoned at the gallows met Harris in the road and showed him his reprive.

'Well,' said he, 'have you shown it to Jesus?'

'No, Mr. Harris, I want you to do that for me.'

The old man immediately descended from his horse in the road, making the man also alight. They both kneeled down, Mr. Harris with one hand on the man's head and the other holding the pardon out. Thus in behalf of the criminal he returned thanks for his reprive and prayed for him to obtain God's pardon also."

It is a striking fact that though Harris was the first to boldly proclaim the new faith in so many different parts of Virginia, yet he suffered little persecution. Taylor explains this saying, "his influence in society previously to his conversion as well as his naturally fearless spirit, contributed much to his advantage." As moderator of the Baptist Association Harris signed the petition presented to the General Assembly in 1780, asking that ministers of all denominations be permitted to perform the marriage ceremony at all times and in all places. The petition was granted and at a Court held for Pittsylvania County in June, 1781, "Samuel Harris, John Bailey, Lazarus Dodson and Lewis Shelton came into court and produced recommendations from the Elders of the Baptist Church as ministers of that Society and are hereby authorized to and empowered to join together in holy estate of matrimony." Bailey, Dodson and Shelton were local preachers.

Harris died at his home in Pittsylvania in 1799, where he was buried, but no stone marks the resting place of the Apostle of Virginia. In his will he requested that his funeral sermon be preached from 2nd Timothy, Chapter 4, verses 7 and 8; and emancipated five of his slaves in reward for their faithful service to him. (Will was witnessed by Christopher Conway, Allen Stokes and George Sutherlin.)

Harris established two early churches in the county, County Line Church in 1771 and Old Banister in 1773. County Line Church is situated at the dividing line between Pittsylvania and Halifax, not far from Peytonsburg, on the old road leading to Booker's Ferry. The first church building was erected that year, and its present constitution adopted. Being deeply sensible of their spiritual duty to their slaves, these early Virginia Baptists opened the doors of the churches to their colored brethren. In 1781 the membership of County Line Church consisted of "34 white brethren and sisters and ten black brethren and sisters." The

[9]Semple.

church minutes record: "August 26, 1786, the church met and drew up plans to build a new meeting house at or near the place where the old meeting house formerly stood, on a piece of land given by Luke Williams for that purpose." This was a brick building and used for 96 years.

Upper or Old Banister was located three miles south of Chatham, near the present Chatham and Danville highway, and in 1774 numbered 200 members in the congregation, being the largest church in the state. Here, many years later, took place that division in the church body which resulted in the Missionary Baptist and the Old or Primitive Baptist Churches. During the year 1927 the Old Baptists erected a new church building near the site of this historic early church.

The oldest Baptist church in the county which has continued an active congregation until today is the Kentuck, or Mill Church, as it was first known. This church was organized in 1770 by John Creel, a Regular Baptist, who in 1765 had moved from Fauquier County down into Pittsylvania. In 1806 "a slave named Adam, the property of the late John Creel, deceased," was emancipated by John Creel, Jr., John Shelton and Abiel Wilson, who were probably fulfilling a last wish of the aged pastor. The Kentuck Church building today is a handsome frame structure and there is an active and large membership.

Whitethorn Church was founded in 1787 by Matthew Bates of Halifax County and is situated on the road leading from Galveston to Mill Creek. This has remained a congregation of the Old Baptists.

John Jenkins, born in Loudon County in 1758, was an early and notable preacher in the county. He moved with his parents to Pittsylvania during the Revolutionary War, in which he served as commissary to the army, and was probably employed by the post at Peytonsburg. In 1796 he was ordained to the ministry and his talents being meager, no great future was expected of him. But he applied himself so diligently to study that he became a proficient scholar, with an understanding of the Greek, Latin and Hebrew languages. 'Twas said of him that he was perhaps the best educated man of his day in the Roanoke Association. Illustrative of his perseverance—when he desired the use of globes in his study and had no money to purchase them, he made a pair with his own hands, "which," 'tis said, "were well executed." Through his untiring efforts he became a preacher of marked ability. In 1795 he established a church at Lower Banister or Riceville; and a few years later a church at Shockoe.

The Shockoe Church was ever mindful of the colored people, and six months after its organization the minutes read: "Alba, a negro woman, the property of John Irby, was received into the membership of the church by experience." This congregation exerted an active religious care over the slaves, reserving the rear of the church for their use at all seasons. In the church yard at Shockoe was laid to rest in 1833 that fearless old soldier of Christ, John Weatherford, who in his day suffered much persecution. Jenkins' tomb is not far distant from the Riceville Church, where a simple slab marks his last resting place.

Griffith Dickenson, another early Baptist minister of the county, was born in Hanover County in 1757, and when a young man came to Pittsylvania, where in 1787 he married Susanna, a daughter of Crispen Shelton, Gent. Like Jenkins he was a veteran of the Revolutionary War. He became a convert under the preaching of Elder Jenkins, and when in 1800 the Greenfields church was organized at Chalk Level (taking its name from the Coles's home), Dickenson became the pastor of the church, and labored there for over forty years. His old home, with adz-hewn beams and corner fire places is still standing; and his tomb in the family burial plot crowns a nearby hill.

Pittsylvania County lies within the bounds of the Roanoke Association, of which Semple wrote in 1810: "It may with safety be said that within her limits the Baptist cause has flourished more than in any section of the State of Virginia, not to say of the United States."

The Methodist Church

Methodism was first introduced into Virginia in 1772 by Robert Williams who preached on the court house steps of Norfolk. The following year Williams was laboring at Petersburg and in the country round about. At the first American Conference, held at Philadelphia in 1773, of the ten preachers stationed, two were in Virginia—Wright at Norfolk and Williams at Petersburg. The latter preached through the counties south of Petersburg with great effect, forming many "societies" as the congregations were first called. The Rev. Devereux Jarratt, the minister of the Church of England for Dinwiddie County and "a pure and zealous[1] preacher of the gospel, was a warm friend of the early Methodist preachers." He and Robert Williams ably assisted one another in their work of saving souls. Brunswick, including Petersburg, was the first circuit formed in Virginia and reported at Conference in 1774 two hundred and eighteen members. In 1775 six preachers[2] were appointed

[1] "Methodism in Virginia," by Bennett, pp. 60-65.
[2] "Methodism in Virginia," by Bennett, p. 74.

to Virginia, nearly one-third of the whole number that composed Conference: Norfolk, Francis Asbury; Brunswick, George Shadford, Robert Lindsey, Edward Drongoole, Robert Williams, and William Glendenning. These men traveled through the country preaching by day and night, "and the word of God fell with power on the hearts of the people, and the flame of revival spread throughout the vast field." One of the greatest religious revivals known in Virginia followed their work, of which George Shadford was the leader. All the adjacent counties shared in the great awakening. Some one of these preachers must have traveled up to Pittsylvania at this time for at the Fourth Annual Conference held in Baltimore in 1776, Pittsylvania was one of the four new circuits added, reporting one hundred members. Isaac Rawlins was appointed to the circuit, and under his charge fifty new members were added. In 1777 the work in Pittsylvania was assigned to John Sigman and Isham Tatum; in 1778 to William Gill, John Major and Henry Willis. These men entered upon their duties with spirit and their labors met with much success, for the membership in the circuit had increased in 1779 to five hundred. A very early church was built at this time in the Southwestern part of the county, called Watson's Meeting-house, but nothing is known of the Watson from whom it took its name. Bishop Asbury preached there several times.

Bishop Francis Asbury, one of the first Bishops of the Church, spent forty-five years of his life traveling back and forth through the Atlantic States, visiting the people, exhorting those of the faith to stand firm and calling sinners to repentance. He lived in his saddle, riding many miles each day through sun and heat, rain and snow, preaching from house to house, for in the early days there were few church buildings. In Asbury's journals there is mention of several Pittsylvania homes which he visited and from which he preached to large assemblies.

The journal reads:[3]

"Sunday, August 13, 1780 I rode to Watson's preaching-house, a round log building after the plan of this part of the country. There were about five hundred people. I spoke of the parable of the sower, a lengthy discourse. There was a moving.

"Monday 14th, I brought Isaac Rawlins to some acknowledgment (of his error) and appointed him to ride Pittsylvania, New Hope and Tar River Circuits till Conference. I hope this will be a warning to him and make him take more care and submit to order. I preached at Col. Wilson's to about two hundred people.

[3]Asbury's Journal, Vol. 1, pp. 392-3.

"Tuesday 15th, I rode thirty miles to Mr. Martin's, the roads and creeks are rendered bad for traveling by the late freshets.

"Wednesday 16th, I preached at Dowdy's store to about three hundred people, some gay ones. The people were attentive. I had been very unwell traveling down Dan River, and among the creeks, am in danger of the fever and ague. We were obliged to swim the horses over Birch's creek, and bring the carriage over the shattered bridge.

"Thursday 17th, I stopped at friend Baker's, being very unwell. This has made it an additional burden to travel, and the sun is so violent, that it appears to me I could not stand it, were it not for the top carriage. I rested comfortable, retired ofter to prayer. I suppose I have ridden better than a thousand miles since Feb. last.

"Friday 18th, I rode twelve miles to Boyd's church, about sixty people. I asked the people if they chose to hear the service (of the English Church); they did and I read as far as the first lesson.

"Saturday 19th, I rode to brother Parish's, ten miles, crossed Shoko Creek at the Fish-trap, a very bad ford, occasioned by the late freshet that rose near forty feet."

Again in 1791, Bishop Asbury recorded[4] a visit to Pittsylvania, entering the County from North Carolina:

"April 1791. We rode seven miles to the banks of Dan River, but knew not where to cross. At length we came to the Fishery, crossed in a canoe, and walked two miles to T. Harrison's.

"Sunday 10th. Dr. Coke and myself both preached at Watson's Church and there was some little effect produced. I spent the evening with George Adams,[5] a true son of his worthy father, Silvanus Adams, for kindness to preachers. We moved from G. Adams to the widow Dick's, and thence next day to brother Martin's.

"Wednesday 13th. Came to Difficult Church where we were honored with the company of some of the great."

In 1799 the now aging Bishop again visited the Pittsylvania Circuit. He recorded in his journal:[6]

"Monday, September 23, 1799. I crossed Staunton River and rode into Halifax County; we made it thirty miles to Hawkins Landrum.

[4]Asbury's Journal, Vol. 2, p. 113.

[5]George Adams' will was proven in August, 1866, in which he named daughters Justina and Lizzie Wilson, Mary E. Dick and Emma E. Wilson; executors John R. Wilson and Robert P. Dick. The slaves had been freed, but he willed to "Ned, Jack and Susan (formerly my slaves) the sum of $50.00, each, in consideration of their faithful service and good conduct towards me." His daughter Emma had married Dr. John R. Wilson, son of Major George Wilson, of "Laurel Cliff," and they established the now well known estate of "Oak Ridge," with its beautiful gardens. Dr. Wilson and his wife, Emma, had two daughters, Lizzie and Jessie, who now preside over the home of their father.

[6]Asbury's Journal, Vol. 2, p. 425.

Tuesday we had a large congregation and an affecting time upon the banks of the Banister River; here I saw only two persons that I was acquainted with twenty years ago—they were brother Baker and his wife.

"September 25th. We rode to Armistead Shelton's in Pittsylvania twenty miles: we stopped to dine, pray and feed our horses at Clement McDaniel's; the roads were much broken in some places and it was as much as we could do to reach Shelton's by sun set. My mind is calm, my body in better health.

"September 26th. A congregation of from three to five hundred attended Divine worship: On Friday we rode twelve miles to Carter's (Thomas Carter of 'Green Rock'), where a large company attended; my subject was, 'What shall the end be of them that obey not the gospel of God'."

Mrs. Carter, formerly Winnefred Hobson of Cumberland County, had become a convert to Methodism before their removal to Pittsylvania, and being acquainted with Bishop Asbury wrote asking him to include her new home in his journeyings north and south. At his coming the people of the neighborhood were notified, who gathered at "Green Rock" to hear the Bishop preach. Being a man of low stature, in order to address the crowd Asbury asked for something upon which to stand. The most convenient thing at the time was one of the liquor cases belonging to Thomas Carter. They were stoutly built and covered with leather, and upon his first visit Bishop Asbury preached from the top of one of the cases. Piqued at her husband's teasing, Mrs. Carter had a pulpit built which she kept in her parlor. Thereafter upon the visits of the clergy the pulpit was carried out on the lawn by the servants and from this elevation they addressed the assembled neighbors.

The journal continued:

"Saturday 28th. We had to travel a most uneven path up Sandy River to George Adams', twenty miles.

"Sunday 29th. I attended at Watson's Meeting-house. Baptized several children, visited brethren Trahan and Church, from Maryland, who have been Methodist twenty-five years. Crossed Dan River at Perkins' Ferry to North Carolina."

James Hinton and James Robinson were early ministers of the Methodist Church who labored in the county. Their bonds for the performance of the marriage ceremony were dated 1785. James Reed was another very early minister in the county and inclosed in his minister's bond is the following note:

"This is to certify that James Reed is a member of the Methodist Episcopal Church, is approved of as a local preacher, and is permitted to exercise his gifts amongst our Societies by way of preaching and exhortation.

Henry Merrill Elder M. E. C.
October 31, 1791. In behalf of Conference."

Though Methodism found many followers in the County, it was not until 1823 that deeds were recorded for the erection of churches. In that year Nathaniel Wray made a deed of gift of one acre to the Methodists for the building of a church. In 1827[7] Rawley Williamson Carter and his wife Anne gave a lot for the erection of a church, making the deed to the following trustees: Augustine H. Carter, Jeduthan Carter, Ira Ellis, Reuben Hopkins, William A. Lilly, Nicholas Ellis and John Pinnell. In the same year Robert Wilson and his wife Katherine gave a lot for a church building "on the road leading from the Courthouse to Crafts." In 1830[8] Robert Devin and his wife Nancy gave one acre for the erection of a church to the following trustees: William, John, Henry, Joshua and Robert Pritchett, William Tarpley, John M. Inge and T. C. Shelton. In the year 1832 there were five Methodist churches built in the county. Walter Fitzgerald gave one acre for the building of a church on the road leading from Pittsylvania Courthouse to Leaksville. Nathaniel Wilson and wife Winnefred gave a lot in Danville on the corner of Wilson and Lynn Streets, the church to face on Wilson Street. Nathaniel and James Sutherlin, attorneys for Adams Sutherlin, gave a lot for a church building on the head waters of Sandy Creek. John Ware and Elizabeth,[9] his wife, gave land for a church, "on the north side of the public road below Bachelor's Hall," naming as Methodist trustees, George Wilson, Robert Wilson, George Adams, Samuel Hairston, Joseph Perkins, Henry Serjeant and William Dupuy. George Tosh and Katherine his wife gave one acre for a Methodist church "on the road leading from Samuel Berger's store to Daniel Crider's mill," naming as trustees, David Berger, Thomas Wright, William Crider, John McCrickard and Robert Thurman.

[7]Deed Book No. 29, pp. 153, 219.
[8]Deed Book No. 32, p. 21.
[9]Deed Book No. 34, pp. 200, 206, 358.

Chapter X

PRE-REVOLUTIONARY DAYS

In 1768 Lord Norbonne de Botetourt, a new governor, arrived in Virginia. He forthwith issued a call for an election of Burgesses, which accordingly met at the capitol in Williamsburg on May 1, 1769.

There was much friction at this time between England and the American Colonies over the question of taxation and Lord Botetourt had been instructed to impress the people with a sense of England's authority and dignity. Col. John Donelson, the county surveyor, and Mr. Hugh Innes, a lawyer, were elected to represent Pittsylvania in the House of Burgesses at this Assembly, and both gentlemen were present and witnessed the elegant scene of Governor Botetourt's arrival at the capitol in a state coach presented to him by the king and drawn by eight milk white horses. Governor Botetourt opened the Assembly with all the formality of a British Parliament, but mere pomp could not dampen the spirit of this enlightened body of men.

Since the governor had no particular business for them to consider, the House began to discuss the subject of taxes. The Stamp Act had been repealed, but later England had laid a tax on paper, glass, tea and painter's colors. The House drew up a set of resolves in which they set forth that "the right of imposing taxes in Virginia is now, and ever has been vested in the House of Burgesses, according to the ancient and established practice." It was further agreed that an address should be presented to the king himself, setting forth their grievances.

The Governor becoming alarmed at these proceedings, summoned the House of Burgesses to the Council Chamber and said to them: "Gentlemen, I have heard of your resolves, and auger ill of their effects. You have made it my duty to dissolve you, and you are dissolved accordingly."

But the House of Burgesses were not one bit awed by the Governor's action and repaired to a private house and continued their meeting. They organized a Non-Importation Association, agreeing not to import or to buy of others things imported from England until the tax was removed from paper, tea and glass. A long paper was drawn up stating their wrongs, followed by eight resolves, which was signed by the gentlemen present, and later circulated through the country for other signatures. The Association was sponsored by George Washington, Thomas Jefferson, Patrick Henry and other great Virginia leaders, and with their signatures[1] are not only those of John Donelson and Hugh Innes but also Nathaniel Terry and John Wilson, representing home thought.

We may well know that a deep sense of the gravity of the situation with the mother country was beginning to invade all men's minds, and that at gatherings on muster fields, at church and at court, the subject of the unjust taxes was discussed with deep interest.

The House of Burgesses was convened again in November of that year, at which time a great many different subjects were considered and laws enacted. It was determined that every burgess should be paid ten shillings a day by his county for his service in attending the General Assembly, and that the burgesses from Halifax and Pittsylvania should be allowed six days for going and six days for returning, the trip being made on horseback. It was at this session that the town of Chatham was established at Pittsylvania Courthouse. A fine of twenty shillings a month was laid on any person building a wooden chimney in the new town as a precaution against fire.

Matters relative to the Indians were also considered and Colonel John Donelson, of Pittsylvania, was appointed to represent Virginia in a conference with the Cherokee Chiefs at Lochabor, South Carolina in 1770. At this conference a treaty was drawn up respecting the boundary lines between Virginia and the Cherokee Nation, in which Virginia's western frontiers were obtained; for the Cherokees claimed that their territory extended eastward to the Peaks of Otter. Colonel Donelson was accompanied at the conference by Major Lankford, also of Pittsylvania.

In 1772 Colonel Donelson was appointed to survey the State Line to the westward, which he did, designating certain limits for the Indians; at this time he marked out a route for emigrants to follow going into Kentucky. He then called the Cherokee chiefs to a conference at the Long Island of the Holstein River and gained their consent to and approval of all that he had done.

Colonel Donelson and Mr. Hugh Innes represented Pittsylvania in the House of Burgesses until 1774, which ushered in the period of the Revolution.

Hostilities which had been smoldering for some time broke out afresh between the Indians and whites in 1774, and a force under the command of Col. Andrew Lewis was organized for defense. Pittsylvania was called upon for troops. A letter[2] from Col. William Preston to Col. Arthur Campbell August 14, 1774, stated: "I have demanded 100 men

[1] Burk's "History of Virginia."
[2] Dunmore's "War," p. 140.

with proper Officers from the County Lieutenant of Pittsylvania to cover the Frontiers in the absence of the Troops. Those will be employed from the Head of Clinch to Culbersons." Major Campbell[3] replied to Col. Preston: "I hope levies from Bedford and Pittsylvania is arrived at New River."

The force under Col. Lewis marched northward toward the Ohio to meet and join forces with Lord Dunmore in order to make an attack upon the Indian towns. The Indians attacked Lewis before he had overtaken Dunmore and the battle of Point Pleasant was fought October 10th, 1774. Samuel Crawley, a Pittsylvanian lost his life in this battle as shown by a petition presented to the General Assembly by his wife, Elizabeth Crawley, asking aid for herself and small children, which was granted, £25 for present relief and a yearly pension of £20.

At the Continental Congress of 1774 it was resolved that the Colonies would neither buy from nor sell to Great Britain, and this agreement to boycott the mother country's trade was called the Continental Association. Towns and counties were authorized to form committees to see that the Association was carried into effect, and Virginia lost no time in carrying out the instructions.

The committees were chosen from among the most experienced and reputable men in the county, and there has been preserved in a newspaper of the day an account of Pittsylvania's selection of her Committee of Safety.

Virginia Gazette, February 11, 1775:

"The freeholders of the County of Pittsylvania, being duly summoned, convened at the Courthouse of the said county on Thursday the 26th day of January, 1775, and there proceeded to make choice of a committee, agreeable to the direction of the General Congress, for enforcing and putting into execution the Association, when the following gentlemen were chosen members of the same, viz: Abraham Shelton,[4] Robert Wil-

[3]Dunmore's "War," p. 194.

[4]Abram Shelton was active in the life of the county, serving as justice, vestryman, militia officer, sheriff and member of General Assembly. He was the son of Crispen Shelton who with his brothers John and Daniel Shelton, moved from Amelia County to Pittsylvania about 1765, and settled in the upper part of the Meadows, where they owned large bodies of land.

Abram Shelton married Chloe Robertson of Amelia, January 16, 1760, (Amelia Marriage Bonds); his will was proven at Pittsylvania C. H. in 1789 in which he named wife Chloe, daughters Lettie, Anne and Jane Shelton, sons Abram, Crispen, (Doctor) Tavenor, Frederick, Meacon, Robertson and William. His home was on Buck Branch, near Chalk Level. Dr. Tavenor Shelton was one of the early physicians of the county.

The will of Mrs. Chloe Robertson Shelton was proven February 20, 1804, in which she left her estate to her beloved daughter, Jane Stone, wife of John Stone.

liams,[5] Thomas Dillard, William Todd,[6] Abraham Penn,[7] Peter Perkins, Benjamin Lankford, Thomas Terry,[8] James Walker,[9] William Peters Martin, Daniel Shelton,[10] William Ward,[11] Edmund Taylor, Isaac Clement,[12] Gabriel Shelton,[13] Peter Wilson,[14] William Short, Henry Con-

[5]Robert Williams and his brother Colonel Joseph Williams settled in North Carolina prior to the Revolution, and married sisters, Sarah and Rebecca Lanier, daughters of Thomas Lanier, an early justice of Lunenburg County, who later moved to North Carolina (Wheeler's "Reminiscences of North Carolina"). Sarah Lanier and Robert Williams were married October 10, 1774 (Marriage bond at Oxford, N. C.), and moved to Pittsylvania County to live, settling near Sandy Creek of Banister River. Here he practiced his profession of law and served as commonwealth attorney for both Pittsylvania and Henry Counties. He died in 1790, and the inventory of his estate showed much silver, books, and elegance of living; he left no will but in 1799 there was a division of his estate as follows:

To Col. John Williams and wife Elizabeth, 617 acres, including Manor Plantation on Sandy Creek.

To Nathaniel W. Williams, 1,540 acres, beginning on John White's line, taking in the mill.

To Micajah Watkins and Sarah his wife, 240 acres and 1,156 acres.

To Patsy Williams, 279 acres, the balance of 2,866 acres land of the Manor Plantation, 147 acres, the mill tract 168 acres on Cascade Creek.

To Fanny Williams 200 acres, 296 acres and 790 acres.

Patsy Williams married John Henry of Woodlawn.

[6]William Todd of Chesterfield County, settled first in Halifax and about 1770 moved to Pittsylvania County where he married Jane Shelton, the daughter of Crispen Shelton. He was active in the early life of the county, filling various positions of trust such as justice of peace, officer of militia and sheriff. William Todd (5) was the son of Richard Todd (4) of King and Queen County and his wife, Elizabeth Richards, who had issue: William Todd (5) of Pittsylvania, Richard (5) of Pittsylvania, Mildred (5) who married Thomas Tunstall, and Thomas (5), who went to Kentucky in 1785 with Harry Inness and became chief justice in 1806. Richard Todd (4) of King and Queen County, who died in 1766, was the son of William Todd (3) and his wife Martha Vicaris, who were married in 1709. William Todd (3) was the son of Thomas Todd (2), born 1660, and his wife Elizabeth Bernard. Thomas Todd (2) was the son of Thomas Todd (1), of Gloucester, who died in England, 1677, and his wife Ann Gorsuch, daughter of the Rev. John Gorsuch, of England, and his wife Ann Lovelace, daughter of Sir William Lovelace (1584-1627) and Anne Barne, his wife. Anne Barne who died in 1632, was the niece of Sir Edwin Sandys and George Sandys, those two staunch friends and supporters of the Early Virginia Colony. (*Va. Magazine of History.*)

[7]Abram Penn lived in that part of Pittsylvania that later became Henry County, and was a member of the Penn family that descended from Moses Penn, who married Catherine Taylor, daughter of John Taylor of Caroline.

[8]Thomas Terry was the son of Joseph Terry, whose will was proven at Pittsylvania Courthouse in 1785, naming sons David Terry, Thomas Terry, Joseph Terry, Shampness Terry, deceased; daughters Anne Barksdale, Lucy Williams, Elizabeth Oliver; executors Beverly Barksdale, Thomas Terry and David Terry.

Thomas Terry was the grandson of Benjamin Terry, Senior, whose will was proven at Pittsylvania Courthouse, September 1771, naming sons Nathaniel, Benjamin, Peter, Joseph and Robert Terry.

[9]James Walker's estate was divided by Court in 1783, his two daughters Susannah and Wilmoth being his heirs. Wilmoth Walker married James Mastin Williams and Susannah Walker married William McCraw.

[10]Daniel Shelton was the son of Mrs. Mary Shelton Clark whose will was written in Amelia in 1750 and probated at Pittsylvania Courthouse in 1770; she named sons Ralph, John, Crispen, Benjamin, James and Daniel Shelton, leaving to Daniel the greater share of her estate. Daniel Shelton's will was probated September 18, 1809, in which he named wife Lettie Shelton, sons Young, Leroy, Tunstall, David and Willis; daughters Milly Taylor, Anne Bailey, Sally Payne, Clary and Polly Shelton.

[11]William Ward was the son of Major John Ward and his wife Anne Chiles Ward, whose home, "The Mansion," lay across Staunton River in Campbell County. Major Ward's will proven in 1813, named following children: 1. William Ward, born 1745, married Mildred Adams. 2. Agatha Ward, married Col. John Calloway. 3. Anne Ward, married 1st Christopher Lynch, 2nd Benj. Dillard. 4. Jeremiah Ward. 5. Thomas Ward married Mildred Walden. 6. John Ward of "Sulphur Springs," Pittsylvania. 7. Henry Ward, married Martha Barbour.

William Ward, and his wife Mildred Adams (daughter of Robert Adams and his wife Penelope Lynch), had issue: Robert A. Ward married Betsy Terrell; John Ward married Tabitha Walden and lived at "Edge Hill" on Staunton River; Sally Ward married Samuel Smith, son of John Smith of "The Pocket"; Mildred Ward married Dr. Lynch Dillard.

Captain William Ward was a man of large property and was active in the life of the county, serving as a justice of the peace, member of Committee of Safety in 1775, captain of the militia, and sheriff of the county in 1792. His home was in the northern part of the county on Staunton River.

[12]Isaac Clement, the son of Captain Benjamin Clement and his wife Susanna Hill, was born 1733. He married Anne Denham of Wales and had issue three sons, Hugh, Stephen and Isaac, Jr. About 1798 he moved to Pendleton District, S. C., and was accompanied by two of his sons:; Stephen, who had married Susanna Palmer of Halifax County, remained in the county and inherited his father's

way, John Payne, Sr., Joseph Roberts,[15] William Witcher, Henry Williams, John Salmon, Rev'd Lewis Guilliam,[16] Richard Walden,[17] Peter Saunders,[18] John Wilson, and Crispen Shelton.[19]

"The Committee then proceeded to make choice of Robert Williams for their chairman and William Peters Martin their Clerk.

"During the time of choosing the said committee, the utmost good order and harmony was observed, and all the inhabitants of the county then present (which was very numerous) seemed determined and resolute in defending their liberties and properties, at the risk of their lives, and if required, to die by their fellow sufferers (the Bostonians) whose cause

---

estate, "Cherry Grove," near Straightstone. Stephen Clement's will proven in 1856, named among other children daughter Anne Denham Clement, wife of Rawley Thompson.

[13]Gabriel Shelton was the son of Crispen Shelton. His will was proven June 1803, naming sons Wyatt, Gregory, Gabriel, Beverley and Samuel. His home was at Chalk Level, joining the lands of Pannell and Buford.

[14]Peter Wilson was a brother of Col. John Wilson, and a son of Peter Wilson, Sr., of Wilson's Ferry. His will was proven November 16, 1801, in which he named wife Sarah, children Ellis, John, Jiles, Peter, William, Meade, Betsy and Nanny.

[15]Joseph Roberts was probably the son of Joseph Roberts, Sr., whose will was proven at Henry Courthouse in 1778, naming sons John, James and Joseph, Jr.

[16]Rev'd Lewis Guilliam was the minister of the Established Church of Camden Parish, Pittsylvania.

[17]Richard Walden, married Candace Hubbard and his will, proven in 1790, named wife Candace, sons John, Charles and Richard; daughters Lucy Hudson, Milly, Mourning, Fanny Bobbitt, Mary Whitworth, and Elizabeth Ballard—"The history of the Walden family is traced from John Walden, son of Lord John Walden of Ravensworth Castle, England, who settled in Leyton, Essex County, Virginia, in 1715, moved later to his home Walden Towers in Caroline, site of which is about nine miles from Bowling Green." A legal firm of Baltimore was employed by the descendants of Lord Walden in Virginia to recover their share in the English estate, but the property had been taken over by the Crown, and the castle converted into a museum (Early's "Campbell County"). Richard Walden's home was in the northern part of the county, near Staunton River, and he bequeathed the Manor Plantation to his son Charles, who married Elizabeth Wall, daughter of Col. Charles F. Wall, by whom he had issue: Martha married Joel L. Adams, Mary married Vincent Snow, Polly married Thomas Goggin, Tabitha married John Ward of Edge Hill, and Richard H. Walden.

In the Halifax wills there is the will of a Samuel Walden, dated 1779, naming sons Richard, Owen, William, Lewis and Elijah.

[18]Peter Saunders lived at "Bleak Hill," on the head waters of Pigg River, in that part of the county that later became Franklin. His will, proven December 1, 1817, named sons: 1. Fleming married Miss Watts and were the grandparents of Judge Edward Saunders of the Virginia Supreme Court. 2. Robert. 3. Samuel married Mary Ingles. 4. Peter, born 1774, died in Pittsylvania County, 1846, unmarried. After his death his adopted daughter, Miss Jane Saunders, purchased Belle Grove and there he and Miss Jane are buried.

[19]In 1762 Crispen Shelton patented 3,000 acres in Pittsylvania along Panther, now Whitethorn Creek, where he settled. His will was proven in February, 1794, in which he bequeathed:

To son Abraham Shelton, six slaves.
To son Gabriel Shelton, four slaves.
To son Lewis Shelton, four slaves.
To son Beverley Shelton, four slaves.
To son Spencer Shelton, four slaves.
To son Armisted Shelton, four slaves.
To son Vincent Shelton, four slaves, also watch and Bible Burket and all lands.
To daughters Elizabeth Hurt, Jane Todd wife of William Todd, Susanna Dickerson wife of Griffith Dickerson, four slaves each.

Crispen Shelton was the son of Ralph Shelton and his wife Mary Pollard of Middlesex County, who were probably married about 1712 for the Parish Register of the County gives the following entries concerning their children:

Crispen, son of Ralph and Mary Shelton, born April 1, 1713, baptized May 17, 1713.
John, son of Ralph and Mary Shelton, born July 19, 1722, baptized August 12, 1722.
Benjamin, son of Ralph and Mary Shelton, born June 18, 1724, baptized July 12, 1724.
Daniel, son of Ralph and Mary Shelton, born May 17, 1729, baptized June 22, 1729.

Ralph Shelton was the son of Sarah Shelton and Richard Gassage of New Kent, and he for some reason retained his mother's maiden name. Tradition says that Sarah Shelton and Richard Shelton were the emigrant children of a ship's captain who was drowned in the English Channel in 1691. After the death of her husband Mrs. Sarah Shelton Gassage married in 1703 Joseph Bickley, of King William County, who was first sheriff of Louisa County.

they consider their own, and it being mentioned in committee that this county had never contributed their proportionable part towards defraying the expenses of the Delegates who attended on our behalf at the Gen'l Congress, that sum was immediately and cheerfully raised and deposited in the hands of Peter Perkins and Benjamin Lankford, Esquires, the Representatives for the said county, to be transmitted by them to whom it ought to have been paid; after which the committee rose, and several loyal and patriotic toasts were drunk, and the company dispersed, well pleased with the behavior of those people they had put their confidence in.

"Ordered that a copy of the above proceeding be inserted in the Virginia Newspapers.

"William Peters Martin, Clerk of the Committee."

The Association was carried out actively and thoroughly in Virginia, where each county was organized as a unit and comprised a little world of its own. In this way toryism was given no chance to develop and Virginia stood solidly for the patriot cause. Feeling at the time was very intense and people were filled with burning zeal for the cause of liberty.

These County Committees of Safety as they were called entered upon their duties with whole-hearted enthusiasm and not only enforced the articles of the Association, but spied out and put down any pro-British sentiment that arose in the county; and at the same time organized the county for military defense. At the least word or action that could be construed to be unfriendly to the patriot cause, the offending individual was summoned to appear before the committee and if no satisfactory explanation could be given, the offender was published in the newspapers as being "inimical to the cause." This was very drastic and severe treatment for it meant a boycott by one's friends and neighbors.

"If the offense taken cognizance of by the county committees had been limited to those set forth in the Continental Association little more could be said in criticism of these bodies than that they discharged their duties somewhat over zealously. Even this criticism would have to be qualified for revolution by its very nature can not tolerate difference of opinion: it means the victory of a part of the population over another part—a triumph of organization no less than arms. The local committees in Virginia, as well as in other colonies where political dissent was potentially dangerous from a military point of view, were driven to suppress loyalist opinion. Committees summoned offenders for intemperate speeches and punished them as ruthlessly as for actual violations of the Association, which in time came to be regarded as a law rather than a boycott.

Examinations of persons for political opinions occurred in all parts of the colony, proving that there were people everywhere attached to Great Britain. Social position and wealth—in all other ways a very great power in Virginia—failed usually to protect such offenders, who long before the Declaration of Independence were regarded as traitors." (Echenrode, pp. 104-106.)

On account of the tax that had been laid on tea, the drinking of tea was banned, to partake of the beverage was considered a virtual act of treason. Captain John Pigg,[20] a vestryman and captain of the local militia, was reported to the committee as one who had violated the Association "by drinking and making use of in his family the detestable East Indian tea." When summoned to appear before the Committee in May 1776, Captain Pigg boldly refused, considering it an impertinent interference in his family affairs and replied that, "he would do as he pleased." In their righteous indignation the Committee at once published him in the *Gazette* as being "inimical to the cause."

After the royal government under the English governor was dissolved Virginia called a convention to take over its powers, which met at Richmond in July, 1775, and at which Pittsylvania was represented by Peter Perkins and Benjamin Lankford. Immediate action was taken to put the colony in a state of defense—two regiments of 1,000 men were authorized to be raised for the Northern Continental Army under General Washington, a body of Minute Men for the State's defense, while the militia was to be reorganized.

In order that the troops called for the Continental Army might be equally proportioned among the several counties, the state was divided into sixteen military districts, of which Pittsylvania, Bedford, Botetourt and Fincastle formed one district and were allotted to furnish one captain, two lieutenants and sixty-eight men, who were to be expert riflemen and attached to the regiments. Each of the sixteen military districts was called upon to raise a battalion of 500 Minute Men, to be divided into ten companies of 50 men each, under the command of a colonel, lieutenant-colonel, and major. In order to render the men "more expert in military exercise," they were to be trained for twenty days under the adjutant as soon as enlisted, then four days out of each month, with a general muster in the district spring and fall lasting twelve days.

---

[20]John Pigg was the son of Paul Pigg of Amelia County, who moved to Pittsylvania when a very old man, and whose will is the first on record in the Clerk's Office. John Pigg was an early settler and Pigg River was named for him. He married Anne Clement and his will was proven February 1785, in which he bequeathed to his only son Hezekiah Ford Pigg the mill tract, his two guns, rifle and silver buckles.

In addition to these military forces "it was adjudged necessary in the present time of danger" that all free male persons between the ages of eighteen and fifty should be trained for military duty, and be formed into companies of militia of not less than thirty-two nor more than sixty-eight men. That every militia man should furnish himself with a good rifle, or tomahawk, common firelock, bayonet, pouch or cartouch box, and three charges of powder and ball; and further that the companies should be drilled every two weeks, with a general county muster in April and October.

The Committee of Safety for Pittsylvania proceeded at once to organize the county for military defense. The military strength of the county was given in a census of 1774 as 1438 men, and these were organized into twenty-seven companies. The record reads:

"At a meeting of the Committee of Pittsylvania County on Wednesday the 27th, September, 1775, the following gentlemen were nominated as officers of the militia agreeable to the Ordinance of the Convention, viz.:

"John Donelson, Esq.—County Lieutenant.

"Robert Williams, Esq.—Colonel.

"William Tunstall, Esq.—Lieutenant-Colonel.

"John Wilson, Esq.—Major.

"Captains: Benjamin Lankford, Peter Perkins, Francis Luck,[21] James Lyons, Robert Hairston,[22] Robert Woods, Daniel Shelton, Jesse Heard,[23] Frederick Rives, John Donelson, Jr., Archelaus Hughes,[24] Joseph Martin,[25] John Dix, William Witcher, Gabriel Shelton, Henry

[21]Francis Luck's will was proven July 17, 1781, naming wife Sarah, sons John, Nathaniel, Richard Hubbard; daughters Joyce, Rhoda, Betty, Sarah, Anne Deadman, Lucy, Caty Evans Luck. His home was in the eastern part of the county at a point now known as "Lucks," though the mansion house has long since disappeared. The place was noted for its elaborate and beautifully laid out gardens, which surrounded the house; unfortunately these too have disappeared.

[22]Robert Hairston, the son of Peter Hairston, a Scotchman of Albemarle County, lived in that part of Pittsylvania that later became Henry County. He married Ruth Stovall, the daughter of George Stovall, and left three sons, Peter and George of Henry County, and Samuel of Franklin County.

[23]Stephen Heard's will was proven at Pittsylvania Courthouse November, 1774. He named wife Mary, children Jesse Heard, Stephen Heard, George Heard, Mary Heard, Anne Gwilim, Susannah Standiford.

[24]Archelous Hughes settled in the western part of Pittsylvania that later became Patrick County. He married Mary, daughter of Samuel Dalton, and had issue: Leander, Archelous, William, Jane, John, Samuel, Reuben, Nancy, Madison Redd, Sally, who married Col. Joe Martin, Matilda who married Gen'l John Dillard.

[25]Joseph Martin had been a "long hunter," of Albemarle County. In 1774 he purchased a plantation in Pittsylvania on Leatherwood Creek to which he moved. He was active in Indian affairs along the frontier, and acted as Indian agent for Virginia for a number of years. He married, 1st, Sarah Lucas and, 2nd, Susanna Graves, leaving the following children: Susanna, William, Elizabeth, Brice, Joseph, Jesse, Thomas, Lewis and Alexander. He served many years in the Virginia Legislature.

Williams, John Salmon, Robert Payne,[26] Jonathan Hanby, William Peters Martin, Jehu Morton,[27] Charles Connors, Richard Gwynne, John Smith, Edmund Lyne, Joshua Abston,[28] and James Hix; Lieutenants: Stephen Coleman, Joseph Terry, Thomas Withers, William Ward, Robert Boreman, Thomas Smith, Charles Burke, Bartlett Williams, Samuel Shields, John Strong, Spencer Shelton, Reuben Payne, Beverley Shelton, John Morton, Isaac Clement, James George, Tully Choice, Jr., Edmund Cheat, Thomas Jones, Sr., George Hairston, Bryce Martin, David Lanier, George Waller, John Cunningham, Frederick Fulkerson, Elisha Shelton, Benjamin Hursely; Ensigns: Charles Irby, Joseph Terry (son of Joseph), George Carter, William Been, Samuel Bolling, Thomas Black, John Wynne, William Dix, John Fulton, Thomas Smith, Edmund Taylor, Armisted Shelton, John Payne, Lyrus Roberts, William Short, Joseph Farrar, William Estes, Levinfield Heit, Peter Vardaman, James Poteet, John Wells, James Taylor, James Anthony, David Chockwell, John Parr, Leonard Carter, John Rentfro."

With such extensive military plans as the state had called for, we may know that the men of Pittsylvania County spent a great part of their time in the autumn and winter of '75-76 on the various musterfields of the county.

The *Virginia Gazette* gives an incident of Pittsylvania life at this time, showing that youth and age alike were bending every effort to prepare for the struggle with the mother country. In the issue of August 1775, there is a statement by Mr. Charles Lynch, whose home lay across Staunton River, in Campbell County (not far from Altavista), in which he said:

"Sometime ago my having made powder was mentioned in your paper, but as I wish for no more merit (should there be any in it) than

[26]Robert Payne was the son of Josias Payne of Goochland and Pittsylvania, whose will was probated at Pittsylvania Courthouse December 19, 1785, in which he bequeathed his estate as follows:
To son John, 200 acres on Little Birch Creek and 400 on James River.
To son William, 400 acres in Fluvanna.
To son Josias, 700 in Goochland.
To son George, 200 acres in Goochland and 200 on the Three Chopt Road.
To Robert, 800 acres in Goochland, the plantation I formerly lived on.
He named daughters, Susanna, wife of William Heale; Anne, wife of William Harrison (of Pittsylvania County) and Agnes Michel. Robert Payne married in July 22, 1763, Anne Burton of Goochland and had issue: 1. Charles Payne. 2. Robert Payne. 3. John Payne. 4. Elizabeth Payne. 5. Keturah Payne. 6. Anne Payne. And 7. Agnes Payne, married Mamaduke Williams.
Colonel John Payne, a brother of Josias Payne, the elder, married Mary Coles, the daughter of William Coles of Coles's Hill of Hanover County, and were the parents of Dolly Payne, who later became the fascinating Dolly Madison.

[27]Jehu Morton was one of the sons of Joseph Morton, Sr., one of the earliest settlers of the County.

[28]Joshua Abston was the son of Francis Abston, whose will was proven in Halifax in 1762, naming sons William, John, Jesse and Joshua Abston. John Ward was a witness to the will. Joshua Abston married Rachel Clement, a daughter of Capt. Benj. Clement and moved to South Carolina.

Clement Hill
Home of Capt. Benjamin Clement who first settled here in 1748
The porches are modern additions

I deserve, I inform the public that Mr. Benjamin Clement[29] is a partner with me in making the powder, and that he was the first in the colony I have heard of who attempted to make it, altho' he did not bring it to perfection. Since our partnership we have brought it to such perfection with salt-petre of our own making that the best riflemen approve of it; and with the little mill we now have, we can make fifty pound weight a day. Salt-petre only is wanting which may very easily be made by observing the following directions; and when it is considered how much we want powder and that salt-petre is the principal ingredient, it is hoped that those who have the good of their country at heart will exert themselves in making it. Without it we can have no powder, consequently no means of defense; but with it we shall soon have both. I am sir, your very humble servant.

Charles Lynch,[30]
August 5, 1775."

Then followed directions for making salt petre by digging up the dirt floors of old meat houses, boiling the soil and straining the liquor through straw in a process somewhat similar to making lye from wood ashes.

Mr. Benjamin Clement lived on Staunton River at "Clement Hill" (now owned by John Hurt, Jr.), and was an old man of some seventy-five years. Captain Clement and Colonel Lynch were neighbors, and together

[29]Captain Benjamin Clement, born 1700, was the son of William Clement of King William County, who in 1735 patented 1,225 acres in Amelia County and moved with his family to the latter. William Clement was justice of the peace and sheriff of Amelia. His will, proven in 1760, named sons Benjamin, William, John and Francis; daughters Elizabeth Ford Ellyson, Anne and Barsheba Major.

Benjamin Clement married Susanna Hill, daughter of Col. Isaac Hill of King and Queen County and moved with his family to Pittsylvania (then Lunenburg) in 1748, establishing his home at Clement Hill, a sharp knoll overlooking Staunton River. The knoll was an excellent site for a pioneer settlement in the wilderness, for its elevation commanded a view of the river and countryside around and could be well defended against marauding bands of Indians. Captain Clement died in 1780 and is buried at the foot of Clement Hill; his estate was appraised at £27,604. In his will he named wife Susanna, and children: 1. Stephen Clement. 2. Isaac Clement, married Anne Denham. 3. Adam Clement, married Agnes Johnson of Louisa County. 4. James Clement. 5. Benjamin Clement. 6. John Clement. 7. Rachel Clement, married Capt. Joshua Abston. 8. Elizabeth Clement, married Isaac Butterworth. 9. Susanna Clement, married William Evans.

The old mansion house at Clement Hill, with its corner fireplaces, typifies a very early period of architecture. Charles Clement, a son of Adam and Agnes Clement inherited the place; in 1803 he married Miss Nancy Hanby of Patrick and made his home there. The property passed into the possession of John L. Hurt, through his marriage with Nannie Clement, granddaughter of Charles Clement, Sr., and daughter of Charles Clement, Jr., and his wife Lucy Hunt.

[30]Colonel Charles Lynch was the son of Charles Lynch, Sr., Burgess for Albemarle County, and his wife Sarah daughter of Col. Christopher Clark of Louisa Co. Charles Lynch, Jr., married in 1755 Anna Terrell and settled on Staunton River, about a mile below Altavista. He represented Bedford County in the House of Burgesses from 1767-75; was justice of peace and colonel of the militia; he died October 29, 1796, age 60 years, and is buried in the garden at Avoca, his home. Col. Charles Lynch and his wife Anne Terrell had issue: 1. John Lynch, moved to Tennessee. 2. Anselm Lynch married Susan Miller, their daughter Mary Anne Lynch married James Dearing and were the parents of General James Dearing of the Confederate Army, Mary Dearing who married Captain Thomas Fauntleroy and Susan Dearing who married Judge Robert Ward. 3. Charles Lynch, the third, moved to Kentucky.

Avoca, the beautiful old home of Col. Lynch, is owned to-day by the family of Captain Thomas Fauntleroy and his wife Mary Dearing.

succeeded in producing a gun powder of good quality. And since the first efforts to make it were at "Clement Hill," it is more than probable that the mill that turned out 50 pounds a day was also located there, and on Sycamore Creek, which divided the plantation.

At the Virginia Convention of December, 1775, six more regiments were authorized to be raised, each regiment to consist of ten companies of sixty-eight men each. Pittsylvania was called upon for one full company with captain, lieutenant and ensign.

Since the eastern part of the state was felt to be in an exposed condition by reason of its many navigable streams, the eight regiments were ordered to be stationed as follows: two between the Potomac and Rappahannock, two between the Rappahannock and York, two between the York and the James; and two on the south side of the James River.

CHAPTER XI

THE REVOLUTION IN PITTSYLVANIA IN 1776

Having gained some idea of the number of troops called from Pittsylvania in the first days of the war, let us see how many names of those brave soldiers history has preserved for us.

A company of Regulars marched from Pittsylvania early in 1776, commanded by Captain Thomas Hutchings,[1] Lieutenant James Conway[2] and Ensign Harden Perkins.

In an old military order book at the University of Virginia are the following items:

"April 4, 1776. Certificate of Review of the Pittsylvania County Regulars of Captain Hutchings.

"June 1776. Warrent to Captain Thomas Hutchings for £107.15 for men of the 6th Regiment whilst in the country and for blankets, leggins, horses and hunting shirts.

"June 17, 1776. Captain Hutchings of the 6th Battalion took the Oath, subscribed the Test and received his Continental Commission."

The oath[3] here mentioned was required of all officers and soldiers and read: "I, ———, do swear that I will be faithful and true to the colony and dominion of Virginia; and that I will serve the same to the utmost of my power, in defence of the just rights of America, against all enemies whatsoever."

The State Regulars were put under the command of General Andrew Lewis, and we have seen how they were ordered to be stationed between the large rivers in eastern Virginia. The 6th Regiment to which the Pittsylvania company belonged was stationed at Williamsburg and the Orderly Book[4] for "that part of the American Army stationed at Wil-

---

[1]Captain Thomas Hutchings was the son of Christopher Hutchings, who lived near Concord; an early road leading in that direction was known as the Hutchings Road. Christopher Hutchings' will was probated May 20, 1807, in which he named wife Elizabeth, children: John Hutchings, deceased. Thomas Hutchings. Aaron Hutchings. Charles Hutchings. Moses Hutchings. James Hutchings. Mildred, the wife of Bryon W. Nowling. Anne, the wife of Samuel Dillard. Jemima, the wife of Joshua Welch.

Thomas Hutchings was an early surveyor of Halifax and Pittsylvania. He married Catherin Donelson, daughter of Colonel John Donelson and had issue: 1. Captain John Hutchings, born 1775, died 1817, a business partner of President Andrew Jackson. 2. Lemuel Hutchings married Miss Owen. 3. Christopher Hutchings. 4. Rachel Hutchings. 5. Mary Hutchings. 6. Elizabeth Hutchings. 7. Jenny Hutchings. 8. Thomas Hutchings. 9. Stockley Donelson Hutchings, married Elizabeth Atwood, and their daughter Elizabeth Hutchings married Andrew Jackson Coffee, son of General John Coffee.

[2]There is an order for a Warrent of £9 to be issued to Ensign Perkins for himself and Lieutenant Conway of Captain Hutchings' Company of the 6th Regiment, for two tents.

[3]Hening's "Statutes."

[4]To be found in the State Library.

liamsburg from March to August, 1776," has been preserved and gives an interesting picture of this early force of the Revolutionary War.

The Orderly Book opens March, '76, with an order to the officers to report how many men in their companies are provided with cartouch boxes, powder horns, and shot bags.

The colonels were advised to have their troops appear as neat as possible in their dress—that their hats should be cut "all cocked in Fashion," and that their hair should be worn exactly the same length, and that officers and men should dye their hunting shirts a like color.

The officers and men of the 6th Battalion were ordered to provide themselves with hunting shirts, short and fringed, "the men's shirts to be short and plain, the sergeants' shirts to have a small white cuff and plain; the Drummers shirts to be with dark cuffs: both officers and soldiers to have hatts cut round and bound with black; the Brims of their Hatts to be 2 inches deep, and cocked on one side with a Button and Loup and Cockades, which is to be worn on the left. Neither men nor officers to do duty in any other uniform. The officers and men are to wear their Hair short and as near alike as possible. Each captain is to appoint a Drummer and Fifer to their respective comp's."

On April the 7th the regimental order was for "Men and officers of the 6th Battalion to parade this afternoon at 4 o'clock to hear the Articles of War read."

On May the 13th Captain Hutchings' Company was ordered to Jamestown where a guard was maintained.

The *Virginia Gazette* records an interesting event of this time. The Virginia convention of May, '76 was sitting at the capitol in Williamsburg, and had drawn up the resolutions instructing our delegates in Congress to declare us free and independent colonies. Word spread through the community of the courageous position taken by the convention, and hearts beat high. In recognization of the occasion the citizens of Williamsburg prepared a celebration, at which the troops were paraded in Waller's Grove before the Convention and inhabitants, after which the resolutions drawn up by the Convention were read. Then patriotic toasts were drunk, accompanied by the discharge of artillery and small arms, to "American Independent States," "the General Congress of the United States," and to "General Washington and Victory to American Arms." The ceremonies being finished, "the soldiers then partook of the refreshments prepared for them by the affection of their countrymen and the evening concluded with illumination and other demonstrations of joy." We can well imagine the high enthusiasm which filled the hearts of the Pittsylvania boys on this momentous occasion.

The Orderly Book records on August 21st: "All troops in the 6th Virginia Regiment in camp to be paraded tomorrow at 7 o'clock with their arms and accoutrements, which I expect to be in the best order, in order to be mustered out." Their term of enlistment having expired the troops were disbanded, but as many as would were at once re-enlisted. Lieutenant James Conway[5] re-enlisted, march north, and was killed near Trenton in Dec., 1776. Harden Perkins also re-enlisted and was made a second Lieutenant Oct. 28, 1776.

Again in October '76 Pittsylvania was called upon for a company for the Continental Line, to consist of four officers and ninety-four men. This was probably the company of Captain Henry Conway[6] who received his continental commission as captain in the 14th Regiment, February 24, 1777. In July, 1777, Joseph Conway took the oath of ensign in Captain Henry Conway's company of Regulars and served to the end of the war. (Pitts. Minute Books.)

It was proven on the oath of Captain Henry Conway that Andrew Laprade, a Pittsylvania soldier in the 14th Regiment, died in the service. Other Pittsylvanians serving in the Regulars of whom there is record were Charles Nicholas, who served three years and ten months in the first Virginia Regiment; Thomas Smith who served three years in the 6th Virginia Regiment; Zacherias[7] Lewis who served three years in the tenth Virginia Regiment. Matthew Clay enlisted as an ensign in the

[5]The Order Books of Pittsylvania County for 1778 read: "Mary Conway, widow and Relict of James Conway deceased, ordered to undertake the administration of her husband's estate."

The will of a James Conway was proven April 16, 1798, in which he bequeathed his estate to his brother Christopher Conway. James and Christopher are thought to be the sons of the young patriot James Conway who gave his life for his country, at Trenton. Christopher Conway was the father of James Washington Conway of Pittsylvania County. James W. Conway was the father of Lysander B. Conway, Sr., and grandfather of Lysander B. Conway, Jr., of Danville.

[6]Captain Henry Conway, Lieutenant James Conway and Joseph Conway were splendid patriots, serving in the Continental Army with distinction. They appear in the early lists of tithables for Pittsylvania County, and it is thought they moved down the Valley from Fauquire County just prior to the Revolution and were the sons of Thomas Conway of Fauquire, who named in his will 1784, sons William, Thomas, Peter, Joseph, Henry and grandson James Conway.

Captain Henry Conway served as a justice of the peace for Pittsylvania County for several years after the Revolution. It is thought that he later moved west.

Heitman's "Historical Register" gives Henry Conway's record in the Revolutionary War as follows:

"Captain 14th Virginia, 24th Feb. 1777; resigned Mar. 12, 1778."

And Joseph Conway's reads:

"Joseph Conway, Ensign 14th Virginia, 24th July 1777; 2nd Lieut. 22nd Dec. 1777; Regiment designated 10th Va., Sep. 14, 1778, taken prisoner at Charleston May 12, 1780, 1st Lieutenant July 15, 1780, transferred to 1st Virginia 12th, Feb. 1781. Served to end of the war."

Joseph Conway was an original member of the Sons of Cincinnati, the society formed by Washington of the officers of the Continental Army.

[7]Zacherias Lewis was the son of Charles Lewis whose will was recorded in Pittsylvania in 1805, naming sons Charles Lewis, Zacherias Lewis, Edward Lewis and James Lewis; daughter Lucretia, wife of Vachel Clement. Zacherias Lewis married Winnefred Mustein, a daughter of Thomas Mustein, and died in 1817, when his estate was settled, leaving no will.

9th Virginia Regiment in Oct. 1776, and was promoted to first lieutenant and regimental quartermaster in 1st Virginia Regiment, serving to 1783.

John Milburn, John Hall, and Abraham Goad died in Continental Service, and their wives were assisted by the State. (Pitts. Order Books.) Leonard Clark stated in a petition to the General Assembly that he enlisted in the Continental Service in 1776 for three years; that he was captured and held a prisoner in a house in New York City without a fire, and as result of his sufferings has lost the use of his limbs.

While Virginia was trying to meet the needs of Continental Congress, affairs at home were developing rapidly. In the summer of 1776 Lord Dunmore, Virginia's last royal governor, had entrenched himself with his band of loyalists and negroes behind fortifications on Gwynn's Island, off the coast of Matthews County. His force had distressed the inhabitants greatly through plundering and burning the estates along the bay. Patrick Henry, the newly elected governor, ordered an armed force to march against Gwynn's Island.

One company of Minute Men marched from Pittsylvania against Lord Dunmore and there may have been others of which there is no record. In June,[8] 1776, Captain Thomas Dillard, Lieutenant Jesse Heard and Ensign Robert Dalton commanded a company of which David Irby, Thomas Davis and Avory Mustein[9] are the only known members. They marched from Pittsylvania through the counties of Halifax, Charlotte and Dinwiddie to the town of Petersburg, crossed James River at Cobham, and proceeded on to Gwynn's Island. Here they were stationed several weeks under General Andrew Lewis and took part in the battle fought there July 9, 1776. A steady cannonading had been going on for a day or more when the enemy from their lookouts, perceiving our men taking boat, cried out, "The shirtmen are coming!" and fled precipitously. Lord Dunmore feared the deadly aim of the shirtmen, as the soldiers of the up-counties, clad in hunting shirts, were called. Dunmore did not desert his post at the capitol until it was reported to him that the shirtmen were marching on Williamsburg, when he fled to a man-of-war on the river.

When the minute men reached the Island they found it deserted, Lord Dunmore had left Virginia forever.

---

[8]Pension papers of Avory Mustein.

[9]Avory Mustein was the son of Thomas Mustein, whose will names sons Avory and Jesse, and daughters Anne Buckner, Milly Kezee, Tabitha Bruce, Winny Lewis and others.

Avory Mustein's will was recorded Sept. 16, 1832, in which he named the following children: 1. Joe Mustein. 2. Haley Mustein. 3. Shadrock Mustein. 4. Thomas Mustein. 5. Drury Mustein. 6. Elizabeth Shelton. 7. Polly Dove.

While the Virginia troops were still in their entrenchments at Gwynn's Island an express arrived from the governor ordering them to march at once against the Indians along the western frontier. The inciting of the Indians to their cruel barbarities against the defenseless frontiersmen is the darkest blot on England's fair name during the Revolutionary War. Her great statesman, William Pitt, openly denounced such a course of warfare in the Hall of Parliament. Conelly and Stewart, who had formerly been Indian agents for the British Government, now went among the tribes and having much influence among them, persuaded them to make war upon the whites. Due to the outrages committed by the Indians, the inhabitants of the frontier were crowded together in forts, suffering from the confinement and lack of food.

Virginia sent a force of 1,600 men against the Cherokees, while North and South Carolina sent out expeditions at the same time. Virginia's troops rendezvoused at the Long Island in Holstein River, where in the early summer a fort had been erected and named Patrick Henry in honor of the newly elected governor.

Captain Thomas Dillard's company of Pittsylvania Minute Men was ordered from Gwynn's Island to the frontier, and the married men being given the priviledge of returning home, Captain Dillard resigned and Lieutenant Jesse Heard was made captain, Robert Dalton lieutenant and Tully Choice ensign of the company. They marched first to New Castle where they awaited reinforcements which arrived under Colonel Haynes Morgan, of Pittsylvania, who commanded the 2nd Battalion of Minute Men. The troops then proceeded together by way of New London, Bedford County, crossing the Blue Ridge in Franklin County, and New River at English's Ferry.

Other companies of Pittsylvania Militia served in the Cherokee Expedition, one of which was commanded by Captain Peter Perkins and left Pittsylvania in July, 1776, following the route through Franklin County to Long Island. This company was composed of 102 men, and the names of only two are known to us, Charles Colley and Jesse Gwynn. Captain Joseph Martin raised and commanded a company from Pittsylvania in this campaign. Captain William Witcher also served and no doubt he too led a company of Pittsylvania militiamen.

The Cherokees lived on the Tennessee River, and all things being in readiness on October the 1st, the troops set out from Fort Patrick Henry for a march of 115 miles through the wilderness to the Indian towns. Captain William Witcher was left with a guard of 200 men for the Fort.

On the approach of the troops the Indians were found to be massed 3,000 strong on the opposite side of the river, and a battle seemed imminent. But the red men did not dare risk open conflict with the whites and they suddenly fled into the mountains. However, to punish them for their unprovoked attacks upon the settlements, several of the Indian towns were burned. The troops feasted upon the Indians' store of corn and potatoes, which Colonel Christian reported to be as much as 50,000 bushels of corn and 15,000 bushels of potatoes, again giving evidence of the extensive farming operations of the Southern Indians.

Finding it impossible to overtake the enemy the troops made their way back through the woods to Fort Patrick Henry, and the Indians suing for peace, the Pittsylvania militia was marched home and discharged by Colonel Morgan a few days before Christmas.

Colonel Morgan,[10] who commanded troops in the Cherokee Expedition, was an experienced soldier, having served through the French and Indian War in the 80th British Regiment[11] under Montague Wilmott, Esq. This regiment was raised in Virginia in 1758 and Morgan enlisted for six years, holding the office of sergeant-major.

When the State Line Regiments were organized[12] in 1776, Colonel Morgan was appointed lieutenant-colonel of the 1st Regiment. While these state regiments were the regular troops for the state, raised in addition to the Continental Line, yet their services were not confined to the state, and several times were sent beyond its boundaries. In June 1777 Lieutenant-colonel Morgan[13] was promoted by the General Assembly to be colonel of the 1st Regiment, which was ordered north to join General Washington. The colonel being a man of family and many business affairs, it was feared lest it might not be convenient for him to go so far from home. The Board questioned him, and while the colonel's answers were "full of Spirit and Delivery," yet it was perceived that he would prefer a station in the state, and Colonel Gibson was

---

[10]Colonel Haynes Morgan was probably a descendant of the Welch family of Morgans who emigrated from Wales to Pennsylvania, and later made their way down the Valley into Virginia and North Carolina. Edward Morgan came to America from Wales and his son Richard Morgan settled in Virginia.

Haynes Morgan, married on October 27, 1774, Mary Thompson (Halifax Marriage Bonds), daughter of William Thompson, whose will is recorded in Halifax in 1780, naming wife Rachel, daughters Mary, wife of Haynes Morgan, Susanna, wife of William Terry, Rebecca, Anne and Patsy. In his will probated January 15, 1790, Haynes Morgan left to his son Haynes his library of books and small sword. Haynes Morgan, Jr., married Elizabeth Shelton, December 23, 1803, and in 1817 he and his wife Elizabeth, and his mother, Mrs. Mary Morgan sold their lands on Banister River to Edmund Fitzgerald, when they probably moved from the county. The Morgan place is owned today by Mr. Sam Stone.

[11]Pittsylvania Minute Books.

[12]*Virginia Magazine History,* Vol. 21, pp. 338-39.

[13]*Virginia Magazine History,* Vol. 21, p. 338.

CALLANDS
Old Moorman Home

appointed in his stead. In November of that year Colonel Morgan was placed in command of all the state infantry.[14]

Colonel Morgan was probably a native of Bedford County since his name appears in the Committee of Safety of that county. He settled in Pittsylvania about the time of the opening of the war, and made his home on Banister River near the great falls below Riceville, where one today can trace the outline of his garden in the terraces. He was a lawyer by profession, and served as commonwealth's attorney for Pittsylvania and Henry counties.

Indian outrages continuing along the frontier, the states forces were ordered to take the field in another Indian expedition in 1777. Two companies from Pittsylvania marched in this campaign, one commanded by Captain John Donelson,[15] Lieutenant Hugh Henry,[16] Ensign Moses Hutchings[17] in which were privates John Neal, John Farthing, Joshua Dodson, David Wray and Abram Chaney; the other was commanded by Captain William Witcher. Both rendezvoused at Pittsylvania Old Courthouse (Callands) in the month of March 1777.

One can picture the scene of the gathering of these troops in the early springtime. Preparations must be made incident to the long march through the wilderness. Each soldier must be well clad in stout hunting shirt and leggins, with blankets, gun and ample ammunition. Patriotic sympathy would draw many people, so that there would be much coming

---

[14]Journal of House of Delegates, November 28, 1777.

[15]Captain John Donelson was the son of Colonel John Donelson, and married Mary Purnell, whose family was from Maryland. He moved with this father to Tennessee, and his daughter Mary Donelson married General John Coffee, who was second in command at the battle of New Orleans. General Coffee and wife Mary had issue: 1. Andrew Jackson Coffee married Elizabeth Hutchings. 2. Mary Coffee married Andrew Jackson Hutchings.

[16]Lieut. Hugh Henry, of Capt. John Donelson's Company was probably a son of that Hugh who first patented land here in 1744 and who married Mary Donelson, sister of Col. John Donelson.
Halifax Deeds show that Hugh Henry and wife Mary sold lands in 1757 to Archibald Gordon. William Wirt Henry in his life of Patrick Henry wrote: "The names Alexander, Patrick and Hugh were common with the Henry family in Scotland and Ireland." Hugh Henry was no doubt a member of the same family as that of the distinguished orator. In 1779 many of the Henrys accompanied Col. Donelson on his trip to Tennessee.
Another Henry family of Pittsylvania was that of James Henry of Accomac County, who owned large bodies of land here. The list of tithables for 1777 showed that he paid taxes on 19,000 acres at that time. James Henry is said to have been a grandson of Alexander and Jean Robertson Henry, grandparents of Patrick Henry; he married Sarah Scarborough and had sons John, Charles and probably others. John was settled on the Pittsylvania lands which lay in the eastern part of the county, and he called his home "Woodlawn." The house is standing to-day and the interior woodwork is elaborately carved. The garden laid off in terraces, is called "a falling garden."
In 1803 John Henry married Martha Williams, a daughter of Robert Williams and his wife Sarah Lanier. The will of Mrs. Martha Henry was proven in 1844, in which she named daughter Sarah B. French and sons Robert W., John S., and James Henry. Robert W. became a lawyer and practiced in Richmond, James studied medicine and lived at Woodlawn, where their portraits hang today.

[17]Moses Hutchings was the son of Christopher Hutchings and stated in his pension declaration that he was born in Culpeper County in 1754. He married Lucy Parks, December 13, 1780 (Marriage Bonds) and had issue: 1. William, married Judith Johns. 2. John, married Anne B. Williams. 3. Nancy, married Thomas Carter, IV. 4. Polly, married Jesse Walton. 5. Samuel, married Lucy Robinson. 6. Margaret, married Samuel Thompson. 7. Robert, married Mary Carter. 8. Stokely, married Nancy Johnson.
Moses Hutchings was sheriff of the county in 1817. He made his home just beyond Dry Fork and there in a rock walled graveyard lie the tombs of himself and his wife.

and going, with a goodly crowd ever around Calland's store. The commanding military officers of the county would be present, who, no doubt, delivered patriotic speeches to the departing soldiers. An old tradition has lingered at Calland's even until today, of a great tree around which the soldiers of the Revolution stacked their arms, and this very probably was the occasion.

On the 9th of April[18] these two companies marched from Pittsylvania through Franklin County, crossing the Blue Ridge at Magotty's Gap. Their line of march was probably about the same as the present Franklin Turnpike, leading from Callands to Rocky Mount. They crossed New River at English's Ferry and proceeded to Fort Patrick Henry on Long Island. This island is four miles long and one mile wide, and today is the site of the city of Kingsport, Tennessee; at that time it was thought to be Virginia territory. Here they were stationed several weeks and searched for Indians, going out in parties of 15 or more and ranging the woods in all directions.

In July a treaty was drawn up with the Indians at the Fort. Colonel John Donelson who had formerly settled many Indian affairs for the colony was present at the making of the treaty. The militiamen were then discharged by their captains and made their way home 300 miles through the woods.

In January 1778, Pittsylvania sent several companies of militia again to the frontier. Captain Thomas Dillard and Lieutenant Charles Hutchings commanded a company that marched direct from Pittsylvania to Isaac Riddle's house, twelve miles above the Long Island on the Holstein; thence to Boonesboro, Ky., where they were stationed three months. While in Kentucky Moses Hutchings, one of the company, acted as Indian spy. In July David Irby, James Irby and Thomas Faris, other members of Captain Dillard's company, were transferred to Captain Montgomery's company and marched with Colonel George Rogers Clark's regiment into the country known as the Illinois, of which they took possession. James Irby[19] died on the march.

In the spring of '78, Captain John Donelson and Captain John Dillard marched their companies of militia to the frontier but had no active engagement.

Colonel John Donelson, the father of Captain John Donelson, had been for ten years or more along the frontier, performing various trusts for the Colony. He was a pioneer settler of Pittsylvania, first patenting

[18]From Pension Papers on file in Pittsylvania Courthouse.

[19]David Irby stated this in a petition to the General Assembly found in Pittsylvania Petitions.

lands here in 1744 when this section was still a part of old Brunswick. Colonel Donelson was the son of John Donelson, Sr., who came to America from London in 1716, and settled in Delaware, where he married Catherine Davies. Mrs. Donelson's brother, Samuel Davies, was a Presbyterian preacher of great eloquence and one of the founders of his faith in Virginia; he was called by the Hanover Presbytery to Virginia in 1748, where he made his home for many years. It is said of him that his influence was greater than that of any other preacher of the gospel in Virginia—"an influence of fervent piety and zeal, directed by a mind of uncommon compass and force." (Howe's "Virginia," p. 294.) Mr. Davies went to England in 1753 in the interest of Princeton College, N. J., and his preaching excited such favorable comment that the King himself came to hear him. He was one of the early presidents of Princeton College.

John Donelson, Sr., and his wife Catherine Davies had two children, Mary, who married Hugh Henry of Accomac and John, who married Rachel Stockley also of Accomac. It was probably from his Davies ancestry that Colonel John Donelson inherited those qualities of force and leadership that made him an outstanding figure in the development of the western country.

When about twenty-five years of age Donelson came to this section and made his home on Banister River, near the mouth of Whitethorn Creek, where the house is still standing with long slooping roof and wide rock chimneys. Here was born in 1767 and grew up to lovely girlhood his daughter Rachel, who in later life was to become the wife of President Andrew Jackson.

Colonel Donelson was a man of ability and education, filling with honor the many positions of trust conferred upon him by his fellow

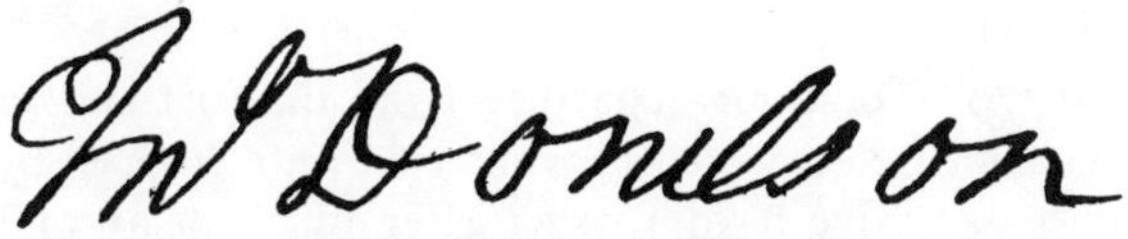

SIGNATURE OF COL. JOHN DONELSON

countrymen. He served as justice of the peace, vestryman, commandant of the military forces of the county, surveyor of Halifax and Pittsylvania Counties, and a member of the House of Burgesses. His position of county surveyor led him to know intimately all parts of this section, and he first successfully developed here the mining of iron. His iron works, known as the Bloomery, were located on Pigg River. In the tax lists for the year 1774 John Donelson was listed at the Bloomery—Hugh Henry overseer, Thomas Bolton, John Holloway, Aaron Tredway and seven slaves. There is on record a deed of trust from John Donelson to Hugh Innes in which Donelson agreed to furnish Innes forty tons of bar iron in eight equal parts within two years time, and offered his home plantation of 1,019 acres and eighteen slaves as security.

When Donelson surveyed the State Line westward in 1772 the Indians told him of the beauty and fertility of the Tennessee land and so aroused his interest that he visited the Great Bend of the River in Middle Tennessee. He found the country to be all that the Indians had represented and finally determined to make his home there. He disposed of his properties in Pittsylvania, selling his home plantation to Colonel John Markham, from whom the place has taken its name, and is known today as "Markhams." His lands on Pigg River, including the iron mine he sold to James Calloway and Jeremiah Early for £4,000 (Deed in Henry County, Book 1, p. 300), who with laudable partiotism renamed the mine, calling it the Washington.

In 1779, with his family, slaves and household effects, Donelson set out for the Tennessee country, and at Fort Patrick Henry was met by General John Robertson and his family and a party of emigrants. It was determined that the men should go by land and the women and children, with the household goods, should make a boat trip down the Holstein and Tennessee Rivers. The boats, some forty in number, set sail in December under the leadership of Colonel Donelson, in his boat the *Adventure*. Colonel Donelson kept a diary of the trip which opens: "1779 Journal of a voyage intended by God's permission in the good boat *Adventure* from Fort Patrick Henry to the French Salt Springs on Cumberland River:

"Dec. 22, 1779. Took our departure from the fort and fell down the river to the mouth of Reedy Creek, where we were stopped by the fall of water and most excessive hard frosts; after much delay and many difficulties we arrived at the mouth of Cloud Creek on Sunday evening the 20th day of February, 1780, where we lay by until Sunday the 27th, when we took our departure with sundry other vessels bound for the same voyage, and on the same day struck the Poor Valley Shoal on which we lay that afternoon and succeeding night in much distress."

MRS. RACHEL DONELSON JACKSON
From a copy of a Portrait which hangs in the Bedroom of the Hermitage

The diary can be read in Putman's "History of Middle Tennessee." It was a perilous trip many hundred miles in length, made in a winter of excessive cold, and the voyagers were frequently attacked by the hostile Indians along the river banks.

Among the members of Col. Donelson's party were Capt. Thomas Hutchings, his son-in-law, Hugh Henry, Sr., Mrs. Henry (widow) and Thomas Henry. The young daughter Rachel was twelve years old at this time, and shared in all the perils of her father's voyage. It was some ten years later when she met and married Andrew Jackson a young lawyer of the new western country.

It was said of Rachel that "those who knew her never tired telling of her beauty, her goodness, her sweetness and natural charm. She is described as being a brunette, with olive complexion and high coloring, black eyes that danced and sparkled in fun; vivacious and kindly."[20] This lovely Pittsylvania girl became the guiding star in the brilliant, though stormy career of her distinguished husband.

Jackson[21] said of his wife in after years: "We lived together, happy husband, loving wife, for nearly forty years. When I entered my room it seemed hallowed by a divine presence. I never heard her say a word that could sully an angel's lips. What I have accomplished I owe to her. * * * She made earth a paradise for me. Without her there could be no heaven."

In 1783 the Governor of Virginia appointed Colonel Donelson and Colonel Joseph Martin, of Henry County, to make a treaty with the Southern Indians, and the following letter was sent by them to chiefs of the tribes, inviting them to a conference:

"To the Chiefs and Warriors of the Shawnas Tribe of Indians: Kentucky.[22] Your Elder Brother the Governor of Virginia having issued his commission, commanding us to wright to you, Signifying his intensions of treating with your Nation for Peace, and that the Peace so Desirable To us, and we make no Doubt to you, may be fixed on the firm principle of honor and Justice. We send you This Talk, to invite such of your chiefs as you may appointe as your Com's for that purpose, To meet us at the Falls of the Ohio, when we shall be glad to meet you and Take you by the Hand as friends and Brothers.

"The United States of American and the English Nation have agreed in terms of peace, and your Elder Brother, the Governor of Virginia,

[20]John Trotwood Moore's "Jackson and His Beloved Rachel."
[21]John Trotwood Moore's "Jackson and His Beloved Rachel."
[22]Virginia Calendar of State Papers.

and his great Council, through a Benevolence of heart, and an ardent desire to put a stop to those Miseries Incident to War, have vested us with full power to Communicate the same To your Nation, and To Invite such of your Chiefs as you may appoint to meet us at the Falls of the Ohio, on the 18th day of next month in order to conclude on such Articles of peace as may be for the future happiness and prosperity of Both Nations, which is the Sincere Wish of

Jos. Martin
and
Jno. Donelson } Com.s."

In 1785 Colonel Donelson visited Pittsylvania to settle some of his business affairs, and on his return trip was murdered by some unknown person. His last letter, written from Campbell County September 4th, 1785, probably at Colonel Calloways, is preserved by the Tennessee Historical Society, which greatly reveres his memory as one of the founders of their state.

CHAPTER XII

PITTSYLVANIA COUNTY IN 1777

Up to this time Pittsylvania had comprised within her boundaries the counties of Henry, Patrick and a large part of Franklin—a real domain within itself. During the year 1776 petitions[1] were made to the General Convention for a division of the county on account of its great size, setting forth that the people "were so often called together to the Court-house on account of our unhappy disputes with Great Britain, being ready and willing to do all in our power for our just rights and liberties."

It was therefore enacted[2] "that the county of Pittsylvania be divided into two counties, by a line beginning at the mouth of Blackwater on Staunton River, and running parallel with the line of Halifax County till it strikes the Country line,[3] and that all that part of the said county which lies to the westward of the said line shall be known by the name of Henry, and that all the other part which lies to the eastward of the said line shall be one other distinct county and retain the name of Pittsylvania."

It was further ordered that the court for Pittsylvania should be held at the house of Richard Farthing until the justices of the peace should select a central point in the county at which the necessary court buildings should be erected.

On January 1, 1777, Pittsylvania assumed its present size, and on the 23rd day of that month a court for the county was held at the home of Richard Farthing. A new Commission of Peace had been appointed by the governor, and the following gentlemen were named: James Roberts, John Donelson, esq., Chrispen Shelton, Thomas Dillard, Peter Perkins, John Wimbish, Benjamin Lankford, William Witcher, John Owen, Abram Shelton, William Todd, Stephen Coleman,[4] William Short,

---

[1]Pittsylvania Legislative Petition.

[2]Hening's "Statutes," Vol. 9, p. 279.

[3]The State Line between Virginia and North Carolina.

[4]Stephen Coleman moved to Pittsylvania from Cumberland just prior to the Revolution, and made his home near Java. He was probably the son of Daniel Coleman of Cumberland, who on May 1, 750, was granted 2,000 acres on the south side of Banister River, below the upper Great Falls. In the first tax list of Pittsylvania, taken in 1767, Daniel Coleman of Cumberland is listed as owning oo acres here.

Stephen Coleman's will was probated September 17, 1798, in which he named wife Sarah, and following children: Daniel, born 1768 in Cumberland County married Anne Harrison, daughter of William Harrison; Stephen; Thompson; Anney Towns, wife of Stephen Townes; Elizabeth McDaniel; Patsy Turner; Lucy and Polly Coleman.

Ruben Payne, Robert Payne, Charles Kennon, George Carter, Daniel Hankins, Joseph Morton,[5] Charles Lynch Adams, and John Dix.

Of the twenty-one appointed eighteen were present at this Court and took the oath of office. In the above list we find missing many familiar names of those who had been foremost in the settlement and development of the section, in the enforcement of the laws and the establishment of civilization. They were no longer inhabitants of Pittsylvania for their homes now lay within the new western county of Henry. We miss Colonel Archibald Gordon and Captain Hugh Innes who so often sat as presiding justices and affixed their signatures to the day's court pro-

SIGNATURES OF ARCHIBALD GORDON, HUGH INNES AND PETER COPLAND

ceedings. Captain Innes had represented Pittsylvania in the July Convention of 1776, at which time he was appointed with Edmund Winston of Bedford, "to take evidence in behalf of Virginia against persons claiming to have purchased lands from the Indians within this boundary." Archelaus Hughes, Peter Copland, John Hanby, Hamon Critz and Robert Hairston were other familiar names now missing from Pittsylvania's records, but their qualifications for leadership were needed in the new county to the west in which their homes were now located.

When Halifax was made a county the court ordered that one dozen volumes of Webb's "Virginia Justice" be purchased for the use of the justices of the county; and Pittsylvania probably did the same judging from the following court orders:

[5]Justice Joseph Morton was the son of Joseph Morton, Sr., who died in 1753, leaving sons Joseph, Jehu, and John. All three brothers served as officers in the Pittsylvania Militia during the Rev. War. (Pitts. Order Book 4, 343-44).

The marriage register shows that Joseph Morton married Clancy Harrison in May, 1778, and that John Morton married Lucy Blakeley in September, 1777, her father James Blakeley giving his consent in a note to the clerk. In 1777 Joseph Morton purchased from his brother Jehu Morton the 400 acres on Sandy River willed him by his father. Jehu later moved to Rockingham County, N. C.

Joseph Morton's inventory was taken in 1818 by his administrator Benj. Watkins, showing that his death occurred that year. Many of his descendants moved to Mt. Sterling, Kentucky.

"November 1774: Edmund Taylor is ordered to apply to Richard Walden a justice of the peace, for the Law Books that he has in Possession."

"June 1775—It is ordered that the law books in the hands of Archibald Smith be delivered to Robert Hairston, Gent, a justice of the peace."

A search through the inventories of the estates of Pittsylvania's early justices show that practically all possessed books, some owning few in number while others had goodly libraries. The inventories of all the early justices are not listed in Pittsylvania, some being found in adjoining counties, while still others had moved westward, as did Colonel Donelson, George Carter and Thomas Dillard. Where the titles are listed we usually find a few law books. In John Wimbush's library there were seventy-eight volumes, among which were Voltaire, Shakespeare, "The Spectator," and Stark's "Justice." Crispen Shelton's library showed the "Revised Code," Hening's "Justice," and "Laws of the United States." William Thomas's library contained Stith's "History of Virginia" and two Law Books. James Walker's books included one old law book and "Sundry Law Books." William Witcher owned one Webb's "Justice." Richard Walden owned three old law books.

More often the books were not named but listed as a "parcel of books" or "sundry books," as in the estate of Thomas Dillard, Sr., John Dix, Daniel Hankins, John Smith and John Wilson. Robert Payne owned twenty-seven books, titles not given, and Theophilus Lacy nine religious books.

The early settler usually brought books among his household effects. Not many inventories were made prior to 1770, but from then on through the eighties we find books generally listed in the settlement of all estates. Books were mentioned in the following early inventories: Joshua Worsham, Patrick Shields, Ambrose Porter, Patrick Still, William Compton, James King, John Fulton, Isaac Dodson, Elijah Harbour, James Hix, John Hutchings, John Creel, Stephen Heard, Thomas Williamson, Samuel Crawley, James Bartlett, John Stewart, Ayres Hodnett, David Nance, Abram Motley, James and Benjamin Clement, William Wynne, Arthur Hopkins, John Lewis (of the Byrd), Constant Perkins, Francis Luck, John Pigg, Hezekiah Pigg, Thomas Jones, Epharodius White, John Hill, William Astin, Thomas Vaughan, Thomas Lester, Thomas Ramsey, John Pannill, James Buckley, Haynes Morgan and many others.

Wherever titles were given religious books predominated. In 1776, Thomas Dillard, Sr.'s, books were listed:

1 Large Bible.
1 Prayer Book.
A parcel of old Sermon Books.

James Hix's books of the same year were:

Erskine's Sermons, 4 Vols.
Religious Books.

In 1777, James Stewarts' books were listed:

9 Bibles.
1 Confession of Faith.
8 Volumes of Sermons.
Parcel of old Books.

Theophilus Lacy's:

Hervey's "Meditations."
1 Prayer Book.
1 Watts' "Psalms and Hymns."
Part of the "Whole Duty of Man."
Part of the Testament.
Beveredge's "Thoughts."
Gray's Fables.
Bailey's Dictionary.

James Walker's:

1 Old Law Book.
Body of Husbandry, 4 Vols.
Shakespeare's Works, 7 Vols.
Peregrin Pickle, 3 Vols.
Sundry Law Books.
History of the Bible, 3 Vols.
Mercer's Abridgement.

Among the officers chosen for the new court were: John Dix, sheriff, John Donelson, Jr., surveyor, Robert Williams, Esq., commonwealth's attorney, Joseph Akin, clerk of the court. The home of William Tunstall now lay in Henry County, and for this reason he was judged to be ineligible for the clerkship; but so great was his popularity that this objection was waived and he was soon re-elected clerk of the County with Akin as his deputy.

John Donelson, Esquire, was ordered to run a line from the "mouth of Straightstone Creek to where the line between this county and Henry County intersects the Country Line and that the center of that line be the place for holding Court."

At the July Court, 1777, "on a view of the Justices of this county for the settling of the Court-House, the same is established on the Lands of Jeremiah Worsham near the Cherrystone Meeting House Spring."

"It is agreed by the Court that the next court to be held for the county to be on the lands of Jeremiah Worsham where the same is established near Hickey's Road." In August 1777, the Court of Pittsylvania was removed to Cherrystone Meeting House Spring, and in the absence of court buildings the meeting house was repaired and given over to the use of the court, where its sessions were held until after the close of the Revolution. The Cherrystone Meeting House Spring is situated in the ravine to the north of Depot Hill, and in this ravine were located the first court buildings at Chatham. The justices presiding on that court day were Thomas Dillard, John Wilson, Benjamin Lankford, Stephen Coleman, Crispen Shelton, George Carter and Reuben Payne. Among the many matters disposed of by the court a license was granted William Short to keep a tavern at the Court House; Joseph Terry was appointed surveyor of the road from the Halifax line to the Old Town, as Peytonsburg was often called; Colonel Wilson, Major Lankford, Captain Witcher and Reuben Payne were ordered to let the building of a prison and also the "Hull of a Courthouse thirty two by twenty four Shingled Ruff."

The General Assembly of May, 1777, enacted that all male inhabitants of Virginia above 16 years of age should take the following oath to the Commonwealth:

"I do swear that I renounce and refuse all allegeance to George III, King of Great Britain, his heirs and successors, and that I will be faithful and bear true allegance to the Commonwealth of Virginia, as a free and independant state, and that I will not at any time do or cause to be done anything injurious to the freedom and independance thereof: as declared by Congress: and that I will discover and make known to the some one justice of the peace for the said state all treasons or traiterous conspiracies which I now or hereafter shall know to be formed against this or any of the United States of America."

The justices of the peace were ordered to take a list of the names of all persons taking the oath before them and send in to the clerk:

"Benjamin Lankford to his company of militia, and those living in his district.

Thomas Dillard to the male inhabitants of the District of Isaac Clement's Company.

Charles Lynch Adams and William Ward to the Company of Joshua Abston.

William Witcher to his own company.

James Roberts to Thomas Black's[6] Company.

Joseph Morton to Jehu Morton's Company.

Daniel Hankins to his own Company.

John Owen to Thomas Smith's[7] Company.

Peter Perkins to John Smith's[8] Company.

John Wilson to Charles Burton's Company.

Robert Payne to John Dix and his own Company.

Charles Kennon to his own Company.

George Carter to Richard Gwynne's Company.

Stephen Coleman to his own Company.

Reuben Payne to his own Company.

Abraham Shelton to Daniel Shelton's Company.

Crispen Shelton to Gabriel Shelton's Company."

The county, now its present size, was laid off into eighteen districts, and a company of militia organized in each district. With an average of but fifty men to a company, together with the officers, this would comprise a fighting force of over a thousand men.

In 1778 Colonel John Donelson resigned his position of county lieutenant of all the county's military forces, and John Wilson was appointed in his stead. At the same time Benjamin Lankford was appointed colonel, Peter Perkins lieutenant-colonel and Daniel Shelton

[6]Thomas Black's will was proven in 1814 in which he named children of a former marriage—Elizabeth Mitchell, Sarah Decus, Skiff Richards and Thomas; present wife Susanna and her children, John, Absolom, Nathan, Polly, and Susanna. A road in the northwestern part of the county is still known as Black's Road.

[7]Captain Thomas Smith was the son of Thomas Smith, Sr., who lived on Sandy Creek of Dan River, and died in 1781, naming the following children in his will: Jane, Edward, Sarah, Martha, Thomas and John. Witnesses to the will were John Fulton, Wm. Orr and John Wilson.

[8]Captain John Smith, Jr., was the son of John Smith, Sr., who lived on Sandy Creek of Dan River and was probably a brother of Thomas Smith, Sr., of Sandy Creek. In the will of John Smith, Sr., proven in 1784, he left to son Drury land bought of Jos. Morton; to son Thomas mill and land bought of Col. John Wilson; to son John lands on Raccoon Branch; to son Joseph land bought of Drury Stith; to son Edward Washington the home plantation; to daughter Jinna a tract of land on Bannister River touching Captain John Pigg's; to daughter Martha land on Pole Bridge; to daughters Anne, Elizabeth and Sarah, negroes; wife Martha, and Col. John Wilson Executors.

Captain John Smith, Jr., left no will, but his brother Thomas Smith, in will of 1809, left his estate to Smith Fulton and William Smith, son of John Smith, deceased. William Smith married Elizabeth Burnett, only child of Captain Henry Burnett (Burnett's will), and had issue: John Henry Smith, James Blakley Smith, William Lynch Smith, Patrick Shields Smith, and daughters Elvira, Mary E. and Martha. Many of this family moved westward, and William Forrest Smith, Tax Commissioner today of the State of Missouri is a grandson of Patrick Shields Smith.

major of the militia. Colonel Donelson was preparing to move to the Tennessee Country. The Court also ordered Benjamin Lankford and William Todd, Esq., to let the building of a prison, stocks and pillory.

With the progress of the war the county committees of safety which were unwieldy because of their large numbers were superseded by Courts of Inquiry, composed of a few persons appointed by the governor from the Committee of Safety and the militia officers. The court was equally active in putting down any disloyalty of the patriot cause.

It was represented to the Governor that after the division of the county two of the commission appointed for the trial of tories were in Henry County, and that John Wimbish, Crispen Shelton, William Todd, William Short and Reuben Payne were suitable and fit persons to form a commission.

Gabriel Shelton was ordered to summon Samuel Calland and the Rev'd Lewis Guillian to appear before the Court on February the 5th 1777 to answer "why they do not depart the colony, they being natives of Great Britain."

Virginia had enacted a law that all persons who refused to take the oath of allegiance must depart the colony. The Court of Inquiry that met on February the 5th was presided over by Benjamin Lankford, Crispen Shelton, William Witcher, Abram Shelton, William Short and George Carter. Although Samuel Calland, the young Scotch merchant, refused to take the oath, yet since he had married a native of the county, Miss Elizabeth Smith, the daughter of John Smith, of "The Pocket," for this reason he was allowed to remain in the colony. Other members of the Calland family were patriots, for at a later session of the court, "it appeared to the Court of Pittsylvania that Samuel Calland was heir at law to James Calland, who died in the Continental Service in Georgia."

The Rev'd Mr. Guilliam, minister of the Church of England, did not appear before the court as ordered, and he and Alex Cummins, were ordered to appear before the next court "to give reason why they do not depart this country, being natives of Great Britain." They probably departed since nothing further is found concerning them.

Abram Shelton was appointed Escheator for Pittsylvania County of properties owned by British subjects. These properties consisted of lands owned by merchant firms such as John Smith, Murdock & Co., John Fisher, Archibald Smith and James Smith. The lands were appraised and sold at public auction.

Pittsylvania was represented in the General Assembly in 1777 by Abram Shelton and Peter Perkins; in 1778 by Abram Shelton and John Wilson; in 1779 by John Wilson and Benjamin Lankford.

In the ten years since the county's formation the population had more than doubled; there were goodly plantations throughout its extent, though the rivers with their rich low grounds were the centers of settlement. Along Staunton River in the northern part of the county were living Thomas Dillard, Richard Walden, Robert Adams, Captain Benjamin Clement, Joshua Abston, Charles Lynch Adams, William Ward, John Smith, Captain William Calloway, Captain Henry Snow and Captain Anthony; along Dan River in the southern part of the County plantations had been settled by John Lewis of "The Byrd," the Irvins, John Dix, William Harrison, John Wilson, Peter Perkins and his brothers, Gideon Marr, Robert and Josias Payne, John Pryor, Joseph Scales and Thomas Smith; while numerous settlements were scattered through the center of county. The list of tithables taken the summer of 1777, after the separation of Patrick, Henry and the lower half of Franklin Counties, numbered fifteen hundred and thirty-five.

Chapter XIII

THE REVOLUTION—THE SOUTHERN CAMPAIGN

The British having conquered Georgia centered their attack upon South Carolina, which in dire distress sent urgent appeals to Virginia for assistance, and they were not made in vain.

An Act of the General Assembly, May 4th, 1780, stated that there was a dangerous invasion of South Carolina, "and as it is incumbent upon this state to assist our friends and fellow citizens in distress, as speedily and effectively as possible," therefore 2,500 infantry were ordered to be marched without delay to Hillsboro, North Carolina, the place of rendezvous.

In making up this number Pittsylvania was called upon for 97 men who were commanded by Captain Isaac Clement and Lieutenant Benjamin Duncan.[1] This company numbered among its members Avory[2] Mustein, John Harris, Joseph Hubbard and Nathaniel Gardiner, and marched from Pittsylvania in June 1780, going by way of Captain Peter Perkins' home on Dan River, where they were met by several other companies probably from adjoining counties. They proceeded to Hillsboro, where they joined the 3rd Va. Regiment under Major Henry Conway, in General Edward Stevens' Brigade and continued their march until they came up with General Gates lying in front of Cornwallis at Rudgeley's Mill. The march southward in the oppressive heat of summer produced[3] much sickness among the troops, so that in order to reach the front Stevens was compelled to rest his brigade through the day and make long forced marches at night which broke the spirit of the men.

General Stevens and his exhausted force reached camp on August the 15th, and General Gates denying them a single night's rest, broke camp at ten o'clock and moving forward in the dark encountered the British

[1]Six of the Duncan family appeared in Culpeper County in 1722. They were Scotchmen and it is supposed that they came up from Drumfries, a Scotch settlement in Prince William County. About 1750 James Duncan moved from Culpeper down to Pittsylvania and established his home in the southeastern part of the County. Between 1762-68 Benjamin, Charles, William, Thomas, John, Martin, Peter and Ambrose Harrison Duncan were patenting lands in different parts of the County. Benjamin Duncan made his home on Staunton River at the mouth of Blackwater. After the close of the Revolutionary War he moved out to Madison County, Ky., where his will was proven in 1796, naming sons Benjamin, Jr., John and Samuel. Here the family multiplied and prospered and among the living descendants of Benjamin Duncan the third (son of Benjamin Duncan, Jr.) are Mrs. Josephine Asbury, William McKee Duncan, Mrs. Preston Pope Rogers, Mrs. Charles Ridgeley Lee and her sons Duncan Rogers and Preston Pope Lee, Miss Jennie Duncan, Mrs. W. S. Elkins, Miss Judith Barnard, and Mrs. Chastine Bradley Smith, Ashby Warren, Mrs. Nellie Duncan Osburne.

Among the descendants of John Duncan, another son of Benjamin Duncan, Jr., are Judge John Duncan Goodloe, Mrs. Jane F. Goodloe of Goucher College, Mrs. Brutus Clay, Mr. James Stone and Mrs. Emily Duncan Pike.

[2]Pension Declarations of Avory Mustein and John Harris.

[3]General Henry Lee's "Memoirs of the Southern Campaign," p. 191.

Army likewise in motion. Both generals prepared for battle, and in forming his lines General Gates placed the same wearied Virginia troops on his left, opposing the veterans of the British right, whereas General Lee said the trained Continentals should have occupied this place.

General "Light Horse Harry" Lee gives the following description of the battle in his memoirs (p. 183):

"The light of day dawned, the signal for battle. Instantly our center opened its artillery and the left of our line under Stevens was ordered to advance. Stevens, exhorting his soldiers to rely on the bayonets, advanced with his accustomed bravery. The British general ordered Webster to lead into battle with the right. Our left was instantly overpowered by the assault; and the brave Stevens had to endure the mortifying spectacle exhibited by his flying brigade. Without exchanging more than one fire with the enemy they threw away their arms and sought safety in flight. The North Carolina brigade followed their shameful example."

The Continental troops of Maryland and Virginia stood firm and resisted assault after assault but the desertion of the militia so crippled the line of battle that these brave soldiers were compelled to retreat. Our losses were disastrous at the battle of Camden, August the 16th, 1780. The blame of the defeat should rest upon the commanding general rather than upon his troops, for Gates had everything to gain by waiting before offering battle to Cornwallis. He could have fallen back from his advanced position and gathered together his forces which were scattered throughout the state; he could have increased his army by a re-inforcement of hardy warriors from the mountains who later won the battle of King's Mountain; and how well he could have employed a few weeks resting and training his raw militia.

General Lee further said that whenever the militia was placed in battle against regulars that "his heart was rent with painful emotions, knowing the waste of life resulting from the cruel policy."

"Though the raw[4] colonial troops broke before the charge of British regulars, it was a general and not a people that had been defeated, as was to be proven." The American Army retreated northward, and Captain Isaac Clement's company of Pittsylvania Militia, and other Virginia troops, were encamped for the night on the edge of a swamp. The men were exhausted and slept soundly. Suddenly the night air was rent with a deafening noise. Captain Clement delighted to tell that his brother who

[4]Turpin's "Short History of the American People," p. 164.

commanded a troop of Bedford Militia leaped to his feet and, drawing his sword, exclaimed, "Gentleman, I surrender!" The noise, however, was not Tarleton's pursuing force, but a mighty chorus of swamp frogs.

After the defeat of Camden General Gates was removed from command of the Southern Continental Army, and on October 3rd, Congress appointed General Nathaniel Greene of Rhode Island to this position. Greene at once journeyed south, stopping over in Richmond where he made arrangements for the defense of the state and for supplies for his army. General Steuben was put in command of a force of 2,000 militia to defend the state against invasion, for Virginia, rich in resources and generous in aid was the backbone of Southern resistance and to her, General Greene looked for the success of his campaign. His army must have food, clothing, arms and ammunition, and from Virginia alone could they be obtained. Colonel Edward Carrington was appointed Deputy Quarter Master General of the Southern Continental Army and Major Richard Claiborne his assistant. In furtherance of their work they devised[5] the plan of dividing the state into nine districts with a central point in each at which supplies for the army were to be gathered and forwarded South. "As the great line of communication for Philadelphia to the Southern Army through this State will be from Alexandria to some part of Staunton and Dan Rivers," it was deemed advisable to locate posts both at Alexandria and on these rivers. The posts were designated as follows: Alexandria, Fredericksburg, Carter's Ferry on James River, Richmond, Williamsburg, Charlottesville, Petersburg and Dan and Staunton Rivers.

The district of Dan and Staunton Rivers comprised the counties of Mecklenburg, Lunenburg, Charlotte, Halifax, Bedford, Pittsylvania and Henry Counties, and Boyd's Ferry[6] on Dan River was first chosen as the depot of the district. After Cornwallis's advance upon Boyd's Ferry the point was considered too open to attack and Col. Carrington gave the following order:

"March 11, 1781. The Enemy having retired from Dan River, Mr. William McCraw is appointed to that station and to keep his principal post at Wimbishes Stores in Peytonsburg."

A few days later Col. Carrington wrote to Major Claiborne: "I suppose you have received mine of the 11th Inst. making a new Disposition on Dan, to-wit: That Terry's stores should be established as a post under

[5]Calendar of Virginia State Papers, Vol 2, 157.
[6]Calendar of Virginia State Papers, Vol. 2, 160.

Mr. McCraw, and stores pushed on upon our first plan upon that Point; from which we are to get them forwarded by public waggons. These Public Waggons are to be those we expect from Virginia; you will therefore lose no time in sending them to the army, properly brigaded, with good conductors and drivers, loaded with provisions."

Let us pause for a moment to picture to ourselves the little town of Peytonsburg at this early time, for today there is no vestige of it left standing, not one stone upon another, and even the place of its location is in dispute. One hundred acres had been laid off into a town in 1759 and in the twenty years following many people had settled there. In early deeds we find the names of some of the streets and early inhabitants. There was a central main street with connecting ones named Randolph, Spring, Forest and Mountain Streets. In 1771 Thomas Spraggins was living on Main Street on corner lot No. 98. Mr. Henry Williams was also an inhabitant of Peytonsburg, where his schoolmaster, John Williams, taught "a reading school." William Williams was also a schoolmaster of Peytonsburg. In 1774 Henry Williams procured[7] a license to keep an ordinary at this house. Hospitality was so largely practiced in Virginia that it was sometimes necessary for a man to procure a tavern license to protect himself against the too frequent guest, else he would find himself "eaten out of house and home," an expression familiar to Virginians. John Martin, a maker of hats, lived at Peytonsburg and secured a tavern license at this time. The following year Richard Bayne and Beverley Barksdale were granted licenses to keep ordinaries at their homes in Peytonsburg. Stores were operated here by John Wimbish, a justice of the peace, and the Terrys, many of whom lived in the vicinity. Court no longer convened at Peytonsburg, but that it was a place of business importance is shown by the number of tavern licenses issued.

Young Dr. Rawley White, of eastern Virginia, located at Peytonsburg to practice the profession of medicine. He had recently returned from aboard where he had pursued his studies graduating from Edinburg in 1763. He married Miss Maacha Spraggins and established his home just outside the village, where it stands today surrounded by ancient box trees.

As soon as the post was established at Peytonsburg the place at once became a point of military activity. Supplies of every kind needful for the life of the army were collected from the inhabitants of the district and stored at Peytonsburg in warehouses, awaiting shipment south. Guns

[7]Order Books of Pittsylvania County, 1774.

were repaired and canteens and horseshoes manufactured here, and for these purposes there were numbers of smith's shops and forges.

In gathering supplies for the army, wagons went from farm to farm, collecting provisions, and in return a receipt was given stating the amount collected. After the successful close of the war Courts of Claims were held at Pittsylvania Courthouse at which the claims were presented and payment received. The records of the Courts[8] show how largely the people of Pittsylvania contributed of their substance toward the patriot's cause. The record book is badly mutilated, but from that part which can be deciphered we learn that the county gave: 1,285 bushels of corn and 220 barrels of corn; 12,842 pounds of bacon and eight hogs; 45,550 pounds of beef and 22 whole beeves; 101 sheep and much mutton; 382 bushels of oats, as well as many sheaves and stacks of oats; large quantities of fodder and straw; much meal, flour, wheat, brandy, cider and chickens. Horses to the number of 55 were taken and 63 guns. Wagons and teams were commanded for various periods of time, ranging from a few days to several months; of these fifty-five were listed. Samuel Harris, the noted pioneer Baptist Minister, wagoned military stores from Peytonsburg to Charlotte Town.

Salt was a scarce and a precious article during the war, and Harris had his wagons bring up salt from Richmond for the inhabitants of the county. The salt allotted to the county was issued "one quart per head to those who have salted their pork and two quarts to those that have not." Peter Perkins' wagons went north for supplies, which were probably of a military nature. Among the unusual articles gathered at the post were bear skins. A post for manufacturing clothing for the soldiers had been established at Albemarle Barracks, and on August 10, 1781, the post reported the arrival of several hundred bear skins from Peytonsburg, "which may do for vests and overalls."

Items from the Claim Records:

"To Robert Williams for one smooth bored gun impressed for the state troops in the march against Wallace, £5.

"To James Buckley for Provisions and Rashings of Licker for fifty-seven men on their march to joing General Greene, £5.13.

"To William Ward for three sheep impressed for Continental Troop, £1.10.

"To William Davis for three horses impressed for state troops, £45.

---

[8]Records of Courts of Claims of Pittsylvania County.

"To Col. John Lewis for three canoes, hire of two negroes three days @ 2/6 impressed for Continental use £15."

Patrick Henry, the ex-governor, was now living on Leatherwood Creek, in Henry County and 228 sheaves of oats were collected from his plantation by "John Redd, waggon conductor for William McCraw." Other wagon conductors for the Post were John Rowland, Robert Ferguson, Samuel Parks, George Elliot, Thomas Glass and William Norton. Wagon brigades plied between the Post and the army in the south delivering the supplies; at one time the Post reported that a brigade of forty wagons had just set out. With all these activities centered at the town we can see what a busy and important place Peytonsburg now became—the daily arrival of wagons laden with supplies for the army and the setting off of brigades for the south; droves of cattle and sheep plodding down the dusty roads; the hurried arrival and forwarding of important despatches by the express riders; and high above all else the incessant din of hammer and anvil from the smith's shops, where canteens and horse shoes were taking shape.

Goodly numbers of men were employed in the different branches of work carried on at the post: Thomas Meade was paid £1.8 for "collecting Beaves for Continental use for seven days." Others who assisted in collecting cattle and driving them on to camp were William Shelton, Richard Todd, Benjamin Dillard, David Irby,[10] Edward Lewis,[11] Lewis Williams,[12] George Shelton, Edmund Fitzgerald,[13] Mattox Mays, Silvanus Stokes,[14] Isaac Gregory,[15] John Buckley and Stephen Terry.[16]

[10]David Irby was the son of Peter Irby whose will was proven February 16, 1795, in which he named wife Elizabeth Irby, sons Francis, David, Abraham, Samuel and William Irby; daughters Amey, Irby, Mary Camp, Anne Grant and Rebecca Irby.

[11]Edward Lewis was the son of Charles Lewis, whose will was proven October 19, 1805, naming sons Edward, Zacheriah, Charles, James, John and William.

[12]Lewis Williams was the son of William Williams whose will was proven May 16, 1780, and in which he bequeathed to "my dearly beloved son Lewis," one eight of his lands. The remainder of his estate was left to his wife Lucy and her seven sons, viz.: James Mastin Williams, Thomas Terry Williams, David Champness Williams, William Mastin Williams, Doctor Crawford Williams, John Williams, Joseph Terry Williams. Attorney-General Samuel Williams was a descendant of this family.

[13]There is a tradition in the family that Edmund Fitzgerald was born upon the highseas, his parents being emigrants to America. He first appears in the Pittsylvania records in 1778, when he purchased 100 acres on the north side of Banister River. In 1814 he and his wife Mellicent (Payne) made a deed of gift of 300 acres on Banister River, which he had purchased from Haynes Morgan, to their son Edmund Fitzgerald, Jr. Here Edmund, Jr. built his home, which is standing today in a fine state of preservation, owned by his grandson, Samuel Stone. The will of Edmund Fitzgerald, Sr., was proven January, 1848, in which he made sons Reuben, Samuel, Edmund, Jr., James and William Fitzgerald; daughters, Nancy, wife of Hardin Wilson, and Elizabeth, the wife of James H. Stone. The latter settled the fine old place, "Oak Grove," with its boxwood gardens.

[14]Silvanus Stokes made his will in 1798, naming sons Allen, Silvanus and Joel Stokes; daughters Susanna May, Elizabeth Allen Neal, Sally Walker Dupuy, and wife Sarah Stokes.

[15]Isaac Gregory is mentioned in the will of his grandfather Robert Ferguson, which was proven September 17, 1798, naming wife Mellicent Ferguson, "grandsons Wm. Gregory, Tunstall Gregory, John Gregory and Isaac Gregory (sons of Isaac Gregory) and Donald McNeal Ferguson, son of my daughter Elizabeth Gregory."

[16]A deed of 1780 shows that Stephen Terry was "the son of Zacheriah Terry, heir-at-law of James Terry, deceased," who about 1755 moved from this section to Orange County, N. C. Stephen Terry's will was proven October 16, 1797, naming wife Sarah Terry, sons Nathaniel, James, William and John Terry; daughters Anne, Elizabeth and Rhoda Terry.

The mail post was an important branch of the service at Peytonsburg. Because of the winter's mud of the more eastern roads the main mail route from the north to the south led by Peytonsburg. Dispatch riders would arrive with important mail and it was the duty of the post commandant to forward the same without delay, and in order to do this it was necessary to keep at the post a number of express riders. James M. Williams served one year as a dispatch rider at Peytonsburg; other express riders as shown by the Claim Records were Sherwood Thompson, William Norton, Drury Smith, Matthew Stone, Samuel Harris, William Shelton, Edward Ware.

John Hay[17] who was bearing important public dispatches from Congress to the south lodged complaint against Charles Lynch Adams,[18] saying that while at Peytonsburg his dispatches were forcibly taken from him and opened by Adams and Edward and Thomas Tunstall.[19] Adams was a justice of the peace and the Tunstalls were kinsmen of the clerk of the county, all men of position, and the explanation given of their conduct was "that the Continental and State affairs had become so blended as to involve both in difficulties"; those who were responsible for the different arms of the service being overzealous, probably, in the dischanrge of their duties.

17Calendar of Virginia Papers, Vol 2, 181.

18Charles Lynch Adams was the son of Robert Adams and his wife Penelope Lynch, a sister of Colonel Charles Lynch. Charles Lynch Adams married a sister of Thomas and Edward Tunstall, and daughter of Thomas Tunstall of Pittsylvania County. The following entries were found in a Bible Dictionary belonging to Shubal P. Barnard:

"Charles Lynch Adams died on Saturday 21st of April, 1804, in the 52nd year of his age.
Charles L. Adams (Jr.) was born July 24, 1782.
Penelope Adams was born Aug. 4, 1788.
Sarah C. Adams was born Dec. 13, 1789.
Elizabeth Adams was born December 5, 1792.
Mildred Adams was born Aug. 23, 1794.
Thomas T. Adams was born June 2, 1796.
Robert Adams was born Aug. 1, 1800.
Elizabeth T. Adams was born April 10, 1768." A portrait of this venerable old lady hangs at "Monteflora" the home of her great grandson Henry Ward Adams.

Elizabeth Adams, the daughter of Charles Lynch Adams and his wife Elizabeth Tunstall, married Shubal P. Barnard, an early Baptist Minister.

19The complaint read:

"John Hay to Robert Williams, State's Attorney for Pittsylvania County.
Sir:— June 22.
Arriving here yesterday on my way to North Carolina with public dispatches, a person named Charles Lynch Adams, accompanied by two persons called Thos. Tonsill and Ned Tonsill, assuming the authority of magistrates did by force of arms seize upon me and my public dispatches, with my private papers all on lawful and necessary business."

Thomas and Edmond Tunstall were the sons of Thomas Tunstall, an early clerk of Halifax County who in 1768 purchased lands on Stinking River in eastern Pittsylvania and established his home there. The will of Thomas Tunstall, Sr., was probated at Pittsylvania Court House in which he named sons Thomas, Edmund, William and daughter Rebecca. He had probably already provided for daughter Elizabeth. Thomas Tunstall, Jr., married Mildred Todd, sister of William and Richard Todd; he represented the county in the Legislature for the session of 1791, 92, 93. In 1794 he removed to Lincoln County, Ky.

Edmund Tunstall married a daughter of his kinsman William Tunstall, the clerk. In 1796 Mrs. Elizabeth Tunstall of Bertie, North Carolina, made a gift of two slaves to her grand daughter, Elizabeth Tunstall, daughter of Edmond Tunstall of Pittsylvania. Edmund Tunstall represented Pittsylvania in the Legislature for the sessions of 1801 and 1802.

A good deal of friction developed between McCraw of the Continental Post and the military authorities of Pittsylvania County concerning field duty for the men employed at the Post. McCraw[20] reported to the Governor at one time:

"I have a number of men in the Public Service at this Post as waggoners, express riders, canteen makers and etc., for whom I have promised to procure a tour of duty provided they work faithfully; otherwise it would be impossible to carry on the work of the department. The Court Martial of Pittsylvania has threatened to declare these men liable to six months service in the army. The southern army is suffering for horse shoes and canteens and can not supply them if deprived of these men."

Again he complained:[21] "The Court martials of the Counties threaten to make six months soldiers of all men I engage. The citizens willing to work, but are deterred. Unless this be stopped I can not furnish the canteens so much wanted by the southern army; the armorers will not be able to repair the damaged guns, nor can I have the horseshoes made, now so much needed."

To solve this difficulty the General Assembly declared that men employed by the various military posts would not be subject to draft for field duty.

It is not difficult to understand the cause of friction between McCraw of the Continental Service and the county military authorities, for constant calls came to the county for men to be drafted for the Northern Continental Army, for the Southern Continental Army, and still others for the state service. The county authorities were expected to put in the field the number of men called for; while McCraw was held responsible for the work of his post. With so much to be done and so few to do it, there is no wonder "that one grew sick of the world," as an officer reported from a Bedford County post.

McCraw advised[22] the state authorities against employing the artificers of his post for twelve months, saying that it was much better to engage them to make two canteens a day, or as smiths for 500 pairs of horse shoes. Much difficulty was experienced in getting a sufficient number of wagons for the post, and McCraw reported that he had never been able to get any of the "State's Brigaded Wagons," and so was entirely dependent upon the people of the district for wagons. At times

[20]Cal. Va. Papers, Vol. 2, 301.
[21]Cal. Va. Papers, Vol. 2, 260.
[22]Cal. Va. Papers, Vol. 2, 398.

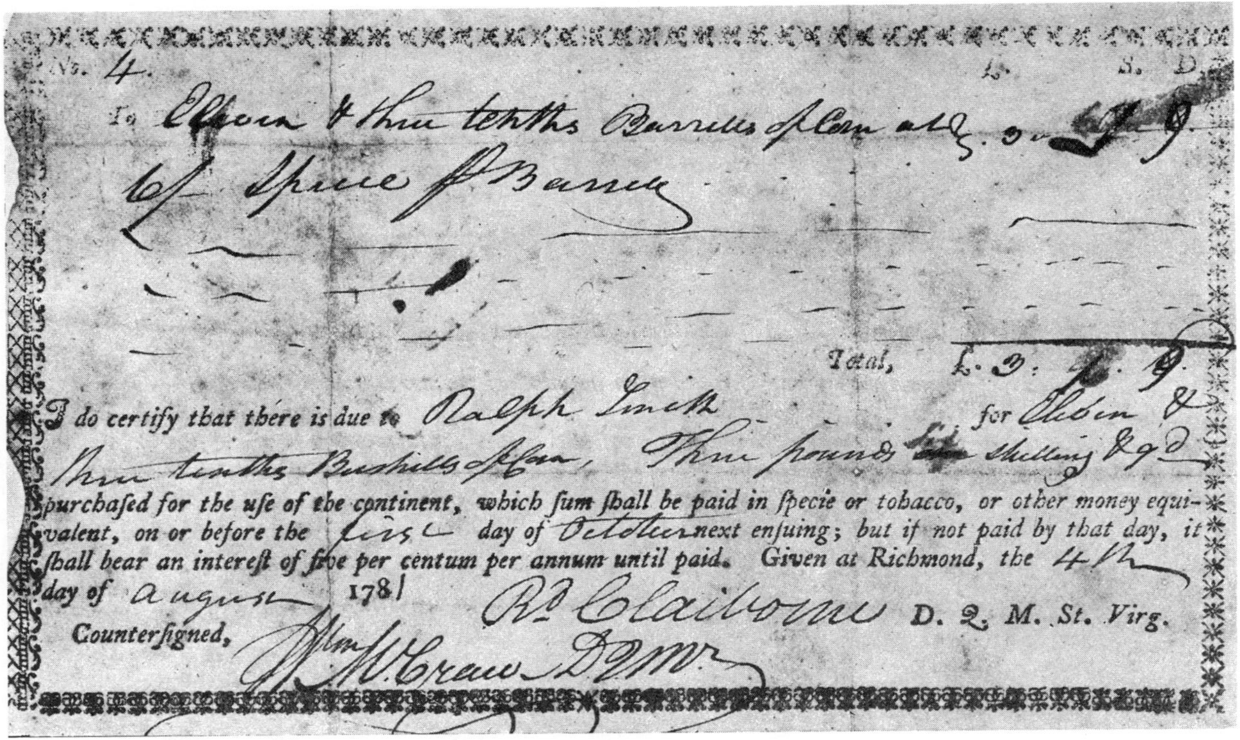

No. 4. £ S. D

To Eleven & three tenths Barrells of Corn at £.3.6.9

6/ Specie ℔ Barrel

Total, £.3.6.9

I do certify that there is due to Ralph Smith for Eleven & three tenths Bushells of Corn, Three pounds six shillings & 9d purchased for the use of the continent, which sum shall be paid in specie or tobacco, or other money equivalent, on or before the first day of October next ensuing; but if not paid by that day, it shall bear an interest of five per centum per annum until paid. Given at Richmond, the 4th day of August 1781

Rd. Claiborne D. Q. M. St. Virg.

Countersigned, Wm. McCraw D.Q.M.

A receipt given by William McCraw, D. Q. M., to Ralph Smith, in August, 1781, for 11 3-10 bushels of corn

in his reports he complained of the worthlessness of the teams and wagons furnished by the people, and again praised them for their generous aid.

Another post of the district was located at New London, in Bedford County, where arms were repaired and ammunition manufactured. The old armory building was standing a few years ago. It was said[23] of these works that the post at Bedford "is of first importance as the operations of General Greene's army entirely depend upon its supplies." Captain Nathan Reid reported from New London that "300 stands of arms ordered to General Lawson; if it was to save life wagons could not be procured within a week. I am sick of the whole world." Again it was reported[24] from New London, July 1781, "Major Mazuret called for all fixed ammunition to be forwarded to Halifax old Court House (Peytonsburg) amounting to ten or twelve wagon loads."

In January 1781, General Greene[25] wrote to the Governor of Virginia that "unless the State of Virginia immediately begins to collect the magazines of provisions on the Roanoke we shall absolutely starve."

Major Claiborne reported[26] to the Governor:

"February 11, 1781, Sir: Your Excellency will observe that among the most weighty articles (to be collected for the use of the Southern Continental Army) are 500,000 bushels of corn and oats to be laid in at the magazines on Dan River from Boyd's Ferry upwards. The price of everything is so enormous that the ½ million will go but a small way procuring them." These magazines were probably located at the ferries such as Boyd's, Dix's, Irvine's, Wilson's and Perkins'.

We have learned in the World War how the tide of war raises the cost of everything. The high cost prevailing at the time of the Revolutionary War is illustrated in the sale[27] of the property of Samuel Hoskins of Halifax Nov. 17, 1780, when steers sold at an average of £300 each, 4 barrels of corn at £244, a cow and calf for £426, and 2 sheep for £100.

Virginia contributed to the northern Continental Army under General Washington 15 full regiments, and at different times calls were made to complete the regiments. In October 1777 there was a draft made from each county for that purpose, and Pittsylvania was called upon for 36 men. In May 1778 Washington needed 2,000 recruits from Virginia, and Pittsylvania and 32 other counties were ordered to furnish each a

---

[23]Cal. Va. Papers, Vol. 2, 156.
[24]Cal. Va. Papers, Vol. 2, 264.
[25]Cal. Va. Papers, Vol. 1, 458.
[26]Cal. Va. Papers, Vol. 1, 506.
[27]Cal. Va. Papers, Vol. 1, 388.

full company of 50 men, with captain, lieutenant and ensign. In October, 2,216 men were needed to complete Virginia's quota for the Continental Army and each county was called upon to furnish 1/25 of their militia for this purpose. In October 1780 Washington again appealed to Virginia for recruits, and the state responded with a call for 3,000 troops, of which Pittsylvania's quota was 45 men.

Virginia's Continental soldier enlisted for three years while the New England soldier enlisted for three to six months. This greatly hampered Washington's movements, for one day he might have a fairly strong force in the field and the next day find himself with a greatly lessened force through the return home of the New England soldiers. Washington urged a three-year enlistment, with which Virginia complied, but New England never heeded. As this long enlistment worked a great hardship upon the families of the married men, at first only the single men were called, but as the war wore on it was found necessary to draft the married men also. This created such distress in the families of the poor that the inhabitants of Pittsylvania petitioned the Legislature against the draft saying:

"We have the highest sense of justness of the Common Cause that we have embarked upon, and have to the utmost of our power contributed to the carrying on of the war with men, money and cheerfulness and are still ready to pour forth our blood and treasure in defense of our country. But many of your petitioners being poor men without slaves, and wives and many small children to maintain, the taking of such of your petitioners from their families would reduce them to the most indegent circumstances and hard grinding want." They further stated that they were ready and willing to serve their country when called upon for a regular "Tour of duty (from 3 to 6 months)" in turn, and to do everything in their power toward the raising of regular soldiers to serve in the Continental Army.

To prevent suffering in the families of absent soldiers the court[28] appointed certain ones to furnish the wives of the soldiers with the necessaries of life.

In May 1777, Crispen Shelton, Gent., was appointed to furnish the wives of Jesse Holder and William Holder, "soldiers now out in the country's service."

Charles Burton was appointed to furnish the wife of John Hall.

[28]Minutes of Pittsylvania County.

In August 1777, Daniel Hankins and Joseph Morton, Gents., were ordered to furnish the wife of John McMahan, "a soldier now in his country's service."

In October 1777, Thomas Black, Gent., was appointed to furnish the wife of John Holt, "a soldier now in his country's service."

In November 1777, James Roberts and William Witcher, Esqs., were appointed to furnish the wives of Francis Henry and Thomas Milburn, "soldiers now in their country's service."

In February 1778, John Donelson, Esq., was appointed to furnish the wife of George Hundley.

In February 1779, Daniel Hankins, Gent., was appointed to furnish the wives of Barlett Atkins, Francis Henry, John McMahan and Peter Hutchison.

In March 1779, John Bays was appointed to furnish Neilly Short's wife.

In 1780, Stephen Coleman, Gent., was appointed to furnish the wife of William Mayes, and Silvanus Stokes to furnish Mary Ann Prosize, the wife of Daniel Prosize, "a soldier in the Continental Service."

We have seen how solidly Virginia stood for the patriot cause in the opening years of the war. As the struggle wore on a sentiment of disaffection arose in the western part of the state largely due to the work of secret British agents sent out from Detroit, who first worked along the western[28] frontiers, then growing bolder, penetrated further east until in 1780 the results of their activities appeared in Bedford and Pittsylvania. The British agents were aided in their work of undermining the people's faith in their cause by the tories of North Carolina,[29] who crossed the boundary line in bands and committed deeds of robbery and violence upon the people. Their work was confined largely to the mountain section where the inhabitants were isolated and more unprotected. Colonel William Letcher of western Henry County (now Patrick), who had married a sister of Captain Peter Perkins, was murdered in his own home in the presence of his wife, by one of these tory bands. The lawless element of the country, seeking an outlet for their unnatural instincts, would join these outlaw bands and the vigilence of the county authorities was required to ferret out and bring to justice the offenders.

[29]Echenrode's "Virginia in the Revolution."

In 1778 William Hyde[30] was tried by the military authorities of Pittsylvania County on the suspicion of treason and was acquitted, but was convicted of divulging false news for which he was fined £50. At the same time Peter Crafford was brought before the Court for "speaking disrespectful to the Common Cause," and fined £25. There were two or three occasions when the offense was of a serious nature, and the offenders were sent on for trial to the higher courts at Richmond.

British agents went secretly among the people representing the inevitable failure of the patriot cause and offered pardon to all who would take the King's oath. So many of the ignorant were imposed upon in this way that the General Assembly of October 1780 offered a general pardon to all in Henry, Bedford, Pittsylvania, Washington, Montgomery and Botetourt Counties who had taken the King's oath but had not committed any overt act.

In September 1780, Governor Thomas Jefferson stated that the disaffection had spread down into Henry and Bedford, and in October he wrote to the delegates in Congress that a conspiracy had been discovered in Pittsylvania, and that the leaders had been taken. (Echenrode.)

Across the river in Bedford County (now Campbell), the disaffected met prompt and summary punishment at the hands of the authorities. Colonel Charles Lynch, whom we have seen making powder in the earlier days of the war, together with his neighbors Captain Robert Adams and Colonel James Calloway, all justices of the peace of Bedford County, held Court at the home of Colonel Lynch and to those judged guilty of disloyalty to the cause the punishment of 39 lashes on the bare back was administered. The cost and inconvenience of transporting the offenders to Richmond for trial before the higher Courts as the law of the state required, caused these three justices to resort to an irregular court which the unsettled state of affairs demanded. On the lawn of Colonel Lynch's old home is still standing the venerable walnut tree under which these Revolutionary patriots held their courts. A trial without the prescribed routine of law and judgment of 39 lashes at once became known as Lynch's Law, but the death penalty was never inflicted. Colonel Lynch himself referred[31] to the law in a report made as superintendent of the Lead Mines, on June 10, 1782, in which he told of an attempted labor strike: "The Welch men entered into Bond not to work for the country unless they should all be employed, supposing the business could

[30]Pittsylvania Minute Books.
[31]Cal. Va. State Papers, Vol. 3, 190.

not be carried on without them. * * * They are mostly tories and such as Sanders has given Lynch's Law to for Dealing with negroes & etc."

These lead mines, situated in Montgomery County and owned[32] by Colonel Lynch and Robert Rubsamen, were the chief sources of lead supply for the ammunition of the south, and were therefore of prime importance. The mines were taken over by the state for the period of the war and Colonel Lynch was placed in charge of them.

[32]Cal. Va. State Papers, Vol. 3, 190.

CHAPTER XIV

SOUTHERN CAMPAIGN CONTINUED

General Nathaniel Greene assumed command of the Southern Continental Army in the autumn of 1780 at Hillsboro, North Carolina, and Virginia at once sent re-inforcements. Several companies of militia marched[1] from Pittsylvania that autumn and winter. Captain John Winn commanded a company in which Robert Ferguson was a member; Captain James Brewer a company in which John Harris was a member; Captain William Witcher a company in which David Wray was a member; Captain Isaac Clement a company in which Joseph[2] and Abram Chaney were members; Captain Joshua Stone[3] a company in which William Jeffress was a member.

On January the 17th General Daniel Morgan with his Virginia Riflemen struck a blow at Tarleton and defeated him at Cowpens, taking about 600 prisoners. Cornwallis determined to recapture the British prisoners and started in hot pursuit of Morgan who retreated northward; and so rapid was the advance that Morgan had just crossed the Catawba on the 29th when Cornwallis appeared on the opposite bank.

Here the hand of Providence intervened in behalf of the patriots, a heavy rain falling during the night which so increased the waters of the river that for two days they were impassable. During this interval Morgan sent his prisoners off to Virginia under the charge of General Stevens and his brigade of Virginia Militia, by a route nearer to the mountains than that intended to be taken by himself.

---

[1]Pension papers of the privates filed at Pittsylvania Court House.

[2]Abram and Joseph Chaney were the sons of Jacob Chaney whose will was proven at Pitts. C. H., Sept. 21, 1801, naming wife Sarah sons Ezekiel, Isaac, Jacob, Joseph, Abraham, Nathan, John, Moses, Charles and Church. Jacob was undoubtedly a firm believer, for he gave to eight of his sons Bible names, and to the ninth the name of Church. He bequeathed to son Charles "the land whereon I now live touching Col. Henry's lines."

[3]Captain Joshua Stone is thought to be the son of Joshua Stone of Richmond County, whose will was proven Feb. 15, 1774, naming sons Joshua, Benjamin, Thomas and James, and grandson Thomas Stone son of William Stone, deceased. Joshua Stone of Richmond County was the son of William Stone of Richmond County, whose will was proven Jan. 13, 1707, in which he named sons Joshua and Philip, son-in-law Robert Schofield and grandson John Glascock. Joshua Stone of Pittsylvania was a surveyor, and he also served as justice of the peace and sheriff of the county; he married July 1769, Mary Hoskins, a daughter of William Hoskins of Halifax County, and lived in the eastern part of the county, near the Halifax line. His will was proven May 20, 1822, in which he named sons William H., Thomas C., Coleman, Samuel, Clack, Joshua, and John Stone; daughter Polly Terry, the wife of Nathaniel Terry, and daughter D. C. Harrison of Tennessee and her four youngest children, Nancy P. Harrison, Coley, Answorth and Clack Harrison.

John Stone, son of Joshua, was the father of Parson James Hoskins Stone who married Elizabeth Fitzgerald and settled on Banister River at the beautiful old place, "Oak Grove," now known as "Tieches," where he reared a large and interesting family. Mrs. Stone's will, proven 1865, named sons Samuel and John, grand-daughters Betty, wife of Dr. George Carter, Emma, daughter of Allen W. Womack, and Susan, daughter of Armistead Nowlin.

The Pittsylvania troops, still forming a part of Stevens' Brigade, had been stationed at Camp Hicks, South Carolina. From this place General Stevens wrote[4] to the Governor of Virginia on January 24th, saying that as the term of enlistment of the men under his command had expired he was ordered to march "in ye morning and take charge of ye prisoners, and conduct them to Virginia." Stevens' Brigade now left the main body of the army, and acting as a guard for the prisoners, proceeded north. Major Haynes, of South Carolina, whom Greene had appointed deputy commissioner of the prisoners, reported[5] to Gov. Jefferson from New London on Feb. 14th, that "on the way from the south many prisoners escaped, the march being very rapid through Henry and Bedford Counties. They are concealed in the country and orders should be given to collect them."

A guard was called out to receive[6] the prisoners when they reached Bedford, and this probably also happened at Henry Court House for David Wray said in his pension[7] paper that he was ordered out to "guard 500 prisoners taken by Morgan at Cowpens, which were guarded from County to County," and he aided in guarding them to Bedford. Stevens' Brigade then proceeded to Pittsylvania Court House where his men were discharged and their "guns stored in the public magazines there allotted for this purpose," as General Lee tells in his Memoirs.[8] Pittsylvania Court House was then located in the ravine near the railway station, and the magazines where the public arms were stored were no doubt hastily constructed log buildings. After storing the arms and dismissing the troops Stevens set out for his home in Culpeper, but hearing a report[9] that General Greene was likely to be overtaken by Cornwallis before he could cross the Dan, Stevens hurried back to Pittsylvania and through the exertions of the county lieutenant, Col. John Wilson, the militia was again called out and marched with Stevens to General Greene's aid. This was no draft, but a call for volunteers to defend their homes against the enemy whose ruthless policy carried fire and sword before him, and who now stood at their very doors.

There is a county tradition[10] that Revolutionary soldiers once camped in the grove at the great spring on top of White Oak Mountain near

[4]Calendar of Virginia State Papers, Vol. 1, 459.
[5]Calendar of Virginia State Papers, Vol. 1, 515.
[6]Calendar of Virginia State Papers, Vol. 1, 510.
[7]Filed at Pitts. C. H.
[8]"Memoirs of the Southern Campaign," by Gen. "Light Horse" Harry Lee, p. 231.
[9]Lee's "Memoirs," p. 232.
[10]Captain Isaac Coles recounted this tradition in 1925.

Shocco, and this was probably the occasion, when the Pittsylvania troops were hurrying to join General Greene. The rumor of Greene's disaster, however, proved to be false, for he made safe his escape from Cornwallis after a retreat of over 200 miles in the dead of winter, over frozen roads, through rain and snow. Greene was not prepared to risk battle with Cornwallis at this time for fear of the loss of his army and in order to escape, it was necessary to cross three rivers, the Catawba, the Yadkin, and the Dan. Cornwallis endeavored to overtake and attack Greene where a river would cut off his retreat, so that the march northward became a race for the rivers. After the Catawba and the Yadkin had been passed Cornwallis sought to cut Green off from the upper shallower fords of the Dan, not thinking he could cross lower down, but this is just what Greene did. Col. Carrington, the quarter master, had collected[11] all the boats on the river—brought down those from Dix's great ferry and Wilson's and Perkins' ferries, and held them in readiness at Irwin's Ferry, 20 miles below Dix's, just over the line in Halifax County; and at Boyd's Ferry, four miles below Irwin's. At these two points the patriot army crossed to safety on February the 12th. A letter from General Greene to Baron Steuben, written[12] February 15th, from "Camp Irwin's Ford on Dan River," stated:

"The enemy at this moment are in full march for the river not three miles from our camp, but we are happy enough to have the river between us, this will give us an opportunity to cross the Banister. Our stores and baggage are ordered over the Staunton. We are in want of arms, pray send us 600 and let them come[13] to Coles' Ferry on Staunton River."

He wrote further that he was uncertain whether Cornwallis would continue the pursuit, but in case he did, that he, Greene, was ready to retreat further across Banister and Staunton Rivers. But his Lordship gave up the chase at Dan River and turned back into North Carolina. The following item from the Claim Records probably refers to these days: "To John Wynne for a negro fellow eight days impressed assisting the Baggage Waggons and Artillery across Dan River—10 sh."

General Stevens and the Pittsylvania Militia found Greene's wearied troops resting safely among the friendly people of Halifax and Pittsylvania Counties. In camp "joy[14] beamed on every face, each one was conscious of having done his duty" and many were the anecdotes told

[11] Lee's "Memoirs."

[12] Cal. Va. State Papers, Vol. 1, 519.

[13] Home of Col. Isaac Coles.

[14] Lee's "Memoirs."

Berry Hill

Home of Col. Peter Perkins. The addition to the right was added after the War Between the States

of the hopes and fears felt during the retreat. The soldiers were received by the people "with the affection of brethren," and volunteers poured in until General Stevens force numbered more than a thousand.

While Greene's army was in this section he established his hospital[15] at the plantation of Col. Peter Perkins, on Dan River, in the south-western part of the county; and Col. Perkins' home not being sufficiently large to receive all the sick, the homes of the neighbors, Constant and Nicholas Perkins and William Harrison were also used. "Berry Hill," Col. Perkins' home, stands on a hill overlooking the river from the north side, and is a fine specimen of colonial architecture. The William Harrison[16] house is also standing, and is a short distance from the lawn at "Oak Hill," but has suffered from neglect in the passage of years. The hospital was established here for three months, and from the Claim Records we learn that it was under the command of Dr. Brown, and that Dr. Elijah Gillett was one of the attending physicians; that Thomas Casey was paid for shoeing 43 horses for the officers and doctors of the general hospital; that Thomas Thompkins served as ferryman to the hospital. Daniel Roberts was forage master and Nicholas and James McCubbins and Charles Oaks were commissaries and gathered supplies for the use of the hospital. William Norton was paid for twenty-one days service in "collecting and bringing flour from Cumberland for the General Hospital."

The Court of Claims held May 11th, 1785, paid for the use of the hospital as follows:

"To William Harrison for the Rent of houses, Beds and etc., for the use of the General Hospital keep at Peter Perkins, three months....£35

To Constant Perkins for the Rent of houses, Beds and etc., for the use of the General Hospital, keep at Peter Perkins 3 months....£40

To Peter Perkins for the Rent of Houses, Beds, etc., for the use of the General Hospital keep at your house three months....£50

---

[15]Claim Records of Pitts. Co.

[16]William Harrison came from Goochland County to Pittsylvania in 1770, when he purchased for £700, 432 acres on Dan River from John Payne the Elder, of Goochland, who had in turn purchased the land through Gideon Marr from William Bean.

In 1773 Harrison purchased 500 acres for £500 lying on the north side of Dan River, touching the line of William Bean and Nicholas Perkins.

On Dec. 23, 1763, William Harrison married Anne Payne, daughter of Josias Payne of Goochland. He represented the county in the General Assembly the sessions of 1785-86. William Harrison's will was proven Feb. 18, 1811, in which he named sons Robert, Nathaniel and William P. Harrison; daughters Sussannah wife of William Ware, Jane wife of Henry Stone, Anne wife of Daniel Coleman, and Polly Dillard Harrison. Polly, or Mary Dillard Harrison married Captain A. G. Walters and had issue: Robert A., Felix, Archibald Edwards, Mary Catherine who married Christopher Holland, and Elizabeth married Calvin Flynn.

In the rock walled grave yard near the Harrison house sleep William and Anne Payne Harrison, their graves unmarked. In his will William enjoined his children to take particular care of their "tender and antient Mother who has many times contributed to their comfort."

To Nicholas Perkins for Rent of house, Beds, etc., for the use of the General Hospital keep at Peter Perkins three months........................(torn)

To Col. Peter Perkins for 90 Days Service as Commissary to the General Hospital keep at his house @ 12/per day....................................£45."

A hospital for the sick and wounded of Morgan's command was established at Henry Court House.

General Greene could not long content himself with the life of ease and plenty which Virginia furnished, and soon recrossed the Dan and offered battle to Cornwallis at Guilford C. H. on March the 15th. Here General Stevens' Virginia Militia atoned for their past defeat and covered themselves and their officers with glory.

In forming the line of battle, General Greene placed his North Carolina Militia in the first line, the Virginia Militia under Generals Lawson and Stevens in the second line, and the Continentals, two regiments of Maryland and two of Virginia formed the third line; while Col. Charles Lynch with a battalion of Virginia Militia was posted on the right flank and Campbell with his Virginia Riflemen on the left flank. When the British advanced an unreasonable panic seized the North Carolina Militia and they rushed from the field; "but," tells Gen. Lee,[17] "noble was the stand made by the Virginia Militia, Stevens and Lawson with their faithful brigades contended for victory against the best officers in the British Army, and so firmly did they maintain the battle that Brigadier O'Hara with his grenadiers and a second battalion was brought into line for support, and then first Stevens and then Lawson were forced to retire, but so resolutely had these troops supported the action that notwithstanding the desertion of some of our forces, every corps of the British Army had been brought into battle and many suffered severely."

The battle was stubbornly contested on both sides and might have been won had not General Greene, who never dared risk serious loss to his army, and not knowing the extent to which the British Army was crippled, ordered a retreat which was performed in an orderly manner.

The day after the battle Major Charles McGill reported[18] from the army to Gov. Jefferson:

"Immediately on the display of their (British) Column an attack was made on our First Line Composed entirely by Militia, who returned their Fire and the greater number from Virginia behaved in such a manner as would do honor to Veterans."

[17]Lee's "Memoirs," p. 231.

[18]Cal. Va. State Papers, Vol. 1, 574.

History has preserved for us the names of but few of the Pittsylvanians who made so noble a stand on that day of battle, though we may well know that every able bodied man in the county who could possess himself of a gun was present. One would judge from the pension paper of Moses Hutchings, a Revolutionary soldier of Pittsylvania, that the whole militia organization of the county served in the battle of Guilford, for he stated that in February 1781, when the British Army was advancing towards Virginia that he and fifteen other young men took their horses and rifles and set out to "harrass the British Piquets." That on their return home they found all the Pittsylvania companies officered, so he entered the company of Captain Thomas Smith as private, and served in the battle of Guilford under Col. Campbell on the left wing. John Smith and John Irby were also members of this company.

No doubt it happened in Pittsylvania as it did in Henry County, where Major Waller reported[19] to the Governor that his order calling the militia out to General Greene's assistance had been received, "but the approach of the enemy being so alarming had caused the militia to assemble, and they had already joined Gen'l Greene in greater numbers than called for."

In the battle of Guilford Captain James Brewer commanded a company of Pittsylvania[20] Militia in which John Neal and David Wray were members, and which served under the command of Col. Peter Perkins; Captain William Dix commanded a company in which Robert Ferguson was a member; Captain Gabriel Shelton, Lieutenant James Maid, Ensign Vincent Shelton a company in which David Irby was a member. Captain Shelton marched his company to Irwin's Ferry and there Captain Thomas Smith took command. Captain Joseph Morton commanded[21] a company of Pittsylvania Militia in the battle of Guilford in which George Dodson served as a private and was wounded by an enemy ball in the knee. Robert Walters and John Terry both made affidavit that they saw Dodson during the battle and knew that he was wounded. He was granted aid by the state. Nathan Rowland was also so severely wounded in the battle that the Court of Pittsylvania in June 1784 recommended him to the General Assembly for aid.

After the battle the company of Captain William Dix, to which John Neal had been transferred marched south with General Greene. The bit of paper recording Neal's honorable discharge from this tour has been preserved and reads as follows:

[19]Cal. Va. State Papers, Vol. 1, 533.
[20]Pension papers of the soldiers on file at Pittsylvania C. H.
[21]Pitts. Legislative Petitions, Archvist Dept.

March 31, 1781.

"This is to certify that John Neal, a soldier hath served a tour of Duty in Genl. Lawsons's Brigade as a militia man from Virginia to the State of North Carolina and is Discharged from the same Certifyed by me.

William Dix, Capt."

In April two other companies marched from Pittsylvania, one commanded by Captain Henry Burnett[22] in which Leroy Shelton and Robert Ferguson were members, and the other commanded by Captain John Buckley.

William Dixon, who was living at this time in Orange County, N. C., stated in his pension papers that after the battle of Guilford it was deemed necessary to destroy or sink the boats and cannon on Dan River between Perkins and Dix's Ferry, and that he and some others were detached for that purpose, and were piloted by Dr. Bryant.

The following is a brief order issued by the military authorities of Pittsylvania County:[23]

"Edmund Pain May 23, 1781.
Philemon Pain
James Taylor
William Watson

Sir,

The men whose names are contained in the above list you are to give notice to appear at the Court House on Monday next in order to March, they being of numbers now ordered out.

I am, sir,
Your obd't
Humble Serv't
Abram Shelton.

Mr. John Lumpkin."

In the summer of 1781 Cornwallis invaded Virginia, and strange to say, General Greene, instead of defending Virginia in her hour of need, marched south into the Carolinas leaving the source of his supplies to the mercy of the enemy. General Phillips and Benedict Arnold, the traitor, had landed forces in Virginia the first of the year and had been pillaging and burning both public stores and private property in the eastern part of the State. The British authorities were fully conscious of the

[22]Captain Henry Burnett, in his will of 1817, left his estate to his daughter Elizabeth, wife of William Smith, and her children—Leroy Shelton married Nancy Lanier and in his will of 1843, named children: Eliza Robertson, Louisa Dyer, Martha Harris, Mary Law, Nancy Walton, Bethenia Harris, and son-in-law, Jesse Leftwich.

[23]In possession of the author.

generous aid Virginia was lending the patriot cause and were determined to destroy her resources, for with Virginia overrun the rebellion in the South would soon be broken. In order to make Virginia's destruction more complete Cornwallis joined his forces to those of Arnold and Phillips, and the Old Dominion became the seat of war.

In addition to Virginia's contribution of men and supplies to the northern Continental Army and the Southern Continental Army, it was now necessary for her to put a third force in the field for her own defense, which must also be clothed, fed and supplied with arms and ammunition. The demands made upon our forefathers at this time by the "turn of war's tide" were so great that only the consciousness of the justness of their cause enabled them to "carry on" successfully in the face of so great odds. Despite General Greene's desertion of the state he still looked to Virginia as the source of all supplies for his army, and both General Washington and Congress urged that the support of Greene be continued. And so the Continental Post at Peytonsburg remained active in all its departments, gathering and forwarding supplies, repairing guns, manufacturing horse shoes and canteens for the use of the Southern Continental Army.

From reports forwarded by the county lieutenants to the Executive[24] Department at Richmond we learn something of the military activities of Pittsylvania and the adjoining counties of Bedford, Halifax and Henry during this period. These reports make mention of orders to the militia calling them out at different times, and we may judge from the orders to one county that the same were issued to the adjoining sister county.

Col. James Calloway who was in charge of the military forces of Bedford County reported[25] in March 1781: "According to your order of January 2nd, 400 of the militia of this county are now near Portsmouth. They are poor men whose families are suffering in their absence," and he begs that they be relieved. "Nearly the same number are now in service with General Greene. These demands upon the county have interferred with making up the quota of the Regular Troops required."

On April the 11th he reported[26] that according to instructions he had ordered out 380 men to join General Greene but from Col. Lynch who was just from Greene's Head Quarters on Deep River he learned that Cornwallis was on his way to Wilmington, and prayed that since the

[24]Calendar of Va. State Papers, Vol. 1-2-3.

[25].Calendar of Va. State Papers, Vol. 1-5-6-7.

[26]Calendar of Va. State Papers, Vol. 2-28.

distance was so great that the militia be allowed to remain at home and tend their crop at this important season of the year.

On June 4th, Col. Calloway reported:[27] "It has not been in my power to move from this county more than two companies of militia in consequence of your order of May 8th. As many men have been called out as it was thought arms could be procured for. The men that have marched are part of those who have just finished a Tour of three months at Portsmouth, in whose absence the whole balance of our militia served and are serving Tours to the Southward, so that it became their turn to serve again on present call. These men are very poor and their families depend upon their labors for subsistence."

On June 18th, Col. Abram Penn, Co.-Lieut. of Henry County reported[28] that he regretted that so many of the militia were called out at this important season, but the enemy, he supposed would not wait "till we sow and reap." Had no arms having sent 100 with the men to General Greene and another 100 with those who went to General Lawson; desired to know whether he should send the men unarmed, and whether they could be furnished below. An express had arrived from Baron Steuben calling for men, was at a loss how to obey the order.

On July the 21st, Col. John Wilson, Co.-Lieut. of Pittsylvania, reported:[29] "The militia of the county are now reduced to about 600 men except officers. 181 are ordered to the South, 150 are below in our state which makes half now in Service and Runaway which will Distress our county very much."

On the same day Col. Robert Wooding reported[30] from Halifax County:

"Sir,

Yours of the 15th advising 1/7 of the militia officered and Equipt should Join Gen'l Wayne on his march to the Southward; to Equip them will be Impossible because our county are in a manner disarmed by the frequent Impressing of arms to put in the hands of those who were called out on former Occasions: which commenced with the Minute Service. We had 14 guns in the field last April at General Muster. * * * We are not only without guns, as I have said, but we are also without ammunition, Tents, Camp Kettles, flints and etc. * * * Criminal neglect of the Law in some quarter has caused the present condition of things, by which the militia, so necessary as this crisis are powerless."

[27]Calendar of Va. State Papers, Vol. 2, 144.
[28]Calendar of Va. State Papers, Vol. 2, 173.
[29]Calendar of Va. State Papers, Vol. 2, 234
[30]Calendar of Va. State Papers, Vol. 2, 232.

He gave the military strength of the county as 1,004 men, "88 of whom are under 18 years of age, 200 fit for Station Duty, 100 fit for no duty at all, 40 condemned to six months service, mostly runaways to Carolina, Washington and Kentucky Counties, those Receptacles of Villians, which reduces the real strength of the militia to about 670, including those under 18: 300 of which is now on Duty under the command of Maj. Genl: Greene and Brig. Genl: Lawson, and an hundred men under marching orders to relieve those under Genl Lawson, which would have been done before now had not their march been retarded by the late movements of Col. Tarleton. * * * All the public stores in the county have long been removed to Peytonsburg in Pittsylvania."

On July 26th, General Robert Lawson of Prince Edward County, wrote[31] to the Governor saying that his order for 1/4 the militia to join General Greene had been received and that he was strongly impressed with the sound policy of supporting Greene's operations in that quarter which could not well be done without speedy reinforcements from this state and that this reinforcement must go from the southern counties. But all arms having been sent out of the county on former occasions it is not possible to arm and equip the number of men now called for * * *. "It is also necessary to observe to your Excellency that several of these counties have sent down the greater part of their men design'd to relief those who have been already in the field.

"I wish also to remark, that the Southern Counties have sent their militia to South Carolina on four different occasions, and have nevertheless done equal duty in the State with these Northern Counties, who have not thus been call'd upon."

From these reports we gain some idea of the heavy demands made at this time upon Pittsylvania and other southern counties. When a force of 5,000 men were ordered to take the field in defense of the state, these southern counties were called upon for the same proportion of troops as the northern counties, and at the same time were sending reinforcements to Greene's Army in the South, for which the northern counties were not called upon; and also furnishing their regular quota of troops to General Washington's army in the north.

In July Governor Thos. Nelson issued the following letter[32] to the Co. Lieuts. of the state:

"Sir:

The Harvest being over. I hope the militia which have been ordered into Service from your county will take the field with the greatest alacrity.

[31]Calendar of Va. State Papers, Vol. 2, 252.
[32]Calendar of Va. State Papers, Vol. 2.

There was never a Time when vigorous measures were more necessary, or when they promised greater advantage. Every exertion will be made by the enemy * * * and a successful opposition on our Part will in all Probability put a happy Period to the war."

The state was faced with the herculean task of feeding, clothing and equipping this third army, and the difficulties which were met and overcome are revealed in the official reports of that period. Col. Davies from Chesterfield Courthouse stated[33] in a letter to the Governor: "I found upon my return hither that all the troops that marched from hence had by order of Baron Steuben come back to this station, from the utter inability to keep the field from the want of almost every species of clothing."

Col. Febriger who took charge of some new levies reported[34] that the men were literally naked and must have clothing and shoes. "Many men are now left about the country with their feet half worn off."

Each county was called upon to furnish clothing and provisions for the state troops. Abram Shelton was appointed[35] Commissioner of Provisions for Pittsylvania County and was allowed by the county court the sum of £2,325 for his trouble and expenses while acting in this capacity. Captain John Buckley also served as a commissioner of provisions for the state troops, and Jesse Heard as a deputy commissioner. Captain Buckley reported[36] to the Governor on Oct. 4, 1781, that "in a few days will send a large drove of beeves to Camp (Yorktown) and will have on hand large quantities of flour and other provisions."

William McCraw, commander of the Continental Post, complained[37] of Captain Buckley as being "a clog to every branch of public business." But Captain Buckley was collecting supplies for the state troops, while McCraw, in his zeal for carrying forward the work entrusted to his care was bent upon getting as much as possible of the State's subsistence for Greene's Continental troops, and it was but natural that their interests should clash. McCraw brought complaint[38] at another time against Captain Buckley and Captain Thomas Smith of Henry County for taking provisions from Mose Wilson a waggoner from Prince Edward, and against Jesse Heard and Captain Martin for "unlawful siezure of 6 bbls. of salt belonging to the Continentals." Both branches of the service

[33]Calendar of Va. State Papers, Vol. 1, 462.
[34]Calendar of Va. State Papers, Vol. 2, 194.
[35]Minute Books of Pittsylvania Co.
[36]Cal. Va. State Papers, Vol. 2, 524.
[37]Cal. Va. State Papers, Vol. 2, 570.
[38]Cal. Va. State Papers, Vol. 2, 597.

were faced with a tremendous work that necessity demanded—men must be fed and clothed, and those who marched the weary miles and fought the battles had also to sow and reap the crops which fed themselves and their dependent families.

The General Assembly of October, 1780, assessed the counties for clothing and beef. Pittsylvania's share was 20 complete suits of clothing and 20 beeves weighing not less than 3,000 lbs. a piece. Each county was also called upon for a good wagon and four horses with driver, for public use.

Daniel Hankins, Gent., was appointed[39] by the Court of Pittsylvania to procure the wagon and team, and in July 1781, he was authorized to hire a wagoner to "transport the Waggon and Team purchased for the Public Use for this county to John Buckley." Indicative of the high costs prevailing at this time the Sheriff of the county was ordered to pay "Daniel Hankins, Gent., £699 for iron and etc., found the waggon purchased for the Public Use."

In order to procure the clothing and beeves for which the county was assessed, Pittsylvania was divided into twenty districts, each district to provide a beef and outfit of clothing. Ralph Smith, son of Mr. John Smith of "The Pocket," was appointed receiver of one of the districts in the following notice:[40]

"At a meeting of the Field Officers and Magistrates, on Friday the 10th, August, 1781, for the purpose of Laying out the County into districts to furnish an Equal proportion of clothes and beef for the use of the Army, Ralph Smith[41] is appointed Receiver to the within district, and it is ordered that he call together the Inhabitants of the same and proceed according to Law.

Teste:

James Roberts
Thomas Dillard
John Dix } County Commissioners.
John Wilson
Ben Lankford

Abram Shelton, Clerk."

[39]Minute Books of Pittsylvania County.

[40]Paper in possession of the author.

[41]Ralph Smith, eldest son of John Smith of "The Pocket," inherited the home and never married.

The inhabitants of the district were named by the commissioners and assessed as follows:

John Barber	£ 6	Lewis Shelton	£ 82
Shad Collier	5	William Smith	9
John Collier	3	Jos. Grymes	4
Jessee Keesee	4	John Lawson	13
Wm. McDowell	5	James Dalton	8
John Parker	13	George Phillip	146
Frank Smith	6	William Goad	6
Nathan Thurman	36	Ro. Goad	11
Wm. Ward, Gent.	206	Ben. Tarrant	84
Wm. Bennett	39	Timothy Dalton	4
Reuben Bennett	32	Richard Bennett	47
Jesse Bailey	4	James Dalton	4
John Dalton	48	James Downey	25
Samuel Dalton	6	Nottley Wheat	5
John Dalton	10	Jacob Bargers	19
Richard Towler	5	Littlebury Patterson	6
Charles Goad	5	Charles Calloway	110
George Herndon	40	James Calloway (Bedford)	6
John Hensley	7	Wm. Baber	32
John Law	6	John Kessee	42
Bryan W. Nowling	40	John Talbort, Esq. (Bedford)	10
David Ross[42]	805	Richard Walden	20
Thomas Ramsey	5	Sam'l Whitworth	10
Thomas Spraggins	6	Ralph Smith	432
			£2,826

[42]David Ross who was assessed so large an amount by the Commissioners lived at "Arrowfield," on James River in Fluvanna County. He was a wealthy merchant, operating stores in different parts of the state, one being located in Bedford County. He owned a large plantation in Pittsylvania on Pigg River, known as "Ross's Quarter" and the tax list of 1785 gave for the Quarter 2 overseers, 41 slaves, 15 horses and 129 cattle.

Ross was an ardent patriot and warmly supported the American cause. Feb. 2, 1781 he was appointed commercial agent for the state. He made a loan to the government of £2,500 and 1,200 hhds. of tobacco (Cal. Va. State Papers).

In a letter to the governor dated March 27, 1781, he wrote: "Virginia now bears an over proportion of the expenses of the war," and suggested calling upon congress for a proportion of the moneys used for general defense. At another time: "From the time of Gates' defeat till the reduction of most of the British Posts in the Southern States I furnished the Army with Bar Iron and horse shoes, and with my own money paid the waggoners for transporting it to the army, for which I received General Green's thanks. Supplies of provisions and horses were drawn from my plantations in common with other planters and Farmers."

The army post at Point of Forks, was situated on his estate in Fluvanna. David Ross died in the City of Richmond, May 4, 1817, and his executor sold his lands in Pittsylvania on Frying Pan Creek to John Ward, Jr. (Pittsylvania Deed Books).

On September 8th, bids were taken for the clothing and beef, and awarded as follows:

George Phillips, 2 Shirts, 1 pr. overall	£200
2 pairs stockings	100
James Flannigan, 1 pr. men's shoes	35
Bryant W. Nowling, 1 Good Wool Hat	70
George Herndon, 1 Beef to weigh 3000 Lbs.	600

We see from the above that money had little purchasing power at this time.

On November 9th all of the clothing except the suit of overalls was delivered to Col. Wilson and the following receipt taken:

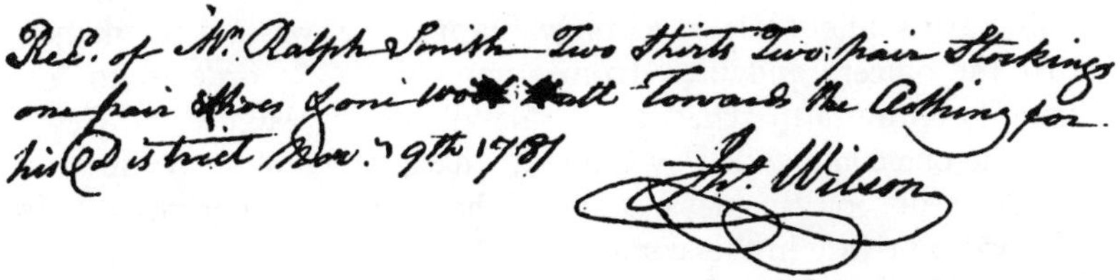
Rec. of Mr. Ralph Smith Two Shirts Two pair Stockings one pair Shoes & one Wool Hatt Towards the Clothing for his District Nov. 9th 1781

Jno. Wilson

Chapter XV

CLOSE OF REVOLUTION—END OF THE CENTURY

After laying Virginia waste with fire and sword, Cornwallis marched his forces down to the Peninsula and entrenched himself behind fortifications at Yorktown.

In the Claim Records[1] is the following item:

"To Richard Todd[2] for Riding Express for giving the militia Officers notice and finding himself for four days in consequence of his Excellency the Governor's Order, to order 1/4 of the militia to the Siege of York."

Again turning to the pension declarations of those few remaining Revolutionary soldiers left in Pittsylvania in 1832, we find the names of some of the officers and men from among the 1/4 ordered to York. Companies of militia marched from Pittsylvania in August and September, and the one commanded by Captain Charles Hutchings rendezvoused at "Stoney Hill," or Buckleys, and marched direct to Yorktown. John Harris[3] was a private in this company.

Captain William Dix,[4] Lieutenant David Hunt[5] and Ensign Clement McDaniel commanded a company which marched from Pittsylvania in August and numbered among its members Lewis Haley, Isham Farmer, John Neal, John Smith, Avory Mustein and William Jeffress. These men were present on that memorable day at Yorktown, October 19th, and witnessed the surrender of the British Army to General Washington.

[1]Claim Records, p. 67.

[2]Richard Todd was the son of Richard Todd of King & Queen County and a brother of William Todd. He married Mary Lankford, a daughter of Benjamin Lankford of Pittsylvania. Richard Todd died in 1795 for in that year his estate was ordered to be appraised. After the death of her husband Mary Lankford Todd went to Kentucky and made her home with her brother-in-law, Justice Thomas Todd, taking with her her four small children. (*Va. Mag.*, Vol. 25, 309.)

[3]Pension Papers of John Harris.

[4]William Dix was the son of John Dix who made his will in 1785, naming among his other children William, to whom he left the ferry.

[5]In 1746 James and Ralph Hunt of Hanover, bought land in Lunenburg and there James Hunt reared his large family, leaving seven sons, viz.: Charles, Nathaniel, James, Elijah, Gilbert, John and David Hunt. David Hunt settled in Pittsylvania on Straightstone Creek where he built his home after the style of an English cottage. He married Nancy Richardson, and died in 1826, leaving a daughter who married George Boyd, and sons David and John; his will was proven at Pittsylvania Court House, leaving much land and many slaves; his library of books was to be divided between daughter Nancy and son John. John Hunt (son of David) married Sally Tate Brown of Bedford, by whom he had five sons and six daughters: 1. Alonza, died in west, buried at Independence, Mo. 2. James married Miss Langhorn, and had Kate and Sally Hunt. 3. Dr. David Hunt moved south. 4. John Hunt married, 1st, Martha Daniel, 2nd, Susan Daniel and had issue: John Pride, Mattie, Alice and Doran. 5. Mary married Mr. Mosely. 6. Sarah married Col. Geo. Coleman, son of Col. Daniel Coleman. 7. Nancy married Captain Jerry Graves. 8. Martha married Isaac Overbey. 9. Ruth married Mr. Jesse Hargrave of Chatham and had issue: Hunt, Almeyda, Sally Tate and Maggie. 10. Lucy married Charles Clement, son of Charles Clement of "Clement Hill," and had issue: Lucy Charles and Nannie Clement. 11. Daniel married Miss Mebane, and had issue: daughter Sally who married Judge Abram Staples, and Bruce Hunt.

Captain William Dix's company formed a part of the guard designated to convey the British prisoners taken at Yorktown to Noland's Ferry on the Potomac, but Captain Dix being sick at the time, Captain Charles Williams of Pittsylvania was appointed to take charge of the company and marched in his stead.

John Neal's honorable discharge from the service, signed by Captain Williams, has been preserved and reads:

Leesburg, November 7th, 1781.

"The Bearer John Neal having Faithfully Served his Tower of Duty is hereby Discharged By Order of Major Jones.

Charles Williams[6] Capt."

While the surrender of Cornwallis brought to an end actual combat on the soil of Virginia, General Greene continued to prosecute an active campaign in the south. He wrote[7] to Colonel Davies of Virginia in December 1781:

"If Virginia does not exert herself for our aid we are inevitably ruined. My Dear Sir, give no sleep to your eyes or slumber to your eye lids till you get the troops on the March."

Throughout the year 1782 Virginia continued active in her efforts to supply Greene's Army with provisions, clothing, ammunition and men. In November 1781, a month after the surrender, the state issued a call for 3,000 recruits for the Southern Continental Line; and in February Col. Febriger complained[8] that as the draft was not set for the same time in all the counties, that the recruits came in very irregularly.

In April 1782, seven places in the state were named at which troops were to be recruited, and the officers appointed for Peytonsburg,[9] one of the points named, were Captain Nathan Reid, Lieutenant Alfred Russell, Ensign R. Rankin. Col. Febriger stated[10] in a letter to Col. Davies, April 10th, "the reasons of my posting Reid at Peytonsburg is that when he has collected a company for your Reg't he is to march it off, and Stith relieve him to go with the 2nd and so on in Rotation."

None of the names of the soldiers who marched south in these companies in the Spring of 1782 have been preserved.

[6]Captain Charles Williams made his home on Dan River (Book of Estrays). His will was proven Oct. 21, 1805, in which he named beloved wife Sally Williams, sons Peter and Charles Williams, daughters Nancy Williams and Susannah Crouch, wife of John Crouch.

[7]Calendar Va. State Papers, Vol. 2, p. 674.

[8]Calendar Va. State Papers, Vol 3, p. 73.

[9]Calendar Va. State Papers, Vol. 3, p. 127.

[10]Calendar Va. State Papers, Vol. 3, p. 127.

Peytonsburg was a Continental Post where food supplies were collected, yet on June 1st Captain Reid complained[11] of the irregularities of the post in furnishing the troops with food and quarters, saying that the commissioner does not consider them continental troops until they have joined the rendezvous. This friction was probably due to McCraw's zeal in forwarding to the army in the field as many supplies as possible, and he did not relish seeing them consumed by the recruits at home.

In May 1782, the state called for 3,000 men for the army of the United States, to be raised by enlisting one man in every fifteen. This was now the eighth year of the war, and the people were exhausted by the long and arduous struggle, yet the demands made upon them could not cease. A tax called the Specific Tax was collected[12] of ½ bu. wheat (or 1 bu. corn, or 5 pk. oats) and 2 lbs. bacon for every man of 21 years of age. The tax from the district including Pittsylvania, Bedford, Halifax and other counties, amounted to 9,544 bushels corn, 3,127 wheat, 3,609 oats, 223 rye, 17,539 lbs. bacon, £472.

The post at Peytonsburg continued active, for in August Deputy Quarter Master Wm. McCraw reported[13] to Col. Davies that he had 2,200 men engaged in making canteens for the army, "for," he said, "Col. Carrington writes from the Army that canteens are necessary in that sickly country."

Peytonsburg became a point on another important mail route when in February 1782 the "route for Expresses[14] to go to the southward from Richmond" was changed to run by Cumberland C. H., Charlotte C. H., Coles' Ferry and Peytonsburg. In this same month Col. Thomas Posey reported[15] that the detachment of men under his command had taken up camp at Peytonsburg where they would remain for a day to rest his men's feet. He was on his march southward with new levies to join General Greene and wrote: "What would you think if I was to tell you that not a man has deserted me since I set out from Prince Edward, C. H."

The signing of the treaty with Great Britain in 1783 brought these troublous days to an end. With the war safely won men were free to turn their thoughts to other matters, and problems of government, questions of state and county affairs, and later those concerning a federation

[11]Calendar Va. State Papers, Vol. 3, p. 203.
[12]Calendar Va. State Papers, Vol. 3, p. 203.
[13]Calendar Va. State Papers, Vol. 3, p. 253.
[14]Calendar Va. State Papers, Vol. 3, p. 73.
[15]Calendar Va. State Papers, Vol. 3, p. 71.

of the states, were subjects of deepest interest and constant discussion. The forming of a new government for a new country was a sport for master minds, and Virginians turned to it with zest. The colonies had passed through a period of momentous events, and men's minds had grown correspondingly great in power and vision. Two great political parties arose of diverse thought, the Federalist led by Hamilton, and the Republican led by Thomas Jefferson. A man's political convictions were intensely personal and upheld and defended with heat and fervor.

The Legislature of Virginia met annually, often with two sessions a year, and among its members were found many intellectual giants as Patrick Henry, Thomas Jefferson, Richard Henry Lee, Thomas Nelson, Arthur Lee, Edmund Randolph and John Marshall. Political questions were the topics of the times and warmly discussed at court, church and on social occasions. Opinion was often divided and when thought crystallized into action the opposing factions presented their views upon the point in question in the form of petitions to the Virginia Legislature, which had succeeded to the powers and duties of the Old House of Burgesses and Council. Pittsylvania was represented in the General Assembly in 1781 by Benjamin Lankford and William Dix; in 1782 by John Wilson and Constant Perkins; in 1783-4 by Benjamin Lankford and William Dix; in 1785 by Benjamin Lankford and William Harrison; in 1786 by Benjamin Lankford and Constant Perkins; in 1787 by Benjamin Lankford and William Lynch; 1788 by Benjamin Lankford and Constant Perkins; in 1789 by Benjamin Lankford and William Dix; in 1790 by Benjamin Lankford and Matthew Clay; in 1791-2-3 Thomas Tunstall and Matthew Clay; in 1794 Stephen Coleman and Matthew Clay; in 1795 by Stephen Coleman and William Payne; in 1796 by Joseph Carter and William Clark; in 1797-8 by Robert Devin and William Clark; in 1799 by Thomas H. Wooding and Theodrick M. Roberts; in 1800 by Thomas H. Wooding and Robert Devin.

These were the formative years of our young country, when the policies of both state and nation were being molded, and in the early petitions presented to the General Assembly we find some of the questions that troubled the people of Pittsylvania. In November 1785 there were two lengthy petitions on the subject of religious freedom with a long list of signatures, one from those citizens who feared lest some favor be shown the Established Church, praying that all denominations have equal privileges; the other petition asking that the bill of October 1784, "which is so liberal and impartial as to preclude the remotest Jealousy of Preference to any Denomination," become a law. At the same time there was presented a petition against freeing the slaves, fearing "lest it bring death and famine to the helpless black, and distress and ruin to the free citizens." Many quotations from the Holy Scriptures were given to bear out this position, such as 1st Cor. ch. 7.20: "Let every man abide in the same calling wherein he is called," and Lev. 25.44-50.

To represent one's county in the General Assembly and share in directing the affairs of the state was deemed a sacred trust, not to be treated lightly; it was an honor eagerly sought. In 1792 four gentlemen offered for election to the House of Delegates—Thomas Tunstall, Stephen Coleman, Matthew Clay and William Clark; and in 1795 there were five gentlemen who stood for election, viz.: James Johnson, John Watson, William Swanson, Stephen Coleman and William Payne. The elections were held at Pittsylvania Court House and the poll papers of these two elections have been preserved.

In 1792 the inhabitants of Pittsylvania petitioned for cross post roads to branch out from the line leading through the state established by the General Government, by authorizing county courts to maintain one post rider in each county and to appoint lines in the most convenient manner for the course of mails. The petition set forth the utility of the press, how "it stimulates industry, improves morals, and contributes to the security of the constitution by teaching people to know and value their rights."

The great mail road from Charleston, South Carolina to Philadelphia, ran through Pittsylvania, passing Danville, Chatham, and at Sonans turning to the right led through the Meadows by "Coles Hill," on to Peytonsburg and north.

The people of Virginia, especially those of Pittsylvania County, were very much disturbed over the Alien and Sedition Acts, passed by Congress. The Alien Act gave to the President the authority to banish any foreigner whose presence was thought to be dangerous to the government. The Sedition Act made it a crime to write or publish any false or malicious matter against the President or any member of Congress. It was charged by the Virginians that the laws were passed chiefly to drive away a number of able Republican (now Democratic) writers of foreign birth, who were doing much damage to the Federalist (now Republican) party.

Feeling on the subject ran very high in Pittsylvania County and the matter was brought before the court on the 15th day of July, 1799.

The presiding justices were John Wilson, Joshua Stone, William Dix, Vincent Shelton, Crispen Shelton, William Clarke, Armistead Shelton, Moses Hutchings, James M. Williams, Robert Devin and Robert Payne. Resolutions were drawn up "setting forth their objections to a compliance with the wishes of the General Assembly to have certain pamphlets containing their resolution on the constitutionality of the Alien and Sedition Laws, and an address by the Assembly to the people of the State distributed to the people of the County, with the determination to have the said papers placed in the office of the Clerk of the County for the perusal of all who desired it." Copies of their proceedings were sent to the Governor and to two of the leading printers of the Commonwealth. They appeared in a Fredericksburg newspaper of the day—(Cal., p. 37).

During the early years of the Legislature Pittsylvania was represented by many able and high minded citizens. In the session of 1803-4-5-6 Colonel Thomas H. Wooding[16] and Colonel Daniel Coleman[17] represented the county and issued a printed letter, which was then the custom, to acquaint their constituents with the various matters brought before the Legislature: "The amount of the expenditures (of the state) for the year Ending the 20th of September 1804 is calculated at 392,689 dollars and 39 cents. And the resources to meet the expense is calculated at 475,325 dollars and 72 cents. Of course no alteration will be made in our taxes the present year, and if prudence directs our Expenditures and no unforeseen event happens, we believe it can never be necessary to make them higher than at present."

These two gentlemen of the old school presided over the courts of the county for many years. In the course of her history Pittsylvania

[16]Thomas Hill Wooding was the son of Colonel Robert Wooding of Halifax. He married Susanna C., and had issue: 1. George Wooding. 2. Nathaniel Wooding. 3. Thomas W. Wooding. 4. John Wooding. 5. Robert Wooding. 6. William Henry Wooding. 7. Louisa who married Echols. 8. Eliza who married Williams.

William Henry Wooding was educated at Chapel Hill, North Carolina where he took his B. A. Degree in 1825; he served in the Senate of Virginia 1855-58. He married Jane Grasty and had issue: George, Thomas Sarchel, Mayor William Harry Wooding of Danville, James, Letitia and Jane.

Thomas W. Wooding, son of Thomas H. Wooding, was born in 1800 and settled the beautiful home of "Meadow Wood," near Chalk Level. For many years he was a presiding justice of the Pittsylvania Court. In his will, proven in 1870, he named following children: Robert, Thomas, George W., Josiah, Nathaniel and William Wooding; Susan Boothe and Eliza Wooding.

[17]Col. Daniel Coleman, the son of Stephen Coleman, was born in Cumberland County in 1769, his father soon afterwards moving to Pittsylvania County. The following incident of his youth is taken from his obituary, written by General Benjamin Cabell: "At 12 years of age he was employed as an express by military commandant of Halifax (Old Town) to convey General Orders forwarded to him by LaFayette, for the commandant of Pittsylvania, ordering troops to the rendezvous, near Irvine's Ferry, for the purpose of aiding General Greene, then actively retreating before the advancing columns of Cornwallis. He delivered the order, the troops marched promptly. Greene crossed the Dan in safety, and Cornwallis chagrined at his escape wheeled about and returned into North Carolina." Col. Daniel Coleman married Anne Harrison, the daughter of William Harrison of Dan River and had issue: 1. Matthew W. Coleman. 2. Stephen H. Coleman. 3. George W. Coleman. 4. Thompson Coleman. 5. Daniel Coleman, Jr. 6. Sally Finny Barker. 7. Anne P. Glascock. 8. Elizabeth W. Dobbs. 9. Judith Coleman. 10. Lucy G. Easley. 11. Susan H. Luck.

Daniel Coleman, Jr., married Margaret Eliza Ayres, and had issue: Mary Ella Coleman who married Mayor Harry Wooding of Danville.

has had many able justices, but Colonel Coleman so won the hearts of all who knew him that he was honored by having his portrait painted by the order of the court and placed on the walls of the court room where it hangs today. Colonel Coleman's home was near Riceville and there he was buried in 1860 at the age of ninety-two years.

Captain Thomas Hill Wooding was the son of Colonel Robert Wooding of Halifax, commandant of Halifax's military forces during the Revolutionary War. His home, a handsome brick structure still stands about three miles east of Chatham, and contains some interesting examples of early interior woodwork.

General Benjamin Cabell[18] was another outstanding early citizen who frequently represented the county in Legislature, in both upper and lower houses, and was a member of the Constitutional Convention of 1829-30. He was the son of Joseph Cabell of Repton, and settled in Pittsylvania about 1820, making his home, "Bridgewater," about a mile above Danville, overlooking Dan River. He held in succession the commission of major, colonel, major-general and brigadier-general of the militia, the last two being by election of the General Assembly.

In 1791, General Washington, in his official capacity as president of this new country, made a tour of the southern states, and on his return visited the scenes of some of General Greene's campaigns during the Revolutionary War. The President kept a diary[19] of his trip and records that he spent a night in Pittsylvania at Peytonsburg. He wrote that after leaving Guilford (now Greensboro) and traveling all day he came to "one Gatewoods" (near the City of Danville) where he spent the night. "June 4th—Left Mr. Gatewoods about half after 6 o'clock and between the house and Ferry (Dix's Ferry over the Dan) passed the line which divides the State of Virginia and North Carolina, and dining at one Wilsons 16 miles from the Ferry, lodged at Halifax Old Town." Halifax Old Town was Peytonsburg, which was often called simply Old Town, and here the Father of his country once passed the night in a

[18]General Benjamin W. S. Cabell, born May 10, 1793, was the son of Joseph Cabell of "Repton" and his wife Pocahontas Bolling. He was educated at Hampden-Sydney College and married Dec. 16, 1816, Sallie Doswell, daughter of Major John Doswell, of Nottoway County. At the outbreak of the war between the states General Cabell sent six sons into the service, all of whom served with distinction. He had issue: 1. Pocahontas Rebecca married Col. John Hairston of Henry Co. 2. Dr. John Roy Cabell, born March 23, 1823, married Martha C. Wilson, daughter of Col. Nathaniel Wilson and his wife, Winnefred Tunstall, of Belle Grove. Dr. Cabell married, secondly, Mrs. Kate Clement, widow of James Clement of "Clement Hill." He settled at Callands where he had an extensive practice throughout his life. He had issue by his first wife: Anne Eliza, Dr. William C. Cabell, Mary W. Cabell, and Nathaniel. 3. Virginia Cabell. 4. William Lewis Cabell, Captain in U. S. Army, became Brigadier General in Confederate Army. 5. Powhatan Bolling. 6. Algernon Sidney, Major in Confederate Army. 7. George Craighead, Col. of 18th Regt. 8. Sarah Epps. 9. Joseph Robert, killed at head of his Regiment. 10. Benjamin Edward Cabell, died 1862.

[19]Washington's Southern Tour.

Mrs. Isaac Coles
By John Ramage

Mrs. Elbridge Gerry
By John Ramage

public tavern. The diary[20] of Richard Venable, a young lawyer who was living at that time in the home of Mr. John Wimbish at Peytonsburg simply states the facts of Washington's arrival. The Venable diary reads: "Sat. June 4th, 1791. Gen'l Washington came in the evening. Stayed at Tavern, set out next morning before sunrise."

Venable does not tell whether fitting preparations were made to receive the president of the United States at the little village tavern or whether the people of the vicinity knew of his coming and gathered to do homage to so illustrious a countryman.

General Washington's diary continues: "Sunday 5th. Left the Old Town about 4 o'clock A. M., breakfasted at one Pridie's (after crossing Banister River 1½ miles) about 11 miles from it came to Staunton River about 12, where meeting Col. Isaac Coles[21] (formerly a member of Congress from this District) who pressing me to it, I went to his home about 1 mile off to dine and to halt a day for the refreshment of myself and horses, leaving my servants and them at one of the usually indifferent taverns at the Ferry that they might be no trouble or be inconvenient to a private family."

A few years after this Col. Coles moved to Pittsylvania and settled at Chalk Level where he had purchased in 1785 5,000 acres of land, extending down the Meadow. Col. Coles represented this district in Congress from 1789 to 1797. While in New York he met and married an English lady, Miss Catherine Thompson, whose brother, Jacob Thompson, was a member of the Queen's Guard, an English body of troops, and whose sister was the wife of Elbridge Gerry, a member of Congress from Mass. It is of interest to note that when the question of slavery came before Congress, Col. Coles of Virginia, voted to abolish the practice of slavery, while his brother-in-law Eldridge Gerry of Mass.,

---

[20]Tyler's Quarterly.

[21]Colonel Isaac Coles was the son of John Coles and his wife Mary Winston, daughter of Isaac Winston. He was born in Richmond, Virginia, February 25, 1747, and married first Eliza Lightfoot, and secondly on Jan. 2, 1790, Miss Catherine Thompson, the daughter of James Thompson, a native of Scotland and resident of New York, and his wife Catherine Walton. Col. Isaac Coles and wife Catherine Thompson had issue: 1. Walter Coles, born Dec. 8, 1790. 2. Catherine Thompson Coles, born Feb. 10, 1795, married Baldwin Payne. 3. James Thompson Coles, born Jan. 9, 1797. 4. John Coles, born April 26, 1799, married Louisa Woodson Payne. 5. Dr. Robert Thompson Coles, born March 15, 1801, married Eliza Patton; first settled in Chatham, building the house now occupied by Edwin S. Reid, and later moved to Alabama. 6. Mary Coles, born Oct. 18, 1805, married James M. Whittle in 1834, and died 1835, leaving one daughter, Miss Mary Coles Whittle, of "Eldon." 7. Jacob Thompson Coles, born Jan. 23, 1808, married Catherine Patton, daughter of Dr. James Dodridge Patton, who moved from Augusta County to Danville. They made their home at "Elkhorn" (an old Sydnor place) and had issue: Judge James Dodridge Coles, of Chatham, Capt. Isaac Coles of "Forest Home," Jacob Thompson Coles, of "Elkhorn," Catherin Coles, who married Mr. Roger Atkinson of Greensboro.

Mrs. Catherin Thompson Coles survived her husband many years, and her grandson, Capt. Isaac Coles spent much of his boyhood at "Greenfield" as a companion to his grandmother. Capt. Coles died in 1926 at the age of 92 years, with his faculties perfectly clear and related many of the incidents contained in this volume.

voted to retain the same. Col. Coles, with prophetic foresight, voted against the adoption of the Constitution of the United States in its present form.

In the campaign for re-election to Congress in 1797, Col. Coles was defeated by Matthew Clay,[22] who with keen political acumen brought no accusation against Col. Coles' qualifications as a congressman, but constantly reminded the voters that when Col. Coles wanted a wife he did not marry some pretty Virginia girl, but went to New York and married an English lady who was a member of the Church of England. And so unreasonable are men in their prejudices and so bitter was feeling against England at this time, that solely for the reason of his English wife was Col. Coles defeated for re-election to Congress. Col. Coles spent his declining years at "Greenfields," his home at Chalk Level, and thither journeyed friends from all parts of the country to enjoy his generous hospitality, his keen wit, and the recollections of his full and active life. The old mansion house was destroyed by fire but in the rock walled grave yard can be seen the tombs of Col. Coles and his wife, which bear the simple inscriptions:

Isaac Coles
Born March 2, 1747
Died June 17, 1813
Mrs. Catherin Coles
Born April 16, 1768
Died July 15, 1848

Clay represented the district from 1797 to 1813. He was the son of Charles Clay of Chesterfield County who had patented much land in eastern Pittsylvania, where the son Matthew Clay made his home near Chestnut Level. He married on December the 4th, 1788, Mary,[23] the

[22]Matthew Clay's will was proven July 1815, in which he named three children, Joseph, Martha and Amanda Anne Clay. He represented Pittsylvania in Legislature from 1790-94. Matthew Clay was the son of Charles Clay, born 1716, and his wife, Martha, daughter of Thomas Green, who had issue: Rev. Eleazer Clay, Matthew, born Nov. 25, 1754, General Green Clay of Kentucky, Thomas, Henry and Martha Clay (Thomas Clay's will was recorded at Pittsylvania Court House Oct. 1777). Charles Clay was the son of Henry Clay of Chesterfield and Henrico counties, who was born 1672, died 1760, and who married Mary Mitchell, having Issue: Charles and John, the grandfather of the great Henry Clay (*Va. Mag. Hist.*, Vol. 7, pp. 124-5).

[23]Mary Williams was the daughter of Joseph Williams and his wife Sarah Lanier, the daughter of Thomas Lanier of North Carolina. Her grave stone reads:

"In memory of
Mary
daughter of Joseph Williams
who was born 16th June, 1770
On 4th December, 1788 she was married
to Matthew Clay
On Sun. 22nd Nov. 1789 she was
delivered of a Daughter named Sally
On Sat. 19th May, 1792, she was delivered of a son
named Joseph

lovely daughter of the late Joseph Williams, a brother of Col. Robert Williams. From the latter's annual reports to the court as guardian, we catch glimpses of a happy girlhood. The following items are taken at random:

"1781 To R. Pamphlett for Schooling.
1783 To Jeduthan Carter for Board and Schooling.
To one Large Sealskin Trunk.
To two Portmantue.
To one Hunting Saddle.
To one pair Silk Shoes.
To Gold for Pocket Money.
To Hand Pin and Gold Locket.
Pd. Benjamine Walker for entrance to Dancing School and going to it.
To James Johnson for your expenses and Board at School.
11 yds. Lutestring of Sam'l Calland.
1 pr. Ear Rings of Jasper.
1 Stone ring of Thomas.
For cash at the Sweet Springs.
Expenses at Sweet Springs and returning."

Mrs. Mary Clay died in 1798 and her rock walled tomb is all that marks the site of their home. Matthew Clay died in 1813, while on a return trip from Richmond and is buried in Halifax County.

Henry St. George Tucker, a son of Judge St. George Tucker and his wife Frances Bland Randolph, the mother of John Randolph of Roanoke, made his home in Pittsylvania about this time, settling about 7 miles from Chatham. He represented this district in Congress from 1815 to 1819, when he moved from this section to northern Virginia. During his long and distinguished career he served as a judge of the Court of Appeals and as professor of law at the University of Virginia. He was the author of several books upon law.

An echo of the capitol's fashionable life at this period is preserved in the letters of a Pittsylvania belle, Miss O. W. Carter written in 1826, to her mother Mrs. Charles Carter, of "Deerwood." Miss Carter had just been present at a Fourth of July Celebration at the Capitol, and writes of the occasion:

On Thurs. 29th March, 1794 she was delivered
of a son named Matthew
On Sat. 12th December, 1795 she was delivered
of a Daughter named Polly Williams
and on Sun. 25th March, 1798 she died in
child Bed much lamented."

It is told that Mrs. Clay's family were deeply hurt by the inscription which her husband had engraved on her tomb, and purposely drove their carriage across it breaking it in half. The halves, however, were set in place.

"Tuesday being the 4th, we all went over to the City, where we were much delighted with all we saw. The parade was splendid, the capitol crowded with people to hear Mr. Jones. We had comfortable seats, smart beaux, and were altogether much delighted. From the capitol we proceeded among a hundred carriages to the drawing room, and I had the honor of making my courtesy to Mr. and Mrs. Adams, leaning upon Shirley Carter's arm, who was a very valuable beau to us the whole excursion, and is a charming young man. Mrs. Adams was dressed in a bobinet dress over lemon colored silk, full trimmed with lace and tied down before with lemon colored ribbons; her cap was of lace and all manner of flowers and flaxen curls * * *. The evening of the Fourth we were at a very handsome party at General Mason's, where we saw all the fashionable ladies of the City and a number of gentlemen of high sounding titles. The yard and the avenue to the house were illuminated and had a very pretty effect. Without vanity I think our two carriages contained the prettiest people there."

Among the friends mentioned by Miss Carter were Lieutenant Hazard with whom they "cut quite a dash," and Eliza Dangerfield and Eugenia Gennis, "two sweet girls."

"Deerwood," the home of the Carters, was situated in the northern part of the county along Staunton River, where today Deerwood Ford marks the location of this old estate.

Walter Coles,[24] of "Coles Hill," like his father, Col. Isaac Coles represented this district in Congress—serving from the year 1835 to 1845. He established his home on lands bequeathed him by his father and built in 1825 a handsome brick residence six miles east of Chatham. So difficult were Virginia roads of that day that Mr. and Mrs. Coles often made the trip to Washington by water, driving in their carriage to some point on the Roanoke River where they took a boat which carried them down the river and up Chesapeake Bay.

In a letter written from Washington in 1835 to her little daughter Helen, in Virginia, Mrs. Coles described some of the social customs of that period. "We were invited to a great dinner last week and did not enter the dining room until candle light, when instead of meat and vegetables the table was covered with artificial flowers, pictures, oranges, sugar candy, nuts, wine and silver vases of hot water to set the plates on.

[24]Walter Coles, eldest son of Col. Isaac Coles, married Priscilla Lettice Carrington, daughter of Judge Paul Carrington, and had issue: 1. Captain Walter Coles, born Aug. 12, 1825, married Lavinia Jordan, and had issue: Walter, Dr. Russell, Harry C., Thomas and Agnes. 2. Lettice. 3. Isetta. 4. Helen. 5. Mildred, married Col. Stanhope Flournoy. 6. Agnes, married Dr. J. T. Cabell, of Richmond.

Walter Coles, Sr., died in 1857 and is buried at "Coles Hill."

We all took our seats and found a piece of bread wrapped up in a nice napkin, and a gold spoon and a silver knife and fork by the side of all our plates. Presently they brought from the next room soup in plates and gave to everybody, then the plates were changed and we all had a piece of turkey and one kind of vegetable, and then some other meat and one kind of vegetable, and so they continued until the plates were changed 15 times for the meat course and twelve times for the desert. Tell Cousin Green this and ask her if she does not think the people here are genteel.

I tell you all this my child to amuse you, and not because I think such things can make us happy. I would have willingly have exchanged this fine dinner for a little fried bacon on a pewter plate, provided it could have been eaten with my dear children.

* * * * * * *

Your father says that they have done nothing in Congress but quarrel so that it will be a good long time yet before we can go home."

William Tredway,[25] a native of Prince Edward County, who had settled in early life at Pittsylvania C. H. to pursue the practice of law, was the representative to Congress for the session of 1851. He was afterwards judge of the county court of Pittsylvania for many years, which honorable position his son, James L. Tredway also held.

That famous lodge of the Order of Masons to which General Washington belonged was organized at Alexandria in 1788; a lodge[26] was also organized at Pittsylvania Court House on September 15, 1788, Pittsylvania Lodge, Number 24. Lodges were numbered in the order of their organization, the first being at Norfolk in 1741. There were present at the first meeting of Lodge No. 24, Colonel Haynes Morgan, Daniel Lovell, Tavenor Shelton, William Shelton, Fred Shelton, Leroy Shelton, John Markham, Thomas Lankford, James George, Jr., Thomas Hoskins, Peter Presley Thornton and Richard Johnson. Officers were chosen as follows:

Master Mason—Haynes Morgan.
Senior Warden—Daniel Lovell.
Junior Warden—John Markham.

---

[25]William Tredway, son of Moses Tredway, was born 1809, at Hampden-Sydney, Prince Edward County. He married in 1831 Nancy Millner, daughter of William Millner, by whom he had issue: 1. Moses Tredway, married Miss Edmundson. 2. Robert, married Letitia Clark, daughter of David Clark. 3. William, married Rebecca Martin. 4. Thomas. 5. Nannie, married Wyatt Whitehead. 6. Pattie, married Fletcher B. Watson. 7. Mary, married Mr. James Lovelace. 8. James Lewis, married Almeyda Hargrave. 9. Sally, married John D. Coleman.

[26]Lodge Records.

Secretary—William Shelton.
Treasurer—Tavenor Shelton.
Dean—Thomas Hoskins.
Junior Dean—Frederick Shelton.

Other first members were: John Wimbish, Thomas Tunstall, Crispen Shelton, Nathaniel Hunt, William Ware, Thomas Todd, William Tunstall, Jr., John Clement, John Bennett, Jeremiah White, George Perkins, Joseph Carter.

The following year a lodge room was built on the land of Charles Lewis in which the first meeting was held Nov. 4, 1789. That lodge room has long since passed away and Pittsylvania Lodge No. 24 today owns a substantial brick building, the second floor of which forms their commodious assembly room.

Chapter XVI

1800-1860

TOWN OF COMPETITION—WAR OF 1812—PERIOD OF DEVELOPMENT

In 1806 a very curious dispute engaged the attention of the people of the county regarding the legality of the position of the court house. After the division of Henry and Pittsylvania in Jan. 1777, it was necessary to choose a more central location for the court buildings than the site at Callands, and the Cherrystone Meeting House Spring near Hickey's Road was the place selected. The road then did not run along the brow of Depot Hill as it does today, but led up the ravine to the north of the hill where are located several springs of good water.

As we have seen, the court house was not built for several years owing to the stress of war, and the meeting house was repaired and used as a place for holding court. In 1782 the court building was erected, not in the ravine, but on top of the hill where the residence of the late Judge James L. Tredway now stands, the two-room brick building on the rear lawn being the clerk's office. The court house, a brick structure with tall white columns in front, was built by David Hunt, at a cost of 4,000 pounds of tobacco.

Some 25 years later a dispute arose over the legality of changing the location of the court buildings from the bottom to the top of the hill. Feeling in the matter ran very high and the question was finally carried before Legislature, the opposing sides presenting lengthy petition with many signatures attached, and the affidavits of some aged citizens within whose memories the change had taken place. One side was led by William Clark[1] and his friends, claiming the location of the court house to be illegal and unjust, to which was attached the affidavit of Joseph Par-

[1]William Clark of Pittsylvania was the son of Thomas Clark and his wife Phoeba Howson of Halifax County. He settled in Pittsylvania at the close of the Revolution, where he amassed a large estate in lands and slaves. He made his home about six miles from Chatham, near Banister River, and built an imposing white columned residence which he called "Pineville." He married Jane White, the daughter of Jeremiah White, who in 1778 moved from Dinwiddie County, settling in the eastern part of Pittsylvania. Jere White's will was proven in 1788, naming wife Jane and the following children: William Jeremiah, John Hamilton and Robert, Nancy, Mary who had married a Hardaway, Jane who had married William Clark, and daughters who married James Hinton and Braxton Mabrey. William Clark was, for a number of years, a magistrate presiding over the County Court. He represented Pittsylvania in the Legislature 1796-1799. He left no will, but that of his wife Jane Clark was proven May 20, 1839, naming the following children: 1. William S(tainbeck) Clark, married Martha Redd. 2. David H(amilton) Clark, married Martha Clark. 3. John A(gustine) Clark, married Elizabeth Fowlkes. 4. Mary Garland, wife of James Garland. 5. Phoeba Howson Stone, wife of Samuel Stone. 6. Lettice W(hite) Stone Claiborne, wife of Col. Leonard Claiborne at Danville. 7. Grandson James White Wooding. Her son General Thomas H. Clark, a brigadier-general of Virginia Militia, had died unmarried in 1829. Her daughter Jane White Clark, wife of Philip Grasty, of "Mount Airy," was not named in the will.

sons. He stated that court was first held in the Cherrystone Meeting House within twenty or thirty yards of land now the property of William Clark and very little further from land belonging to Samuel Hughes. "Court continued to hold sessions there until the year 1782, when on the application of Major Johnson, who at that time had become the purchaser of the land whereon the Court House stood, the jail was taken down and moved from six to eight hundred yards into the body of land Johnson owned, and the Court House, which was directed to be built adjacent to the meeting House Spring, was built near the jail, and the applicant never heard any other reason given as to removal of court house other than that to prevent competition, to prevent others of the advantages of that place, as there were two other stands convenient to the court house whilst continued at Cherry Stone Meeting House Spring, and I believe did as much business on public days as the tavern on the Court House land, as they were nearly as convenient to the Court House Spring as the Court House Tavern.

"One of the stands was fixed on the land of William Clark and the other on the land of Sam'l Hughes. I believe a majority of the Justices favored the C. Meeting House Spring on account of the three tracts of land lying adjoining said spring, and the middle tract was named to set the buildings on, which gives the other two tracts an equal chance with that of the Court House tract, and Court was established there to give fuller and freer competition at the Court House.

"This affiant always understood that Jeremiah Worsham, who was the proprietor of the land when the C. House was established at Cherrystone Meeting House Spring did give up land for the use of the County for Public Buildings.

"It is a fact unanimously known that the removal of the Court House from the place assigned by law to the place where it was last held has established a monopoly at the Court House, which has caused the most passive members of society to complain of extravagant and enormous charges."

Joseph Parsons.

John Watson,[2] Senior, also made a sworn statement similar in intent to Parsons.

[2]John Watson and William Watson were the sons of Thomas Watson known as "the Scotchman." William settled on Harping Creek and John on Cherrystone Creek and Watson's Branch, where the lands are still held by the family. Among John's children was a son named Thomas, born May 1780, who married in 1806 Malinda Watson, a daughter of William Watson. The children of Thomas and Malinda Watson were: John, Thomas Jefferson, born 1809, Amos, Ichabod and Permelia Watson. Thomas Jefferson Watson married Elizabeth Leonard Duffel of Lynchburg in 1838 and had issue Wilbur Fiske, Fletcher Bangs, Thomas J., and Elizabeth Watson. Elizabeth Leonard Duffel was the granddaughter of Thomas Leonard, the English secretary of the Hon. Benjamin Franklin. Fletcher Bangs Watson married Pattie Treadway, daughter of Judge Wm. Treadway.

Richard Johnson,[3] owner of the lands whereon the court buildings at that time stood, stated in the petition submitted by himself and his friends, that court was first held in an old meeting house, "down in a disagreeable Valley, till the Court chose a place to erect thereon a court-house. The situation adopted for the purpose is a truly beautiful one as much so as any within ten miles of the place, elevated and airy, commanding the most agreeable view of the mountains, and on the said tract which was formerly Worsham's, where they were by Law authorized to erect the Courthouse, distant two or three hundred yards from the said old meeting house where court was first held; very convenient to an excellent spring of pure wholesome water." He further stated that court had been held here for twenty-five years. "Lately a doubt had arisen, whether the court is legally established at the place aforesaid, and has been determined by a court held last November that it is not legally established. Whether Party zeal (which has been running very high in the county for some time) private interest, or Good of the Public brought about the discovery of the long concealed error, circumstances and the value of the case sufficiently convince."

Legislature decided the matter by authorizing on January 8th, 1807, the present site of the court buildings to be the legal place for holding court in Pittsylvania County, at the same time establishing a town there, to which the name of Competition was given, in view of the dispute. In those earlier days men's holdings were large, their business interests varied and scattered, and it was the custom of the lawyers to practice not in one court, as they do largely today, but in the courts of all the adjacent counties. Likewise the attendance upon court was a matter of interest to the people of not only the one county in question but of the adjoining counties as well; and as travel was accomplished almost entirely by horseback a very great distance could not be covered in a day, so that the convenience of taverns to court was a matter of general concern.

Richard N. Venable, the young lawyer living in the home of Mr. John Wimbish at Peytonsburg at the time of Washington's visit, recorded in his diary: "Jan. 22, 1791. Went to Henry Court, 65 miles, and from

[3]Richard Johnson was the son of James Johnson, whose will was proven at Pittsylvania, C. H., February 17, 1817, naming wife Jane, son Richard and wife Lettice; granddaughter Jane Hamilton Johnson, daughter of deceased son Fullington Johnson; George Washington Johnson, Letty Shepherd Johnson, James, Nancy, Richard and Jeremiah Fullington.

The will of Richard Johnson was proven Nov. 21, 1826, in which he named wife Lettice, sons Richard and James F. Johnson; daughters Nancy and Mary Anne Johnson.

there to Franklin C. H., 37 miles, returned by Sam Callands to Peytonsburg 55 miles, from thence to Prince Edward C. H., 65 miles, and returned to Peytonsburg, February 11th."

Each county had its monthly court lasting several days, and a lawyer's life was indeed a busy one.

The Act of the General Assembly for determining the location of Pittsylvania Courthouse read:

"Be it enacted that 8 acres of land, the property of Richard Johnson, adjoining the south end of the court house shall be laid off by Daniel Coleman, Rawley White, John Dabney, Thomas M. Clark, Jabez Leftwich, William Tunstall, Joseph Sandeford, Jeduthan Carter, Francis Dabney, Joseph Carter and William Yancey, gentlemen trustees, into lots of ½ acre each, with such streets and alleys as they may think convenient, and be established a town by the name of Competition."

The county seat of Pittsylvania bore the name of Competition until 1874, when it was changed to the more appropriate name of Chatham. This had been given in 1769 to that earlier court house on Sandy River, but had been dropped after the removal of the court and the name of its principal store, Callands, substituted in its place. When the resolution for this change of name was brought before the General Assembly, Henry St. George Tucker, then Clerk of the House of Delegates, wrote on a blotter the following lines:

"Immortal Pitt! How great thy fame,
When Competition yields to Chatham's name!"

The ancient custom of "processioning," or re-marking boundary line trees, continued in use. This duty formerly belonged to the vestry of the Established Church. Another custom of colonial days that was retained under our Republican form of government was that of having each county organized for military defense. The following order for processioning gives the militia companies in the county at the time:

"At a court held for Pittsylvania County, June 1803, it is ordered that the following persons do Procession Lands in their respective Precincts, between the 1st day of October and the 30th of March next:

Ainsworth Harrison and Isham Farmer in said Harrison's Company of Militia. Jeremiah White and Gardner Mays in said White's Company of Militia. Jackson Walters and Josiah Atkins in said Walters' Company. William Stamps and John C. Russell in said Stamps' Company. William White and Washington Thompson in John White's Company of Militia. James M. Williams and Martin Farmer in Captain Thomas

Tanner's Company. James Soyars and Allen Stokes in Soyars' Company. William Beavers and William Sutherlin in Captain Adams Sutherlin's Company.

William Smith and William Ware in Captain Wm. Smith's Company. Robert Harrison and Philip Jenkins in Captain Nicholas Perkins' Company. Joseph Morton and Clement Nance in Captain Thomas Ragsdale's Company. Daniel Boaz and James Fuller in Captain Boaz's Company. Jonathan B. Dawson and Joseph Faris, Sr. in Captain Nathaniel Crenshaw's Company. Nelson Tucker and Stephen Clement in Captain Nelson Tucker's Company. Charles Bailey and Abram Shelton (son of Gabriel) in Captain Young Shelton's Company. John Adams, Sr. and Thomas B. Jones in Captain Richard Johnson's Company. Charles Walden and Winston Dalton in said Walden's Company. James Noland and Edward Hatchett in said Noland's Company. Peyton Graves and John Allen in said Graves' Company. Joseph Davis and James Blakeley in said Devin's Company. Robert Devin and James Hopkins in said Robert Devin's Company. It is ordered that they shall take and return to the court an account of every person's lands they shall so procession, and the names of the persons present at the same."

These many companies of Militia were organized into two full regiments, the 42nd in the southern half and the 101st in the northern half of the county. Dr. Henry G. Calloway, of Callands, was appointed surgeon to the 101st Regiment in the following order:

"Doctor Henry G. Calloway,

Sir, By section 54 of an Act.

Entitled "An Act to amend and reduce into one the Several Acts of the General Assembly for regulating the Militia of the Common-Wealth,"

It is made the duty of the Lieutenant Colonel Commandant to appoint a Regimental Staff. In compliance with that duty I have thought proper to appoint you Surgeon to the 101st Regiment. You will therefore please to consider yourself in that character attached to the Regiment and exempt from all duty in any particular Company.

I have the pleasure to be your

Very Huml Serv't

Tho. H. Wooding Lieut-Col^{o}. Com^{d}

101st Regiment

29th October 1806."

THE FLAG OF PITTSYLVANIA COUNTY

The only known County Flag in existence

A field of William Hames' was selected at this time as the place of annual muster for the 101st Regiment.

Virginia loyally sustained the action of the Federal Government in the War of 1812-14, and Pittsylvania sent many sons to the front. Col. Daniel Coleman served throughout the war as colonel-commandant of the 42nd Regt., which was stationed both at Norfolk and in Maryland. It was probably at this time that the regiment conceived the idea of regimental colors of their very own and had designed and painted a beautiful flag, which has been preserved through all the vicissitudes of war and time. It was found in the State Library a few years ago and returned to the county. The flag is painted in oils on white taffeta and the smoothly worn staff gives evidence that it has seen much service.

Captain James M. Lanier[4] commanded a troop of cavalry in the 42nd Regiment, in which John H. Lanier was a lieutenant and James May the cornet. Other officers serving in the 42nd Regiment at this time and who took the oath of office at Pittsylvania Court House were Peter Wilson,[5] Nathaniel Wilson[6] and Thomas Ragsdale,[7] majors; Robert

---

[4]James M. Lanier was a lawyer by profession (license to practice 1817) and made his home near Whitmell. He married Mary Merrimon Johns, the daughter of Mrs. Gâtrehood Glover Johns of North Carolina (who married secondly, 1799, Mr. Charles Lewis of "The Byrd" and had issue Lucy, who married Fielding Walker and Nicholas), and had issue: 1. James Lanier. 2. John Lanier. 3. Lucy Washington Lanier born Sept. 18, 1817, married July 2, 1834, James Carter of "Greenrock." 4. Cecilia Virginia Lanier, married Feb. 28, 1844, Morris Pollock of Scotland. 5. Mary Johns Lanier, married July 14, 1831, Green R. Hill and moved to Mississippi. 6. David Lanier, of White Oak, married Anne Carter.

James Lanier was the son of Captain David Lanier of Brunswick County, who in 1772 purchased land on Marrowbone Creek in Henry County and moved thither. During the Revolutionary War he commanded a company of Henry Militia; in 1796 he represented Henry in the Legislature.

David Lanier was the grandson of Sampson Lanier and his wife Elizabeth Washington, the daughter of Richard Washington of Surry, son of John Washington, the emigrant. Sampson Lanier was the son of John Lanier, the emigrant, whose will was proven in Surry in 1717, naming sons John, Nicholas, Robert and Sampson. The emigrant John Lanier is thought to be the son of John Lanier of London (whose will was proven 1650), and his wife Eleanor, whose will was proven 1652, leaving to son John a ring, his father's picture, and all his books; and "whereas my late husband John Lanier left me his executrix and bequeathed me his whole estate and several sums still due, same to my said three children equally, John and Elizabeth being under eighteen years of age and unmarried." (*Va. Mag. Hist.*, Vol. 38, 340-42). Both John Lanier and his wife Eleanor were buried in St. Giles Church Yard, London.

The Laniers in England were distinguished for their artistic talent in music and painting. Nicholas, brother of John above, gathered on the continent for Charles the First of England, in 1625, the Royal Collection of paintings and statutes by the Masters, and is said to be one of the first to appreciate their true worth. This talent has been inherited by the American branch of the family as is demonstrated in the poets Sidney and Clifford Lanier and the distinguished musician, John Powell, who is of Lanier ancestry.

[5]Major Peter Wilson was the son of Col. John Wilson and purchased from Col. Peter Perkins his home on Dan River, "Berry Hill," when Col. Perkins moved from the county. His gravestone bears the record that he was born Jan. 25, 1770 and that he died Dec. 1, 1813.

Major Wilson married Ruth Stovall Hairston only child of Peter and Elsie Perkins Hairston, and left an only child, Agnes J. P. Wilson, who married Sam'l Hairston and settled "Oak Hill." Samuel and Agnes Hairston had issue: Peter, George, Robert, Samuel, Henry, Ruth and Alcy. Samuel Hairston, Jr., succeeded his father in ownership of "Oak Hill," and married Miss Elizabeth Leech of North Carolina; their son Samuel Hairston, married Miss May Joplin of Danville, and is the present owner of this beautiful estate.

[6]Nathaniel Wilson was another son of Col. John Wilson and married Winnefred, daughter of William Tunstall of "Bellegrove."

[7]Thomas Ragsdale married Lucy Lanier, a daughter of Captain David Lanier of Henry County.

Wilson, John Wilson, Robert Bullington and James Nance, captains; William Hutchings, David Neal, Thos. Chaney and William L. Terry, lieutenants.

In the 101st Regiment, Jesse Leftwich served as major; William S. Clark and William Swanson as captains; and Ephriam Giles and Jeremiah Walker as lieutenants. Walter Coles, son of Col. Isaac Coles was appointed captain in the regular army of the U. S. and served on the Canadian frontier. His commission has been preserved at "Coles Hill" and bears the signature of President James Madison. Sam'l Hairston, Jr., served as 2nd Lieut. in the regular army of the U. S. and his commission has also been preserved and hangs at "Berry Hill."

In 1852 the Federal government issued land bounties in blocks of 40, 80, and 160 acres to the surviving soldiers of the War of 1812. These lands being located in the far west, it was impractical for the aged men to do aught but sell them and agents in New York and Washington Cities handled the sales. Many of the lists of warrants[8] made out preparatory to the sales have been preserved, and from them we learn of the great number of troops sent out at this time by Pittsylvania. Captain Calland, a son of Samuel Calland, commanded a company in which served Samuel Craddock, Jesse Fuller, Samuel Mitchell, and Jonathan Elliot; Captain Wm. Pritchett a company in the 41st Regt.; Capt. Thos. Ragsdale a company in the 5th Regt.; Capt. Townes a company in the 3rd Regt., in which served Stephen C. Townes, Geo. Hall, Johnson Farmer, Wm. Dodson, Elijah Grubbs, Francis Epperson, Thos. Williams and Pleasant Haley; Capt. T. Shelton a company, privates, Thos. Mustein, William Gregory, Daniel Shelton, Mayo Mease and Spencer Hammond; Captain Clarke a company, privates Charles Lewis, Hiram Haskins, James Nance, Moses Hall and Jesse Chaney; Captain Dyer a company in the 5th Va. Regt., John Clark private; Capt. Wilson a company, Lieut. Richard Parrish; Captain Lawson, privates Sampson Dodson, Elijah Beggarly, Joseph Simms; Captain Jesse Carter a company in the 7th Regt., privates John Giles, Benjamin Terry, Sam Dawson, Thos. Davis, William Waller, Nathan Hutcherson, Rawley W. Carter, Abner Bennett, Hezekiah Hubbard, Phillip Price, William Riddle, Thomas Parrish, Vincent Shelton, John Hall. In Captain James Lanier's troop of cavalry were Thomas Chattin, Rawley Thompson, John Birch and Edward Robertson.

---

[8]Papers in the possession of the late Mr. George W. Jones of Chestnut Level.

In this list of soldiers of the War of 1812 we find the sons and grandsons of the soldiers of 1775, who like their forefathers were willing and eager to defend their country.

The officers of the 42nd Regt. presented a petition to Governor John Floyd (1830-34) asking that the place of annual general muster of the regiment be changed from Danville to a more central location, such as "at or near the tavern house of Mrs. Elizabeth Beavers[9] some eight miles north of Danville, where ample accommodations can be had at but little expense, and that the place is very near the center of the Regiment." Of the 57 officers of the regiment, 39 voted in favor of the change, which was accordingly made. Great crowds attended these annual musters which lasted for several days, and a fine show was made by the commanding officers in full regimental regalia, mounted on horses, with the plumes from their hats sweeping in the wind. No guns were used, only sticks and cornstalks were carried by the soldiers, and since little knowledge of military tactics was possessed by the officers, many amusing contre temps occurred. As for instance when the commanding officer marched his troops against a large out-building, and not knowing how to extricate them, gave the order to break ranks and make a fresh start.

On another occasion the commanding officer, full of pomp and ceremony was fearful lest he forget the commands, so wrote them on a slip of paper which he placed inside his hat. Before giving an order the officer, mounted on his fiery steed, would turn to the assembled crowd and bow with a sweep of his plumed hat. After intently studying the inside of his hat for a moment, he would replace his head piece and with a show of much military dignity give the command. This ceremony of bowing to the assembled crowd preceded each order, much to the general amusement of the onlookers. (Mr. Isaac Coles.) Yet these officers and men upon the outbreak of war in 1861, proved themselves to be as gallant and great soldiers as ever trod a battlefield.

An old yellowed sheet from the adjutants book, preserved in the papers of Major Langhorne Scruggs, gives the officers of the 101st Regt. in 1846, as follows:

[9] Mrs. Elizabeth Beavers, widow of Major William Beavers, was the daughter of Moses Fontaine and his wife, Elizabeth Ballard. See Note 1, Chap. 17.

Col. Coleman D. Bennett[10]; Lt. Col. Wm. Rison[11]; Major Tarpley White[12]; Captains, Joab Watson,[13] Washington Patton, Christopher Davis, John G. Murrell, Griffith R. Neal, Edward Hatchett, William G. Dickenson, Charles W. Yeatts; Staff, L. Scruggs,[14] R. Griggs, Fred Rorer, John Gilmer,[15] W. A. Anthony, B. A. Rives, ——— Shelton, —— Shelton, T. A. Drean.

In February 1841, there was organized at Danville a volunteer company of light infantry known as the Danville Blues, with George E. Welsh captain and George White, John Patterson, Joseph B. Terry and Thomas D. Neal lieutenants. The company was attached to the 42nd Regiment of Pittsylvania Militia, 11th Brigade and 1st Division.

In the early years of the county, all elections were held at the courthouse. But as the number of inhabitants increased, for the convenience of the people, other points were named as polling places. In 1823 the General Assembly enacted that a separate election be held at Danville for that part of the county between the North Carolina line and Dan River, "that used to be held at the court house." And in 1829 three other points were named in the county in the following act: "When an election is held in Pittsylvania County, at the same time a separate poll shall be opened at the residence of Abram Rorer, in the northwest part of the county; at the store of Wier and Smith at Mount Airy in the northeast, and the home of Benjamin Walker in the southwest parts of the county."

With the establishment of our new republican form of government in which the people were given the right to participate through their vote, it was realized that the safety of the nation lay in having an intelligent

---

[10]Col. Coleman D. Bennett was a merchant at Pittsylvania, C. H., and represented the county in the Virginia Legislature for the session of 1842-43. He married first Mildred Jones, daughter of Mr. Richard Jones of Sheva, and had issue three daughters: 1. Mildred, married Major Langhorne Scruggs. 2. Mary, married Jacob Franklin of Lynchburg. 3. Sally, married Mansell Smith.
Col. Bennett married, secondly, Miss Parrish and had issue: Willie, Lucy, Lelia, Preston, Mollie, Mattie and Tunstall Bennett.

[11]William Rison was born Aug. 24, 1813, in Chesterfield County of Huguenot descent (name originally spelled Raison), the son of John and Jane Foster Rison; and died 1902 in Danville, where he had made his home since 1856. He served for 27 years as Clerk of the Corporation Court. He married Sally Anne Towns, daughter of George and Elizabeth Tunstall Townes, and had issue: 1. Elizabeth, married Pleasant R. Jones of Danville. 2. Emma, married Edwin Barber of Richmond. 3. George Townes Rison of Chatham. 4. John Foster Rison of Danville. 5. Whitmell T. Rison of South Carolina. 6. Sally, married Rev. John M. Oakey.

[12]Col. John White was the son of Dr. Rawley White of Peytonsburg. He was a wealthy old bachelor, who lived at Pittsylvania Court House and maintained a very fine stable of racing horses.

[13]Joab Watson was a grandson of William Watson of Harping Creek. He died without issue leaving his property to his nieces and nephews.

[14]Langhorne Scruggs was a lawyer by profession, served as Clerk of the Court and represented Pittsylvania in Legislature in 1871-77. He married Mildred Ward Bennett and had only child Sallie, who married Col. Edwin Sidney Reid, president of Chatham Savings Bank.

[15]John Gilmer, of Albemarle County, settled in Chatham in early manhood to practice law. He built a beautiful home on an eastern hill overlooking the village where the Chatham Hall now stands. He represented the county in the General Assembly from 1857-65. He married Miss Eliza Patton of Richmond and had issue: John Patton, William W., Tazwell, Mercer, James, Lindsay, Mary R. and Isabelle.

voting populace, and the education of the masses gave the leaders of our country grave concern. Thomas Jefferson fought for a system of free schools, but failed in his efforts. As a substitute with the proceeds arising from the sale of the churches and rectories belonging to the Church of England, in Virginia, was founded a Literary Fund which was used to pay for the schooling of the very poor children of the state.

A report of the School Commissioners of Pittsylvania County to the president and directors of the Literary Fund for the year 1823 reads: "Within the year ending the 31st day of December, 1823, there have been in operation in the said county schools of all sorts of which fifteen were partly attended by poor children. That from the best information that can be obtained there are in the said county 254 poor children entitled to the benefit of the fund, 112 of whom have been educated for different periods. For the year 1822-23 have expended $1,014.00, leaving in the hands of the Treasurer for future use on application $2,827.00." The report for year 1825 gave 22 schools which had been attended by poor children, of whom there were 381 in the county, 168 having received instruction. This plan was never very successful for the reason that in order to share in the benefits of the fund the father was required to declare publicly that he was unable to provide schooling and books for his children, thus putting the stigma of pauperism upon himself and family; and more often before a man would do this he would allow his children to grow up in ignorance.

The system of private tutors and private schools for the families of means continued in vogue. The following notice appeared in the *Virginia Gazette* of Sept. 28, 1803:

"Pitts. 10th Aug., 1803.

Notice

On Cascade Creek about two miles above the confluence thereof will commence on the 12th of Sept. next a Latin Grammar School under the direction of Mr. John W. Caldwell, a gentleman of much respectability, who has been greatly applauded for his former attention paid to his pupils. He will teach the Latin and Greek languages to perfection; also, English he will teach in its various branches. The terms of tuition are, 16 Dollars for Latin scholars, and half price for English. Any gentleman wishing to have his son or sons taught by said Mr. Caldwell, may have them boarded at either of the subscribers' houses, both which are very contiguous to the Academy. The price of boarding will be forty Dollars per annum.

Permenas Williams
David Rice.

N. B. Any number of Boarders will be taken."

In their need of higher education for their children the citizens of the county established in 1802 an academy about six miles east of the courthouse on Banister River, which was known as the Banister Academy. In response to a petition from the inhabitants, the General Assembly enacted in December 1801, that, "Thomas H. Wooding, Edmund Tunstall, William Tunstall, Edmund Fitzgerald, Allen Womack, Thomas B. Jones, John Adams, jun., Armistead Shelton, John White, William Wimbish, Edward Robertson, Samuel Calland, William Clark, Moses Hutchings, William White, Joseph Carter, John Smith, James M. Williams and Rawley White shall be and are hereby constituted a body politic and corporate by the names of the Trustees of Banister Academy, with power to take and hold any estate for use of the Academy.

"2. That said trustees or any five of them shall be a sufficient number to constitute a board and have power to appoint a principal, tutors and etc."

The school was established at once and Mr. William L. Turner, a Presbyterian preacher from Bedford County, was chosen the first principal. To provide funds for the academy the trustees appealed to the General Assembly for permission to hold a lottery, then a popular means of raising money. On January 12, 1804, the permission sought was granted in the following act:

"Be it enacted that it shall and may be lawful for Isaac Coles, Senior, Samuel Calland, William Clark, William Tunstall, John Wilson, Stokesley Turner, William Wimbish, Joseph Carter, Jesse Leftwich, Daniel Coleman and Thomas H. Wooding, Gents., to raise by way of lottery $10,000 for the benefit of Banister Academy."

The academy building was a wooden structure and was situated on the road leading from Sheva to Clarke's Bridge. The school flourished for many years and among its teachers was Mr. Richard Jones,[16] an

[16]Richard Jones was the son of Thomas B. Jones of Pittsylvania and his wife, Miss Burton, who had issue: John, James, Richard and Allen Jones. Thomas B. Jones and Emmanuel Jones were the only sons of Thomas Jones, Sr., and his wife Mary, of "Mountain Top" (White Oak Mountain), near Shocco, who moved to Pittsylvania County prior to the Rev. War, in which Thomas served as an officer. Richard Jones was educated at Hampden-Sydney College, being a very fine Latin Scholar, and taught school for two years at a Lynchburg College. He married Mildred Ward Smith, daughter of Mr. Samuel Smith, of "Clifton," Bedford Co.

The following testimonial of his merits as a teacher was given Richard Jones by his friends and neighbors:

"Feb. 1808.

"In a free and extensive country where learning is encouraged and useful improvements and discoveries rewarded, it will naturally result that young and ingenious minds will forever be exerted to excell in the most plausible pursuits. A young man sincere and moral in all his deportments will hardly fail to meet with the friendship and patronage of every good man, but when those virtues shine in a conspicuous manner with sentiments polished and refined by a classical education, we may and do expect such a one to meet not only with respect but encouragement in whatever business his qualifications shall induce him to undertake. These we conceive and these we recommend to be the dispositions and qualifications of Mr. Richard Jones of the County of Pittsylvania and State of Virginia, being personally and intimately acquainted with Mr. Jones, etc."

The letter was signed by Dr. Reuben Fitzgerald, Edmond Fitz Gerreld, Armisted Shelton, John B. Dawson, Allen Womack, William Tunstall, Edmond Tunstall, John Adams.

educated gentleman whose home was nearby, who taught the Greek and Latin classes. In later years the management of the academy was taken over by the Clark family and taking its name from the home of the Clarks, became the Pineville Academy.

The following is an account of a pupil to the Pineville Academy in 1845:

"1845. Received of Richard Jones $3.00 for last session and $6.00 for this session to the Pineville Academy of Mildred Bennett.[17]

D. H. Clark, Adm. of
John A. Clark, Dec'd."

There were academies at Callands and Whitmell; while at the Court House there were always private schools for girls and boys. The old building standing in the field south of the Chatham cemetery is an old school house in which Mr. Sidney Buford taught in antebellum days. The Rev. Pike Powers, a noted educator of his day, was another who taught school at the Court House.

The most widely known academy in the county was the Woodbourne Classical School taught by Mr. Samuel Miller[18] at his home in the northern part of the county. Mr. Miller was a very fine Greek and Latin scholar and was said to be "the most distinguished classical teacher in all that part of Virginia that lies west of Petersburg." When a mere youth he opened a boarding school at New London, Campbell County, in which venture he was assisted by his mother, Mrs. Anne Ball Miller. Miss Frances Elizabeth Fitz Patrick of Pittsylvania County, a niece of John[19] and David Pannill, of Chalk Level, was a student at New London, and a romance developing between master and pupil, they were married in

---

[17]Mildred Bennett, daughter of Col. Coleman D. Bennett, and grand-daughter of Mr. Richard Jones of "Sheva," by whom she was reared.

[18]Samuel Thomas Miller, born in Richmond, Nov. 22, 1789, was the son of Thomas Miller of Maryland and his wife Anne Ball, of New Kent County, Virginia. Mrs. Anne Ball Miller made her home with her son and died at Woodbourne in 1840. Mrs. Sarah Elizabeth Fitz Patrick Miller was the daughter of David Fitz Patrick, who was a large land owner and died at an early age in 1807, directing in his will that his children be well educated. He had married Sarah Baily Morton Pannill, a sister of John and David Pannill of Chalk Level. Samuel Miller and his wife had issue: Anne Ball, Sarah Pannill, Frances Patrick, William Alexander, David Patrick, John Maffitt, Mary Maffitt, Samuel Hartshorn, James Ball, Elizabeth, Alfred Henry, Thomas Cecil, Catherin Agnes and George Francis. Mr. Miller built a second and more commodious home on his estate, which he named "Cedar Forest," and where he laid out extensive gardens and orchards. His diaries contain frequent mention of his flowers: "March 5, 1859. Few jonquils and hyacinths in bloom."

[19]John Pannill who first settled Chalk Level operated a store there; he married Nancy Wimbish, a daughter of Mr. John Wimbish of Peytonsburg. John Pannill died in 1793 and his wife removed to her father's; his brother David took charge of the store. He in turn died in 1803 leaving a widow and two infants, William L. and Elizabeth Pannill, but in his thirty-three years he amassed a large estate, owning stores at Chalk Level and Sandy River, and one-third interest in following concerns: William Wimbish & Co., Jesse Leftwich & Co., and Grasty & Pannill.

David Pannill named in his will brothers Samuel, Morton, George and John, deceased; sisters Polly, Nancy, Fanny, Sarah B. M. Pannill and Sarah Davis, who were the children of William Pannill of Orange and his wife Anne Morton, daughter of Jeremiah Morton.

1817. About 1824 Mr. Miller moved to northern Pittsylvania to his wife's estate of some 600 acres which she had inherited from her father the late David Fitz Patrick. Here the Millers established their home, naming it Woodbourne, and reared their large family of fourteen children. A school house was soon built and the Woodbourne Classical School, a boarding school for boys, was opened, which became increasingly popular as time went on, and youths not only from Pittsylvania but from adjoining counties and Lynchburg were educated there. Among the boys who were Woodbourne scholars were: William Lovelace, Robert Wade, Thomas Glass, Isaac, Robert, Willie and Thomas Coles, Sam Lacy, Dr. John Hutchings of Dry Fork, James Neal of Danville, David Pannill, John and Abram Wimbish, Beverley Conway, Sam. Hubbard and Elisha Barksdale. Colonel Robert Withers, who was also a student, described in his memoirs the studious and religious atmosphere of the school. On Sunday afternoon the boys were required to learn "by heart" hymns and psalms. It has been said of Mr. Miller: "What an influence streamed forth from his school room for fifty-two years. All over the country there are advocates that reason more clearly, farmers that till more intelligently, engineers that calculate more accurately, and ministers who preach more effectively because Sam Miller lived and taught." One of Mr. Miller's greatest achievements was the education of his blind son Hartshorn Miller, who lost his sight through an accident when twelve years of age. Cumbered with the care of a large plantation, many slaves and a large school, yet he found time to open for this son the door to the literary world, and make of him a fine French, Greek, Latin and Hebrew scholar. Much of their work was done in his study before breakfast. Mrs. Miller was a woman of great executive ability and to her skill and management was due much of the material success of the school.

The tutors and teachers of Virginia at this period were generally from the north and one of the most noted of northern tutors in the county was Joseph P. Godfrey, who was educated for the navy. Having become lame as the result of an accident, Mr. Godfrey made teaching his profession, and taught and trained two generations of the young people of Pittsylvania. He died at an advanced age at Pigg's Mill, where a simple monument has been erected to his memory by a former pupil.

The University of Pennsylvania drew the medical student of Virginia. In the year 1833 there were thirty-three graduates from the state of Pennsylvania and thirty-nine graduates from the state of Virginia. (Hazards' Register, Vol. II, pp. 236-7.)

In 1808 young Lynch Dillard, the son of Benjamin and Anne Ward Dillard, wrote from the University of Pennsylvania, where he was then a student, to Dr. Henry G. Calloway, a young physician at Callands:

"Philadelphia, January 1808.

Sir, in a former letter you wished me to make some enquiries to know if Dr. Rush had made any late publications. * * * I have made some enquiry into the manner which Doctor treated consumption but I find nothing that I think will be new to you. Notwithstanding I will mention his treatment. In the first stages he begins with depleting remedies such as bloodletting, purging and blistering. And after he has reduced the system properly he makes free use of mercury and by that means in many cases completes a cure.

Dr. Rush a few days ago had one of the students bound over for fighting in his Lecture room he had to part them himself. Some blamed the Doctor very much for having them Bound over but I think, he was right as it was very insulting to the Doctor."

Dr. Calloway had been a student of the University of Pennsylvania from 1799-1803, and died in 1809 at an early age. He was succeeded in his field of practice at Callands by Dr. George W. Clement, who was student at the University in the years 1809-10.

The successful growing of silk in Virginia was a dream long cherished by the Europeans—the gnarled old mulberry trees found standing today at Jamestown and Williamsburg being mute reminders of their efforts in the early days of the colony. We find from legislative petitions that this old dream of silk growing in Virginia was renewed in Pittsylvania in almost modern times, where it also came to naught, and only a few old mulberry trees testify to the fruitless effort.

Morris Pollok,[20] of Glasgow, Scotland, a silk manufacturer, stated in a petition to the General Assembly, in 1837, that he had inherited

[20]The will of Morris Pollok, Sr., of Scotland is recorded at Pittsylvania, Court House, March 15, 1869, and reads:

"I, Morris Pollok, Silk Throwster in Govan considering that by contract of copartnery of even date with these presents entered into between me and Morris Pollok younger, my son, Silk Throwster at Govan aforesaid, I for the love, favor and affection I have and bear to him make as a free gift one of the whole property, heritable and movable now belonging to me and etc."

"I, Sir Archibald Alison, Baronet, Commissory of the County of Lanoch, considering the late Morris Pollok, Silk Throwster in Govan and residing there, died at Govan upon the 9th day of March, 1862, said Morris Pollok nominated and appointed his son Morris Pollok younger, Silk Throwster, Govan Factory, Govan, to be his executor, and etc."

"At a Court held at Pitts. C. H. March 15, 1869, a duly authenticated copy of the will of Morris Pollok, deceased, formerly of this county, but at the time of his death residing in Govan, Scotland, * * * it is ordered that same be recorded as will of said Morris Pollok, deceased. On motion of Morris Pollok (younger) devisee and legatee of Morris Pollok, deceased, he entered into bond for $25,000 with Harrison Robertson and Berryman Green his securities."

the estates of two of his brothers who had lived in Virginia where their fortunes had been made; that he would like to do something for Virginia in appreciation of this inheritance; and since he had introduced the manufacture of silk in Scotland, he contemplated establishing the silk industry in Pittsylvania County, where he believed climatic conditions were suitable. He sought permission as an alien to hold property in Virginia in fee simple, for he could not relinquish his citizenship in Great Britain since he owned a silk factory near Glasgow. The petition was accompanied by a petition from the inhabitants of the county, asking that this right be given Mr. Pollok.

In a letter to Norman Stewart of Richmond, 1838, Morris Pollok stated that he gathered his mulberry plants in Italy and Spain, and started them growing in his gardens in Scotland before transplanting them to Virginia. Lands near Fall Creek were secured for a site for the silk factory and the mulberry orchard, and a nephew, young Morris Pollok,[21] came over from Scotland to take charge of the industry. When the trees had become well established and were growing in long straight rows, the eggs of the silk worms were shipped, packed in large cakes of ice, which, before the long sea journey was over, had melted to the size of marbles. The venture was working out successfully, the silk worms thriving and feeding on the vigorous young mulberry trees, when Morris Pollok the elder crossed the seas to visit his Virginia silk plantation. He criticized the method of cultivation used by his nephew in the mulberry orchard, and ordered that the young trees be ploughed and cultivated closer to their roots. These instructions were followed with the dire result that all the young trees died, and with them perished the infant silk industry in Pittsylvania.

The lure of a new country was as strongly felt by the Virginians of this period as in the previous century, and thousands of Virginia's sons responded to the call of the far west, and taking their families and household goods, faced toward the setting sun. Nurtured in the Old Dominion and bred to a high sense of civic duty and honest endeavor, these transplanted sons of Virginia maintained their standards of life in their new home. Had Pittsylvania's sons but remained within her borders, she would blossom today like a garden.

---

[21]Morris Pollok, Jr., a nephew of Morris Pollok, Sr., remained in Pittsylvania after the failure of the silk factory. He married Miss Cecilia Virginia Lanier, daughter of Captain James M. Lanier, and had issue: Nicholas Lewis Pollok, of Danville, Robert, Ferdinand, Emma, Agnes and Virginia.

One of those who made the west to blossom as a garden was a grandson of Pittsylvania, James Smith,[22] the renowned horticulturist of Iowa. He was the son of John Smith, of Sandy River, who in 1800 moved with his family out to Kentucky. The son James, born in Kentucky in 1810, upon reaching manhood moved on further into the new west and settled in Iowa, at Fort Des Moines. Having always been interested in growing fruits, he collected and carried with him to Iowa a peck of apple seed, and there established a nursery in 1857. Through his skill in grafting and producing new fruits he acquired an interstate reputation as an horticulturist, and when the great Centennial Exposition was held at Philadelphia in 1877, he was appointed judge of the fruit exhibit. His son, John Smith of Iowa, was the first to use the arsenic spray on apple trees.

The study of genealogy, the tracing of families in their movements from one place to another, has shown what great numbers of Pittsylvania's inhabitants have gone south and west. United States Senator Henderson[23] of Missouri, one of the seven Republicans who voted to acquit President Andrew Johnson in his trial for impeachment, was born in Pittsylvania and reared in Missouri. Wilson Lumpkin, governor of Georgia from 1830-35, was born in Pittsylvania; he was the son of George Lumpkin and his wife Isbell Wilson, a sister of Col. John Wilson of Dan's Hill. John Motley Morehead,[24] governor of North Carolina from 1840-45, was born in Pittsylvania; he was the son of John Morehead and his wife Obedience Motley, daughter of Joseph Motley. Gov. Morehead was a man of marked ability and an outstanding figure in the development of his adopted State. Other North Carolina governors whose fathers were from Pittsylvania were Albert M. Scales and Robert Brodnax Glenn.

The grandfather and grandmother of "Mark Twain," Samuel Clemens and Pamela Goggin Clemens, once lived in the adjoining county of Campbell. Their distinguished grandson was brought up in Missouri.

[22]James Smith of Iowa was the son of John Smith who was born in Pittsylvania in 1772 near Sandy River, married in 1795 Elizabeth Bradford, of Caswell County, N. C. and in 1800 moved west. John Smith's tomb in Kentucky records that he is the son of E. and R. Smith and is thought to be the son of Captain Edward Smith of Henry County, and grandson of Thomas Smith, Gent., whose will was proven in Pittsylvania County in 1781, naming wife Sarah, youngest son Thomas, sons John and Edward, daughters Jane, Sarah and Martha. Among the descendants of James Smith, of Iowa, are the Misses Stella and Mary Smith of Des Moines.

[23]Senator Henderson made his home in Washington City in his latter years and was acquainted with Mrs. Lizzie Lyons Swanson, first wife of Senator Claude Swanson. Upon one occasion he told Mrs. Swanson that he was born in Virginia, near the little town of Competition.

[24]John Morehead is said to have been a Scotch emigrant from Pennsylvania. Obedience Motley was the daughter of Joseph Motley, who in 1778 purchased a thousand acres in Pittsylvania County and moved thither from Amelia County. The will of Joseph Motley named wife Elizabeth, sons David, Daniel, Samuel, John, daughters Martha Stewart, Obedience Morehead, Sally Anderson, Amey Carter, Delilah Terry, and Grandson Joseph Tanner.

Among the many who left Virginia during the early part of the last century were the Quakers, a people not generally wealthy, for it was against their religious scruples to own slaves or to take an oath of office, but they were honest, peacable and industrious, making the best of citizens. From the large Quaker settlements in Louisa County numbers of families had moved down into Bedford, Campbell and Pittsylvania, among whom were the Johnsons, Moormans, Lynches, Terrells, Anthonys, Wests, and others. They built the old Stone Quaker Meeting House near Lynchburg as a place of worship. Later many of these same families and others into which they had intermarried moved to Ohio and settled in Highland and Warren Counties, forming Quaker communities there. An old Quaker lady, whose family had gone to Ohio from these parts, wrote in her reminiscences: "In my childhood days I knew nobody but kinsfolk (Quakers), they were honest, quiet, kind and loving. There were no millionaires among them, but they all had homes and plenty, were contented and happy." Among the Quakers settling in Pittsylvania was the family of Owen West, who is said[25] to have been the brother of Benjamin West, the noted American artist of Revolutionary times. They were Pennsylvania Quakers and moved first to Louisa County, Virginia, later settling in the north eastern part of this county near Straightstone. Some of them, too joined the Ohio migration.

The discovery of gold in California drew numbers of young men from Pittsylvania to the far West. But tragedy stalked in the wake of those who made the long overland trip in 1849. Young Adam Clement wrote from St. Louis, March 27, 1849:

"We had a very disagreeable trip to Kanawha, it rained nearly the whole time. On the boat we came up on there was one case of cholera, which killed him in twenty-five hours. He was a man of family and was on his way to California. There are a great many on their way to California. We leave here this evening for Independence."

Independence is now near the great metropolis of Kansas City and there one of a party from Pittsylvania fell a victim to the plague—young David Hunt, son of Col. John Hunt. When the news of his death reached Virginia, his mother sent a check of $100.00 to the post master at Independence and asked him to have a stone placed at her son's grave. The post master carried out the wishes of Mrs. Hunt, and when Mr. Hunt Hargrave, of Chatham, a nephew of young David Hunt, visited the cemetery in 1925, he found the stone, though it was much overgrown with vines.

[25]Family tradition.

This little band of Virginians continued their journey westward but had not gone far when disaster again overtook them. Adam Clement and young Scott, two other members, fell victims to the scourge. A letter notifying the family of young Clement's death reads:

"In Camp near Independence,
May 7, 1849.

"He (Adam) died of cholera on the 5th of May, after an illness of ten hours. His little party was camped about twenty miles from us, but sent in for Dr. David C. Ward, Edward Alexander and myself. We set off immediately but reached camp only in time to see him die. Scott came for us and died in less than twenty-four hours after Adam.

Charles B. J. Clement."

Dr. Ward, Edward Alexander and Charles Clement were from the adjoining County of Campbell, traveling together in a party. A letter from another member of the party, described the westward journey as follows:

"April 30, 1849.

"The plains are the most monotonous of all the works of nature that I have ever seen, there is no object that the eye can rest upon. You may travel from day to day without seeing any wood, it seems that you are all the time in a large plantation. There is a great deal to amuse the traveller, especially at this time, when you can look before and behind and see trains of waggons just as far as your eyes will permit. Also at no time scarcely but what you see hunters in full speed after antelope, elk and buffalo.

"I do not think there has been a day since I left Independence but what I have seen graves where persons have died with various diseases, but two thirds at least died with cholera. In Missouri it has swept them off by scores. We have had a troublesome trip."

That part of Virginia lying south of the James River was known as "the black belt" for the number of slaves owned there. Their presence in such large numbers was due to economic reasons, for it was found that the areas drained by the Roanoke and its tributaries were the true home of the tobacco plant; that here in the famed "bright tobacco belt," it flourished and grew a silkier leaf than elsewhere in Virginia. The culture of tobacco required more and more virgin soil, that that which had been under cultivation might rest, for the plant is a gross feeder; therefore the large tobacco grower was constantly adding to his acreage. Since the plant required constant attention there was a need for a great body of workers, and in this way grew up those great plantations and their many slaves. In Pittsylvania there were many large slave owners possessing a hundred or more, among whom were William L. Pannill of "Chalk Level," David Clark of "Cedar Hill," the Wilsons along Dan River, Dr. George Clement of "Turkey Cock," and Samuel Hairston of "Oak Hill."

In 1840 Halifax ranked[26] first among Virginia counties in number of slaves owned, possessing 14,216; Pittsylvania ranked fifth, with 11,588. This same census showed that Pittsylvania ranked high in many things at this time; in population second, with 26,398 inhabitants, Henrico first with 33,000. In number of scholars in school it stood fifth with 1,012, while Henrico again stood first with 1,800. Pittsylvania stood first in the cultivation of tobacco growing 6,439,000 pounds, in corn second with 674,000 bushels.

Tobacco was frequently manufactured on the plantation where it was grown, and occasionally one sees standing today the old brick factory of former years, now long silent and unused, as at Swansonville and Leatherwood. The notice of a sale of a foundry and machine shops located near Pittsylvania Court House, which appeared in the *Danville Register* of October 29, 1859, stated that this property was "situated in the midst of seventy tobacco factories in the county and immediate vicinity," showing how generally tobacco was manufactured on the plantations prior to the formation of the great tobacco companies.

The question of slavery occupied the minds of the people of Virginia more and more with the passage of the years, both from a moral and economic viewpoint. When one gentleman[27] visited another spending the day or night, as was the custom, the subject of slavery was a main topic of conversation, for these Virginians were practical men and realized that slavery was proving to be an economic loss to the state. The owner of many slaves (with their numbers ever increasing) having so many dependants for whom he must provide, needed more and more land to cultivate. Against this system the farmer of small means felt that he could not contend, and in great numbers they left Virginia. Their loss was deplored and felt to be a blow to the economic welfare of the state for the industrious farmer of small means is the backbone of every nation.

But what was to be the remedy? From every point the matter was viewed; these helpless blacks had come as an inheritance and were felt

[26]Howe's "Virginia," pp. 161-2.

[27]Recollections of the Rev'd Chiswell Dabney of Chatham, Va.

to be a great responsibility. Colonization was tried by some, but the people of the western states bitterly resented having the negro settled among them.

As early as 1785 Nehemiah Norton[28] emancipated his eight slaves, stating that he had become "convinced of the iniquity of keeping negroes in a slavish bondage" (Pitts. Deed Book). In 1826, John Ward of "Sulphur Springs," now Gretna, son of Major John Ward of the "Mansion," by the terms of his will freed his seventy slaves. He bequeathed to each one over fifteen years of age twenty dollars, except certain ones to whom he gave $150. They were all taken to Ohio and settled in Lawrence County.

To prevent the separation of husband and wife, when a slave from one plantation wished to marry a slave from another, it was the general custom in Virginia for one master or the other to sell. Griffith Dickerson, in his will, 1842, admonished his executors, "in disposing of my negroes I desire every feeling of humanity to be regarded in parting husband and wife, parent and child."

Prior to 1861 the Fourth of July was celebrated with much pomp as was fitting for the birthday of a great nation—there were speeches of patriotic fervor, great dinners with barbecued meats, horse races and tournaments in which the gallants rode, wearing their lady's colors. The day closed with a brilliant ball at the Court House, for which at times the wines and cakes were especially ordered down from Baltimore. It is recalled that Colonel Elisha Keene attended some of these balls accompanied by his lovely young daughter, Nancy, who later became the mother of the distinguished Lady Nancy Astor, of England.

At this time there were race courses laid out to the south of the Court House on the Danville Road, and to the north on the Gretna Road. "Blue Dick" and "Fly-by-night" from the stables of Col. John White, of Pittsylvania Court House, were among the great race horses of the day. "Fly-by-night" was imported from England by Col. White, but "Blue Dick," a product of his own stables, proved to be the faster horse. An oil painting of "Fly-by-night" and the hoof of "Blue Dick" are prized possessions today in Col. White's family.

The period following the close of the Revolutionary War and extending up to the opening of the War Between the States may be called the golden age of Pittsylvania's life. Throughout the extent of the county were goodly estates with comfortable mansion houses surrounded by

[28]Nehemiah, William and John Norton were brothers. They settled along Dan River and intermarried with the Stonestreets, who had moved down to Pittsylvania from Maryland. Many of their descendants moved to Tennessee and south.

lawns, gardens and well tended fields, where a wholesome and cultured country life was lived, and from which a generous hospitality was dispensed.

Of life in Southside Virginia, Dr. Philip Alexander Bruce, the historian, says: "It was the most characteristically Virginian of all. The spirit of colonial times lingered there longest after Yorktown; the spirit of ante-bellum lingered there longest after Appomattox. Because Southside Virginia remained, during both eras, the greatest scene of tobacco culture in the State. This meant that it was the principal site of the plantation system, upon which the fabric of rural Virginian social life rested from the beginning."

Each plantation was an industrial unit within itself, supplying its own needs through the work of the slaves, who not only tilled the broad acres of the fields and performed the household tasks, but were trained to be carpenters, shoemakers, wheelwrights, weavers, and etc. Domestic manufacture was practiced throughout Virginia, and was left largely to the women slaves who worked under the close supervision of the mistress; the labor of the men being required in the fields and shops. Cloth was woven, dyed, cut and sewed to provide clothing; the hides of cattle were tanned and made into shoes. The making of dyes was understood and indigo was a common garden plant; cornstarch was manufactured in the home. In fact everything needful to the life of the plantation, with the exception of coffee and sugar, could be produced there and life was active and absorbing, requiring great executive ability from both master and mistress. Each plantation formed a miniature village within itself, where the industry of the farm was carried on; there were the carpenter shops and blacksmith shop, the meat house, the weaving house, the dairy, and granary, the great stables, the numerous tobacco barns and the many slave cabins. The census of 1790 reported from Virginia that home manufacturing was largely practiced: "The culture of tobacco requiring so much labor, in the middle counties manufacture is left largely to the female slaves under the eye of the mistress; so that clothing for the slaves is largely purchased, using Kendall's cotton, Osnaberg and hempen rolls. * * * No country under the sun could produce more raw material than Virginia." The year 1865 brought emancipation not to the slaves alone, but also to their mistresses who were relieved from their tremendous responsibilities.

Yet despite many cares time was found for a delightful social intercourse between the neighboring plantations, in which dinings with a

Garden at Oak Hill

Home of Samuel Hairston; built 1823

rich mid-day meal was the favorite mode of entertainment among the elders. The making of beautiful gardens with terraces, flagged walks and much boxwood lent dignity to the life of that period; and viewing the garden with an exchange of flowers was a part of the day's pleasure when visiting a neighbor.

The early Pittsylvania matron was well versed in the art of garden making although she lacked the aids which we have today in garden magazines and books, landscape architects and the ever-convenient nurseryman. She created from an innate sense of beauty and achieved places of great loveliness, peace and content. Here and there we find some of these old gardens that have survived the wreck of time, as those of "Oak Hill," which were planned and built by Mrs. Agnes Hairston in three months, using the labor of seventeen slaves and an overseer. In the Moorman garden at Callands stands a unique and lovely summer house, planted a century ago. For it is a living summer house, with walls of tree box grown in a circle, and sheared smoothly inside and out. A cedar tree planted in the center whose branches rest high upon the box wood wall, forms a perfect cover and shade. Its very simplicity bears the mark of a master gardener.

There are some few of the ante-bellum homes yet standing where the traditions of a gracious past are maintained, but the greater number have long since disappeared, given over to fire and decay, and there is little to mark their site today save the silent rock walled family burial plot, where amid a tangle of vines and weeds we may read the names of those who lived in this charmed and vanished era. Among those early Pittsylvania homes whose memories are fragrant of a gracious hospitality and cultured living may be mentioned the Wilson homes of Dan Hill, Oak Ridge, Windsor and Belle Grade; Oak Hill and Berry Hill of the Hairstons; the Coles's homes of Greenfields, Elkhorn and Coles' Hill; the Pannill places of Chalk Level and Whitethorn; the Wimbish, Terry and White homes of Peytonsburg; the Daniel and Stephen Coleman places near Shockoe; Pineville and Cedar Hill of the Clarks; Cherry Grove, Clement Hill and Turkey Cock, the Clement homes; Mountain View, Mountain Top, Forest Home, Sheva and Bachelor's Hall, the Jones places; Belle Grove, the Tunstall home; Glenland, of the Hunts; Samuel Callands' home, now owned by Mr. Cabell Cobbs; Parson Stone's place now owned by Cabell Shelton; the George Townes' place, now owned by Mr. Jerry Whitehead; the Edmond Fitzgerald home of White Falls; the Moorman home at Callands; Oakland, Greenrock and Deerwood of the Carters;

Shareswood, home of the Millers; Bridgewater of the Cabells; Meadow wood of the Woodings; Eldon, the Whittle home; Swansonville, home of the Swansons; the Byrd, home of the Lewis's; Woodlawn, of the Henry's; the Pocket, of the Smiths; Mount Airy, of the Grastys; Woodside, of the Logans; Edgehill, home of the Wards; Laurel Grove, of the Andersons; Calloway's Level; the homes of the Paynes, Harrisons, Keenes, Adams, Robertsons, Womacks, Scales and a host of others who in their gracious interpretation of life gave to it that rich and mellow flavor which distinguished the social order of old Virginia.

HAND-CARVED MANTEL AT SWANSONVILLE
Portraits over the mantel are the parents of Senator Swanson
Photographed by Dunsford's, Danville

Chapter XVII

THE FOUNDING OF A CITY

Low rounding hills by the side of a stately, beautiful river form a situation designed by nature for man's abode. The Indians were quick to perceive the fitness of the location and established one of their towns there. But it is to the tobacco plant which has wielded so tremendous an influence upon Virginia life that we owe the founding of the City of Danville.

There was a point on Dan River known as Wynne's Falls named in honor of William Wynne, a very early settler who had moved with his family to this section from Brunswick County. At the falls there was a ford across the river over which ran the great mail road from north to south. The cultivation of tobacco was the main industry of the people of Pittsylvania County, and the burden of carrying their product to Richmond and Petersburg for inspection was so great that the inhabitants of the county petitioned Legislature in October 1793 for an inspection of tobacco at Wynne's Falls on Dan River. The petitioners further stated that "the situation of the place is suitably calculated for a Town, which will make the convenience of the Inspection more Servisable," and asked that a town be established "on the south side of Dan River, adjoining Wynne's Falls on the lands Larkin Dix sold to John Barnett"—Signed John Wilson, John Wilson, Jr., William Ramsey, Joel McDaniel, George Adams, William Harrison, Robert Harrison, William Ware, Fra Mayberry, Robert Somerhays, James Paine, Peter Perkins, John Sutherlin, George Sutherlin, Sr., Thos. Fearne.

In answer to the petition Legislature enacted on November 23, 1793: "That 25 acres of land, the property of John Barnett adjoining Wynne's Falls, on the Southside of Dan River, in Pittsylvania County, shall be and they are hereby vested in Thomas Tunstall, Matthew Clay, William Harrison, John Wilson, Thomas Fearne, George Adams, Thomas Worsham, Robert Payne, John Dix, John Southerland, John Call, Thomas Smith, gentleman trustees, to be by them or a majority of them laid off into lots of half acre each, with convenient streets and established a town by the name of Danville." Many of the names of these twelve gentlemen trustees are already familiar to us; Thomas Tunstall lived on Stinking River, below Chalk Level; Matthew Clay was a young lawyer who lived near Chestnut Level; William Harrison's home was on Dan

River, near Wenonda; John Wilson was living up the River at the Ferry; Robert Payne was a neighbor of William Harrison; John Dix was the owner of Dix's Ferry; John and George Sutherlin lived nearby on Dan River; Thomas Smith lived on Sandy River.

On May 4th, 1795, the trustees of Danville offered for sale the lots into which the town had been laid off, the purchasers of the lots obligating themselves to build upon them within five years "a dwelling house sixteen feet square at least with a brick or stone chimney." In December 1799, the owners of several unimproved lots petitioned that a further time of three years be allowed them to build thereon, which petition was signed by Beverly Barksdale, George Williamson, William Beavers, William Spiller, James Colquehoun, James Arnett, John Sutherlin, early citizens, some of whose names are preserved in the streets of the city.

As a place of tobacco inspection, warehouses were erected at once for the reception of the tobacco, and there is on record in the clerk's office at Chatham a report from the inspectors as follows:

Dan River Danville Warehouse
a List of Tob. received from 22 Sept. 1795
Til 19th September 1796—
18 hhds. of Tob. Shipped by Thos. Barnett.
44 hhds. of Tob. Shipped by Col. John Wilson.
28 hhds. of Tob. Shipped by James Colquehoun.
29 hhds. of Tob. Shipped by Ro. Payne & Co.
7 hhds. of Tob. Shipped by George Baskerville.
1 hhd. of Tob. Shipped by John Jones.
1 hhd. of Tob. Shipped by George Cook.
7 hhds. of Tob. prized heavy by John Wilson & James Calquahoun.
70 hhds. of Tob. remaining in the Warehouse.

249. Sept. 17, 1796.

John Sutherlin & John Dix.

The location of the town of Danville—a slight elevation by the side of the broad river with excellent water power from the falls, was one calculated to induce growth, and indicative of its rapid expansion are three interesting petitions which were offered to Legislature in December 1801. In order to educate their children the first citizens of Danville established the Danville Academy, for as they said "being in a remote part of the estate we have found it attended with great inconvenience and expense to get our children educated, and have undertaken to build an academy near the said Town, to be known as the Danville Academy." The petitioners sought permission to hold a lottery to complete the building. A few years later permission was granted for the trustees of the academy to be made a "body politic and incorporate," and the following gentlemen signed the petition and no doubt also formed the body of trustees: William Beavers, James D. Patton, Dan'l Sullivan, William Lynn, Nath. Wilson, John Barnett, John Noble, Dan'l Price, John Ross, Thomas Stewart, Harold Haralson, Jeduthan Carter, George Townes, Thomas Clark, William Tunstall, and George Tucker. The academy was a two-story brick structure which at this time stood outside the village, but with the growth of the city the highway upon which it faced came to be Wilson Street.

The second petition of 1801 shows that the foundation of one of Danville's leading industries had been laid at that early time, when flour inspection for the town was sought, "as the flour manufactured here is generally shipped down Dan River and has to be inspected lower down." The third petition sought permission for the erection of a tollbridge over Dan River from the land of John Barnett to the land of Thos. Worsham, to charge the customary rate of toll. A petition from the proprietors of the toll bridge in 1818, asking to raise the rate of toll stated that the bridge was built in 1802, just below the great falls opposite the town of Danville, and was 325 yards in length. "Owing to the great changes in the times, the progress which has been made and is making in the navigation of Roanoke River, and its Branches, and the rapid growth of the town of Danville," an increase in toll rates was deemed necessary to keep the bridge in repair; for "the road which passes through the counties of Halifax and Pittsylvania to Danville and from there through the State of North Carolina is one of the most public in the United States, being the principal Highway of Travellers from the south and southwest to Richmond, the city of Washington, Baltimore, Philadelphia, and other large commercial towns of the north and east."

The petition was granted and the rate of toll was fixed as follows:

Horses, 4 cts.; man, 4 cts.; Hhd. Tob., 4 cts.; 4 wheel carriage, 24 cts.; 2 wheel carriage, 8 cts.; neat cattle, 4 cts.; hog, ¾ cts.

There was a famous inn on this highway about seven miles north of Danville, known as Beaver's Tavern, which was a favorite stopping place with travelers. The tavern was owned by Major William Beavers,[1] a gentleman of good standing, a justice of the peace and major of the militia. As a rule the southern tavern was ill kept and uninviting, the host a man of few opportunities in life—so that Beavers Tavern was the great exception, with a genial gentleman for the host and one's needs comfortably supplied. The tavern is now the home of Mr. John Blair, and has recently been remodeled into a modern dwelling. It sets well back from the road in a wide grassy lawn, flanked by rows of boxwood. Across the road stood the stables in a grove of great oak trees. Here the southern statesmen were wont to await one another and from here continue the journey to Washington in company together. Calhoun of South Carolina, would spend days resting at Beaver's Tavern, in his journeys to and from the capital; you can picture to yourself the great statesman walking in the grove nearby, deep in thought, or conversing pleasantly with the genial major.

With the assembling of a few families there on the banks of the Dan, a pleasant social life developed at once. And as the Fourth of July Ball was generally held at the Court House, preceded by the races and a barbecued dinner, so the Washington Ball was usually held at Danville, to which came the socially élite of the county. The following invitation was sent by William Clark of Danville, in 1804, to young Dr. Henry G. Calloway,[2] at Callands:

[1]Major Wm. Beavers married Elizabeth Fontaine in March 1802 (marriage bond at Pittsylvania County Courthouse).

His will was proven at Pittsylvania Courthouse in Nov. 1822, naming sons William, Edwin R., and John Fontaine Beavers; daughter Mary Gatewood, and wife's mother Mrs. Elizabeth Fontaine. Mrs. Elizabeth Fontaine's will was proven January 1845, in which she named sons Thomas B. Fontaine, Peter Fontaine, William Fontaine and B. F. Fontaine; daughters Tabitha Thompson and Elizabeth Beavers; Edwin Beavers and William W. Keen Executors.

Mrs. Elizabeth (Ballard) Fontaine was the wife of Moses Fontaine, a younger son of the Rev. Peter Fontaine, of Westover Parish, Charles City County, Va., who died in 1755, owning about 6,000 acres in this section. Moses Fontaine moved to these western lands. (Records of the Huguenots.) Edwin R. Beavers, son of Major William Beavers, married Elizabeth Carter, daughter of Col. Jeduthan Carter, and had issue: 1. Elizabeth Fontaine, married John Daniel Coleman of Chatham, Va. 2. Martha, married Mr. C. A. Pritchett. 3. Anne Wesley, married Col. John Herndon, son of Captain Aaron Herndon. 4. John. 5. William. 6. Jeduthan.

[2]Dr. Henry Green Calloway was the son of Col. John Calloway, of "Flat Creek," Campbell County, and his wife Agatha Ward, a daughter of Major John Ward of "The Mansion." A few months after the Washington Ball Dr. Calloway married Miss Anne Calland, a daughter of Samuel Calland and his wife Elizabeth Smith. Mrs. Elizabeth Calloway, named in the invitation, was a sister of Miss Anne Calland. When setting up housekeeping Dr. Calloway turned to the old Washington Iron Works for his kitchen iron ware. These works had been established by Col. John Donelson and successfully worked many years prior to the Revolutionary War. The following acknowledgment was made to Dr. Calloway's order:

"Washington Works, August 19, 1805.

Dear Sir,

I received yours of the 16th Inst., by the Bearer Mr. Augustin Dishon and have sent you by his return the different castings you wrote for as stated below except the six Gallon pott of which we have none on hand at this time. We shall shortly be in blast again, if you should want any other article of castings shall be glad to furnish you.

I am Dear Sir
Very Respectfully
Yr M o Ob't
Wm Crump.

1 10 Gallon pott	£0.16.8
1 Large oven	0.14.0
1 Middle Size "	0.12.0
I Large Skillet	0. 5.0
1 Deep "	0. 3.0
1 pair Fire Dogs	0.15.0
	3. 6.2"

"Callands, 1804.

Dear Sir,

I have got this far on my way to court where I thought it possible I might have the pleasure of seeing you, but the weather being so intensely cold I have declined going any farther. I now write you by your connection M. J. Calloway (of Franklin) informing you that we purpose having a Ball on the 22nd February next, and I flatter myself we shall have the pleasure of your company. I left home without bringing tickets for Miss Anne Calland and Mrs. Elizabeth Calloway. You will oblige me by writing tickets for them, sealing them and conveying them to them. The tickets are wrote in this form 'The pleasure of Miss ——— company is requested to a Ball at the Eagle tavern in the Town of Danville on the 22nd of February next.' This is signed 'The Managers.' If enquiry should be made of you who the Managers are, you may inform them that W. Hillyer (counsellor-at-law) Doctor Patton and myself are to act in that capacity. I will only add that I expect a large, elegant and genteel company will grace the Ball room on that evening.

I am with Esteem

Yours Sincerely

Wm Clarke."

The Calland home stood two miles beyond Callands, so that the drive to the ball was a ride of some twenty-five miles in a carriage. Doctor Patton, one of the managers of the ball, was Dr. James Doddridge Patton, a young physician from Rockbridge County who had recently located at Danville. He married Miss Mary Fearn, of Pittsylvania County, and was a leading citizen in Danville's early life.

At the time of the founding of the city of Danville the waterways were the chief means of conveying produce to market. The fact that the rivers which drained this section—the Dan, the Staunton and the Roanoke, flowed into North Carolina brought about very close trade relations between the two sections. It was in North Carolina that much of the produce of Pittsylvania found market. The clearing and opening of the waterways was a matter of such concern to the people of south mid-land Virginia that the subject was brought before the General Assembly, and on November 24, 1796, George Carrington, John B. Scott, Richard N. Venable, Henry E. Coleman and Clement Carrington, or any three of them, were appointed "to wait upon the Governor of North Carolina and enter into proper mutual stipulations for improving the navigation of

Roanoke River." Men caught the vision of a great waterway of trade formed by the Roanoke and its tributaries, with boats and batteaux ladened with produce swiftly covering the many miles to market. The project offered relief from the weary miles of rough travel over the roads leading to the Richmond and Petersburg markets.

In their eagerness the people of Virginia did not wait upon the commissioners appointed to confer with North Carolina, but set to work at once. In December 1796 a bill was introduced in Legislature for clearing and extending the navigation of Pigg River from its mouth to the Washington Iron Works in Franklin County, and Swinfield Hill, Benjamin Cook, Josiah Woods, Samuel Duval and James Calloway were appointed trustees for the work. In January 1798 a bill was introduced for improving the navigation of Staunton River from Booker's Ferry to the mouth of Pigg River and the trustees named for the work were Philip Payne, William Ward, David Hunt, Charles Calloway, John Ward, Bryan W. Nowling, William Witcher and John Law.

After many conferences between the Virginia and North Carolina commissioners the Roanoke Navigation Company was formed by Act of the General Assembly of Virginia in December 1804, for the navigation of the Roanoke River and the tributaries. In order to raise $100,000 to carry out the project, shares in the company were offered for sale, and the committee named by the Assembly to sell and receive moneys for the company in Pittsylvania County were Nathaniel Wilson and John Barnett; in Henry County Benjamin Jones and Patrick H. Fontaine; in Patrick County Greenville Penn and Charles Foster.

An interesting document of this period is "the journal of a trip by water from Danville to Norfolk in May and June 1819, in company with Col.s Cabell (Benj. W. S.) and Lawson Carter," written by young Captain Walter Coles. The three gentlemen probably formed a committee appointed to make observations in view of the further development of the navigation of the Roanoke River. Captain Coles writes:

"I set out from Danville on the 24th May and arrived at Rock landing (Roanoke Rapids) on the evening of the 28th. There are about twenty falls from Danville to the Rock which have from two to five feet in the distance of from fifty yards to a quarter of a mile and about twenty-five miles of the way is interrupted by shoals which are from 100 yards to 12 miles in length. Eaton's and Pugh's falls have a pitch of four feet each and a fall of ten feet in the quarter of a mile. The Balance of the river affords two or three feet water in common seasons and presents several beautiful sheets of many miles in length. The observations upon this part of the river were general, but the opinion was strongly impressed that considerable improvement would be necessary for convenient and profitable Batteaux Navigation, and by a small additional expense boats of heavier weight might be used and by an expense not very enormous, perhaps less than $1,000.00 per mile sieam boats might ply between Danville and the falls.

"It is absolutely necessary that temporary improvements should be avoided and some permanent system of improving the upper navigation adopted; which if it does not aspire to the use of larger boats, may at least prevent the useless waste of money and insure a profitable Batteaux Navigation. If the present spirit for Town speculation should continue and the rivalship between the different Towns should be kept alive, the improvement of the river will meet with obstacles from the separate interests of the Towns.

"Rock Landing is situated at the upper end of the canal (built around the rapids), upon three elevated ridges running down to the canal at right angles. In the beginning of the year 1817 the Directors of the Roanoke Navigation Company had a log house built for the accommodation of themselves when in session and of their clerk. Shortly afterwards commission houses were established and warehouses built for the reception of produce that it might be waggoned to the lower end of the falls.

"In the spring of 1818, when the whole country was excited by a mania for town speculation, Col. Jones the proprietor, was prevailed on to lay off his lands into lots, a few were sold at $50.00 and $100.00 each, but the balance soon rose to four or five thousand, and in one year the place has sprung up almost to the size of Danville. To return to the canal which was frequently visited during a stay of a week at Rock Landing—for particular calculations and estimates, I must refer to paper mark A. B." (The Roanoke Navigation Company constructed a canal around Roanoke Rapids. Rock Landing was situated at the upper end of the rapids and Weldon at the lower end.)

"The canal it was supposed would be constructed so as to admit boats of the lower river. This is not the case but might be by a small expense.

"June 4th Friday at two o'clock left Weldon in the Hariot freighted with 54 Hhds. of tobacco and commanded by Captain Young. Having prepared a good sounding line we commenced taking accurate soundings of the River." (Then following pages of observations regarding the depth of the river, height of banks and etc.)

"Halifax Town about 7 miles below Weldon is an old Town which took its rise almost with the settlement of the country, and contained some thirty years ago near 1,000 inhabitants; it was then the seat of trade, of wealth, taste and fashion. The country immediately around it is exceedingly rich, and it purchased the produce from and furnished foreign goods to an extensive back country. It was a considerable tobacco market and shipped all the corn, peas and fish of the adjoining country. But alas, how great is the instability of human affairs. The improved market at Petersburg has bereft it of its tobacco trade and the rise of many Towns in other parts of North Carolina has completely cut off its back country trade. The decay of Halifax and the crop trade to Petersburg from the very banks of the Roanoke below the falls are certainly strong evidence that we cannot expect our produce to pursue a channel that the produce below the falls has long since deserted. And that we must look to some other outlet to the ocean than has heretofore existed.

"June 7th arrived at Plymouth, a shipping point for tar, pitch, lumber, corn and fish. Fifty thousand barrels of corn are yearly stored at Plymouth and shipped from that place to West Indies and different parts of the coast. The distance between Weldon and Plymouth is 120 miles. There are five boats carrying from 40 to sixty Hhds. of tobacco and 45 river boats carrying from 200 to 500 barrels of corn. These boats all have five men, a captain and boy to manage them. The Norfolk boats are ultimately intended to ply between Weldon and Norfolk through the river, sound and swamp canal, but the canal not being in a situation to receive them, they either unload at Plymouth and the produce is shipped to Norfolk by sea or they proceed to Elizabeth City where the canal boat meets them and finish the route.

"Accomplished the distance of twenty miles between Plymouth and Edenton in two hours and 10 minutes. Edenton is situated on the North side of and fronting the sound. It has about 1,000 inhabitants who are remarkable for their industry, neatness and respectability. Liberality without extravagance, morality without austerity, and elegance without ostentation mark the character of these people. The bordering country is rich as is all the country extending along the north side of the sound."

Captain Coles likened the beauty of Albemarle Sound to Lake Champlain (New York), describing it as one of the finest sheets of water in the world. He said that in the Sound and its waters were caught annually around 100,000 barrels of fish. The journal closes with the statement that "an engineer has been sent for to Europe who is expected shortly, chiefly for the purpose of examining the subject of sand bars," which obstruct the entrances to the streams on the North Carolina coast. To obviate this difficulty a canal was built through the Dismal Swamp leading to Norfolk.

The Roanoke Navigation Company flourished for many years, adding greatly to the prosperity of this section. With exclusive rights and state aid the company opened navigation from Weldon, N. C., up the Staunton to the mouth of Pigg River; and up Dan River to Meade, N. C. Howe said in his History of Virginia, 1850, that Dan River was navigable for batteaux carrying from 7,000 to 10,000 pounds as far up as Meade, N. C. Batteaux plied regularly up and down the Dan and Staunton Rivers, propelled by long poles, and the blowing of the batteau horn gave notice of its approach at the landing places where hhds. of tobacco, cargoes of flour, wheat and other produce were loaded on to be conveyed to market. Batteaux on the Staunton continued in use until recent years, bringing their cargoes to the R. R. bridge at Hurts, where by means of pulleys it was loaded into freight cars.

The river batteaux were long narrow boats and were the invention of Robert Rose and Anthony Rucker. It is said the idea was suggested by the Indians' custom of lashing their light canoes together with poles when a very heavy load was to be carried. The batteaux on James River at Lynchburg were described in 1796 by Isaac Weld as "boats from 45 to 54 feet in length, but very narrow in proportion to their length. Three men were sufficient to navigate one of these boats." (*Wm. and M. Q.*, Vol. 2, 154.)

The building of a canal through the Dismal Swamp opened uninterrupted water carriage from this section to Norfolk. With the benefit of open navigation to the ocean, Danville grew rapidly and in a petition for a bank in 1822, it was stated that in a few months there would be open water communication between the town and Norfolk. A rock canal with locks was built by the navigation company around the falls at Danville, and so substantial and enduring was their work that the canal is in use today by the cotton mills.

In 1835 the General Assembly enacted a bill for improving the navigation of Banister River from Meadeville in Halifax County to Clark's Bridge (six miles east of Chatham). The books were to be opened at Pittsylvania Court House by William H. Tunstall, Coleman D. Bennett,

Robert Coles and George Poindexter; at Riceville by Daniel Coleman, Raleigh Thompson, William Logan, David Berger and Edmund Fitzgerald.

Meadeville and Riceville were both river villages which had grown up during this period when the waterways were the chief means of transportation. They flourished for a period, with their flour mills and tobacco factories, but with the railroads came a change of trade centers, and these villages then gradually faded away. Riceville was incorporated a town in the year of 1835, with the following gentlemen trustees: Daniel Coleman, Vincent Dickerson, Nelson Tucker, John W. Power, Wm. L. Pannell, John B. Jennings, David Logan and David Berger. The town was situated upon the bluffs above the White Falls of Banister River.

The year 1828 was a memorable one in the annals of the city, for in that year was established the first cotton mill, known as the Danville Manufacturing Company; and among the promoters were Eustace Hunt, George Craghead, Samuel Pannill, Ed. Carrington, John W. Paxton, John Ross, James M. Williams, John Noble, Robert Payne, Nathaniel Wilson, James Lanier, James Patton, Ben Cabell and others. Eight years later the company's stock was increased to $300,000.00. This plant was the forerunner of the great Dan River and Schoolfield mills of today.

The necessity for improved highways over which to move the farm products to market was engaging the attention of the people. In 1832 a petition was presented to the Legislature from Pittsylvania, Henry, Patrick, Grayson, Floyd, Montgomery, Franklin, and Wythe Counties for a turnpike from Danville to Evansham in Wythe County, to be built after the manner of the Kanawha Pike. It was considered that $50,000.00 would be sufficient funds to construct the road. A map of the road was surveyed at this time.

In 1837, Pittsylvania, Franklin and Botetourt petitioned for a dirt turnpike to be built from Danville by Rocky Mount and Big Lick (now Roanoke City), to Fincastle, and stated that the road from Danville to Rocky Mount be constructed at $300.00 per mile. This road it was thought would be of great benefit to travelers from the south seeking the mineral springs of Virginia. Books were to be opened at Danville under the direction of John Dickenson, Robert W. Williams, Thomas Rawlings, Robert Wilson, John Ross and George Townes; at Pittsylvania Court House under George H. Gilmer, Coleman D. Bennett, James M. Whittle,

William Rison, James F. Johnson and William H. Tunstall; at Jabez Smith's Stores under Vincent Witcher, Jabez Smith, James Hopkins, James Mitchell and W. B. Roger.

The road was surveyed by Crozet, the French Engineer, and was built at once. It ran from Danville to Rocky Mount, leading by Swansonville and Callands, and was known as the Franklin Turnpike. It proved to be a great artery of trade, being the outlet to market for the mountain counties of Franklin, Grayson, Floyd and Carrol. Along its dusty way traveled droves of horses, cattle, sheep and hogs; flocks of turkeys; wagon loads of chickens, apples and produce of all kinds seeking the market of Danville. It was a rare sight for the country boy who was not so fortunate as to live on the Turnpike, to be permitted to stand for an hour on the roadside and watch the traffic down this busy highway of trade.

In 1842 a turnpike from Danville to Lynchburg was chartered, which led by Chatham and Chalk Level, crossing Staunton River at Ward's Bridge where it entered Ward's Road and led on to Lynchburg. A stage coach plied daily between the two towns, a distance of some seventy-five miles, and the turnpike was known as the "Stage Road." Porter Flagg had the mail contract for years. Four horses driven at a long gallop were used to the stage, and relay stables were placed at Chatham and Chalk Level, where the horses were changed. The approach of the stage was heralded by blowing a horn, and its passing was a picturesque event of each day.

The building of railroads as an improved and quicker mode of transportation next engrossed the minds of the men of this section. A brilliant and gifted son of Pittsylvania, Whitmell P. Tunstall, was the leader in a determined movement for a railroad from Richmond to Danville. A railroad was a revolutionary idea at this time in which many people had no confidence, and Tunstall met with strong opposition from those who considered him a vain dreamer, as well as from the Roanoke Navigation Company, which feared lest Tunstall's dream be realized and they find a rival in the transportation business.

Tunstall was a lawyer by profession and for many years a member of the Legislature. With firm belief in his plans and the future development of his country, he pursued his course with pursuasive eloquence. A railroad convention met in Danville October 5, 1835; and another in Richmond on June 11, 1836, at which Danville was represented by Ben

Cabell,[3] George Townes,[4] Thos. Rawlins, Robert Williams and John Price; Pittsylvania by William Swanson,[5] Walter Fitzgerald, and Vincent Witcher.[6] At this convention it was resolved that the Legislature of North Carolina incorporating the Roanoke-Danville and Junction R. R. Co. was liberal, and requested Virginia to do the same.

Mr. Tunstall introduced the bill to charter the Richmond and Danville Railroad, Apr. 1838, in a strong and eloquent speech. Again in 1845 Pittsylvania County petitioned that the railroad from Danville to Richmond be built, and pointed out the advantages which the state would receive from the expenditure in building the road—that only through this railroad could the products of this section of the state reach the Richmond markets, which would furnish "an outlet of trade for the counties of Franklin, Roanoke, Floyd, Carrol, Grayson, Wythe and other western counties to the Tennessee Line." That no other section of the state could furnish to eastern markets so great a quantity of products.

After a struggle of nine years the charter was granted on March 9th, 1747, with state aid assured, and in a letter to his brother-in-law, Col. George Townes, written one hour after the passage of the bill Mr. Tunstall wrote: "'Tis the proudest day of my life and I think I may now say I have not lived in vain." The first train entered the city of Danville on June 19, 1856, but Mr. Tunstall did not live to see the completion of the railroad of which he had been elected the first president, but his vision has been more than fulfilled in the expansive development of his native section, accomplished through the work of the railroad. Whitmell P. Tunstall[7] passed away at the early age of 44 years "and with him

[3]Ben Cabell was General Benjamin B. F. Cabell of Bridgewater.

[4]George Townes was the son of Halcutt Townes whose home was in eastern Pittsylvania, near Keeling, and whose will was proven July 18, 1803, naming sons George, Stephen, Robert and Edward. George Townes represented his county in the Senate of Virginia in 1830, and again 1859-61; in the convention of 1829-30; and in the House of Delegates at different sessions extending from 1818 to 1852. He married Eliza Tunstall, sister of Whitmell P. Tunstall, and settled the estate now owned by Mr. Jere Whitehead, who married a great granddaughter of Col. Townes.

[5]William Swanson, son of William Swanson, Sr., frequently represented his county in the General Assembly, and was great grandfather of Governor and Senator Claude A. Swanson.

[6]Vincent Witcher was the son of William Witcher, Jr., and his wife Molly Dalton, married in 1782, and had issue: Vincent, William married Lucy Graves, Caleb married Fanny James, Ephraim, James married Polly Swanson, John Reuben, and Nancy who married Capt. John Keen. Vincent Witcher was a grandson of Capt. Wm. Witcher, of the Revolutionary War. He represented Pittsylvania in both the Senate and the House of Delegates for a number of years, serving in the lower house from 1823-39, and again in 1843-44. From 1845-50 he served in the Senate, and was again in the House of Delegates from 1850-57.

[7]Whitmell Pugh Tunstall, born Apr. 1816, died Feb. 19, 1854, was the son of Col. William Tunstall and his wife Winnefred Pugh. He married first the beautiful Mrs. Doneche, who lived only a short while, and secondly, Mary Liggot, Sept. 29, 1840, by whom he had issue: John L. born 1845, Alex Augusta, Norman. He served in House of Delegates from 1836 to 41; the session of 41-42 he was elected to the Senate; from 1845-48 he was again in the House of Delegates. He was forceful in debate, quick with repartee, and withal such a genial, pleasing personality that he made for himself a host of friends. His portrait hangs on the walls of the Court House of Pittsylvania.

BELLE GROVE

Built 1798 by William Tunstall, Jr., now home of Miss Laura Crews

perished much of genius and worth." He was buried at "Belle Grove," his ancestral home.

At the close of the war in 1865 the Richmond and Danville Railway, the pride of the city, was in a most deplorable condition, with the trackage largely destroyed and the bridges burnt. At this crucial point another brilliant and gifted son of Pittsylvania and Danville was called to take charge and was made president of the railroad, Col. Algernon Sidney Buford.[8] For twenty years he held this responsible position and through the trying period of reconstruction, when the south was battling for its existence, with meager resources at his command he extended the line to 3,000 miles of trackage, and thus established the great system known as the Southern Railway, which had its inception in the Richmond and Danville Railroad. Col. Buford was the son of William Buford of Lunenburg and his wife Sarah Robertson Shelton of Pittsylvania, and spent his boyhood in Pittsylvania, being brought up in a school taught by his father. For awhile he himself taught a school for boys in Chatham. Later he graduated in law at the University of Virginia and began the practice of his profession in his mother's native county of Pittsylvania, but soon removed to Danville, where in addition to his practice he became the owner and editor of the *Danville Register.* He represented Pittsylvania in the House of Delegates for the session 1853-4 and 1861-65.

Another outstanding figure in the founding of the City of Danville who was also a builder of railroads, was Major William Sutherlin,[9] a son of Pittsylvania. He was born in 1822, and was educated at the Danville Academy and in the private school of Joseph Godfrey, that famous teacher who trained so many of the youth of the county. William Sutherlin was a manufacturer of tobacco and a man of vision, who planned for the development of the resources of his native section. He built two railroads, the Milton and Sutherlin and the Danville and New

[8]Algernon Sidney Buford was born Jan. 2, 1826. In 1854 he married Emily W. Townes of Pittsylvania County, sister of George Townes, by whom he had a daughter, Emily, now Mrs. Clement Manley, of Winston-Salem, N. C. He married secondly Katie Wortham of Richmond, had issue, Kate T. Buford. He married a third time, Miss Mary Cameron Strother, issue: Mary Ross, Algernon Sidney, Jr., William Erskine Buford. Ambrose Buford was living in Pittsylvania at the time of the Revolutionary War, and died in the service. His will was probated in 1780, and wife Mary was his executrix.

The will of Gabriel Shelton, 1803, mentions that his lands adjoin those of Pannill and Buford. Gregory Shelton married Elizabeth Buford, daughter of Mrs. Elizabeth Buford, in 1792. Gabriel Shelton married Mary Buford in 1814.

[9]Major William Thomas Sutherlin was born near Danville April 7, 1822. He was the son of George S. Sutherlin, and his wife Polly Norman. He served as major and quarter master of the Confederate Army, being stationed at Danville throughout the war. Served in the House of Delegates in 1873. He was deeply interested in the subject of agriculture, and was largely instrumental in the establishment of the Virginia Agricultural College at Blacksburg. He married Jane E. Patrick, and left one daughter, Janie Sutherlin, who married Mr. Smith and left an only daughter, Janie Smith Barrett. Major Sutherlin died July 22, 1893; his portrait hangs in the State Library at Richmond.

The will of George Sutherlin, Sr., was proven at Pittsylvania, June 18, 1804, naming sons George, Thomas, William, Adams and James. He owned lands on Dan River and Sandy Creek.

River. He was deeply interested in the science of farming and aided in reorganizing the State's Agricultural Society of which he was president for four years. Major Sutherlin's beautiful home in Danville is preserved as a Memorial Mansion and houses the public library of the city.

Through the navigation of the streams, the building of the highways and railroads, Danville grew and developed as a market and industrial center. As the plantations in the surrounding country multiplied in number and increased in acreage, more and more tobacco was bought and brought to Danville to feed the many tobacco factories there. It was not until 1860 that the first auction warehouse was opened for the sale of the plant.

The growth of education had kept pace with the growth of the city and just prior to the outbreak of the War Between the States there were four excellent private schools for girls in the city of Danville, viz.: the Southside Female Institute, of which Mrs. E. E. Nottingham was principal; the Danville Female Academy, of which Dr. Geo. W. Dame, the Episcopal Minister, was principal; the Danville Female College under the auspices of the Methodist Church; and the Baptist Female Seminary, with Mr. J. J. Averett and Mr. Nathan Penick as associate principals. In recognition of the worthy service of Mr. Averett the school today bears the name of Averett College, while the Danville Female Institute has become the well known Randolph-Macon Institute for girls.

The story of Danville's great industry of cotton manufacture is one of modern times and began in the year 1882, when Thomas B. Fitzgerald of North Carolina and his associates the three Schoolfield brothers of Henry County, John H., James E., and Robert A., founded the Riverside Cotton Mill in a very modest way. Through their wise management the business grew and expanded until today it comprises eleven large mills, being the largest textile manufactory in the south.

Around some of these mills has grown up the village of Schoolfield, with a population of 6,000 people, who have been supplied through the beneficent wisdom of the mill directors with every advantage that would lend itself to their health, comfort and uplift—in the best of modern schools, libraries, Y. W. and Y. M. C. A., with the result that where other mills have suffered strikes, the most friendly and cordial relation exist between the directors and the workers. No strike has ever sullied Schoolfield's record.

Chapter XVIII

THE WAR OF 1861-65

The history of Pittsylvania County during the four years of that mighty conflict between the states was in no wise different from her sister counties. When Virginia decided upon secession as the only honorable course left to her and sent forth the call to arms, her sons responded alike from all parts of the state—the lawyer left his office, the doctor his profession, the teacher his school room, the farmer his fields, the merchant his counter, all eagerly going forth to defend Virginia's rights.

There were many great leaders produced in that struggle, and we glory in the greatness of Lee, Jackson and Stuart; but we should not forget that "the real hero[1] is the private soldier. It was he who won the victories that distinguished his commanders. It was he who stood sentinel at the lone midnight hour; faced cold, hunger, nakedness, peril, with no hope of promotion or fame; pointed the rifle, wielded the saber, fired the belching cannon, defied overwhelming odds, all for the sake of loyalty to his State. * * * No grander, no more tragic figure has ever trod the arena of history" than the Confederate soldier.

Pittsylvania sent hundreds of men into the Confederate ranks, her numerous companies following Generals Lee, Jackson, Stuart and Johnston in their different campaigns. Company I, of the 53rd Regiment, participated in the battle of Bethel, the opening engagement of the war on Virginia soil. A detachment from the company escorted the first prisoners of war to Richmond, and word of their coming having preceded their arrival, the whole city turned out to meet them. Company I, of the 21st Regiment, was with Jackson in his celebrated Valley Campaign. Pittsylvania cavalry stood side by side with Stuart on that fatal day at Yellow Tavern. Pittsylvania's men charged with Pickett across that field of death at Gettysburg bearing aloft the flag of the 53rd Regiment.

There is a charge laid at our doors by our northern friends that we, the descendants of the noble men who have made illustrious Virginia's history, are strangely lacking in appreciation of their deeds of valor and courage, failing to record even the names of those who have fought her battles and thus shaped her destiny. And the accusation is not without

[1]John Leslie Hall's, "Half Hours in History."

truth for we have not a complete list of all the companies from Pittsylvania that served in this great struggle. The 38th Regiment was commanded by Col. Isaac Carrington of Pittsylvania Court House, in which were:

Company A, Captain David Townes.
Company B, Captain John Cabell, called the Pittsylvania Vindicators.
Company C, Captain William B. Simpson.
Company D, Captain R. C. Herndon.
Company E, Captain Joseph R. Cabell.
Company H, Captain Joseph M. Terry.
Company K, Captain George R. Griggs.

53rd Regiment, Col. Aylett; Lieut.-Col. R. W. Martin, of Pittsylvania Courthouse:

Company I, "Chatham Greys," Captains Werth and William Tredway.
Company G, Captains Ross Carter, W. S. Penick, R. A. Mustein.
Company F, Halifax Border Company.

18th Regiment, Cols. Robert Withers and George C. Cabell, of Danville:

Company I, Spring Garden Blues, Captain James Luck.
Company A, Danville Blues.
Company B, Danville Greys.

57th Regiment, Col. William H. Ramsey, of Pittsylvania:
Company I, Pittsylvania Life Guards.
Company E, Pigg River Greys.

21st Regiment:
Company I, Turkey Cock Greys, Captain Ad. Witcher.
Company H, Captain Sherrod Mustein.

46th Regiment:
Company C, Pigg River Invincibles, Captain Isaac Watson.

6th Virginia Cavalry, Col. Thomas S. Flournoy:
Company E, Pittsylvania Dragoons, Captain Cabell Flournoy.

13th Virginia Battalion of Artillery:

Company B, Riggold Battery, Captains Stamps and Crispen Dickenson.

Green's Battery, of Danville.

6th Virginia Reserves:

Company C, Danville, Captain R. J. Moorman.

Pittsylvania C. H. Home Guard, Captain Chesley Martin.

Danville became a military post of many activities—there were established hospitals, arsenals, commissary departments, woolen mills and prisons for Federal soldiers. Dr. Robert E. Withers, of Danville, Colonel of the 18th Regiment, after sustaining severe wounds which incapacitated him for further field duty, was placed in command of the post. There were some six or seven thousand prisoners to guard who were housed in the large tobacco factories, and this was performed by a company of enlisted men detached for the duty because of disease or injury unfitting them for field service, aided by many companies from adjoining counties composed of persons between the ages of 16 to 18 and 45 to 50.

A Prussian by the name[2] of Charles de Nordendorf, a graduate of one of the finest military schools in that kingdom, was at this time teaching music in the Methodist Female College of Danville and he was pressed into service by Col. Withers, commandant of the post. It was necessary to construct fortifications for the defense of the post against raiding parties which might attempt to liberate the prisoners. Under the direction of Nordendorf redoubts and rifle pits were erected on the hills overlooking Danville, the remains of which can be seen today.

A Freedman's Bureau was established at Danville at the close of the war, to which came one day a negro man asking for his land. A rumor had gone through the country that the Federal government would give to each ex-slave of 21 years a mule and ten acres of ground. When the Federal agent replied that the government had no land to give away, the negro, with keen insight into the situation, said: "I belonged to marster and you took me from him," and the inference was, why not his lands, too.

---

[2]Dr. Robert E. Withers, has preserved in his Memoirs many interesting events of this trying period. His efforts to feed and care for the Yankee prisoners in his charge, despite the scarcity of food in the latter days of the war was favorably reported by them to the Federal authorities, saving Col. Withers from imprisonment in a Federal prison. After the close of the war he moved to Wytheville; and later was appointed consul to China. Of Col. Withers eleven daughters, one married Mr. Williams of Martinsville, and Mrs. Robert Paxton of Danville, and Mrs. Albert Gravely of Martinsville are his granddaughters.

The struggle of the War Between the States, its battles, the gallant bravery of the soldiers, the strong courage of the women, is all too well known to need repeating in this brief history. But in all the annals of time nothing finer has ever been recorded than the courage displayed in Pickett's charge across the field of Gettysburg, and the following extracts are taken from the written statements of three Pittsylvania soldiers who participated in the charge—Col. Rawley W. Martin[3] who commanded the 53rd Regiment, and James Carter[4] and Wyatt Whitehead,[5] member of Company I, of the 53rd Regiment:

"About one o'clock our artillery opened fire which was immediately answered by the enemy's guns. For about 1½ hours the Yankees shelled us with all the power they had, but the shells passed over us doing us but little damage. This is when Col. Aylett was wounded and Lieut.-Col. Rawley W. Martin was called to command the 53rd Regiment, Armistead's Brigade." (Whitehead.)

"Armistead called attention and instantly every man was on his feet. He walked to the front of the 53rd Regiment, his battalion of direction and addressed the Color-bearer, 'Sergeant, are you going to put those colors on the enemy's works over yonder?'

" 'Yes, General, if mortal man can do it.'

"He then exhorted the men to follow their colors and to remember the brave words of their color bearer." (Martin.)

"The Brigade moved promptly forward and arrived at the top of the hill which until now had protected us. As we advanced toward the valley the enemy's artillery re-opened fire upon us and it seemed to me the whole of Cemetery Ridge was a blaze of fire and the blaze continued

---

[3]Col. Rawley White Martin was the son of Dr. Chesley Martin of Chatham and his wife Rebecca White, who had issue: Rawley, Rebecca married Capt. William Tredway son of Judge William Tredway, Mattie, Mollie married Rev'd Mr. Penick. Mrs. Rebecca White Martin was the daughter of Dr. Rawley White of Peytonsburg.

Dr. Rawley White Martin married Miss Ellen Johnson, step-daughter of Col. Tarpley White, and had issue: Rawley, James, Chasley, Nellie, Douglas married Sterling Thornton and Rebecca married Dr. Robert Taliaferro.

Dr. Martin was born Sept. 20, 1835, and after the close of the War became one of the leading physicians in Virginia; he served on the State Board of Physicians and was one of those who were instrumental in establishing Catawba Sanatorium.

[4]James Carter, born April 9, 1842, died March 20, 1916, was the son of James Carter, Sr., and his wife Lucy Lanier. He married Bettie Pigg, daughter of Hezekiah Ford Pigg and had issue: Rutledge married Annie Pollock, Lanier married May Belle Moon, Maud married Nathanie E. Clement, and James Shirley married Katherine Coles.

[5]Wyatt Whitehead was taken a prisoner at Gettysburg and carried to Johnson Island. He was the son of Richard Whitehead, and grandson of Richard Whitehead, Sr., of Pittsylvania County. He was a prominent merchant of Chatham and first introduced oil lamps in this vicinity, having purchased them with his goods in Baltimore. He married Nannie Tredway, daughter of Judge William Tredway, and had issue: William, Wyatt married Lucy Lockett, Langhorne married Eula Shepherd, Park married Foot Wooding, Emma married John Jones, Howard married Miss Drewry, Edgar married Emma ———, and Lewis married Patsy Oliver.

until the Confederate forces had marched through this valley, which was four or five hundred yards wide, and gotten within charging distance of the stone wall.

"General Kemper's Brigade was in front and when we were about half through this valley Kemper rode up to Armistead who was in front and said to him, 'Armistead, I am going to charge those heights and carry them and I want you to support me.' Armistead replied, 'I'll do it! Look at my line. It never looked better on dress parade.'

"This took place under the heaviest artillery fire that in my opinion the world ever saw, and still under this fire Armistead's Brigade was marching at quick step, as if on parade. Just at this point Armistead took off his hat, put it on the point of his sword, and kept it there through the entire charge. He kept fifteen or twenty steps in front of his brigade all the way, was cheering all the time and calling his men to follow. After getting within 40 yards of the stone fence (not a gun had been fired by the Confederates up to this time) there came an order all along the line to charge, and we did charge, and just behind the stone wall rose up the Yankee infantry and poured into our ranks such a murderous fire as no human tongue can describe. Kemper's and Garnett's Brigades had almost entirely disappeared now, for forming the front line of attack they had received the brunt of the enemy's merciless fire and were lying wounded and dead upon the valley across which we had come. After a desperate fight the Yankee's gave way and as they fell back from the stone wall our men began to climb over." (Whitehead.)

"When the brigade reached the stone wall there were very few men left, and General Armistead turning to Lieutenant Colonel Rawley W. Martin said: 'Colonel, we can't stay here.'

"To which Colonel Martin replied: 'Then we'll go forward.'

"And over the wall the remaining few went, but there were only seven or eight men left now, General Armistead, Col. Martin, Lieutenant H. L. Carter,[6] Thomas Tredway,[7] James C. Coleman, and a few others. Lieutenant Carter grasped the regimental colors from the hands of Robert Tyler Jones, the wounded bearer, and ran forward among the enemy's artillery which had been abandoned. But reinforcements coming up, the enemy returned, retook the guns, there being no one to hold them,

[6]Hutchings Lanier Carter, born May 2, 1832, died Nov. 1892, was the son of James and Lucy Lanier Carter. He married Eliza Poindexter, daughter of Mr. James Poindexter and Matilda Calloway, of "Calloway's Level." Lieut. Carter and his wife had issue: James T. Carter, married Kate Prescott, of North Carolina, Edgar Carter, Major Henry P. Carter, U. S. A. and Nellie Carter.

[7]Thomas Tredway was a son of Judge William Tredway. He died of his wounds received at Gettysburg.

and opened fire again on our line. General Armistead was fatally wounded while trying to turn one of the enemy's guns; Col. Martin was severely wounded; his friend Thomas Tredway, who ran to his assistance was shot and fell across his body. The others fell also and Lieutenant Carter finding himself alone in the enemy's lines, surrendered himself and the flag of the 53rd Regt., which had been carried to the farthest point in the enemy's lines that day" (James Carter, color corporal).

"As Armistead was carried from the field he met Hancock as he was hurrying to the front. They recognized each other and Hancock (a federal officer) dismounted and grasped his hand and told him how sorry he was to see him wounded. Armistead returned his kindly expressions, and told him the wound was mortal and that he had on his person some things that he wished to entrust to him to be returned when opportunity presented to his people in Virginia. Hancock accepted the commission and tried to persuade Armistead to look on the bright side, that he probably was not so seriously hurt as he feared, excused himself by saying he was compelled to hurry to the front, left Armistead promising to see him next day. In a short time he was wounded himself and they never met again.

"This was related to me as I lay on the ground back of the battle lines where hundreds of wounded were carried after the fight, by one of Hancock's Staff, who rode up just about dusk. When he found that I was of Armistead's Brigade he said, 'Armistead, Armistead, I have just left him, he is mortally wounded. I will have you taken care of'." (Martin.)

While lying in a Federal hospital Col. Martin wrote to his father, Dr. Chelsey Martin, of Chatham:

"General Hospital Gettysburg, Pa.,
September 10th, 1863.

"My Dear Father: Your letter of the 13th of August has just been received. Oh! how glad I was to hear from home, that you were all well and praying for my recovery. I am anxious for you all to know that I have so many good friends and they are so kind to me, and among those friends ladies who know how to take care of wounded Rebs.

"I send you a little slip I cut out of a paper. You can see from it how I talked, and though I was mild I was firm and determined to let the enemy know that although my life was despaired of by the surgeons I would be true to my God and my country.

Hon. Claude A. Swanson
Governor of Virginia, 1906-10; United States Senator, 1911-

"Your letter was sent me from Johnson's Island by Wyatt, who is there with H. L. Carter and several other of my officers. Wyatt and the other officers there express great gratification at my prospect for recovery and are very anxious to see me. I expect to be with them at Sandusky or Johnson's Island in a short time. I am not able to walk yet on account of the tenderness of the left leg where it was shot. Some of my wounded comrades are going off this morning. I guess I shall see them again soon.

"My love to all at home, and tell them to pray for me and for the success of the Confederate cause, which is so near to the hearts of us all. Oh, my country, my country!

"Send my letters under ground to Miss Mary A. Weimer, care of Col. J. C. McConnell, Baltimore.

"Your affectionate and devoted son, R. W. Martin."

Captain William H. Ramsey,[8] who commanded the Pigg River Greys (Co. E, 57th Regt.) on this fatal day, was promoted to colonel of the 57th Regiment for his gallant conduct in the charge.

Of the great military leaders of the Confederacy, none was more greatly beloved than "J. E. B." (James Ewell Brown) Stuart, who spent much of his boyhood in Pittsylvania with his grandmother, Mrs. Bethenia Pannill.[9] He was the son of Archibald Stuart of Patrick County and his wife Elizabeth Letcher Pannill, the daughter of David Pannill of "Chalk Level," Pittsylvania, and his wife Bethenia Letcher, only child of Col. William Letcher, of Patrick, who was murdered by Tories during the Revolutionary War. David Pannill died very early in life, leaving his wife with two infant children, William Letcher and Elizabeth Pannill. Upon the marriage of her two children, Mrs. Pannill built and settled "Whitethorn" about two miles from "Chalk Level," overlooking Whitethorn Creek, and it was here that young Stuart passed much of his youth

[8]Col. William H. Ramsey, born 1837, was the son of Henry Ramsey, of Pittsylvania. He married Rebecca Mahan, who was born near Callands in 1836 and died in 1908. They had issue: Dr. Oscar Lee Ramsey of Gretna, who married Miss Susie Fitzgerald, daughter of Edmond and Virginia Crews Fitzgerald; and William Edgar Ramsey, present treasurer of Pittsylvania County, who married Nannie Anderson, daughter of Mr. James Anderson of Tomahawk. The Ramsey family is of Scotch origin.

[9]Mrs. Bethenia Letcher Pannill, widow of David Pannill of "Chalk Level," is buried at Chalk Level by the side of her husband, and on her tomb is the following inscription: "In memory of Bethenia Pannill, whose maiden name was Letcher. She was born in Patrick County, Virginia, the 21st day of March, 1780, Died 25th day of February, 1845, a pious and exemplary member of the Methodist Episcopal Church." Her will was proven March 17, 1845, in which she named the children of her daughter Elizabeth Stuart as follows: Bethenia F. Chevalier, David Pannill Stewart, William Alex Stewart, Mary Tucker Stewart, John Dabney Stewart, Columbia Lafayette Stewart, Victoria Anguela Stewart and James Brown Stewart (General "J. E. B.).

She also named the following children of her son William L. Pannill and his wife, Maria Bruce Banks, daughter of William Banks: James Bruce Pannill, David Henry Pannill, Susannah Pannill, Francis Anne Pannill, William Banks Pannill, Samuel Hairston Pannill.

To Zion Methodist Church Mrs. Pannill left seven acres for a public burying ground and a school, and $500 to the Missionary Society; to her grandson, James Brown Stewart, also $500.00.

in the companionship of his grandmother. The old home is standing today, seven miles north of Chatham, though much altered and changed in the passage of the years.

Mrs. Bethenia Pannill was a woman of great strength of character and deep piety, and reared her family in an atmosphere of strict morality. The force of her teaching is shown in the beautiful incident related[10] of the closing hours of General Stuart's life.

Stuart had received his mortal wound at Yellow Tavern and had been removed to a hospital in Richmond, where life was fast ebbing, when an attending physician held a glass to his lips and said:

"Drink a little of this, General, I think it will help you."

Upon taking a mouthful Stuart found it to be brandy, and after holding the liquid in his mouth for a moment, spat it out, saying:

"I promised my mother I would never take a drink of liquor, and I can not do it now."

To Danville is accorded the melancholy distinction of being the last capital of the Confederacy. Upon the evacuation of Richmond, President Davis, his cabinet and their departments came to Danville where they remained from Monday, April the 5th to Monday, April the 12th, 1865, carrying on the business of the fast failing Confederacy. The beautiful and imposing home of Major William Sutherlin was proffered for the use of the president and his cabinet, while the old brick academy which had been built in 1801 for the education of the first youth of the town now became the seat of the executive departments. The sad tidings of the surrender of General Lee at Appomattox were brought to President Jefferson at the Sutherlin Mansion and the inevitable dissolution of the government followed.

Many troops from the far south were with General Lee at Appomattox and after the surrender passed through Pittsylvania and Chatham on their return march home. One of the matrons of Chatham, Mrs. Lucy Lanier Carter,[11] when she learned of the coming of these southern soldiers determined to offer them refreshment, although her pantry contained nothing but several bushels of black eyed peas and some corn meal. Large iron pots were placed out in the yard, fires built and all the peas cooked, while the meal was baked into small pones—a few faithful

[10] Related by Mr. Roswell Page.

[11] Mrs. Lucy Lanier Carter was the daughter of Captain James M. Lanier and his wife Mary Merriman Johns. She was born Sept. 18, 1817, married July 21, 1834, James Carter, and had issue: Mary Thomas married James P. Johnson; Hutchings Lanier married Eliza Poindexter; Samuel Ross married Sallie Lucke; James married Betty Pigg; Ellen married William B. Hurt; John Dale; Scott married Belle Ragsdale; Hugh Lawson; Ada Binny; Williamson married Carrie Dufur.

slaves assisting in the preparations. When the soldiers came they were invited into the dining room and each asked to take his tin cup full of peas and a pone of bread, then to pass on to the lawn where refreshing water was to be found at the well. Upon the offer of some of the soldiers to contribute a share of the meal in their knapsacks for the cheer of others to follow, a barrel was placed by the dining room door and the baking of the small pones continued actively day after day. These weary disheartened men passed in a stream for four or five days, a disorganized body of troops, unofficered and hundreds of miles from home, yet in all that time there was only one instance of disorderly conduct, and that was occasioned by a soldier insisting upon a second cup of peas. And like the miracle of the loaves and fishes, at the end of the five days there was more meal in the bin of this generous southern woman than when she began the task of feeding a famished army.

The months that followed were full of sadness and gloom, "for no people ever suffered greater losses by the termination of a war than the people of Virginia. At one blow their entire slave population was emancipated, their value entirely lost, and their accustomed labor instantly stopped—the circulating medium, State and Confederate was rendered worthless, no Federal money in circulation, houses, barns, fences, mills given to conflagration—lands impoverished and having no money value, and they themselves entirely powerless to purchase, and for the want of buyers equally powerless to sell" (Code of Va.).

The complete destitution of the people is illustrated by the following incident. Dr. Leigh,[12] a physician of a neighboring county, was one day called in to prescribe for a sick member of a detachment of Federal soldiers and was paid 50 cents in U. S. money for his service. Confederate money was of no value and this one-half dollar comprised the entire money possession of the good doctor, and its expenditure was a matter of grave concern. He and his wife sat far into the night talking the matter over, to determine the one thing most needed on the plantation or in the household. Food sufficient to maintain the family could be produced on the plantation and clothes could be managed. After mature deliberation a wooden wash tub won the decision.

The men of the south had set about the work of rebuilding their civilization and though the task was a heavy one faced it resolutely, when a second blow befell them more disastrous than the loss of their properties. By an act of the Federal government these men who had founded

[12]Dr. Leigh of Halifax, father of Judge William Leigh of Danville.

a nation, converted the wilderness into a civilized state, established governments and builded cities had their rights of citizenship taken from them and vested in their former slaves. And then a horde of unscrupulous men from the north poured down into the south to fill the offices which the slaves through unfitness could not hold, and who bled the south of the pittance that she had left. A man named Lehigh from Pennsylvania became sheriff of Pittsylvania County, who defaulted costing the county $30,000.00. A carpet bagger from Maine named Tucker was commonwealth's attorney and was very active inciting a spirit of resentment among the negroes toward the white people. These northern visitors had no kindly feeling for the colored people and never as slaves had they suffered anything like the cruelty meted out to them by Lehigh, the sheriff. For such minor offences as pig and sheep stealing he would have the culprit hung[13] up by the thumbs for two hours, with suffering almost beyond endurance.

In March 1867 Congress passed an act that before the seceding states would be allowed representation in Congress they must form a new constitution, drawn up by delegates duly elected and not disenfranchised by participation in the late rebellion. On December 8th, there assembled in Richmond a most remarkable body of men for the purpose of forming the new constitution for Virginia. It was composed largely of "carpet baggers" and negroes and has always been known as the Black and Tan Convention. Pittsylvania was represented by a "carpet bagger" named Thayer and Herbert A. Wicker, a native of the county. There were two clauses in the constitution framed by this convention, which, if allowed to remain, would produce a situation in Virginia intolerable to the Anglo-Saxon blood of her people:

"First—No one who has engaged in insurrection or rebellion against the United States or given aid or comfort to the enemies thereof can hold any office, civil or military, under the United States or any State.

"Second—The following oath must be taken by all City, County and State officers before entering upon their duties: I do solemnly swear that I have never voluntarily borne arms against the United States, that I have given no aid, counsel, countenance or encouragement to persons engaged in armed hostility thereto, and etc."

This meant that the unscrupulous carpet baggers and the former slaves would become the judges, clerks, magistrates and sheriffs of Virginia. A delegation of the leading men of the state went to Wash-

[13]Witnessed at Chatham by Mr. Hunt Hargrave when a small boy. The sight of such suffering would send him home on flying feet in great agony of mind.

ington and interviewed President Grant, telling him that such a thing could not be. He give his permission for the constitution to be voted upon with and without the clauses. Then followed days of intense strain when there was no thought and talk of aught but the coming election and the constitution—the white people struggling for the existence of their race.

The negroes under the leadership of the carpet baggers held nightly meetings, with much oratory. One old darkey was heard arguing in favor of the much talked of clauses along the following lines: "Cose I'se gwin ter vote for de claus. How de constitution gwin to hol' wid out claus? How kin 'er cat clamb er tree wid out claws?"

Such logic seemed irrefutable to his hearers.

On court days great crowds gathered at the Court House, as many as four and five thousand people, with every man armed. On one occasion when there were at least five thousand people assembled Judge Gilmer got up on a box out in front[14] of the courthouse to address the crowd, and was denouncing Tucker for his ugly work among the negroes when he was interrupted and called up into the court room to attend to some business.

Tucker tried to resent Judge Gilmer's accusations but a very large man who was standing near named Zery McDaniel ascended the box Judge Gilmer had just vacated and expressed himself against Tucker in the strongest terms. He said: "I have lived in many parts of the earth, under fifty-two different governments, and I have beheld every kind and variety of criminal; I have looked into the face of murder, arson and every crime known in the catalogue of sin, but," and pointing his finger at Tucker, who was standing near, "that man standing there embraces in his features every characteristic of every crime known to man! None have I ever seen depicts so low a type of criminal as that cowardly scoundrel!"

But Tucker did not stir.

On another court day when the town was full of men, armed as before, one of the negroes had some trouble with a white man and the blacks grew very ugly and sullen and gathered in a mass at the lower end of Main Street. The white men gathered at the upper end of the street and the divergent crowds began approaching one another. The white

[14]Related by the Rev'd Chiswell Dabney, who at that time, as a young lawyer, had just settled in Chatham to practice his profession. He served as an aid on General Stewart's Staff during the war. He was the son of Mr. John Blair Dabney of Campbell County, and married Lucy Fontaine, by whom he had issue: John, Chiswell, Louise, Lucy, Edmond and Bessie Dabney. In his mature years he entered the ministry of the Episcopal Church and spent the remainder of his life serving the people of the County, who hold his memory in great respect and love.

men were led by a man named Whit Bradshaw who carried a long pistol, and as he came opposite the courthouse he waved the pistol around his head, crying, "Clear the way," and brought his gun down to aim on the approaching negroes. The latter began running in every direction through alleys, behind stores, anywhere to get out of reach of those guns. But not a gun had been fired. The white people had no desire to hurt their former slaves. When they saw danger threatening they met it coolly and thus averted it.

One day when there was no gathering of men at the courthouse—just the few town people who were residents being present—a large number of negroes were seen coming down the street. Three white men[15] were sitting on the porch of Carter's Hotel, and when the negroes halted out in front of the hotel the white men arose, went to the edge of the porch and stood calmly waiting to see what the negroes intended doing. The crowd seemed to hesitate and after talking among themselves and repeatedly looking at the white men they dispersed. The next day one of the gentlemen who had been on the porch, meeting with one of the negroes, asked him what they were about the day before. The man replied that they had held a meeting and determined to come down town and demand some of their rights from the white folks, but when they saw him and those other two gentlemen standing there on the porch, just looking at them, they got afraid somebody might get hurt and they decided they had better go home.

When the memorable 6th of July, 1869, finally came and the vote was cast the constitution was ratified without the two objectionable clauses. The vote was 84,000 for the clauses but 124,000 against them. The white men had voted that everybody should be allowed to vote, while the negro and "carpet-bagger" had voted that nobody but themselves should vote. The Congress of the United States accepted the constitution thus ratified by Virginia and January 20th, 1870, the Old Dominion was again admitted to the Union.

So passed this agonizing period of Virginia's history, and it is with pain that we recall the harsh and brutal incidents of the Reconstruction Period. But never should be forgotten the memory of the men who with calm patience and strong courage, met and solved the difficult problems of those dark days. Out of the chaos and wreckage of their pre-war civilization they brought order, and laid the foundations on which we have built our prosperous commonwealth of today.

---

[15]James Carter, Sr., Dr. Chesley Martin, Judge Gilmer.

Chapter XIX

WORLD WAR

Pittsylvania, the largest of Virginia's one hundred counties, would be reckoned today a modern and progressive agricultural section, with excellent railway, highway and educational facilities. So have the people of Virginia, in the sixty years following the overthrow of their civilization, risen from the defeat of 1865, and through their own unaided efforts, builded anew this old commonwealth.

Pittsylvania is primarily an agricultural section, the three principal crops being tobacco, corn and wheat. Excellent marketing advantages are afforded through the main line of the Southern Railway which passes north and south through the center of the county, and the minor branches —the Richmond and Danville and the Danville and Western roads. There is a network of 1,500 miles of public roads throughout the county, 300 of which are improved. State Highway No. 14 connects Danville, Chatham and Gretna with Lynchburg, and Highway No. 12 connects Danville with Richmond and Martinsville. The county itself has built over 200 miles of improved roads, leading out to the surrounding counties of Campbell, Halifax, Henry and Franklin. The state's system of public schools is well maintained with eleven high schools, among which is the well known Rural Life School of Whitmell. There are also two splendid church preparatory schools at Chatham—Chatham Hall, a school for girls, established by Dr. C. O. Pruden and the Rev'd Chiswell Dabney in 1894; and the Hargrave Military Academy, a school for boys under the auspices of the Baptist Church.

When we look back to the Virginia of 1865 and survey the Virginia of today, we know that a people of indomitable will, courage and vision has labored and striven through the years.

The men of '65, after the close of the war, attempted to adjust their lives to the changed conditions, and to carry on the old life of the plantations through the hire of their former slaves; they did not forsake their standards of life and reared their families in an atmosphere of "high thinking and plain living." But the transition was too great for their efforts to be clothed with financial success, and the sons of those fathers forsook the parental homes to seek their fortunes in the world. In this way the old plantations of hundreds of acres have come upon the market, been divided up and sold, until today few indeed in Pittsylvania are left in the possession of their original owners. The cities drew these young men, and though their pockets were penniless their aims were high—they were filled with a determination to make their way in life and at the same time to maintain the good names given them by their fathers. Their pluck and energy have made of Virginia's cities the industrial centers that they are today.

Danville being situated in a large tobacco growing section, the tobacco trade there was seized upon, developed and a great market established. The warehouses where the loose leaf is sold at auction are enormous structures, some covering near an acre of ground. A large export trade with European countries has been established. Danville has become the largest market for bright loose leaf tobacco in the Old Belt Section and one of the largest in the world. During the season of 1926-27 there was sold 50,592,300 pounds for a total of $12,455,642.18, an average of $24.62 per hundred pounds. Many of the largest plants in the South for rehandling and re-drying tobacco are located here. The storage warehouses have a capacity of 100,000 hhds. The excellent water power of Wynn's Falls was harnessed and utilized for many different kinds of factories, such as the Riverside Cotton Factories, the Dan Valley Flouring Mills, Knitting Mills and the very numerous tobacco factories, where the leaf is converted into the cigarette, the cigar and the chewing plug.

Six outstanding figures in the tobacco world of finance all of whom were Pittsylvania boys are William T. Clarke,[1] president and founder of the Clarke Export Company; Lloyd Belt,[2] president of the P. Lorillard Tobacco Company; W. Harley Jefferson, vice-president of P. Lorillard; the late John E. Hughes,[3] president and founder of the Hughes Tobacco Company, who by the terms of his will established the Hughes Orphanage at Design, Pittsylvania County, for the benefit of the unfortunate children of Virginia and North Carolina; and Garnett Cousins[4] and Flournoy

[1]William T. Clark is the son of the late Mr. William Clark of Pittsylvania and his wife Betty Johnson, step-daughter of Col. Tarpley White, who had issue: William T., John, James, Ellen, Lizzie, Janie and Garland Clark; grandson of John Augustine Clark, of "Pineville," and his wife Elizabeth Fowlkes, who had issue, William, Letitia, married Robert Tredway, Bettie married John Hughes. William T. Clark married Mary Howell of Tarboro, N. C., and has one child, Romaine Clark.

[2]Lloyd Belt is the son of the late Dr. Singleton Humphrey Belt, of Whitmell, and his wife Mollie Daniel, who had issue: Dr. Singleton Humphrey, Jr., Lloyd and Mary Belt. He began his business career in Danville, but now resides in New York City.

[3]Col. John E. Hughes was the son of Mr. John Hughes and his wife, Bettie Clark, daughter of John A. Clark of "Pineville." He entered the tobacco business at an early age and by his industry and wise judgment amassed a large fortune. Besides founding an orphanage, Col. Hughes left a large bequest to the Danville Hospital.

[4]Garnett Cousins is the son of the late Mr. William Cousins of Callands and his wife Fannie Turner, who had issue: Benjamin, Ella married Henry Swanson, James, William, Dora, Henry, Garnett, John, Walter, Fannie married Thomas Morrison, Archer, and Bessie.

Cobbs,[5] directors of the British Cigarette Company of Shanghai, China and London.

The world of political affairs as well as business drew the attention of Pittsylvanians and here too, they have won signal honors. George Craghead Cabell, a son of Gen. Benjamin Cabell of Bridgewater, represented the 5th District in Congress from 1875 to 1887. Today the Senior U. S. Senator from Virginia is a son of Pittsylvania, the Honorable Claude A. Swanson.[6] Mr. Swanson, born March 31, 1862, is the son of Mr. John Swanson and his wife Catherine Rebecca Pritchett, of Swansonville. He graduated from Randolph-Macon College in 1885, and received his degree in law from the University of Virginia in 1886. He began the practice of law at Chatham and from earliest manhood has had a distinguished public career, serving the lower House of Congress as representative of the 5th District from 1893 to 1906; as Governor of Virginia from 1906 to 1910; and as United States Senator from 1911 to date. During his term of governorship Mr. Swanson was a strong advocate of better schools and good roads, and may be said to have inaugurated Virginia's present progressive policy along these lines.

Pittsylvania again represented the 5th District in Congress when the Hon. Rorer A. James[7] of Danville served from 1920 to his death 1921;

[5]Flournoy Cobbs is the son of the late Hon. William W. Cobbs of Pittsylvania, and his wife Louise Cabell Flournoy, daughter of Col. Thomas S. Flournoy, of the 6th Virginia Cavalry, C. S. A., who had issue: Mary Love, Mildred Anne, Louise married John Inge Pritchett, Cabell, Nannie, Bueno, Allie, Katie, Elizabeth married Claude Pritchett, Flournoy, Walter and John Cobbs. Mr. W. W. Cobbs was consul to Panama under McKinley's administration. Col. Thomas S. Flournoy (Halifax County) represented the 5th District in Congress from 1846 to 1851.

[6]William Swanson, founder of the Pittsylvania family, was living in Albemarle County in 1750, and it is presumed that he like so many others moved down into Virginia from Pennsylvania. The name indicates Swedish origin. In 1768 he was living in Western Pittsylvania County, having purchased 500 acres which later became a part first of Henry, then of Franklin Counties. When the oath of allegiance was being administered in all Virginia Counties, in 1777, William Swanson, Sr., was listed in Henry County, and his age was given as 57 years. The will of William Swanson, Sr., was proven in Pittsylvania in 1827, naming sons William and Francis; he was probably the son of William Swanson, of Bull Run (Franklin Co.), for his age would be too great to be one and the same person. William Swanson, the third, lived on Pigg River in Pittsylvania and took an active part in the life of the County. He represented Pittsylvania in the House of Delegates for a number of years, serving the sessions of 1813-14; 1818 to 1823; and still again from 1831-36. He was actively interested with Mr. Tunstall in establishing the railway from Richmond to Danville, and was one of the representatives from the County to the Railroad Convention held in Richmond in 1836. John Swanson, son of William Swanson of Pigg River, was born in 1799, and established his home, "Swansonville," on the Danville and Franklin Turnpike, about seventeen miles north of Danville. Here his son, John Muse Swanson, born 1829, lived and reared his family of four sons and three daughters: John M. Swanson married Catherin Rebecca Pritchett, daughter of Major John Pritchett of Brunswick County and had issue: William G. Swanson, of Swansonville; John Pritchett Swanson, of Danville; Claudius Augustus Swanson, U. S. Senator; Henry C. Swanson, of Danville; Blanche Swanson; Julia Swanson; Sallie Hill Swanson.

[7]Rorer A. James, born March 1, 1859, was the son of Dr. John Craighead James and his wife Angeline Rorer; grandson of John James and Katherine Craighead. On his maternal side Rorer James is the grandson of Captain Abram Rorer and his wife Mary Wright, daughter of Thomas Wright. The emigrant Rorer or "Rohrer," was a native of Switzerland and settled near Philadelphia; one of his sons Abram Rorer moved to Virginia in a colony led by Harmon Cook. Young Rorer married a daughter of Harmon Cook's and had four sons, Abram, Jr., Rudolph, Charles and David. Abram, Jr.'s daughter, Angeline, became the mother of Rorer A. James.

Young James was a graduate of V. M. I. and took a law degree at the University of Virginia. He represented the county both in the House of Delegates and the State Senate. He was owner and editor of the *Danville Register* and wielded a wide influence through the medium of his paper. He married Annie Marshall Wilson, daughter of Col. Robert A. Wilson of "Dan's Hill" and his wife Ruth Hairston, by whom he had issue: Wilson, Rorer, Bruce and Annie James.

Joseph Whitehead[8] of Chatham is the present representative, serving from 1925 to date. This county has the distinction of being the birthplace of the first woman to sit in Great Britain's House of Parliament. In Danville was born Nancy, the third daughter of Col. Chiswell Dabney Langhorne, and his wife Nancy Keen (daughter of Col. Elisha Keene[9]), who married Viscount John Jacob Astor, of "Cliveden," England. Lady Astor, in her charm of manner and gracious womanhood typifies all that is best in Virginia culture and has won for herself an enviable place in the home of her adoption. A return visit to the place of her nativity made by Lady Astor in May, 1920, was the occasion of a great demonstration of pride and affection for this gifted daughter on the part of her countrymen.

The Honorable Beverley B. Munford, one of Virginia's most distinguished and best beloved sons, spent much of his early manhood in Pittsylvania. Upon leaving college young Munford made his home at Chatham, where he studied law in the office of his brother-in-law, Judge J. Dodderedge Coles, Judge of the County Court. He later practiced his profession here for many years with marked success, and represented the county in Legislature until his removal to Richmond.

---

[8]Joseph Whitehead is the son of the late Richard Whitehead, treasurer of Pittsylvania County, and his wife Sally Graves, who had issue: Jere, married Annie Norman; Joseph, married Ruth Tredway; John Hurt, married Elizabeth Jones: Nannie; Clencie, married Mr. Millner; Katie, married Fletcher B. Watson, Jr.; Douglas, married Minnie Gatewood; Walter married Miss Leslie; Ethel married Paul Crider.

Joseph Whitehead is the grandson of Andrew Jackson Whitehead, who represented the county in the House of Delegates 1853-54; and great grandson of Richard Whitehead, whose will was proven at Pittsylvania Court House in 1843, naming wife Pincey (daughter of William Camden), sons—Andrew J., Marble, Richard and James Whitehead; daughters—Malinda, wife of William H. Markham; Rhoda Scruggs, Nancy Tankerslay, Jane Tucker, Polly Glenn, Pincey Palmer and Lucy Whitehead. Richard Whitehead, Sr., was the son of John Whitehead of Amherst County and his wife Sally Burcher.

[9]Colonel Elisha Ford Keen was the son of Captain John Keen, a native of Franklin County, who married in 1807 (Pittsylvania marriage bonds) Nancy Witcher, daughter of William Witcher and his wife Molly Dalton of Pittsylvania. Captain John Keen commanded a company of Pittsylvania militia in the war of 1812 and showed an active interest in the political issues of his day. His obituary which appeared in the *Danville Register,* Dec. 1878, reads:

"Death of Capt. John Keen

A noble landmark has been removed by the stern and rentless hand of death. Information was received here yesterday that the well known and highly respected citizen of this county had departed this life. Captain Keen was nearly ninety years of age, and at one time was a prominent and influential politician enjoying a reputation throughout the state. We regret our inability at this time to sketch even an outline of this remarkable man. For many years he was the leader of the Whig party in this county, and was honored by his party with a seat in the State Legislature which position he filled with distinguished ability reflecting credit on his constituents, and establishing for himself a character for efficient integrity rarely equaled. He was a contemporary of the venerable Vencent Witcher, the old style horse of the Whig party, who yet survives. No man ever lived who excelled the deceased as a man of infallible honesty. True to every interest he represented boldly and without fear or favor devoted his energy to the accomplishment of his purpose. His habits were good and remained so to his death. Capt. Keen married Miss Nancy Witcher a daughter of Vencent Witcher of this county, and reared a large family of whom Col. Elisha Ford Keen perhaps was the most distinguished having represented Pittsylvania in both houses of the State Legislature."

Captain John Keen, and his wife had issue: Elisha Ford, William Witcher and Charles Keen; daughters, Kitty, Polly, Emily, Harriet and Frances who married Stokely Carter of "Stoney Mill."

William Witcher Kenn married Elizabeth Ballard Fontaine, and made his home in Danville.

Col. Elisha Keen represented the county in the Senate of Virginia from 1863-67. He married Mary Anne Perkins and left two daughters—Nancy, the wife of Chiswell Dabney Langhorn and mother of Lady Nancy Astor; and Elizabeth Frances, wife of William Henry Jones of "Bachelors Hall," Va.

Lady Nancy Astor

The Honorable Andrew J. Montague was an adopted son of Pittsylvania, making his home at Stokesland, near Danville, when selected by the people of the State to fill positions of great honor and trust. He served as attorney general of Virginia from 1898 to 1902, and as Governor of the State from 1902 to 1906.

Other sons of Pittsylvania have ventured into the field of science where their efforts have been rewarded with success. Dr. Russell Coles,[10] son of Capt. Walter Coles the second, of "Coles' Hill," was an authority upon deep sea fishing, and received from Brown University the honorary degree of Doctor of Science, for his discoveries in this untried field of knowledge. Being a pioneer in deep sea fishing it was necessary for Dr. Coles to invent and have made the harpoons and other implements used in catching the monsters of the deep. Hon. Theodore Roosevelt accompanied him on one of his fishing expeditions when he hunted devil fish in the Gulf of Mexico, and a warm friendship developed between the two great hunters.

Dr. Thomas Watson,[11] son of the late Fletcher B. Watson, Sr., of Chatham, was a distinguished geologist and at the time of his death in 1925 had held the chair of geology at the University of Virginia for many years. He accompanied Peary upon one of his expeditions to the North Pole.

Mr. Henry H. Hurt,[12] son of the late William B. Hurt, of Chatham, is a chemist who has been of great value to his state. He was employed by the great paper mills of Covington to find some use for the mills' refuse which could no longer be thrown into the streams of the state. After months of experiments he evolved three by-products from the waste material, one of which is an excellent road binder, being used in such far away countries as Japan.

In the realm of medical science Dr. Austin I. Dodson, son of Mr. Beverly Dodson of Ringgold, is a recognized authority on urology. The report of the *World's* finding in urology for the year 1926, devoted one entire page of this condensed report to Dr. Dodson's work.

---

[10]Dr. Russell Coles was born at "Coles' Hill" in 1865, received his education at V. M. I., and entered the tobacco business in Danville in early manhood, in which he has been very successful. His study of science has been pursued during his vacation from business affairs.

[11]Dr. Thomas Watson was the son of Fletcher B. Watson, Supt. of Public Schools of Pittsylvania County, and his wife Pattie Tredway, daughter of Judge William Tredway, who had issue: Thomas, Marshall, Fletcher B., Jr., Lizzie, Nannie, and Dr. Wilbur Watson of V. P. I. Dr. Watson married Adelaide Stephenson of Atlanta, Ga., and had issue: Adelaide, Thomas, Pattie, Robert, John and Duffle Watson.

[12]Henry Hicks Hurt is the son of William B. Hurt of Chatham and his wife, Ellen Hicks Carter, daughter of James and Lucy Lanier Carter. He received his education at V. P. I., married Emily Adair of Richmond and had issue: Wm., Henry, Joan, and Emily.

Major Henry P. Carter, U. S. Army, son of the late Hutchings L. Carter, of Chatham, has won distinction by his work in sanitation in the United States Army. He freed the City of Ancon, in the Panama Zone, from the menace of mosquitos and fever.

And so the people of Pittsylvania were busily pursuing the even tenor of their lives in 1914, developing the resources of the county, sowing and reaping their crops, and feeling perfect security in the protection of their government against the might and power of any nation. Suddenly the tocsin of war sounded through the world; but with the scene of conflict in far off Europe, no fears were entertained at first for our own security. Our thoughtful people followed the progress of the war in their reading, and when President Wilson declared on April the 6th, 1917, a state of war to exist between the United States and Germany, they heartily approved of his action.

The United States was faced with the problem of preparing at once for the mighty conflict and according to the will of the President, it was determined that the army which this country must put into the field should be raised through a selective draft. June the 5th, 1917, was the day set for the first registration of men from 21 to 31 years of age, and there were enrolled in the United States more than 9,000,000 men, 4,477 of whom were in Pittsylvania County. Then followed the filling out of the questionaries by the registered men, and so puzzling they seemed to many that the members of the legal profession of Chatham, Judge James L. Tredway, Nathaniel E. Clement, William Smith and others freely offered their services to the registrants and spent the greater part of their time for months in writing out these papers. There were also to be found in every community patriotic citizens who gave assistance to the young men.

To the Draft Board was committed the grave responsibility of determining who were fit soldiers; and according to their fitness the men were designated as being in classes A, B, and C, and given a number which was forwarded to Washington. The first draft took place July the 20th in Washington, when certain numbers were drawn and the men bearing those numbers throughout the country were called to the service. The draft was carried out with amazing success, never had so many men been called into military service with so little friction.

Pittsylvania's first draft, consisting of eleven men left Chatham on September the 5th, 1917, and were among the first soldiers to arrive at Camp Lee; they were Ernest T. Adams, Claude DeBoe, Carson Cox, Roy

DR. RUSSELL COLES AND HON. THEODORE ROOSEVELT
Receiving Honorary Degrees from Brown University

Chatham, Charlie Chumley, Eugen Fox, William Sours, Gray Sours, Curtis Simpson, Eddie Hines and Walter Owen. In the second draft[13] which followed on September 19th, eighty men were called; and other drafts followed in close succession. These men were trained at Camp Lee, becoming a part of the 80th Division, which sailed from Virginia ports in May, 1918, disembarking at Brest, France without mishap from enemy craft. After further training in various camps they participated in the American offensive under General Pershing in the autumn of 1918.

The Draft Board of Pittsylvania County, appointed in the summer of 1917, was as follows: Dr. James Semple Haile, chairman, Dr. Coleman D. Bennett, health officer, Walker Hurt, clerk. January 1st, Mr. Hurt resigned and was succeeded by Lee Paul who served as clerk to the end of the war. In July 1918 Dr. Haile, who was also postmaster at Chatham, finding the work of the draft board so heavy as to interfere with his duties as postmaster, resigned; he was succeeded by David Alexander Jefferson, as chairman. In September, 1918, Dr. Coleman Bennett[14] enlisted in the Navy and was stationed at the Naval Hospital, Hampton, Virginia. He was succeeded by Dr. Oscar Ramsey as examining officer, and by D. T. Williams on the board. The gentlemen who composed the Draft Board conducted the work upon the high plane of justice to all and favors to none, and the people of the county felt that their trust in them was not misplaced.

In the second draft of September 1918, of men from 18 to 21 and from 31 to 45 there were registered in Pittsylvania 5,488 men, making a total registration of 9,965. Of these 1,588 were classified in Class 1.A; 1,283 were called for service, and 1,165 accepted. Of the 1,165 men drafted for the county 746 were white, 419 were colored.

---

[13]Second Draft—Alley, Henry Warner; Amos, William Avery; Bennett, Ernest Arthur; Billings, Dorsey Robertson; Brown, John; Brown, Henry Thomas; Brown, Henry Boyd; Baker, Homer; Bennett, James Gordon; Blair, Wade Henry; Bradley, Clarence Conway; Barber, John Willie; Bernard, Benjamine Joseph; Brown, Wylie Carson; Barker, James Irvine; Boswell, Giles David; Campbell, William Edgar; Carter, Rufus, Jr.; Chattin, John Barksdale; Curry, Arthur Thomas; Cratts, Thomas Willard; Cook, Archer; Checker, William; Collins, Lee Roy; Carnell, Martin C.; Davis, Charles Henry; Dalton, Raymond; Dawson, Luther L.; Dodson, Luther B.; Dewey, William T.; Dishroom, Roy B.; Davis, James M.; Davis, James; Earles, Green H.; Farmer, Boaze; Griffin, John Daniel; Haynes, Edgar L.; Hilliard, William H.; Haley, Ollie L.; Hushey, Henry; Hylton, James Abner; Lumpkin, Robert J.; Motley, Adrian Jackson; Meadows, Robert; Neal, Ernest Loyd; Nelson, Louis; Oslin, Preston Northington; Oakes, Frank Harmon; Parker, Charles James; Poindexter, Eslie Douglas; Pugh, James Leslie; Pickerel, Lester; Powell, Posey Dameron; Ragsdale, Hugh Clifton; Rice, Darnell Floyd; Robertson, Roy; Robertson, Robert H.; Robertson, Grady; Snyder, James Boyd; Scruggs, L. A. George; Shepherd, Elmer Robert; Smith, Rufus Edmond; Slayton, Lewis Edward; Slayton, Charles Lester; Simpson, Walter Dennis; Senteel, Henry Graves; Shropshire, Luther; Scott, Charles Anderson; Smith, Charlie Keen; Taylor, Anderson; Tuck, Albert L.; Terry, Henry Thomas; Tuck, Henry Anderson; Venron, George W.; Wells, Bennie H.; White, George W.; Watson, Russell Carrington; Yeatts, Willie David; Yeatts, James William.

[14]Dr. Coleman Douglas Bennett, born 1873, is the son of the late Jonathan Bennett and his wife Mildred Bailey of Toshes, Pittsylvania and grandson of Reuben Bennett, a brother of Col. Coleman D. Bennett. The Bennett family were very early settlers of the western part of the county and were no doubt of the Scotch-Irish migration from Pennsylvania. Dr. Bennett married Miss Sally Hogan of the County and has an only son, Hubert Bennett.

There were some incidents connected with the draft which we like to treasure, and one is the story of a great affection between two brothers. Their name is Short, and they are fine upstanding young men. One of the brothers was called in the draft and the other was not, and thereby comes the story. On the day appointed for the drafted one to appear in Chatham, he came accompanied by his father and brother. The father appealed to the Board, saying:

"My boys are twin brothers and have never been separated a day in their lives; they work together and play together. Now you are going to send one overseas to war and leave the other at home, and they can not bear the separation—you will have to let his brother go, too—"

The boys were eager, assuring Dr. Haile that if he would just let both go, they would get those Germans. Both were sent, bore an honorable part in the battles of the American Army, and returned home safe from overseas.

Another incident of the draft touches the heart in its pathos. This boy whose very name has been forgotten, lived in the Brushy Mountain district with his aged mother. Their little farm was situated in a thinly settled section of the county, having no near neighbors. He was his mother's sole support; but through some error he was called for the service. He appeared before the Board on the day appointed, bringing his mother with him, and explained her dependant condition. The Board, realizing that a mistake had been made, told the boy to go back home, assuring him that he would not be called for the present.

And then in a few weeks there swept over Pittsylvania that terrible plague of influenza, taking its toll of young and old alike, and the boy's mother was one of the first victims. After her death he put his affairs in order as speedily as possible, and then again appeared before the Board, saying simply, "I'm ready to go."

The drafted men assembled at Chatham to take the train to Camp Lee. The citizens of the town and county, sensible of the fact that these young men were going forth to battle for them, bade them affectionate farewells. On one occasion "an enthusiastic meeting was held at the Town Hall Tuesday night for the purpose of giving a suitable send off to the boys (about ninety in number) who were to leave for camp the next day. These young men, who were from all parts of the County, were the guests of the people of Chatham until they departed for Petersburg Wednesday morning. The boys were escorted into the Town Hall by the Home Guard, and on the platform were two members of the Draft Board,

Doctors Haile and Bennett. The speakers for the evening were the Rev's C. O. Pruden, A. L. Kenyon, F. W. Kerfoot, R. G. McLees, and Mr. J. H. Whitehead, each being introduced by Dr. Haile in his inimitable manner.

"We know of no time when the community has been treated to such a display of local talent, and the interest both on the part of the young men and of the audience was intense throughout the meeting. Dr. Pruden presented soldiers' kits to the young men on behalf of the Red Cross—Chatham wishes them God speed, and a safe return." (*Chatham Tribute Enterprise.*)

Besides the 1,165 drafted men in the National Army there was a notable number of volunteers from the county. Many joined volunteer companies in Danville and adjacent cities; others went into the marines, the hospital service and aviation. A number of young men from Chatham joined Battery E, first Virginia Coast Artillery, which was mustered at Danville July 25, 1917; they were Richard Whitehead, Sam White, William Rison, Henry Oliver, Judson Morris, John Law, Edgar Jones, Henry G. Bennett, Randolph Overbey and William White.

Some of the young men who volunteered from the county won high recognition for their valiant service. Hunter Pannill,[15] son of the late David and Mrs. Augusta Hunter Pannill, who was reared at "Whitethorn," home of his great grandmother (Mrs. Bethenia Pannill), went overseas in 1916 with the Canadian forces. At the battle of Vimy Ridge, April 8, 1917, when his superior officers had all been disabled he took command and led the force forward to victory. For the bravery and valor displayed upon this occasion by young Pannill he was decorated with the Victorian Cross at Buckingham Palace by King George of England, and was promoted to the rank of captain.

Lieutenant Pannill was slightly wounded at Vimy Ridge; upon his return to England he was hailed as a hero and warmly received by the English people. Upon his return from "Cliveden," where he had been the guest of Lord and Lady Astor, he wrote the following letter to his mother in Chatham:

[15]Captain Augustus Hunter Pannill, born February 21, 1882, is the son of the late David and Mrs. Augusta Hunter Pannill who had issue: Maria, married James D. Jones; Harry, married Grayson Lavendar; Augustus Hunter, married Hazel Campbell of Canada; William; Samuel, married Miss Hudspeth.

Captain Pannill is now engaged in lumber business in Ontario, Canada.

"The Royal Overseas Officers Club,
Pall Mall,
London,
June 5, 1917.

"My dear Ma:

Your letter of May 7th was received a day or two ago. I was in camp for a couple of weeks but am in London now. I am all well of my wound (received at Vimy Ridge). * * * I have been meeting a lot of very interesting people. I have a snap shot which was taken at the Astors of a group containing the Duke of Connaught, Princess Patricia, several other prominent people and myself. I have met a number of nice people here in London.

"There are a lot of doctors here from the U. S. Army. I don't know what they expect them to do as I know of hundreds and hundreds of Canadian doctors who have been here for six to twelve months with nothing to do. There are also a great many American nurses here. My love to the family,

Your affectionate son,
Hunter."

Richard Willis,[16] son of the late Dr. Richard and Mrs. L. May Willis of the Chatham Episcopal Institute, was another who volunteered his services to the allies before America's entrance into the war. Being a medical student he joined the ambulance corps and was assigned for duty with the French. He was cited and decorated with the Croix-de-guerre by General Petain for his gallant action in rescuing the wounded from battlefields under heavy bombardment.

Langhorne Barbour, son of Mr. Ennis Barbour, was signally honored in being selected by General Pershing for one of "Pershing's Fifty," who were sent back to the States from France to tour America in the interest of the war. Young Barbour was brought to General Pershing's notice through having rescued his commanding officer from a trench which was being raided and bombed by the enemy.

Paul Sanford,[17] of the aviation, witnessed from his plane the surrender of the German Feet at Scappa Flo. He stayed aloft an hour and a half watching the scene, which he described as wonderful, "between the

[16]Richard Willis is the son of the late Dr. Richard Willis of Orange, Virginia, who died suddenly while in charge of the Chatham Episcopal Institute, and his wife Mrs. L. May Willis, who was for many years principal of the Institute. At the close of the war young Willis completed his course in medicine at the University of Virginia and is now practicing his profession in New York City.

[17]Paul Sanford is the son of Rev. Ryland Sanford and his wife Miss Nevitt, and brother of Dr. T. Ryland Sanford of the Baptist Church. He married Miss Nathalie Moses of Lexington, Virginia, and resides at Stuart, Patrick County, where he practices his profession of law.

double lines of English, French and American warships steamed first of all the most powerful dreadnaughts of the German Navy, followed by the torpedo boats and destroyers."

The county paper recorded such items of the volunteers as: "Mr. and Mrs. J. C. Anderson have received a cable announcing the safe arrival of their daughter Rebecca 'over there.' She is a member of the University Unit No. 41."

"Mr. Lee Inman received a telegram announcing the death of his son Samuel, a volunteer member of the United States Marines serving in France."

Several of Pittsylvania's sons served with honor in the regular military and naval service of the United States. Colonel Edward Anderson,[18] Colonel Harry C. Clement, Jr.,[19] and Major William Parish Currier in the United States Army; Captain William Wirt Gilmer,[20] Commander Jules James,[21] and Lieutenant Commander Samuel A. Clement, of the United States Navy; Lieutenant Clifton Hunt[22] in the United States Engineers. Major Henry Poindexter Carter, who had already distinguished himself in his work of sanitation in the United States Army, won recognition from the government for his able work along this line. He planned and executed the sanitation of Camp Lee. After completing this work he was called wherever disease broke out in Camp, to ferret out and correct the trouble. Upon the signing of the Armistice he was ordered to Germany and stationed for two years with the Army of Occupation.

[18]Col. Edward Anderson is the son of Mr. Otey Anderson and his wife Nancy Smith, of "Tomahawk," who had issue: James Anderson; Rev'd George Anderson; Dr. John Anderson of "Mineola"; Charles Anderson of "Tomahawk"; Louise Anderson, married Edgar Crider; Fanny Anderson, married Mr. Charles Shepherd; Edward Anderson, Col. in U. S. Army. Col. Anderson is a graduate of West Point; he married Miss Amelie Duncan and has two children, Fanny and Edward.

[19]Col. Harry C. Clement, Jr., was the son of the late Henry C. Clement, Sr., and his wife Harriet Morrison, who had issue: Harry C. Clement, Jr., married Jane Rose, of Indiana; Caroline Clement; Bushrod Morrison Clement, married Margaret Lee of S. Carolina; Mary Royall Clement; Nathaniel Elliot Clement, married Maude Carter; James Turner Clement, Judge of the Seventh Judicial District; Stephen Preston Clement, tobacconist of China, married Margaret Clary; Samuel A. Clement, U. S. Navy, married Agnes Taliaferro.

Henry C. Clement, Sr., received his education at Emory and Henry College, served in Flournoy's Cavalry, 6th Regt., during the Confederate War; and represented his county in the Legislature the session of 1899-1900. He was the son of Dr. George W. Clement of "Turkey Cock," and great grandson of Captain Benjamin Clement of "Clement Hill."

Col. Harry Clement served through the Spanish-American war, taking part in both the Cuban and Philippine Campaigns; in the latter he was cited and decorated for bravery under fire. He died in 1924 and is buried at Arlington Cemetery.

[20]Captain William Wirt Gilmer is the son of the late Mr. John Gilmer, and his wife Eliza Patton, of Chatham.

[21]Lieut. Com. Jules James is a son of Mr. John James of Danville, and nephew of the Hon. Rorer A. James.

[22]Lieut. Clifton Hunt is a son of the late John Pride Hunt and his wife Mollie Tredway, who had issue: John P., Jr., Edna, Rosalie, Russell, Clifton, Raymond Hunt. Lieut. Hunt is a great-great-grandson of Captain David Hunt of "Glenland," who served with the Pittsylvania troops in the Revolutionary War.

The great organization that is built up when a nation goes to war is wonderful to contemplate; in it there is a place for each man, woman and child in the country, who by "doing his bit," can materially help in winning the war. The 110,000,000 citizens of the U. S. rallied to their country's call to arms, and what they accomplished through their united efforts in camp, in field, at home and abroad, reads like a miracle of old.

Pittsylvania was far removed from all the great centers of war activity such as camps and embarkation points, yet when we view the efforts of her people as a whole no one will deny that she faithfully performed her duty.

Being an agricultural district, one way in which the county could lend material aid was in increased production of food, and to this end the citizens turned with a will. In the summer and autumn of 1917 the Council of Defense and a number of other gentlemen spoke throughout the county urging the farmers to plant more and more food stuffs; week after week this question of winning the war by planting more corn and wheat, raising more hogs and cattle was discussed among the people of the county. To maintain the farms at normal production was difficult at this time owing to the shortage of labor. In many cases the able bodied sons had been called to the colors, as were the sons of the white and colored tenants; in other cases labor, both white and colored, had sought the high wages of munition plants and the various camps being so hastily constructed. To increase the production of food in Pittsylvania entailed real hardship, yet it was done. In 1919 the 50,175 acres planted in corn yielded 858,306 bushels, the 31,440 acres planted in wheat yielded 289,841 bushels, while in 1909 there had been only 45,037 acres in corn and 26,583 in wheat.

Due credit should be given the school children of Pittsylvania for their share in food production and conservation. The boys through their corn clubs and pig and poultry clubs added materially to the county's food supply, while the girls through their canning clubs labored and conserved the food. Farm agents were employed who directed the work of the boys and girls, and the deep interest and enthusiasm evinced by the 20,000 school children of the county reflected the atmosphere of their homes.

The county was organized as a unit for war work through the churches, schools, red cross chapters, councils and committees, each and every one being called upon to contribute his share in winning the war. The county-seat was the center from which the "drives" were made, but in each vicinity were men and women whose high sense of patriotic duty and qualifications made them leaders in the war work of their communities. There was continuous speaking at churches, schools and stores in the interest of the Liberty Loans, War Savings Stamps, and Red Cross, food production and various other war activities.

The expense of the war was financed through the sale of bonds and war savings stamps and through increased taxation. Five loans were floated, the first four of which were called Liberty Loans. The fifth the Victory Loan, was made the occasion of a great demonstration of patriotism, and while the county was assigned $226,000.00, bonds amounting to $412,000.00 were sold. The sale of War Stamps was entirely satisfactory, many citizens purchasing as high as a thousand dollars worth. Mr. Thomas J. Coles, at that time treasurer of the county, served as chairman of the sale of stamps. He appointed a chairman for each of the seven Magisterial Districts as follows:

Staunton River District—N. E. Clement, Chairman.
Pigg River District—J. W. Marks, Chairman.
Dan River District—T. J. Coles, Chairman.
Tunstall District—Judge E. J. Harvey, Chairman.
Banister District—J. M. Jones, Chairman.
Callands District—Judson J. Patterson, Chairman.
Chatham District—G. E. Thompson, Chairman.

July the fourth, 1917, was made the occasion of a patriotic rally at Chatham, at which thousands of the citizens of the county were present. There was a parade of beautiful floats and hundreds of school children; and many speakers, chief of whom was Governor E. Lee Trinkle, who journeyed down from Richmond for the occasion. Through the efforts of our patriotic women a Red Cross Chapter was organized at Chatham in the summer of 1917, under whose jurisdiction was placed five of the seven Magisterial Districts of the county, the other two being given to the Danville Chapter. The work of establishing auxiliaries in the five districts was vigorously pushed with the result that 41 chapters were organized with a membership of 2,500. There were three auxiliaries among the colored people who did good and faithful work.

At Chatham a work room fitted with sewing machines was kept open all the time, and here materials were issued and the finished garments received from the branch chapters. When we contemplate the amount of sewing accomplished by the Chatham Chapter and the forty-one auxiliaries, of which some items were 681 bed shirts, 664 helpless shirts,

466 pajama suits, 750 pairs of knitted socks and 942 comfort kits, we realize the devoted service of Pittsylvania's women. Mrs. J. Lawson Carter and Mrs. Maria Carrington Watkins were awarded the Red Cross Medals by the National Association for their faithful work.

In the second Red Cross Drive for funds the Chatham Chapter and its auxiliaries gave $13,142.52, which was almost three times the amount of their allotment. The Red Cross Chapters of the county and their chairmen were as follows:

Gretna—Mrs. Robert Owen, Chairman.
Spring Garden—James S. Jones, Chairman.
Greenfield—Miss Hattie Peters, Chairman.
Hollywood—C. A. Thornton, Chairman.
Straightstone—Miss Isla Blair, Chairman.
Climax—Mrs. C. C. Shepherd, Chairman.
Edge Hill—G. M. Moses, Chairman.
Mill Creek—Mrs. L. R. Blair, Chairman.
Museville—Mrs. O. E. Hedrick, Chairman.
Dry Fork—Rev'd O. B. Newton, Chairman.
Piney Fork—J. C. Adams, Chairman.
Green Bay—J. C. Adams, Chairman.
Dame Memorial—J. H. Jones, Chairman.
Piney Grove—A. J. Farmer, Chairman.
Mount Pleasant—L. A. Bryant, Chairman.
Concord—C. J. Ragsdale, Chairman.
Spring Road—Mrs. L. G. Jacobs, Chairman.
Riceville—T. J. Walker, Chairman.
Sheva—Miss Fannie Hunt, Chairman.
Jefferson School—Y. E. Shelton, Chairman.
St. Johns—Mrs. Grace Price, Chairman.
New Prospect—J. H. Allen, Chairman.
Marian—Miss Mattie Giles, Chairman.
Round Pond—H. B. Coffee, Chairman.
Whittles—Mrs. C. A. Adams, Chairman.
Zion—Mrs. J. C. Hunt, Chairman.
Oak Grove—J. B. Forbes, Chairman.
Somerset—Wade H. Ramsey, Chairman.
Salem—W. B. Towler, Chairman.
Hopewell—W. C. Elliot, Chairman.
Liberty—Mrs. J. I. Arnn, Chairman.

New Bethel—Mrs. Geo. Stone, Chairman.
Siloam—Dr. R. W. Bennett, Chairman.
County Line—H. A. Reynolds, Chairman.
The Tabernacle—Rev. W. C. Clarke, Chairman.
Providence—Mrs. G. C. Adams, Chairman.
Chestnut Level—H. T. Carter, Chairman.
Olive Branch—C. W. Easley, Chairman.
Ebeneza, Snow, Chatham —Colored Chapters.

The church, "our help in ages past, our hope in time to come" was a "very present help" in this trying period of war. A pure unselfish patriotism was the keynote of her message, urging the people to give of themselves and their substance to the needs of their country and suffering humanity. Members of the congregations absent in the army were constantly remembered with prayer, gifts and through the service flags, bearing a star for each absent one. The church being the general place of meeting in rural communities, it was through the church that notices were given and the people called together in the interest of various patriotic purposes. Items from the county paper at this time read:

"At St. John's Methodist Church last Sunday the Hon. Harry Wooding of Danville addressed a large and enthusiastic meeting in the interest of the Liberty Loan—$3,100 worth of bonds were taken and the week before $1,700 was raised for the Red Cross."

"There will be a patriotic rally at Marion Baptist Church Sunday, October 1st, at eleven o'clock, in the interest of the 4th Liberty Loan. Everybody come and help put this auxiliary over the top."

Fifty-one sons of Pittsylvania made the supreme sacrifice in the great war, and their names have been preserved in enduring bronze on a tablet placed upon the wall of the courthouse by a grateful people:

Batton, Julius; disease, son of W. F. Batton, Danville.

Blair, Joseph W.; disease, Witt.

Brown, Wallace E.; disease, Schoolfield.

Brightwell, Benyon; disease, Schoolfield.

Boswell, Charles David; killed in action, son of Mrs. David Boswell, Chatham.

Cross, Willie A.; disease, Cascade.

Chattin, Matthew; disease, Dry Fork.

Collins, Andrew J.; killed in action, Schoolfield.
Craig, George; killed in action, Schoolfield.
Dodd, Doctor D.; disease, son of Mrs. Julia Dodd, Whitmell.
Farmer, William; disease, son of James Farmer, Sycamore.
Farthing, Raymond; disease, son of W. J. Farthing, Witt.
Geyer, Clarence; killed in action, son of J. B. Geyer, Chatham.
Gregg, Willie; disease, Dry Fork.
Edmonds, Chesley A.; disease, son of James C. Edmonds, Long Island.
Grant, Russell; killed in action, son of I. T. Grant, Whitmell.
Hedrick, Dr. Oscar; disease, Museville.
Hawker, Allie; disease, Keelings.
Inman, Samuel; killed in action, son of W. L. Inman, Whittles.
Jefferson, John Daniel; killed in action, son of W. T. Jefferson, Sandy Level.
Large, Gaines; killed in action, Schoolfield.
Lockett, William; killed in action, County.
Lewis, Willie O.; killed in action, son of W. B. Lewis, Sutherlin.
Littles, William D.; Hurts.
Kerfoot, Rev. Franklin W.; Chatham.
Mitchell, Nelson D.; Chatham.
Myers, Western; Ringgold.
Merritt, Wm. Henry; son of Mrs. Alice Merritt, Dry Fork.
Norcutt, Roy; killed in action, Whitmell.
Oaks, Frank Harmon; killed in action; Cascade.
Price, William D.; Dry Fork.
Peatross, Charles D.; Cascade.
Reynolds, Homer; son of Wm. Reynolds, Callands.
Richardson, Otis C.; Sutherlin.
Roe, Edward G.; killed in action, Schoolfield.
Snyder, James B.; killed in action, Schoolfield.
Sentall, Henry G.; killed in action, Schoolfield.
Shivers, Harry C.; Schoolfield.
Short, Flournoy; killed in action, son of Mrs. Rachel Short, Hurts.
Smith, Gurney; killed in action, Schoolfield.
Stone, James B.; killed in action, son of T. B. Stone, Chestnut Level.
Strickland, Charles A.; killed in action, son of C. A. Strickland, Witt.
Terry, John B.; Java.
Spangler, Franklin W.; Schoolfield.

Thompson, Lonnie H.; killed in action, Schoolfield.
Wyatt, Walter B.; Mt. Airy.
Shields, Henry; Spring Garden.
Walker, Willie B.; Hurts.
Wright, Dr. Crispen; son of Dryden Wright, Sandy Level.
Yeatts, Alexander D.; killed in action, Chatham.
Steel, James; killed in action, Witt.

PITTSYLVANIA

By DUVAL PORTER

Grand old Pittsylvania! deserving every way
The pride of all thy children and homage they should pay!
Thy record bright and glorious shines out at every stage
And merits place the foremost upon Virginia's page.

Before the Revolution, aye in Colonial Days,
Her sons were ever ready, for so the record says,
To brave the trackless forest when duty bade them go,
To fight the cunning savage who sought their overthrow.

And when the Revolution, that stubborn strife began,
The sons of Pittsylvania fought for the right of man
As bravely as the bravest, on many bloody fields,
Until the haughty Briton at Yorktown humbly yields.

Nay, more, she furnished sinews for that protracted strife,
By giving to Greene's army its nourishment and life;
For Peytonsburg supplied him with food for man and beast,
Else they must have perished or given up at least.

And yet what is far greater remains as yet unsung,
Surpassing all achievements of days when she was young.
To Virginia of the "Sixties" no other county gave
So many to defend her as Pittsylvania brave!

Ye sons of Pittsylvania! come listen as I tell
Of Gettysburg immortal! Well may your bosom swell
At the glorious charge of Pickett upon that bloody day,
Your fathers were the foremost in that terrific fray.

Who are those few brave heroes, with Armistead at the Wall?
Through shot and shell they've fought their way, and with their leader fall!
'Tis Carter, White and Tredway, their names will ever shine
With Rawley W. Martin's, that dauntless son of thine!

And in the living present thou hast another son
Bestowing now upon thee, the fame that he has won;
Beginning life a plow boy, unaided and unknown,
By virtue of his talent he came into his own.

The name of Claude A. Swanson, thy most distinguished son,
In halls of State and Congress with many honors won,
Will shine as one belonging to that illustrious roll,
Whose brilliance the historian will on his page extol.

Be proud, ye sons and daughters, of the historic worth
That crowns your grand old county, the county of your birth!
Resolve that never, never shall any act of thine
Dim the brightness of the glories that on Pittsylvania shine!

Appendix

I

FIRST LIST OF TITHABLES OF PITTSYLVANIA COUNTY, YEAR 1767

A List of Tithables Taken by George Jefferson in Pittsylvania County and Cambden Parish for the Year 1767

Levy Shockley.
Francis Kirby.
Elisha Estis.
Jacob Hubbard.
Joshiah Kirbey.
William Young.
John Kirby & Jesse Kirby.
Daniel Collins.
George Peak & William Peak.
Charles Lucas & John Lucas.
David Kirby.
James Shockley.
John Kirby, Jr.
John Peak (Pr. Edward County).
William Mullins & William Mullins, Jr.
Robt. Neilly.
George Jefferson (Mecklenburg), John Davis, overseer, & Negroes, to-wit: Sam, Chance, Pompey, Phillis, Patt & Lacy.
William Terrell Mills & Thomas Hudson, Joseph Toler, John McLin, Handy, Sam & Israel, negroes.
Elizabeth Irwin (Bedford), John Carter, Ov'sr & negroes Tom, Dick, Sam, Estes, Lucy & Iris.
Jeremiah Salesbury & negro Lacbey.
John Smith & Henry Hains.
William Justice.
John Lucas.
William Neilley.
Isham Hodges.
John Hodges.
Robert Hodges.
Robert Frazier.
William Dillingham.
Fredrick Rives & negro Phillis.
William Stegal.
John Glass & Stephen Thompson.
Thomas Ramsey.
Fulker Fulkerson.
Total 56.

A List of Tithes, Etc., Taken by John Donelson 1767

Francis Bucknall.
William Holder.
Robert Martin.
Charles Rigney.
Thomas Greenwoods List, Peter Brooks, Ov'sr, negroes Duk, Sam Matt & Judith.
Hall Hudson & negro woman.
Ralph Shelton.
John East.
Arthur Kesee.
Joseph Hale.
Chas. Faris.
David Barber.
John Barber.
Thomas Doss.
Thom. Mustein.
John Walrope.
Jas. Walrope.
Richard Hamock.
Thomas Bennett.
Stephen Bennett.
Richard Bennett.
John Bobbitt.
William Bobbit & Jas. Bobbit.
Eliz^th Bobbit & negro Joe.
Wm. Bennet & Chas. Goad.
Joseph Farris.
John Bayes.

John Bayes, Jr.
James Faris & James Faris, Jr.
John Donelson, Thomas Henry, negroes Peter, Caneer, Tobe, Hannah & Sall.
Bryan Ward Nowling.
Jas. Logan & negro Phillis.
Crispen Shelton, Shenor Shelton, negroes, Tom, Lucy & Primus.
Thomas Chandler (Dinwiddie).
Joseph Cunningham (Charlotte).
Gabriel Shelton, Abraham Payne, negroes Zachery & Vilet.
Lewis Shelton, negro Patt.
John Chandler.
Isaac Sibbly.
John Justice (shoemaker).
William Williams.
James Leak.
Joseph Leak.
Robt. Leak.
Alexander Caldwell, negroes Tom & Phillis.
The estate of W. Lightfoot, Dec[d], John Henry, Ov'sr, negroes Peter, Chasl, Sam, Lawrence, Will, Lutis, Moll, Ester, Ross & Sarah.
Uriah Cammeron.
Edmond Hodges.
Henry Blanks.
Abraham Shelton, Edgecomb J. Williams.
James Milum.
Richard Prewet.
Henry Prewit & Joseph Prewit.
John Payne, John Payne, Jr., & Greenwood Payne.
Thomas Farris & Michael Farris.
Elijah Farris.
Richard Keezee & John Keezee.
Joseph Bayes & negro Silfox.
Tully Choice & negro Sarah.
William Hall.
Robt. Large.
John King, Malachi King, negro Phillis.
William King.
Benjamine Lawless.
John Sargent.
Moses Swinney.
John Swinney.
Josiah Maples.
Reuben Payne.

A List of Tithables for Pittsylvania County Taken by John Wilson, Gent., in Year 1767

John Stone & son John.
George Lumpkin, son Robert & son George, John Travis, negroes Jack & Betty.
Absolom Bostick, negro Pato.
Nathan Bostick.
Thomas Garner, negroes Harry, Lillis, Cate & Peg.
William Shelton.
John MacMillion.
William Munkers.
Richard Ardin.
Daniel Sallahan.
John Yates & son John, negroes Bob & Cate.
Charles Little.
Barsheba Beverly (Mulato)
Moses Ridle (Indian)
William Ridle
John Wynne
Robt. Worsham.
John Ferrol.
David Lay.
Robert Macconoway.
John Simmons.
Zachariah Scags.
Henry Stone and Son William, Mason Combs, negro Sarah.
Henry Greens Land.
John Owen & Sons William & John, negro Sam.
George Holms Gwin, negroes Lill, Lucy, Fillis & Gwin.
Dextrous Musick.
William Nelson.
James Sartain.
Peter Grimsted.

John Owen (Cain Cr.).
Small Wood Owen.
Timothy Stamps, John Stamps & Thomas Stamps.
Benjamine Thrasher & negro Luck.
Wm. W. Hodges.
Goram Brown.
William Watson.
William Rice.
Isiah Watkins & Edward Lester (Miller).
Peter Perkins and James, son, negroes Lownon & Hannah.
John Wilson, negroes, viz: Roger, Will, Charles, Isaac, Betty, Lin & Doll.
Isaac Sartain.
Richard Adams.
Valentine Hatcher & negroes Matt, Beck and Charles.
David Stephins.

A List of Tithes Taken by Theop'l Lacy 10th of June 1767

John Madding, John Madding, Jr. & William Ingram.
Peter Terry.
Thomas Waters, negro Lucy.
John Hall.
Robt. Warters & Wm. Warters.
Richard Colyer.
Christopher Sneed.
Thom. Cole.
James Connor.
Wm. Lynch.
Bob. Terrys List of Tithes himself and son Jo Terry.
Robt. Terry's List—Rob. Terry, negroes Sammy, Jack, Harry, Gregory, Abram, Jenney, Abby & Phillis.
Daniel Coleman (Cumberland).
The Revd Alexander Gordon's List, Thom. Riddle, overseer, Davis & Harry.
Capt John Quarles List, Jopph Ferguson, overseer, negr Crozier Elijah King.
Capt Jos Terry's List, Jos Terry Jun, negroes Savoey, Abraham, Cupid, Betsey & Sarah.
Thos. Straton.
David Terry's List, negroes Cate, Matthew, Dourkkin & Sal of Champ Terry.
John Fitzgerald.
Thos. Dodson's List, negroes Peter, Adam, Joseph, Dinah, Sall, Winny, Lucy & Nora.
John Creel.
Lazarus Dodson.
John Piggs List, negroes Harry, Bob, Sam, Sary, Beck.
Griff Dickenson, Jun'r.
Rich. Murphy & Bob. Scott.
Geo. Dodson.
James Thompson & Jno. Terry.
Jas. Roberts, Jun, & negro Isbell.
Ambrose Haley & Ben. Haley.
Richard Persons for his son John.
James Panley.
Thos Fee.
Isaac Jones.
Masses Poor.
Thos Townsend.
Joseph Austin.
Jacob Chaney, Jas. Chaney & Ezekiel Chaney.
Wm. Astin & John Astin.
Wm. Compton
Andrew Polson.
Thom. Hill.
John Pedler.
Wm. Davin & Son Jas Davin.
John Bulard.
Nich Baker.
Theop. Lacey's List Mark. Hardin Overseer, negroes Dove, Abraham, Rachell and Bess.

List of Tithables Taken by Thomas Dillard, Jr., in June 1767

Joshua Abston, Edm[d] Turner, negro Lucy.
John Abston.
John Bolinger.
Thomas Boulding.
Benjamin Clement, James Clement, negroes Yourk, Robert & Tamor.
Benjamin Clement, Jr.
Isaac Clement.
Benjamin Cadle.
Adam Clement.
William Collins & negro Dick.
John Chisom.
James Chisom.
Wm. Check, Joseph Luck, overseer (negroes) Peter & Jane.
Francis Caloway.
Thomas Dillard, Sn, negro Will & Sarah.
Thomas Dillard, Jr., Wm. Gregory, negroes Hinory & Race.
James Doss & John Dikes.
Richard Deakens.
Zacheriah Doss & John Doss.
Jacob Farris.
Jonadab George.
Edward Hubbard.
John Harness.
Thomas Henderson.
Edmond Hodges.
Jonathan Jones.
James Jones.
Edmond King, negro Juday.
Francis Luck, negro Isom.
James Lyle.
Benjamin Lankford, negro Moll.
Richard Morton.
Wm. Owen, Thomas Owen.
John Smith, negroes Dick, Daniel, Jack, Cyrus, Breachey, Vall, Chloe, Kate, Lucy, Edy, Delsey.
John Owen.
John Pemberton, Constable.
Byrd Prewet.
Jessy Pattey & Chas. Pattey.
Phileman Payne.
Benjamin Potter.
John Short.
To Micajah Terrell, George Hearden, overseer, negroes Toby, Daniel, Leason, Sarah, Diner.
George Thomas.
John Vaughn.
Mathew Vance.
George Wilcox.
Geo. Wilcox, Jr., negro Philis.
Col. Richard Whitton for Land.
Thomas Robertson.
George Evans, negro Cate.
John Ward for John Lynch.
Christopher Gorman & Son Wm.
Richard Farthing.
George Parsons.
Joseph Parsons.
Jesse Abston, negro Casar & Nann.

A List of Tithables Taken by Robert Chandler for 1767

Elisha Walling & negro Jake.
Francis Kinton.
John Blevins (son of Daniel).
Benj. Hubbard.
Richard White.
Thomas Hubbard.
James Sams.
Geo. Daniel.
William Rice.
William Sams.
James Wilson and Moses his son.
Merry Webb, Jr.
Henry Bates, Isaac Bates, Henry Bates, Jr., Mathew Steed & negro Samson.
Jas. Blevins, Jr.
John Ray.
Abner Harber.
John Bolling.
John Bowman.
John Blevins, Sr.
Geo. Rowland, negroes Samson, Winey, Hannah, Mimsey, Luck.

John McGuffey.
Wm. Dugger.
Jas. Guinn.
Shockley F. Simmons.
Martin Webb.
Chas. Burns.
Alex. Burns.
Thomas Baby.
Pyerce Guinn.
Sam'l Hall.
Arch Boling.
Sam'l Burns.
Merry Webb Sen., Bartley O'Neal, negroes Robert, Brinter, Judy, Jeanx, Jas. Webb the son of Merry.
Dillion Blevins.
Benj. Bullington.
Jno. Acoff.
Thomas Wilson.

A List of Tithes Taken by John Wimbish, Gent., for the Year 1767

Robert Adams.
Mrs. Sarah Piggs Tithes, Richard Pigg, Phillis, Jim, Lucas, Dorcas & Peter.
James Pigg.
Henry McDaniel.
Jeremiah Worsham.
Joseph Gorman.
Thomas Hardy.
Jonathan Jennings.
Thomas Hardy, Jr., & Jno. Bailey.
Richard Thurman.
Nathaniel Christian.
Adam Clement.
Capt. John Wards Tithes.
John Cleveland, Thos. Hardy, Peter Lee, Harry, Jack, Abram, Bess, Tom, Ben, Nant, Jack, Dick, Matt, Tom, John, Thomas & Nant.
John Nichols.
Samuel Smith, Jack, Tom, Will, Hannah, & Bess.
Edward Polley, Jr.
John Adams, John Adams, Jr.
Alan Adams.
Charles Beasley.
William Pigg.

A List of Tithables Taken by John Hanby, Gent., for Year 1767

William Hinton.
John Panill.
John Condaman.
William Huntsman.
James Lyon.
John Bollin.
William Bollin.
William Stevens.
James Anderson.
Daniel Wells.
Joshua Bewclett.
Jac. McPais.
Abraham Brend.
William Brend.
Beni Sanders.
John Hall.
Nathan Bewclett.
Daniel Con.
John McGown.
Bedford Jinkins.
Eliphes Shalton.
George Cowton.
——— Shelton.
George Carrail.
John Williams.
Ralph Shelton, Sen.
John Hanby.

A List of Tithables Taken July 17, 1767 by Peter Copland, Gent.

John Kendricks.
James Roberts.
Dauzwell Rogers.
Thom. Nunn.

Rich White.
John Rowland, John Palfery, Jack & Pegg.
Capt. William Blevins, Dawl & Peter.
Daniel Newman Jun.
Dennis Bryan.
Thomas Wright.
John Rice.
Neel Roberts.
James Wallen.
Charles Scaggs.
Edwd Callaham.
D'o. Baker.
Harry Dillen.
Wm. Young.
Wm. Baily Jun.
Rich. Baker.
Little William Blevins.
Frederick D. O. Daniel.
William Bailey, Senr.
Wm. Ashart.
David Shadwell & Bob.
John Handy.
Jacob Cooger & Son Henry.
James Filley.
Wm. Reed.
David Hailey.
Robt McVatta.
Wm. McVatta.
John Barker.
Jeremiah Claimck, Jun.
John Newman.
Kave Bailey.
Thomas Cooper, Sen.
Wm. Reeding.
Thomas Shanam & David Cazey.
Jesse Bound & Pompey.
Engium Nunn.
Joseph Nunn & Nan.
Thomas Gazaway.
Joseph Wallen.
Elisha Wallen Senr.
Thomas Cooper, Jr., Terence Daniel, negroes George & Winney.
William Ross.
Elisha Harbour.
Elijah Harbour & negro Hannah.
Forsyth Bradberry.
James Merrydeth.
Barclay Merrydeth.
William Merrydeth, constable.
Thomas Webb.
John Wells.
William Thomas, John Davis, Benj. Davis & Charles Mitchell.
Waters Dunn, Waters Dunn, Jr., Richd Dunn, Richd Bradberry, negroes Tom, Moll & Lilly.
Peter Copland, Richd Copland, Dan'l McBride & negro Hannah.
Ambrose Jones, negroes Dinah & Judy.
Thomas Cooper, jr.
Philip Ryan.
John Talbot.
James Calk.
John Cox, Sr., John Cox, Jr., Negs Lucy.
Nenian Prater, Nemiah Prater.
Charles Semple.
Matthew Small.

A List of Tithables and Land Taken by Archibald Gordon, Pittsylvania County, 1767

John Wimbish, James Mitchell, negro Cyrus, Orange Sall, Pegg in all.
John Martin, Joseph Cox.
William Candler, Arestripes Baghan, negro Chester.
William Stanley, John Stanley, Wm. Stanley, Jr.
William Pain.
Thomas Stone.
John Stone, junr.
James Stone.
Thomas Justice.
Israel Justice.
Simeon Justice.
Samuel Gordon.
Archibald Gordon, negroes Dick, Kildare, Lucy, Sarah.
John Hickey.

A List of Tithables Taken by Hamon Critz, Gent., for the Year 1767

Thomas Walling.
William Hays.
Cillis Ratlift.
Arch'l Hughes.
Geo. Allan.
Henry France.
David Gowing.
Nicholas Langford.
James Fee.
Geo. Poor.
Robt Crump, Junr.
Robt Crump, Senr.
Frederick Fulkerson.
Alexr Deputy.
Adam Loving.
William Loving.
Joseph Cameron.
John Pluk.
Zacheriah Cook.
Thos. Harbour.
David Witt.
Paletiah Shelton.
Geo. Gibson.
John Wildrich Bender.
John Parr.
William Denson.
William Tirpin.
Geo. Gray.
William Harrald.
John Jinings.
Peter Rentfro.
John Koger.
John France.
John Camron.
David Lyles.
Miles Jinings.
Lambath Dodson.
Phillip Buzzard.
Thom. Murry.
Solomon Smith.
John Spain.
John Gooch.
James Pritchard.
Haman Critz.

A List of Tithables Taken for Pittsylvania in 1767 by John Dix.

John Armstrong Annica.
Thomas Ayers.
Daniel Ayers.
Moses Ayers.
John Bynum.
Arthur Bynum.
Lawrence Barker.
William Barker.
Edward Burges.
John Bynam, Jr.
Moses Cornelius.
Thomas Colley.
William Cornelius.
William Colley.
John Chipman, Constable.
James Collie.
Thomas Dudley.
Henry Dixon, Jas. Durough, Jas. Borough.
John Dix, Ephraim Dismunkes, James Evalto, Will, Joe, Minkes, Ben, Lett, Old Janney & Janney and 1 chair, deduct 2 tithes being ferrymen.
William Durrett, Peter.
Edward Floyde.
Lewis Green, William Green.
John Hamilton.
Samuel Harris, Bob, Honeyball, York Pompey, Janney, Sally Lucy.
James Hogan, William Hogan.
John Hensley.
Thomas Pistole.
Samuel Pruett.
Hugh Mahone.
John McClane.
Thomas Merriwether, William Meriwether, Jason Bowcock, Paul, Frank, Southsea, Betty, Nann, Hannah, Nann, Nedd, Sue, Judy, Creshea, Joe, Paul, Jacob, Cate, Peter & Judy.

William McDaniel, Tom, Dick, Daniel, Lovoney, Milley, Liddy & Janney.
Daniel Ober.
William Owen.
John Roberts, Jas. Roberts & Jas. Roberts, Jr.
Gabriel Richards.
David Ross.
Geo. Sutherland.
John Southerland.
Jacob Stillwell.
Philip Southerland.
John Stamps.
Timothy Stamps.
James Terry.
William Travis.
William Thomas, Arthur & Janny.
William Tredwell.
William Wynne, Prince, Peter, Nedd, Cale & Judy.
Thomas Wynne & Lucy.
Robert Wright.
William Wynne, jr., Saunders Southerland & Prince.
John Worsham & Sirus.
Joshua Worsham, Will, Frank, Abram, Lucy, Judy & Pegg.
Robert Wynne.
Thomas Wynne, jr.
John Wheler.

List of Tithables Taken by Peter Perkins for the year 1767

George Chadwell, land.
Dutton Lain, tith, land.
David Terrill, land.
Edward Sweeton, tithe.
Jehu Morton, tithe, land.
James Burnett, tithe.
Davie Fields, tithe.
George Russell, land.
George Young, 1 negro woman, 1 land.
Christopher Bowlin, son William.
Joseph Bowlin, 1 tithe.
James Bowlin, 1 tithe.
Ephram McGoff.
George Thompson.
Richard Churchwell, tithe.
John Rich, tithe.
——— Conoway, 1 tithe.
Archibald Thompson.
Rodden Thompson.
Randolph Gipson, tithe, negro Bomber, land.
Thomas Calaway, sons Charles and Richard's land.
John Court & Son-in-law Jas. Coursey Peterson.
John Frederick Richel, 1 tithe, land.
William Rice Sadler.
Patrick Still, 1 tithe.
Thomas Smith, son Thomas, land.
Edward Smith, negro Will, land.
John Fulton, 1 tithe, land.
John Smith, negro Dinah, land.
Henry Lansford, negro Judy, land.
Ralph Elkins, Jun.
Richard Elkins, 1 tithe.
Nathaniel Elkins, son Jessey.
John Rukey, son James.
Thom. Gresham.
Christopher Bowling, Jun.
John Gresham son of Phil Gresham.
Edward Perogog, tithe.
James Elkin on leather wood.
Samuel Shields, land.
John Gresham son of Thom Gresham.
Jesse Elkins, 1 tithe.
John Cox.
John Givins.
William Shields.
George Button.
Henry Burnett.
Thom. Cunningham, Jun.
James Shields, 1 tithe, land.
James Strong.
Benjamine Croley, negro Peter, land.
Thomas Strong.
Charles Oaks, tithe.
Benjamine Croly, 1 tithe land.
John Strong, Joseph Martin.

Jeremiah Walker, negro.
Joseph Cunningham, 1 tithe, land.
Joseph Morton, 1 tithe, negro Dinah Land.
Abraham Passley, 1 tithe.
Martain Dunkin.
John Scags.
James Edwards, 1 tithe, land.
Thom. Bullock.
Richard Bullock.
John Lankford, 1 tithe, land.
Joseph Cotton.
James Presnall son James, negro Jane.
George Hide, 1 tithe.
Owen Wait.
Joel Certain, 1 tithe.
Shadrack Turner sons John & Josiah.
Thomas Watson, 1 tithe, land.
John Watson, Jun., land.
James Gravely, Jun'r.
John Watson, sen tithe & land.
John Warring.
Thom. Gravely.
James Garner, 1 tithe.
Thomas Garner, 1 tithe.
Thomas Horgeth, tithes.
John Morton Tithes Negroes dogery & seftis.
Arthur Fuller.
Daniel Hankins negroes frank, Nan & patt and land.
Nicholas Perkins 1 tithe negro moll.
Joseph Harris.
David Harris.
John Harris, Constable.
Benjamine Neal, Constable.
John Roach, 1 tithe.
John Oaks.
John Rice.
Henry Dunlop.
John Gwin.
John Sams.
William Bean & son Wm., land.
John Hardiman son Thomas, land.
Constant Perkins negro Jacob.
John Chadwell negro Farmer & Tiller, land.
Zacheriah McCubbins.
John Been, Jun.
John Jones, 1 tithe, land.
John Join, land.
William Edwards son Thom., land.
Robt. Perriman.
Thomas Billings.
William Murphy.
Thom. Edwards, negro Andrew, land.
William McCubbin.
Henry Rice, land.
Nathan Carter.

A List of Land and Tithes Taken by Hugh Innes for Pittsylvania County Anno. Dom. 1767

Samuel Collins.
Rowland Judd & Nathaniel Judd.
James Keith.
Charles Atkinman.
Morris Atkinson.
Abner Cochrum.
John Law John Law jr. negroes Jeany & Keat.
Henry Atkinson, jr.
Thomas Hall.
William Hall & Lansford Hall.
Jesse Hall.
William Hall, jr.
William Hill.
Isom Hall.
Thomas Dunkin, Jr.
Thomas Jones.
Thomas Anderson & James Anderson.
William Griffith.
Joseph Clements, Gabriel Clements & Vardiman Clements.
Francis Easom & Wm. Hungett, John Hungett & Chas. Hungett.
Christopher Shot & Christopher Shot, jr.

Benjamine Barten.
John Ferguson & negro Dinah.
John Savory, Jr.
William Bramby.
Samuel Walker & negro Judd.
William Davis.
Joseph Bird.
Reuben Kieff.
Robert Hill, Swinfield Hill & Thomas Hill.
Swinfield Hill.
Austin Shot.
Thomas Shoat.
John Vanbibber.
Henson McDonal.
Francis McGuier.
John McGuier.
Thomas Carter.
John McGuier, Jr.
Merry McGuier.
Paul Henson.
John Henson.
William Henson.
James Standeford.
William Murphy.
Miller Dogget.
Richard Hough.
Joshua Barton.
David Barton.
Isaac Barton.
William Ferguson.
Thomas Miller & William Sumers.
Francis Bird.
Andrew Ferguson.
Joseph Rentfro.
Robert Jones, Thomas Jones & Henry Jones.
John Jones.
Robert Jones, Jr.
Philip Smith.
William Cook.
John Fushon.
James Rentfro, jr.
James Rentfro Sen, Joseph Rentfro & Peter Rentfro.
Veath Dilingham & negro Jeany.
Peter Vanbiber, jr.
Isaac Vanbiber.
Mack Foster Sen.
Richard Peari's tithes are William Lowry, negroes: Jack, Harry, Jeany, Hannah & Silviah.
Anthony Litle.
Christopher Lackenair.
John Meadly.
John Dilingham.
James Lamb.
William Webb.
John Ramsey.
Joshua Weaver & Isaac Weaver.
Holden McGee.
Edward Richards.
William Dilingham & Joshua Dilingham.
Amos Richardson & negro Moll.
Benj. Jenkins.
Robert Tormet.
John Hall.
Francis Farley.
Wm. Heard, George Heard & Wm. Beans.
Thomas Bird.
Richard Shoat.
Jeremiah Muray.
John Stevenson.
John Callaway, negroes Flemen, Asher, Nan & Nell.
Abraham Motley & Negro Peter.
Stephen Heard & Jesse Heard.
Hugh Innes, James Parberry, negroes Juba, Keat & Peat.
John Heard.
Stephen Heard, jr.
Lewes Jenkins & negro Jack.
John Justice Constable.
William Henson.
William Witcher & negro Sawney.
William Keeny.
James Wade.
Daniel McKenzie.
William Atkinson & Owen Atkinson.
John Good, jr.
Joseph Deal.
Richard Shockley.
Daniel Witcher.
David Dalton & Benj. Dalton.

Samuel Paterson.
John Witcher.
Robt. Dalton, John Dalton & Robt. Dalton, jr.
John Dalton.
Richard Walding, John Walding & negroes Jed, Jeffry, Greace, Phoebe & Lucy.
Richard Adkinson.
William Lawson.
William Hodges & Thomas Neville.
John Hensley.
David Polly.
James Dalton.
Henry Atkinson.
Jacob Seartin.
James Stewart & James Stewart, jr.
Arch Graham & negro Robin.
George Philige, Thom. Lawrence, John Blackesley, negroes Tobias, Robin, Tom. Madey, Betty.
John Hunsman.
Richard Remington.
John Heard.
William Beams.
William Graham.
Nicholas Alley.
John Willis.
Benjamine Griffith.
Jonothan Davis.
Jacob Adkinson.
Edward Wade & negro Pegg.
David Wade.
William Tyrie.
Jacob Stober.
Jeremiah Stober.
William Hodges.
Sherwood Adkins.
Thomas Potter.
John Simons.
Bragan Prunty & Robt. Prunty.
Benj. Dunkin.
John Anderson.
Richard Perryman & negro Billiak.
John Midleton.
Nathaniel Evans.
Hezekiah Pigg.
Adam Stilts.

II

EARLY SHERIFFS

1767. Benjamin Lankford.
1769. James Roberts.
1771. Archibald Gordon.
1772. John Short.
1773. Theophilus Lacy.
1775. John Wilson.
1777. John Dix.
1779. Peter Perkins.
1780. Crispen Shelton.
1782. John Owen.
1784. Abram Shelton.
1786. Wm. Todd.
1789. William Short.
1790. Daniel Hankins.
1792. William Ward.
1794. David Hunt.
1796. Joshua Stone.
1798. William Harrison.
1800. James Johnson.
1802. Vincent Shelton.
1803. Crispen Shelton.
1805. Crispen Shelton.
1806. Samuel Calland.
1813. David Hunt.
1817. Moses Hutchings.

III

EARLY JUSTICES OF THE PEACE

1767. See chapter eight.
1769. James Roberts, Jr., Archibald Gordon, Thomas Dillard, Jr., Hugh Innes, John Donelson, Theophilus Lacy, John Wilson, Peter Copland, John Dix, George Jefferson, Peter Perkins, Hamon Critz, John Wimbish, Robert Chandler, Ben-

jamin Lankford, George Carter, Crispen Shelton, Richard Walden, Robert Payne, John Owen, William Thomas, William Witcher, John Rowland, Archelaus Hughes.

1774. James Walker, Robert Hairston, James Smith, and James McGound were added to the lists of Justices.

1776. Abraham Shelton, William Todd, Stephen Coleman, Charles Kennon, Charles Lynch Adams and William Short were added.

1777. See chapter twelve.

1780. William Harrison, John Parks, Jeremiah White, Henry Conway and David Hunt were added.

1783. Commission of Peace:

James Roberts, John Wilson, Benj. Lankford, Crispen Shelton, Robert Payne, William Witcher, John Owen, Abram Shelton, William Todd, Stephen Coleman, William Short, Daniel Hankins, William Ward, Joseph Morton, Reuben Payne, John Parks, Jeremiah White, David Hunt, Constant Perkins, Joshua Stone, Lemuel Smith, William Dix, Lodowick Tuggle, Thomas Smith, Peyton Smith, Gents.

"The following gentlemen were struck out of the commission for the reasons as follows: Thomas Dillard, removed, John Donelson, same. John Dix resigned, John Wilbish refuseth to act, George Carter removed. Charles L. Adams neglect to act. Charles Kennon removed, William Harrison refuseth to act, Henry Conway removed."

1790. James Johnson, Vincent Shelton, Crispen Shelton, Jr., William Wilkerson, William Clark, Gilbert Hunt, William Durrett, George Adams and Samuel Callands were added to the list.

1797. Armistead Shelton, John Briscoe, Moses Hutchings, John Smith, Charles Walden, Robert Walters, James N. Williams, Robert Devin, Richard Johnson, Thomas Fearn and Robert Payne were added to the list.

1799. Isaac Coles, Philip Jenkins, William White, Robert Harrison, Joseph Morton and Daniel Coleman were added to the list.

1801. Thomas H. Wooding and Clement McDaniel were added.

IV

MEMBERS OF THE HOUSE OF DELEGATES FROM PITTSYLVANIA AND THE CITY OF DANVILLE, 1776-1928

1776. Benj. Lankford, Robert Williams.
1777-78. Abram Shelton, Peter Perkins.
1778. Abram Shelton, John Wilson.
1779. Benj. Lankford, John Wilson.
1780-81. Benj. Lankford, Thomas Terry.
1781-82. Benj. Lankford, Haynes Morgan.
1782. John Wilson, Constant Perkins.
1783. Benj. Lankford, William Dix.
1784-85. Benj. Lankford, William Dix.
1785-86. Benj. Lankford, William Harrison.
1786-87. Benj. Lankford, Constant Perkins.

1787-88. Benj. Lankford, William Lynch.
1788. Benj. Lankford, Constant Perkins.
1789. Benj. Lankford, William Dix.
1790. Benj. Lankford, Matthews Clay.
1791. Thomas Tunstall, Matthews Clay.
1792. Thomas Tunstall, Matthews Clay.
1793. Thomas Tunstall, Matthews Clay.
1794. Stephen Coleman, Matthews Clay.
1795. Stephen Coleman, William Payne.
1796. Joseph Carter, William Clark.
1797-98. Robert Devin, William Clark.
1798-99. Robert Devin, William Clark.
1799-00. Theoderick McRoberts, Thomas H. Wooding.
1800-01. Robert Devin, Thomas H. Wooding.
1800-01-02. Edmund Tunstall, Thomas H. Wooding.
1802-03. Edmund Tunstall, Thomas H. Wooding.
1803-04. Daniel Coleman, Thomas H. Wooding.
1804-05. Daniel Coleman, Thomas H. Wooding.
1805-06. Daniel Coleman, Thomas H. Wooding.
1806-07. Daniel Coleman, Rawley White.
1807-08. Rawley White, Thomas H. Wooding.
1808-09. William Walton, Thomas H. Wooding.
1809-10. Daniel Coleman, Thomas H. Wooding.
1810-11. Daniel Coleman, William Walton.
1811-12. Daniel Coleman, Thomas H. Wooding.
1812-13. Rawley White, William Walton.
1813-14. William Swanson, William Walton.
1814-15. Rawley White, William Walton.
1815-16. George Tucker, Thomas H. Wooding.
1816-17. George Tucker, Thomas H. Wooding.
1817-18. Thomas H. Clark, Walter Coles.
1818-19. William Swanson, George Townes.
1819-20. William Swanson, Jr., Thomas H. Wooding.
1820-21. Rawley White, Sr., Thomas H. Wooding.
1821-22. William Swanson, William Walton.
1822-23. William Swanson, William Walton.
1823-24. Benj. W. S. Cabell, Vincent Witcher.
1824-25. Benj. W. S. Cabell, Vincent Witcher.
1825-26. Benj. W. S. Cabell, Vincent Witcher.
1826-27. William Walton, Vincent Witcher.
1827-28. William Walton, Vincent Witcher.
1827-28. William Walton, Vincent Witcher.
1828-29. William Walton, Vincent Witcher.
1829-30. William Walton, Benj. W. S. Cabell.
1830-31. William Swanson, Vincent Witcher.
1831-32. William Swanson, Vincent Witcher.
1832-33. William Swanson, Vincent Witcher.

1833-34. William Swanson, Walter Coles.
1834-35. William Swanson, Vincent Witcher.
1835-36. William Swanson, Vincent Witcher.
1836-37. Whitmell P. Tunstall, Vincent Witcher.
1838. Whitmell P. Tunstall, Vincent Witcher.
1839-40. Whitmell P. Tunstall, John Keen.
1840-41. Whitmell P. Tunstall, John Keen.
1841-42. Robert W. Williams, John Keen.
1842-43. Coleman D. Bennett, John Keen.
1843-44. James Lanier, Vincent Witcher.
1844-45. James Lanier, Vincent Witcher.
1845-46. James Lanier, Whitmell P. Tunstall.
1846-47. James Lanier, Whitmell P. Tunstall.
1847-48. James Lanier, Whitmell P. Tunstall.
1848-49. George Townes, Thomas Grasty.
1849-50. George Townes, Griffith D. Neal.
1850-51. Vincent Witcher, Griffith D. Neal.
1852-53. George Townes, William H. Wooding.
1853-54. Algernon S. Buford, Andrews J. Whitehead.
1855-56. Richard M. Kirby, Thomas W. Walton.
1857-58. John Gilmer, E. F. Keen.
1859-60-61. John Gilmer, E. F. Keen.
1861-63. John Gilmer, A. S. Buford.
1863-65. John Gilmer, A. S. Buford.
1865-67. Daniel Ragsdale, William T. Clark.
1869-71. WalterColes, W. J. Fulton, M. H. Clark, T. H. Gosney.
1871-73. W. T. Sutherlin, L. Scruggs, Geo. T. Berger.
1874-75. Wm. A. J. Finny, L. Scruggs, Jas. Lamkin, Wm. T. Clark.
1875-77. W. A. Witcher, L. Scruggs, Jas. Lamkin.
1877-79. J. H. Watson, Green Pace, J. J. Wilkinson.
1879-80. I. H. Watson, W. A. J. Finny, J. J. Wilkinson.
1881-82. Beverly B. Munford, Joel Oliver, Beverly A. Davis.
1883-84. Beverly B. Munford, T. W. Keen, R. J. Anderson.
1885-87. Beverly B. Munford, T. W. Keen, Crispen Dickenson, Jas. Schoolfield.
1887-89. Daniel Coleman, Dryden Wright, S. T. Mustain.
1889-90. Rorer A. James, Beverly A. Davis, R. J. Anderson.
1891-92. Rorer A. James, J. W. Gregory, R. J. Anderson.
1893-94. Eugene Withers, Nathan Hall, J. I. White, R. I. Anderson.
1895-96. J. W. Gregory, J. I. White, S. H. Wood, W. H. Cocke, Henry Berger.
1897-98. C. G. Watson, W. T. Wilson, Henry Allen, A. M. Darnall.
1899-00. H. C. Clement, Sr., J. W. Gregory, R. L. Dodson, W. H. Buntin.
1901-04. John E. Taylor, J. D. Reynolds, Logan Coleman, Geo. C. Cabell, J. W. Bruce.
1904. J. W. Bruce, J. W. Gregory, Jas. B. Pannill.
1906. S. F. Clement, J. E. Taylor, W. N. Brown, Samuel H. Wilson.
1908. S. Fletcher Clement, W. N. Brown, Samuel H. Wilson.
1910. S. Fletcher Clement, W. N. Brown, Samuel H. Wilson.
1912. Chas. W. Anderson, W. N. Brown, J. W. Gregory.

1914-15. S. Fletcher Clement, R. L. Dodson, Berryman Green.
1916. Nathaniel E. Clement, R. L. Dodson, Berryman Green.
1918. Nathaniel E. Clement, P. J. Hundley, John W. Carter.
1920. Chas. R. Warren, C. J. Blair, W. H. Buntin.
1922. Chas. R. Warren, B. S.Warren, Joseph B. Anderson.
1924. Chas. R. Warren, H. D. Shepherd, Robt. T. Carter.
1926. Chas. R. Warren, H. D. Shepherd, H. B. Watkins.
1928. Harry Ficklen, H. D. Shepherd, L. A. Bryant.

V

MEMBERS OF THE SENATE OF VIRGINIA 1776-1928

1776-83. Edmund Winston.
1784-90. Charles Lynch.
1790-91. Robert Clark.
1792-96. John Trigg.
1797-1805. George Penn.
1805-10. John Dabney.
1810-17. Edward Watts.
1817-21. George Hairston, Jr.
1821-25. Nathaniel H. Claiborne.
1825-29. Joseph Martin.
1829-30. George Townes.
1830-33. Benj. W. S. Cabell.
1833-41. David Dyer.
1841-42. Whitmell Tunstall.
1842-45. Clark Penn.
1845-49. Vincent Witcher.
1849-51. Crawford Turner.
1852-54. Vincent Witcher.
1855-58. William H. Wooding.
1859-61. George Townes.
1861-63. James M. Whittle.
1863-67. Elisha Keen.
1869-73. Abner Anderson.
1874-75. Michael H. Clark, W. T. Clark.
1875-77. W. T. Clark.
1877-94. John L. Hurt.
1895-96. Jas. L. Tredway, Eugene Withers.
1897-98. Rorer A. James, Eugene Withers.
1899-00. Rorer A. James, Joseph Whitehead.
1901-03. Joseph Whitehead, W. A. Garrett.
1904-22. Geo. T. Rison, W. A. Garrett.
1922-27. Nathaniel E. Clement, W. A. Garrett.
1928. Edwin S. Reid, W. A. Garrett.

VI

EARLY MINISTERS' BONDS

1785. Samuel Harris, Baptist.
1785. Lazarus Dodson, Baptist.
1785. James Robinson, Methodist.
1785. David Barr, Presbyterian.
1786. James Hinton, Methodist.
1788. Richard Elliott.
1790. Clement Nance, Baptist.
1791. Matthew Bates, Baptist.
1792. James Read, Methodist.
1793. Thomas Payne, Methodist.
1793. John Norment Jones, Methodist.
1794. John Jenkins, Baptist.
1796. James Tompkins, Baptist.
1797. Nimrod Scott, Methodist.
1797. James Jones, Methodist.
1801. Thomas Payne, Methodist.
1802. Griffeth Dickinson, Baptist.
1802. James Nelson, Baptist.
1803. David Nowling, Baptist.
1803. James Tompkins, Presbyterian.
1804. James Patterson, Methodist.
1804. Thomas Still, Methodist.
1804. Willis Hopwood.
1805. William Blair.

1805. William L. Turner, Presbyterian.
1805. Johns Terry, Presbyterian.
1808. Thomas Boaz, Baptist.
1810. Samuel Elliott, Methodist.
1811. Ellis Evans.
1814. Matthew Sturdevant, Methodist.
1814. Erasmus Stinson, Methodist.
1814. Shadrack Mustein.
1814. James Beek.
1814. Joel Burgess, Baptist.
1815. James Thomas, Methodist.
1818. Richard Beek.
1822. Clement McDonald.
1823. James Reed, Methodist.
1824. Eben Angel, Baptist.
1825. John G. Mills, Baptist.
1826. William Plummer.
1826. Joel T. Adams, Baptist.
1827. Crispen Dickenson, Baptist.
1828. Robert P. Bailey, Methodist.
1830. Clement Nance, Methodist.
1830. Charles P. Moorman, Methodist.
1830. Thales McDonald, Methodist.
1832. Zebedee Rush, Methodist.
1833. James Hoskins Stone, Baptist.
1834. Wm. C. McLeroy, Presbyterian.
1834. Jesse Roukin, Presbyterian.
1835. Samuel Bryant, Methodist.
1836. Archie W. Eanes, Baptist.
1836. Thompson Bird, Presbyterian.
1836. James P. Owen, Methodist.
1836. Hartwell Chandler, Baptist.
1836. Robert A. Burton, Methodist.
1837. John W. Power, Methodist.
1837. Charles Weatherford, Baptist.
1838. Daniel Culbreath, Methodist.
1839. William Plunkett, Baptist.
1839. Thomas R. Owen, Presbyterian.

VII

CLERKS OF PITTSYLVANIA COUNTY

William Tunstall 1767-1790
William Tunstall, Jr. 1790-1832
Wm. H. Tunstall 1832-1858

The new constitution of 1850 provided for separate clerks for the county and circuit courts.

CIRCUIT CLERKS

Wm. H. Tunstall 1850-1858
Tarpley White 1858-1864
John L. Hurt 1864-1873
Stanhope S. Hurt .... 1873 to date

COUNTY CLERKS

Langhorne Scruggs 1850-1874
Henry P. Jones 1874-1879
Wm. B. Shepherd .... 1879-1904, when office was abolished.

VIII

JUDGES OF PITTSYLVANIA COUNTY

Circuit Judges, First Appointed in 1809

Paul Carrington, Jr. 1809-1816
Fleming Saunders (of Franklin County) 1816-1843
Norbonne M. Taliaferro 1844-1852

George H. Gilmer (Pittsylvania County)......1853-1860
G. A. Wingfield (Bedford County)......1861-1869
L. M. Shumaker (Pittsylvania County)......1869-1870
William M. Tredway (Pittsylvania County)......1870-1879
Berryman Green (Pittsylvania County)......1879-1881
Stafford G. Whittle (Henry County)......1881-1882
Henry M. Ford (Henry County)......1882-1887
Stafford G. Whittle (Henry County)......1887-1901
Edward W. Saunders (Franklin County)......1901-1906
Edward J. Harvey (Pittsylvania County)......1906-1918
Hughes Dillard (Pittsylvania County)......1918-1921
Archer M. Aiken (Pittsylvania County)......1921-1922
J. Turner Clement (Pittsylvania County)......1922 to date

County Court Judges, First Appointed in 1870

James Dodderidge Coles......1870-1880
Horatio Davis......1881-1886
James D. Coles......1886-1896
James L. Tredway......1896-1904, when office done away with

INDEX

INDEX

A

B

C

D

E

F

G

H

K

L

M

N

O

P

Q

R

S

T

V

W

Y

Z